INFORMATION
AND LIBRARIES
IN THE
ARAB WORLD

INFORMATION AND LIBRARIES IN THE ARAB WORLD

Compiled and edited by
Michael Wise
Editor, *Focus on international & comparative librarianship*
and
Anthony Olden
Senior Lecturer, School of Technology and
Information Studies,
Thames Valley University

Library Association Publishing
London

027.0956
I47

© Compilation: Michael Wise and Anthony Olden 1994
© Articles: the contributors 1994

Published by
Library Association Publishing Ltd
7 Ridgmount Street
London WC1E 7AE

First published 1994

This book forms Volume 3 in the series *Information and libraries in the developing world*.

British Library Cataloguing in Publication Data
A catalogue record for this book is available from The British Library

ISBN 1-85604-085-2

Typeset from author's disk in 10/11pt Palatino by Library Association Publishing Ltd
Printed and made in Great Britain by Bookcraft (Bath) Ltd

Contents

List of abbreviations   vii

The contributors   xiii

Introduction   xv

1   Libraries in the Middle East: an overview   1
    Mohammed M. Aman

2   National libraries in the Arab world   12
    Mahmoud Ahmad Itayem

3   A survey of education for library and information   26
    science in Egypt, the Maghreb countries, and Sudan
    Mohammed Fathi Abdel-Hadi and
    Abdelmajid Bouazza

4   Education and training of librarians in the Maghreb   41
    (Algeria, Morocco, Tunisia)
    Halima Semra

5   Children's library services in Algeria   55
    Azzedine Bouderbane

6   Library science programmes in the State of Bahrain   68
    Robhi M. Alian

7   Egyptian university libraries   81
    Sandy Macmillen

8   Libraries in Iraq: a short report   96
    Amer I. Al-Kindilchie

9   Library and information services in Jordan   104
    Najeeb Al-Shorbaji

10 School libraries in Kuwait: before and after the
    Gulf War   131
    Mohamed H. Zehery

11 Public libraries in Saudi Arabia   140
    Hisham A. Abbas

12 LIS consultancy in the Arab world: the Sudanese
    experience   155
    Alhaj Salim Mustafa

13 Library and information services in the Sudan   181
    Cecile Wesley

14 The Assad National Library, Syria   190
    Ghassan Al-Lahham

15 Infrastructure of information and libraries in Tunisia   196
    Souheil Houissa

16 Medical libraries and their services to the health
    sector in the United Arab Emirates (1971-1993)   214
    Mohamed Sadiq Jaffer

17 Economic and social changes in the Emirates:
    is the information adequate?   240
    Bakri Musa Abdul Karim

Index   261

List of abbreviations

ACML	Arab Centre for Medical Literature
AGRICOLA	Agricultural on-line access (formerly CAIN)
AGRIS	Agricultural Information System (FAO)
AHSF	Abdul Hamid Shoman Foundation
AIB	Arab Information Bank
AIDO	Arab Industrial Development Organization
ALA	American Library Association
ALDOC	Arab League Documentation Centre
ALECSO	Arab League Educational, Cultural and Scientific Organization
ALIT	Advanced Technology Light Twin
AOPA	Arab Organization for Public Administration
ARABSAT	Arab Satellite Communications Organization
ARISNET	Arab Regional Information Systems Network
ASMO	Arab Organization for Standardisation and Metrology
ASRT	Academy of Scientific Research and Technology (Egypt)
AUC	American University in Cairo
BASIC	Beginner's all-purpose symbolic instruction code (computer language)
BDL	Business Definition Language
BLDSC	British Library Document Supply Centre
BRS	Bibliographic Retrieval Services, Inc. (USA)
CDN	Centre de Documentation Nationale (Tunisia)
CD-ROM	Compact Disc Read-Only Memory
CDS/ISIS	Computerized documentation service/Individual service information system
CEHANET	Centre for Environmental Health Activities Network
CERIST	Centre d'Etudes et de Recherche en Information Scientifique et Technique (Algeria)
CINAHL	Cumulative index to nursing and allied health literature
CIP	Cataloguing-in-Publication

CND	Centre National de Documentation (Morocco)
CNDA	Centre National de Documentation Agricole (Tunisia)
CNI	Centre National de l'Informatique (Tunisia)
CNUDST	Centre National Universitaire de Documentation Scientifique et Technique (Tunisia)
CPN	Comité Pédagogique National (Algeria)
DBA	Documentaliste - Bibliothécaire - Archiviste
DDC	Dewey Decimal Classification
DESS	Diplôme d'Etudes Supérieures Spécialisées
DEUA	Diplôme d'Etudes Universitaires Appliquées
DGJDPGO	Directorate General Judiciary Decree, Propagation and Guidance (Saudi Arabia)
DIALOG	A technical database service of Information Services, Inc., the Lockheed Corp. (USA)
DLP	Direction de la Lecture Publique (Tunisia)
DPGS	Diplôme de Post-graduation Spécialisé
DSB	Diplôme Supérieur de Bibliothécaire
ELA	Egyptian Library Association
EMA	Emirates Medical Association
ENA	Ecole Nationale d'Administration (Tunisia)
ENAL	National Enterprise of the Book (Algeria)
ENSTINET	Egyptian National Scientific and Technological Information Network
ESI	Ecole des Sciences de l'Information (Morocco)
FID	International Federation for Documentation
FMHS	Faculty of Medicine and Health Sciences, United Arab Emirates University
GAI	General Authority for Information (UAE)
GCC	Gulf Co-operation Council
GDHMS	General Directorate of Holy Mosque Supervision (Saudi Arabia)
GDP	Gross domestic product
GENIOS	[Economic network information on-line system, Germany]
GPO	Government Printing Office (USA)
IBI	International Bureau of Informatics
IBLA	Institut des Belles Lettres Arabes
IBM	International Business Machines Corporation (USA)
ICL	International Computers Ltd. (UK)
IDRC	International Development Research Centre (Canada)

IDSC	Cabinet Information Decision Support Centre (Egypt)
IFLA	International Federation of Library Associations and Institutions
IMEMR	Index Medicus for the Eastern Mediterranean Region
INFORM	Information for Minnesota
INFOTERRA	International Information System for the Environment
INIS	International Nuclear Information System
INTELSAT	International Telecommunications Satellite Consortium (USA)
INTERNET	International Network (International Project Management Association)
INTIB	International Technical Information Bank (UNIDO)
IPSI	Institut de Presse et des Sciences de l'Information (Tunisia)
IRSIT	Institut Régional des Sciences Informatiques et des Telecommunications
ISBD	International Standard Book Description
ISBN	International Standard Book Number
ISD	Institut Supérieur de Documentation (Tunisia)
ISDN	Integrated Services Digital Network
ISO	International Standards Organization
ISSN	International Standard Serial Number
IUC	Inter-Universities Council for Higher Education Overseas (UK)
IUP	Information Utilization Potential
JLA	Jordan Library Association
KACST	King Abdul Aziz City for Science and Technology
KISR	Kuwait Institute for Scientific Research
LIS	Library and information science
LISA	Library and information science abstracts
MEDLARS	Medical Literature Analysis and Retrieval System
MEDLINE	MEDLARS On-line
MINISIS	A microcomputer-based acquisition-cataloguing-information retrieval system developed by IDRC
NASA	National Aeronautic and Space Administration (USA)
NATIS	National Information System (UNESCO)

NDC	National Documentation Centre (Sudan)
NIC	National Information Centre (Jordan)
NIDOC	National Information and Documentation Centre (Egypt)
NIS	National Information System (Jordan)
NML	National Medical Library (UAE)
NSTIC	National Scientific and Technical Information Centre (Kuwait)
NTIS	National Technical Information Service (USA)
PAAET	Public Authority for Applied Education and Training (Kuwait)
PADIS	Pan-African Development Information System
PGI	General Information Programme (UNESCO)
ORAN	Organization Régionale Africaine de Normalisation
POPLINE	Population Information On-line
RETC	Rehabilitation Education and Training Centre (Bahrain)
RURAL	Abstracts on rural development in the tropics
SAEB	Spacecraft assembly and encapsulation building (NASA)
SSI	Social sciences index
STI	Scientific and technical information
TANIT	Traitement Automatisé National de l'Information Tunisienne
TECHLIB	Battelle BASIS-based turnkey system by Information Dimensions, Inc. – a full-text system with the capacity to store chapter headings from books
TUNIS	Thesaurus Usuel National Informatisé et Selectionné
UAE	United Arab Emirates
UBC	Universal Bibliographic Control
UCCI	Union of Chambers of Commerce and Industry (UAE)
UDC	Universal Decimal Classification
UNDP	United Nations Development Programme
UNESCO	United Nations Educational, Scientific, and Cultural Organization
UNIDO	United Nations Industrial Development Organization
UNISIST	United Nations information system in science and technology. Also: Universal system for science and technology

UNRWA	United Nations Relief and Works Agency
USAID	United States Agency for International Development
UTLAS	University of Toronto Library Automation System
VSO	Voluntary Service Overseas
VTLS	Virginia Tech Library System
WIPO	World Intellectual Property Organization

Exchange Rates, September 1992

Algerian dinar (DA)	£1 = 30DA
Bahrain dinar (BD)	£1 = BD0.56
Egyptian pound (£E)	£1 = £E5
Iraq dinar (ID)	£1 = ID0.46
Jordan dinar (JD)	£1 = JD1
Kuwait dinar (KD)	£1 = KD0.5
Libyan dinar (LD)	£1 = LD0.44
Moroccan dirham(DH)	£1 = DH14
Saudi Arabia riyal (SR)	£1 = SR5.6
Sudan dinar (SD)	£1 = SD19.6
Syrian pound (S£)	£1 = S£32.4
Tunisian dinar(TD)	£1 = TD1.53
UAE dirham	£1 = Dirham 5.5

The Contributors

Hisham A. **Abbas**, Faculty of Arts and Humanities, King Abdulaziz University, Jeddah, Saudi Arabia

Mohammed Fathi **Abdel-Hadi**, Department of Library Science, College of Arts, Sultan Qaboos University, Muscat, Sultanate of Oman

Bakri Musa **Abdul Karim**, Etiisalat College of Engineering Library, Sharjah, United Arab Emirates

Robhi M. **Alian**, Department of Educational Technology, College of Education, University of Bahrain, Bahrain

Amer I. **Al-Kindilchie**, Department of Library and Information Science, Al-Mustansiriya University, Baghdad, Iraq

Ghassan **Al-Lahham**, Assad National Library, Damascus, Syria

Najeeb **Al-Shorbaji**, CEHA/CEHANET, Amman, Jordan

Mohammed M. **Aman**, School of Library and Information Science, University of Wisconsin-Milwaukee, USA

Azzedine **Bouderbane**, Institut de Bibliothéconomie, Université de Constantine, Constantine, Algeria

Abdelmajid **Bouazza**, Department of Library Science, College of Arts, Sultan Qaboos University, Muscat, Sultanate of Oman

Souheil **Houissa**, London, UK

Mahmoud **Ahmad Itayem**, Library consultant, Amman, Jordan

Mohamed Sadiq **Jaffer**, National Medical Library, Al-Ain, United Arab Emirates

Sandy **Macmillen**, VSO, Cairo, Egypt

Alhaj Salim **Mustafa**, Omdurman, Sudan

Halima **Semra**, Institut de Bibliothéconomie, Université de Constantine, Constantine, Algeria

Cecile **Wesley**, National Council for Research, Khartoum, Sudan

Mohamed H. **Zehery**, Ohio State University – Lima Campus Library, Lima, Ohio, USA

THE ARAB STATES

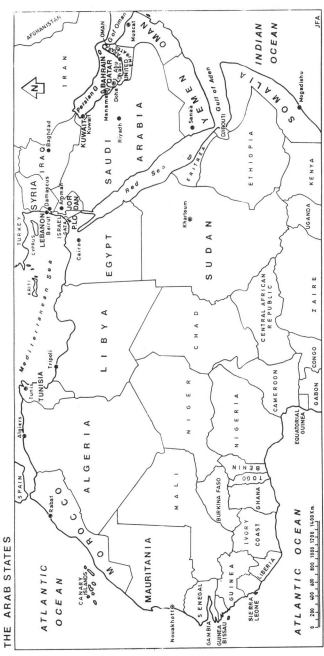

Source: Statesman's yearbook, 1993-94, p.61

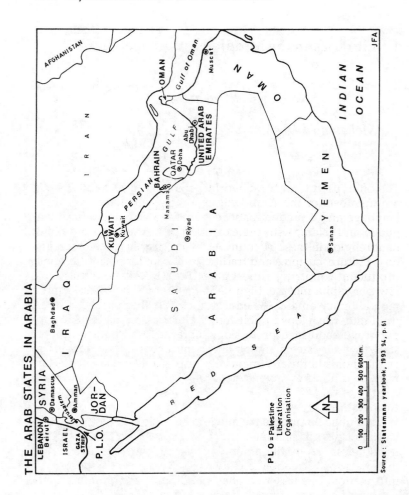

1 Libraries in the Middle East: an overview

Mohammed M. Aman

The often used term 'Arab world' refers to the 21 countries that are members of the Arab League and which share a common language and a predominant religion. Arabic is the official language and Islam, with the exception of Lebanon, is the dominant religion in these 21 countries.[1] They also share common history, culture, customs and traditions. Except for a handful of oil-producing countries, almost all of the 21 Arab countries have low per capita income, high illiteracy among the masses, and a high aliteracy among the educated class. Other problems result from underdeveloped publishing industries, an inadequate supply of well-educated professional librarians and library-support staff, low self-esteem among librarians, and a stifling bureaucracy that holds librarians financially responsible for any books lost from their libraries' inventories.

Readership
While public libraries leave much to be desired in terms of physical facilities, collections, and services, they remain popular nonetheless, especially among young people. They use library materials for recreation and to a lesser extent for education or information. The lesser emphasis on library use for educational purposes may be due to the method of teaching in schools, which relies heavily on rote learning and pre-assigned textbooks.

School libraries, when they exist in schools, even in the Arab oil-producing countries, have poor and outdated collections and almost no current reference books. Library hours are not conducive, since they close early in the day.

Library services for children are also limited. In Kuwait, for example, the only public library that provided services for children, dropped them, leaving children with no other alternative but their school libraries, which close at the end of the school day at 1.00 p.m. In Egypt, library services for children were revitalized when Mrs. Susanne Mubarak led a national campaign to build libraries for young people in Cairo and other major cities. Funding for these libraries came from both private and public sources. Their locations are ideal in relation to demographics and the attractiveness of their surroundings, usually in public parks or near recreational facilities.

One result of the Gulf War has been national awareness of the value of current information to Arab decision makers. The war has highlighted the significance of information in modern warfare and international politics.[2]

Status of librarians
The status of librarians in the Arab countries leaves much to be desired. With the exception of Saudi Arabia, most other countries have chosen to appoint non-library-trained individuals to head their major national or university libraries. In Egypt, the heads of the National Library and Cairo University Library have no formal education in library and information science. In Kuwait, the head of the department of School Libraries is a non-librarian. In both the United Arab Emirates and Qatar, the heads of the university libraries are non-librarians. Saudi Arabia provides an excellent example by employing credentialed librarians as heads of the National Library, the Directorate of Information at King Adbul Aziz City for Science and Technology (KACST). Deanships of university libraries, however are filled by faculty members who do not possess library science degrees.

The absence of national role models for young librarians in the Arab world, and the absence of formal and visible library associations, have deprived the library profession of the positive image that could attract individuals to the library profession, and has made communication and networking among librarians almost non-existent. Egypt has revived its library association, which benefits only librarians working in Cairo. Jordan, Morocco, Tunisia, and Saudi Arabia also have active library associations.

Education for library and information science
Library education may have to take some of the blame for the poor image of Arab librarians and their correspondingly poor status. While some of the educational programmes have recently begun to catch up with non-traditional concepts, and have changed their curricula to incorporate new and exciting developments, the lack of adequate tools, materials, and faculty expertise has made the desirable changes difficult to achieve. The library and information science programmes at Cairo and

Rabat have been strengthened by the acquisition of new IBM (International Business Machines) compatible personal computers, and are developing specialists on their faculty to teach the use of computer and library software applications.

Because of lack of orientation to new concepts and technologies of information handling, many of the newly established information centres in the public and private sectors have engaged staff without library science qualifications. In Egypt, the head of the information centre in the Council of Ministries is a non-librarian, as are the majority of his staff. The same situation can be observed in Kuwait, Saudi Arabia, Tunisia, and the United Arab Emirates. It is hoped that the faculty and administration of library education programmes throughout the Arab world will be able to convince decision makers that their graduates should most appropriately form the staff of these new and modern information centres. Library education programmes must also take an active part in promoting themselves and the positive aspects of the profession, in order to attract the brightest entrants for training. At present, many such programmes take a passive role in a system that distributes students among disciplines primarily according to their final grades in a national high school examination, regardless of their skills, aptitudes, or desires.

Providers of training programmes for librarians include the ministries of education (especially for school and public libraries), library associations (a good example is the Jordan Library Association)[3] and some organizations of the Arab League: Arab League Educational, Cultural and Scientific Organisation (ALECSO); Arab Industrial Development Organization (AIDO), and the Arab Organization for Public Administration (AOPA) are the most active.

In addition to the improvement of library science education, there is an urgent need for better service conditions and salaries, so that bright young librarians can be persuaded to stay with their profession, and thus work to improve its public image.[4]

National information policies
There is a general international agreement that the key to global information exchange is to have workable national policies. A national information policy for any or all of the Arab countries could result in the elimination of duplication, and better co-ordination of information resources and services within a country.[5]

Attempts were made in the mid-1980s to establish an Arab information network. The main effort was spearheaded by the Arab League Documentation Centre (ALDOC), which was established and later expanded in Tunis, when the Arab League Secretariat was moved from Cairo to its temporary headquarters in Tunis in 1980.[6] Funded by the UNDP (United Nations Development Programme) through UNESCO (United Nations Educational, Scientific, and Cultural Organization), ARISNET (Arab Regional Information Systems Network) had the goal of establishing an Arab information network to maintain bibliographic descriptions of the holdings of major Arab libraries and information centres, and to provide access to this information. Plans also called for the exchange of bibliographic and non-bibliographic information via the Arab Satellite Communications Organization (ARABSAT).[7] Unfortunately the concept of ARISNET was abandoned due to lack of funds, technical and technological difficulties, lack of agreement among Arab librarians, and because of the absence of supporting legislation.

A further problem was the reluctance of Arab librarians and their supervisors to give full support to, and work with ALDOC in implementing the goal of setting up a comprehensive Arab information network. Such a concept cannot be developed in the vacuum that presently exists in the Arab library world. To achieve that goal, each country needs to develop an information policy, establish a library infrastructure and thus provide the backing needed for a pan-Arab network. Few major libraries have used computers in a productive manner. No local libraries are connected electronically, and staff expertise in library automation and information technology is still rare.

In addition to the failed attempts of ALDOC to establish an information network, ALECSO has launched initiatives to develop standards and tools, and to organize meetings with the aim of improving communications among Arab librarians. These formerly promising efforts have declined through lack of leadership, and a current lack of funds and administrative support for its activities.

Legislation
In order for libraries and information systems and services to develop and flourish, there must be effective legislation to provide guidance and stimulate funding for their provision. It is encouraging to see the progress among Arab countries in setting up national libraries that are properly supported by legislation in support of their functions. Among these are the introduction of copyright and legal deposit laws, standards for bibliographic description, cataloguing in publication, publication of national bibliographies, regulations for interlibrary loan, and such like.

Introduction

The enormous differences in economic level of the countries that comprise the Arab world enable this third volume of *Information and libraries in the developing world* to show how inappropriate is the designation 'developing country'; yet that label is applied generally by the countries of the North to most of the world outside Western Europe and North America, the so-called South. Some countries, notably those that share the Mediterranean seaboard, contain ancient seats of learning, with libraries that have contributed to the development of world civilization. Some have the advantage, in addition to their ancient heritage, of riches from the exploitation of oil that have given them the means for developing information services that would be envied in developed countries. Yet others are continually afflicted by adverse economic circumstances that leave only meagre resources for libraries, in competition with their people's more obvious need for basic food supply and health services.

Content in this volume has been determined partly by the state of professional development in libraries, and partly by ability to communicate with colleagues in these countries. Contributors who undertook some of the regional or country surveys are known to have experienced difficulty in getting information on which to base their writings. For instance, Professor Aman's well-informed opening chapter, which was intended to present an overview of the entire region, was eventually restricted to the Middle East proper, the central focus of the Arab world. It follows that restrictions on access to information have affected the content of some other chapters, even though their authors are respected members of our profession in their own countries.

The Arab world uses variants of certain place names, possibly not easily recognizable to all readers, yet acceptable in different regions. Decisions on definitive spellings have been taken from the usage of *Europa yearbook*, and companion volumes issued by the same publisher. It will be noticed how certain authors show by their style of writing that French is their second language, and some French versions of place and institutional names have been retained, although each chapter is in English. A few instances of Islamic dates, especially in bibliographic citations, have not been transposed to the universal calendar, which differs by approximately 579 years. Thus, at the time of writing, November 1993 is the sixth month of AH 1414 in the Islamic era.

There is mention of geographical groupings whose composition may not be entirely familiar to every reader:

1   The League of Arab States, more commonly called The Arab League: Algeria, Bahrain, Djibouti, Egypt, Iraq, Jordan, Kuwait, Lebanon, Libya, Mauritania, Morocco, Oman, Palestine Liberation Organization, Qatar, Saudi Arabia, Somalia, Sudan, Syria, Tunisia, United Arab Emirats, Yemen (Statesman's yearbook, 1993–94, p. 61).

2   Maghreb, or Maghrib: Peoples and cultures of the north coastal region of Africa included in Morocco, Algeria, Tunisia and the western part of Libya. Bounded on the south by the Sahara (*New Encyclopaedia Britannica: Micropaedia*, 1983, vol. 6, p. 668).

Sincere thanks go to all the contributors, whose response to deadlines helped to get this volume ready on time for the planned progression of the series, and especially to A. S. Mustafa, who suggested names of several authors and helped in making contacts; to Alan Clark and his colleagues at the Information and Library Studies Library in Aberystwyth, who answered numerous enquiries during the editorial process; and to Angela Wise for help in preparing copy for publication.

Thanks also to John Antwi in Kano for drawing the regional maps of the Arab World, and to Sandy Macmillen for preparing the map that accompanies his chapter.

Michael Wise   Anthony Olden
Department of Library Science   Thames Valley University
Bayero University   St Mary's Road
PMB 3011   Ealing
Kano   London W5 5RF
Nigeria   United Kingdom

April 1994

Following the introduction of computers and electronic networks, there is an urgent need for national guidelines and standards for developing, or adapting computerized information systems from abroad. Legislation should also remove barriers to importing library materials and library hardware and software that meets national standards, and provide libraries with telecommunication access for the development of databases.

Funding for libraries
On the whole this can be described as poor, even in the oil-producing countries. In the poorer countries like Egypt, Jordan, Sudan, Syria, and Yemen there is a problem with the availability of hard currency to pay for books and other library materials. UNESCO book coupons have helped, but have not made up for lack of funding and foreign exchange. Shortage of funds has handicapped, in varying degrees, all Arab libraries and information centres. Younis describes 'the vicious loop' which libraries in Jordan face. His definition can be extended to apply to a good number of Arab countries:

> they have shortages of trained staff, impoverished collections (qualitative as well as quantitative) and inadequate library premises and equipment. Therefore, libraries become incapable of meeting their users' information needs, thus reducing level of services as users turn away to other information sources. Libraries will then be viewed by officials as less important.[8]

Preservation
As a consequence of their long and eventful histories, several of the Arab countries have accumulated valuable collections of rare books and manuscripts, unsurpassed elsewhere. Unfortunately they are suffering from years of neglect, unsuitable housing conditions, polluted environments and lack of professional care, arising from ignorance or lack of concern.

To rectify this situation, national and international efforts should be exerted to salvage these valuable materials. In the past UNESCO, through its cultural preservation programmes, has microfilmed books and manuscripts, depositing copies in national and research libraries in these countries. With the advent of newer technology it may be possible to consider producing electronic images of these rare items, and making them available on optical disks, or other appropriate emerging formats, to libraries around the world. The originals of these books and manuscripts need careful restoration and preservation treatment, to prevent their further deterioration.

Automation

Almost every head of library in the Arab world aspires to introduce computer operations in their library. Unfortunately there has been no general agreement on what system or systems will be most suited to the needs of these libraries and their patrons. In some cases, there seems to be a lack of understanding or appreciation of the complexities of and prerequisites for automation.

As a consequence of over-anxious sales representatives coming to the area from Europe and North America, there have been questionable negotiations when introducing computers into certain libraries. For example, minimal regard has been given to the necessity of Arabizing computer systems to suit the requirements of the libraries and their users. Many of the practising librarians have an inadequate command of the English language for understanding screen messages, and for implementing systems manuals and documentation.

A pioneer in the use of computers in libraries was the University of Petroleum and Minerals, currently known as King Fahd University for Petroleum and Minerals, in Dammam, Saudi Arabia. Its library acquired the DOBIS/LIBIS system, which was designed originally at Leuven University in Belgium.[9] The IBM hardware-specific system was hailed by Saudi and some Gulf-States librarians as being the one that would bring automation to Arab libraries. For lack of technical support by IBM or other western companies, Saudi librarians were left, after a few years, with an antiquated system, and plans for multilingual capability were abandoned. King Saud University Library, which adopted DOBIS/LIBIS several years ago, is seriously considering moving to another system, because of lack of system support at national and international level, as well as increasing obsolescence. At the Egyptian National Library in the mid-1980s, a similar disappointment was encountered with International Computers Ltd (ICL) and its by then antiquated system, which disregarded the need for bilingual information processing for Arabic materials.

In Kuwait, the Ministry of Planning, which has been vested with responsibility for overseeing any automation activity in the public sector, attempted and later failed to deliver a library automation system capable of handling Roman and Arabic characters. Negotiations are currently under way with representatives from companies producing systems such as VTLS (Virginia Tech

Library System), TECHLIB, and UTLAS (University of Toronto Library Automation System) to introduce one or more of these in the Gulf States. Other libraries in Egypt, Jordan, Morocco, Saudi Arabia, Sudan, and Tunisia have found the MINISIS software to be sufficient for their present needs. A member of the ISIS (Individual service information system) family, the MINISIS system, and its micro version, CDS/ISIS (Computerized documentation service/Individual service information system) were Arabized by ALDOC in the late 1980s. The two versions have been made available to developing countries through the financial support of UNESCO and UNDP. So far, these libraries have found no reason, perhaps for lack of money, to migrate to another system. MINISIS is currently in use at King Fahd National Library and the King Abdul Aziz Public Library in Riyadh, Saudi Arabia, in the Ministry of Agriculture in Tunis, and the National Documentation Centre in Rabat, Morocco.[10]

Most recently a number of libraries have acquired databases on CD-ROM (Compact Disc Read-Only Memory). This nucleus of the electronic library has the advantage of introducing Arab library users to computerized information searches, even though in a foreign language, usually English. Because of their user-friendly presentation of information, librarians have been eased into the latest state of the electronic communication age. CD-ROM products are marketed throughout the Middle East by Arabian Advanced Systems, which is based in Riyadh, Saudi Arabia, and has offices in other Gulf States. However, there is a continuing absence of production and distribution of Arabic information sources such as bibliographies and reference works in the CD-ROM format.

The advent of other technologies, such as hypermedia and interactive video should soon introduce Arab libraries to this new information arena. There already exist Arabic hypermedia products which have been tested on children and adults. They range from informational products about Islam[11] and instructional products to teach English to Arabic speakers, to literature and storytelling for Arab children.[12] These programs were designed at the University of Wisconsin-Milwaukee and were field-tested in Kuwait and Egypt.

Direct on-line access to databases such as DIALOG, BRS (Bibliographic Retrieval Service), INFORM (Information for Minnesota) and MEDLINE (MEDLARS On-line) have been available in national, scientific, technical, and medical information centres in many of the Arab countries for quite some time.

INTERNET (International Network) can be accessed in Saudi

Arabia at the King Abdul Aziz City for Science and Technology, and at the American University in Cairo. However, most of the use is limited to electronic mail, without taking advantage of the numerous databases made available on the network. There is a terrible preoccupation with technology, and much less attention is paid to collection development, services, quality management, and staff development. Some administrators have the false notion that the introduction of computers in libraries will somehow transform them to American-type libraries, reproducing all the glamorous impact that they experienced during their brief visits or when using such libraries.

The Future
While there are many negatives in overall library development in Arab countries, there are also hopeful signs that here and there some good examples are emerging.

In Alexandria, Egypt, for example, contracts for the prestige project, Bibliotheca Alexandrina have been signed, soil tests completed, and construction equipment assembled on-site. The next stage of funding will be towards the acquisition of library materials, and it is hoped that the library will open to the public before the end of this decade.[13]

In Saudi Arabia, the new King Fahd National Library is near completion, having been under construction since 1985. The main building has four levels, including one underground, and occupies 25,000 sq. ft. of land.[14] Its construction combines modern architecture and traditional Islamic and Arab design, topped off by a fine dome, and set in a beautifully landscaped park. The library has been carefully designed to allow for future expansion of up to half a million publications. At present it contains under one-fifth of that quantity.

The most prominent special library and information centre in the Arab world is in King Abdul Aziz City for Science and Technology. The city was founded in 1977, and is responsible for the formulation of national science and technology policies, and for the co-ordination and promotion of applied scientific research in Saudi Arabia. A special Directorate for Information Systems was established at KACST to provide a wide variety of support services to the country's academic and research communities. These services include production of national science and technology databases, provision of online search services, and operation and maintenance of data communication networks. The Directorate maintains Gulfnet, which is a store-and-forward network. It can be used to transfer files, text, data, or programs to other modes, to receive or send electronic mail to one or more network users, and to query remote computerized databases on the system. KACSTNET is a dial-up communication network, which connects some 16 research institutions and libraries via the central computer at KACST.[15]

Kuwait University, for the first time since it was founded in 1966, expects its first central library to be completed in 1996 – on the Khaldiya Campus. In 1998 and 2000, two more central university library buildings will be completed on the Sheweikh and Kefan campuses. The Public Authority for Applied Education and Training (PAAET), also in Kuwait, is expected to have new library buildings on one, or at most two, campuses, instead of the scattered and temporarily housed 16 libraries (eight for men and eight for women) now serving the students and faculty.

An impressive centre for scientific and technical literature operated in Kuwait until the Iraqis looted its contents and destroyed the facility during the Gulf War. Located within the compounds of the Kuwait Institute for Scientific Research (KISR), the National Scientific and Technical Information Centre (NSTIC) was the pride and joy of many Arab scientists in general, and of the Kuwaitis in particular. Efforts are currently under way to restore KISR and NSTIC facilities and resources to the pre-1991 condition.[16]

Political stability, economic prosperity and the introduction of democracy in the Arab countries will in the near future place more emphasis on free and unrestricted access to information. It will soon become evident to policy makers and the masses alike that access to libraries and information can no longer be ignored. The Arab world cannot afford to turn its back on the impact, upon everyone, of the telecommunications and information revolution that brought the Gulf War live to the television screens of the majority of Arab homes.

References

1 The 21 Arab League countries are: Algeria, Bahrain, Djibouti, Egypt, Iraq, Jordan, Kuwait, Lebanon, Libya, Mauritania, Morocco, Oman, Palestine, Qatar, Saudi Arabia, Somalia, Sudan, Syria, Tunisia, United Arab Emirates, and Yemen.

2 Aman, Mohammed M., 'Libraries and information systems in the Gulf States: after the war', *Journal of information science*, **18**, 1992, 447–451.

3 Younis, Abdul Razeq, 'Professional library development, manpower education and training in Jordan', *International information & library review*, **24** (1) 1992, 15–43.

4   For further information on library education, see: Al-Ansari, Husein, *A Study of supply and demand of library and information workers in Kuwait ...*, PhD. dissertation, Tallahassee, FL, Florida State University, 1992, 192 leaves; Al-Sereihy, Hassan, *Continuing library education: practices and preferences of the university and major research library personnel in Saudi Arabia, with special emphasis on technical services staff*, PhD dissertation, Bloomington, IN, University of Indiana, 1993, 212 leaves.

5   Aman, Mohammed M., *Towards a national scientific policy, in general, and scientific technical information (STI), in particular*. Kuwait: Kuwait Institute for Scientific Research, 1992.

6   Aman, Mohammed M., *Broad system outline for the Arab League Documentation Center*. Paris, UNESCO, 1980.

7   Henchman, Walter, 'Al-Qamar el-Sina'i al-'Arabi al-Duwali (INTELSAT) wal-Shabaka al-'Arabiya lil-Ma'lumat (INTELSAT and the Arab Information Network)'. In: *Information for development in the Arab world: based on papers presented at the First Technical Meeting on ARISNET, Tunis 8–12 May 1987*, Tunis, ALDOC, 1988, 1011–21.

8   Younis, Abdul Razeq, 'Library automation in Jordan', *International library review*, **22** (1) 1990, 19–29.

9   Ashour, Salih, 'University library planning: the experience of the University of Petroleum and Minerals', *International library review*, **15** (3) 1983, 283–9; Ashoor, Saleh and Zahiruddin Khurshid, 'User reactions to the online catalog at the University of Petroleum and Minerals Library', *Journal of academic librarianship*, **13** (4) 1987, 221–5.

10   *Al-Taqrir al-Sanawi al-Awwal li-Maktabat al-Malik Abdul Aziz al-'Amah'an al-fatra 1989–1990 (First annual report of King Abdul Aziz Public Library for the period 1989–1990)*. Riyadh, King Abdul Aziz Public Library, 1990.

11   Mohamed, Mamdouh N. and Nadeem Malik, *The Religion of Islam*, Fairfax, VA, Institute of Islamic and Arabic Sciences in America, 1992, 2 computer disks (Macintosh System 7).

12   University of Wisconsin-Milwaukee, School of Library and Information Science, *Arab children's literature in hypermedia format*. Milwaukee, WI, University of Wisconsin-Milwaukee, 1993.

13   For further information on the building of the New Alexandrian Library, see: Aman, Mohammed M., *The Bibliotheca Alexandrina: a link in the chain of cultural continuity*, Milwaukee, WI, School of Library and Information Science, 1991, Occasional paper 3.

14   *King Fahd National Library*. Riyadh, King Fahd National Library, 1992.

15   King Abdul Aziz City for Science and Technology, *Brief description*

of services provided by the Directorate General of Information Systems, Riyadh, King Abdul Aziz City for Science and Technology, 1991.

16 Aman, Mohammed M., 'Damage to Kuwait's information and library service', *Bulletin of the American Society for Information Science*, April/May 1992, 24–5; Aman, Mohammed M., *Destruction of an institution: Iraq's legacy*, Kuwait, Kuwait Institute for Scientific Research, 1993.

2 National libraries in the Arab world

Mahmoud Ahmad Itayem

There are three designations in Arabic for the term 'National Library': Maktaba Wataniya or Qawmiya, Dar al-Kutub al-Wataniya, and al-Khizana al-Wataniya. The last of these is peculiar to Morocco, while other Arab countries use one or other of the first two.

Five Arab countries, Djibouti, Kuwait, Oman, Sudan, and Yemen, have no national libraries, although Oman has a nucleus for one, and Kuwait, Sudan, and Yemen have libraries and information centres that perform part of national library functions. The national libraries of Lebanon and Somalia are not operating at present. They have suffered from the effects of civil war; their buildings have been damaged and part of their collections destroyed or stolen. Therefore they are not included in this survey. Regarding the others, only libraries that have been designated as national libraries are covered. It should be noted that the following countries have, additional to the national library, other libraries and information services that operate nationwide. For example:

Algeria:	Bibliothèque nationale des études historiques
Egypt:	Cabinet Information Decision Support Centre (IDSC)
	Egyptian National Scientific and Technological Information Network (ENSTINET)
	National Information and Documentation Centre (NIDOC)
Jordan:	National Information Centre (NIC)
Morocco:	Centre National de Documentation (CND)
Saudi Arabia:	Information Centre of King Abdul Aziz City for Science and Technology
Tunisia	Centre de Documentation Nationale (CDN)
	Centre National de Documentation Agricole (CNDA)

Centre National Universitaire de Documentation Scientifique et Technique (CNUDST)

Some national libraries are also national archives, as in Egypt,
Iraq, Jordan and Morocco.

History

The first national library, in the modern sense, in an Arab country
was that of Algeria, established in 1835; the most recent, at the
time of writing is the National Library of Jordan, in July 1990.
Table 2.1 shows the date of establishment, any change of name,
and administrative attachment of the national libraries comprised
in the content of this article.

Table 2.1

Country	Library's present name	Previous name(s)	Date founded	Administered by
Algeria	Bibliothèque Nationale d'Alger	— —	1835	Ministry of Culture
Bahrain	National Library	—	1990	Ministry of Education
Egypt	National Library	Khidaiwi Library; Egyptian Library	1870	Ministry of Culture
Iraq	National Library	Assalam Library	1920	Ministry of Culture and Information
Jordan	National Library	—	1990	Ministry of Culture
Libya	Libyan National Library	—	1950	Centre of Green Book Studies
Mauritania	Bibliothèque Nationale	—	1965	Ministry of Culture
Morocco	Bibliothèque Générale et Archives	—	1926	Ministry of Culture
Qatar	Qatari National Library	—	1962	Ministry of Information and Culture
Saudi Arabia	King Fahd National Library	—	1990	Presidency of Council of Ministers
Syria	Assad National Library	—	1984	Ministry of Culture
Tunisia	Bibliothèque Nationale	—	1985	Ministry of Culture
UAE	National Library	—	1981	Cultural Complex

Thus it can be seen that two libraries were founded in the nineteenth century, and of the remaining eleven, six date from the
1980s onwards.

Functions

The libraries' objectives and functions have been defined in the
legislation that set them up, or in the case of the older foundations, ensured their continuance, and extended their responsibilities. The traditional function of preservation of the national her-

itage has usually been accorded precedence, and has affected neg-atively their role in the development of a national library and information service. The administrative attachment of each national library, set out in Table 2.1, is an indicator of the impor-tance or otherwise accorded to that role. The following essential functions are summarized, together with a note of the limitations experienced in various countries:

Preservation of national heritage

Except for United Arab Emirates (UAE), which has no legal deposit law, all national libraries claim to perform this function by implementing their respective legal deposit legislation. But none of them can claim that they have achieved comprehensive deposit because not all publications have been included in the legislation; they may have been assigned for deposit in other national institutions, or simply ignored when drafting the laws. For example, Egypt assigned the depository for dissertations to Ein-Shams University Library, and in Tunisia printed music goes to the National Music Conservatoire. Audiovisuals and machine-readable products are almost invariably ignored by legislation, and although government publications may have been included, libraries fail to give the time necessary to tracking them down and securing copies from their publishers.

Although all libraries, with the sole exception of Morocco, claim that they collect materials relating to their respective countries, or written by citizens and published abroad, it is unlikely on the evi-dence available that they are being comprehensive in their collect-ing.

Bibliographic activities based on national products

1   *The national bibliography*   All national libraries except those of Jordan and Mauritania issue their national bibliography at regu-lar intervals. Usually issued annually, it appears each quarter in Egypt, and semi-annually in Algeria. The Jordan Library Association (JLA) has published the annual Jordanian national bibliography since 1979. The contents vary between countries as some are limited to commercially published books, and others more comprehensively include government publications, school textbooks, dissertations and periodicals. None includes audiovisu-al materials.

2   *Lists of periodicals*   Lists that are separate from the national bibliography tend to be published at irregular intervals. No lists at all have been issued in Algeria, Bahrain, Libya, Mauritania, or Morocco.

3   *Indexes of periodical articles*   National lists have been issued only in Egypt, Morocco, Saudi Arabia, and Syria.

Bibliographic activities based on national holdings

1   *Union lists of periodicals*   This activity reflects the secondary role of national libraries in national library and information service; it is performed only by the national libraries of Saudi Arabia and UAE, although other national institutions undertake it in some countries. In Egypt it is carried out by ENSTINET, in Jordan by the Abdul Hamid Shoman Public Library (private sector), and by CND in Morocco. This is not due to deliberate delegation of responsibility by national libraries, but has been taken on by others to make up deficiencies in the national library service.

2   *Union catalogues*   Only the King Fahd National Library, in Saudi Arabia is trying to achieve this. Others, in countries such as Egypt, Jordan, Morocco, and Tunisia are indifferent to their obligation. In some countries their role is taken up by other institutions, as in the union catalogue of reference works among university libraries in Syria. It is to be hoped that the advent of automation networks may improve the scene in the foreseeable future.

3   *Specialized bibliographies and/or indexes*   These are compiled and published by the national libraries of Algeria, Egypt, Iraq, Morocco, Qatar, Saudi Arabia, and UAE.

Other publications

These variously include research reports, annual reports, directories and major publicity materials. They are known to have been issued by Qatar, Saudi Arabia, Syria, and UAE.

Circulation

The national libraries of Bahrain, Egypt, Mauritania, Morocco, Qatar, Syria, and UAE also act as public libraries. Two of them extend to branch library service; there are 26 branches in Cairo, and in Qatar, six are placed in various parts of the country. Other national libraries confine use of their reading rooms. Table 2.2 overleaf shows reported statistics of members, annual usage, and reader places.

Answering enquiries

All the libraries report that enquiry services are supplied, but no statistical or evaluative data is available.

Table 2.2

Country	Membership	Total annual usage	Seats
Iraq	—	17,327	111
Jordan	—	—	50
Morocco	1,672	40,000	—
Qatar	10,857	—	—
Saudi Arabia	200*	—	—
Syria	42,373	102,000	638
Tunisia	7,500	30,000	250
UAE	1,000	90,000	360

* Research workers only.

Training
The national libraries of Algeria, Egypt, Jordan, Morocco, Syria, Tunisia, and UAE actually do, or are willing to receive staff from other libraries for training. Activity in this area is determined by how relevant a particular national library's operations are to trainees from different backgrounds. Other institutions, notably information and documentation centres, do challenge and sometimes excel their national libraries in this respect.

Other activities
The national libraries of Qatar, Saudi Arabia, and Syria each play an active role in organizing local, and international book exhibitions of Arabic materials.

Resources

Human resources
Only three of the thirteen countries surveyed in this article, Mauritania, Qatar, and UAE, have no library schools offering training at any level. Four of the countries that have not been included, Kuwait, Lebanon, Oman, and Sudan do have library schools. Six out of the fourteen member countries of the Arab League with their own library schools actually have more than one; they are Algeria, Egypt, Iraq, Jordan, Libya, and Saudi Arabia.

There are library associations of some kind in nine of them, Algeria, Egypt, Iraq, Jordan, Lebanon, Morocco, Sudan, Syria, and Tunisia. Their designations, functions, and efficiency in serving their members and the profession are variable. Only the Jordan Library Association has a continuous record of activity and publication since it was founded in 1963.

Recorded personnel resources at the national libraries of the countries in this survey are set out in Table 2.3.

Table 2.3

Country	Subject graduates	Professional graduates	Professional non-graduates	Clerks	Janitors	Total
Algeria	—	—	—	—	—	—
Bahrain	—	—	—	—	—	—
Egypt	405 (37%)	405 (37%)	225 (20.6%)	29 (2.7%)	26 (2.4%)	1090
Iraq*	15	49	31	—	—	—
Jordan	13 (27%)	4 (8.9%)	9 (18.8%)	8 (16.6%)	14 (29%)	48
Libya*	—	—	—	—	—	—
Mauritania*	—	—	—	—	—	8
Morocco	9 (11%)	8 (9.6%)	4 (4.8%)	52 (62.7%)	10 (12.5%)	83
Qatar	8 (5.8%)	18 (13%)	41 (30%)	17 (12.4%)	53 (38.7%)	137
Saudi Arabia	6 (2.9%)	73 (35.8%)	56 (27.5%)	44 (21.6%)	25 (12%)	204
Syria	82 (27.5%)	16 (5.4%)	24 (8%)	120 (40.3%)	56 (18.8%)	298
Tunisia	8 (5%)	21 (13%)	40 (25%)	26 (16.3%)	65 (40.6%)	160
UAE*	—	16	13	17	8	54

* Incomplete data available to the author in respect of these countries.

This shows the variations in types and levels of staffing. In the absence of complete returns from some libraries it is difficult to draw general conclusions. However, the following observations about individual library services may be made:

- Egypt and Qatar operate branches.
- The generally low numbers of clerical staff may indicate that clerical duties in many libraries are carried out by technicians.
- The absence of library schools has not affected the recruitment in certain countries of professionally qualified graduate staff. This suggests that citizens have studied outside their country of origin, and also that expatriate staff have been recruited.

Collections

The size of respective collections is very much influenced by the length of time a particular library has been established, as well as the availability of funds. Legal deposit legislation in favour of national libraries has decided the inclusion and exclusion of certain types of materials. The additional functions for some of being public libraries, and custodians of national archives have affected ultimate size, staffing, and size and type of collections. Table 2.4 gives a summary of size of collection, setting out statistics of major categories of stock, as far as they have been supplied to the author.

Table 2.4

Country	Books vols.	Periodicals Titles	vols.	Theses	AV	Manu-scripts	Maps	Others
Algeria	950,000	—	—	—	—	—	—	—
Bahrain	—	—	—	—	—	—	—	—
Egypt	697,795	7,750	291,720	—	30,399	57,000	—	—
Iraq	575,744	129	37,250	15,280	5,298	—	4,205	8,060,615[a]
Jordan	50,000	600	—	—	120	10	30	2,000[b]
Libya	—	—	—	—	—	—	—	—
Mauritania	10,000	—	—	—	—	4,000	—	—
Morocco	500,000	600	—	7,185	400	10,994	600	2,000[c]
Qatar	354,327	—	—	306	4,125	1,821	—	—
Saudi Arabia	232,417	789	3,328	11,817	22,508	850	6,070	51,306[d]
Syria	170,374	2,476	—	3,103	8,755	19,114	114	—
Tunisia	1,500,000	13,000	—	15,000	—	40,000	5,000	—
UAE	310,000	2,000	35,000	—	13,500	9,000	—	—

[a]   Original documents administered as national archives. Additional to, 4,000,000 pages on 2,000 reels of microfilm, and 68,652 microfiche.
[b]   Reports.
[c]   Linear metres of shelving.
[d]   Government and private documents. The library also has a numis-matic collection of 190,000 coins.

Collections of printed materials are, at the least bilingual, and more usually multilingual, bearing in mind that the major foreign language is English in the countries of the Mashreq[1] and French in the Maghreb.[2] The largest collection is that of Tunisia, where the Bibliothèque Nationale inherited some European libraries that were moved there during the Second World War.

Books form the major element of the collections, not as a result of legal deposit, but rather from foreign acquisitions. Periodicals are also generally acquired and it is estimated that about 2,000 titles are published throughout the Arab world. Because of this relatively small number it should have been feasible to index them by co-operative indexing between the national libraries, and thus avoid the duplication of effort by unco-ordinated indexing in the various libraries.

Dissertations are not all obtained through legal deposit. University libraries compete with their national libraries, especially because of the limitations on use that may be imposed. In 1986, the Union of Arab Universities designated the University of Jordan library as a depository for dissertations accepted by member universities.

Audiovisual materials are most usually video recordings and photographs. They are not often well-organized and therefore are under-utilized. Libraries at present lack facilities for easy use of their audiovisual materials, and therefore impose constricting limitations on access to them.

Manuscripts are not always originals, but may be, very usefully, copies in various formats of relevant items located elsewhere in the world.

Maps do not form part of the collections in most national libraries. Geological surveys and departments of land and surveys usually have better collections. There is in every country a shortage of current maps. The publication of these materials may improve with advances in printing techniques.

Premises
A few of the libraries supplied basic data on the overall capacity of their premises: Iraq, 41,400 sq. m.; Jordan, 2,000 sq. m.; Saudi Arabia, 28,000 sq. m.; Syria, 22,000 sq. m.; Tunisia, 6,000 sq. m.; UAE, 5,000 sq. m. Jordan's library occupies temporary premises during the construction of a purpose-designed building of 16,000 sq. m., which has been financed by China.

Tunisia has the largest collection and almost the smallest area. Although a new building was constructed for its use, this was eventually occupied by another institution. A fresh project for rehousing the library is said to be in progess, but no details have become available.

Financial resources
None of the libraries has supplied any financial data.

Library operations

Technical processing

The only national library that influenced technical processing practices, particularly cataloguing, was that of Egypt, which published cataloguing rules in 1938, based on the 1908 precursor of AACR. Their application underlies continuing controversy about preferred entry of names, by family name, or in the natural order of Arabic usage. Its effects have not been confined solely to Egypt, because of the part played by Egyptian librarians in developing libraries elsewhere, especially in the Arab Mashreq. Since then, no national library has played a significant part in developing cataloguing rules. In 1962 a set of descriptive cataloguing rules, based on the American Library Association (ALA) rules of 1949 was prepared by Dr Mahmoud Shinaiti and Mohammad Mahdi, both Egyptians. In the last two decades the Arab League Educational, Cultural and Scientific Organization (ALECSO) has undertaken the Arabization of International Standard Book Descriptions (ISBDs), and their new sectional editions, but only ISBD(G) and ISBD(PM) have been published.

The most significant achievement in this field has been the Arabization of AACR2, produced as a co-operative venture between the Jordan Library Association and ALECSO in 1983, which has been widely adopted throughout the Arab world.

Closely related to this is the application of Cataloguing-in-Publication (CIP), which has been implemented through the national libraries in Iraq and Jordan. International Standard Book Number (ISBN) operates in Egypt and Morocco, and negotiations for its adoption in Jordan, Saudi Arabia, Syria, and Tunisia are at an advanced stage. International Standard Serial Number (ISSN) has been adopted by some journals in the region, although not in Morocco. Saudi Arabia has recently signed an agreement with ISDS for this purpose.

The international standards for ISBD and ISSN have been translated into Arabic and issued as Arab Standards 521 and 581, respectively. Morocco maintains databases for each of them.

Regarding classification, the French edition of Universal Decimal Classification is used in Algeria, Morocco, and Tunisia. Egypt developed and uses its local scheme at headquarters, but has applied Dewey Decimal Classification (DDC) in its branches. All other national libraries report the use of DDC, although in different editions, sometimes even in the same library system. DDC is the only major, general classification scheme to be formally translated and modified. Translation of the abridged eleventh edition was undertaken by ALECSO, which is also negotiating to translate the full twentieth edition.

In subject analysis, libraries use different lists of subject headings for Arabic and foreign materials. No lists for general use have been developed in any of these national libraries, although Saudi Arabia is working on lists for internal use, to make up the deficiencies of existing published subject headings. In the interim, ALECSO has prepared a unified list and plans for publication in 1994.

Although thesauri are considered worthwhile, only two libraries, Syria and UAE are attempting to use one. This arises because there is no comprehensive thesaurus covering all fields of human knowledge. A co-operative venture between the Abdul Hameed Shoman Foundation (Jordan), Juma'a al-Majed Foundation for Culture and Heritage (UAE), and Dubai Municipality (UAE) is expected to provide such a tool. It will be trilingual, in Arabic, English, and French, to serve both Mashreq and Maghreb libraries, and help to solve problems of multilingualism. This should make up for deficiencies in existing subject heading lists.

Automation
There has been slow progress in adopting advanced information technology. Saudi Arabia alone has taken up general automation of library service activities.:

- Algeria: no data available
- Egypt: catalogue automation is under way, using MARC. There are two databases:
  1 Foreign books, started in 1983. It contains 5,800 titles.
  2 Arabic books, started in 1991. No retrieval is yet possible on either database.
- Iraq: CDS/ISIS (Computerized documentation service/Individual service information system) is in use. The following databases have been implemented:
  1 Deposited books, 1992–
  2 Iraqi intellectual heritage, 1989–1991.
  3 Iraqi dissertations.
  4 Iraqi and foreign documents (archives).
- Jordan: CDS/ISIS used at present (6,900 records), but MINISIS has been selected and hardware ordered, to provide the major system into the foreseeable future.
- Mauritania: no library automation.
- Morocco: CDS/ISIS used. The following databases are available:
  1 KANZ (periodical indexes – 1600 records).

    2 ISBN data base – 1100 records.

    3 ISSN data base – 400 records.

- Qatar: no library automation.
- Saudi Arabia: MINISIS (version G.01) in use. The library has the following databases:

  1 Catalogue database – about 60,000 Arabic and 21,000 English records.

  2 Subject headings database – about 22,000 Arabic and 19,000 English records.

  3 Kingdom of Saudi Arabia information database – 51,306 documents.

  4 Library and information science database.

  5 Numismatics information database – about 19,000 records.
- Syria: 4th Dimension and Oracle packages are used on Macintosh and Bull DPX2000 computers. The library has the following databases:

  1 Catalogue – 59,000 records to date.

  2 Syrian legislations – 51260 records to the end of 1992.

  3 Political speeches.
- Tunisia: the library has partial automation, and has generated the database for the Arab Maghreb catalogue.
- UAE: the library was until recently using a locally developed package on Wang. The decision has been taken to move to another system, but no alternative has been agreed.

Some libraries have acquired off-line, or have access to foreign databases:

- Iraq: NTIS (National Technical Information Service), 1985–9; POL TOX, 1991–2. Also has access to DIALOG.
- Saudi Arabia: BDL (Business Development Language); BIP ONCD; GPO (Government Printing Office (USA)); LIA; SSI (Social Sciences Index) Full Text.
- Syria: AGRIS (Agricultural Information System); MEDLINE (MEDLARS On-line). Also has access to DIALOG.

Evidently progress in automation throughout this large region is rather uncoordinated, especially since other libraries and information centres in some of the countries are doing much better. This may be the reason why national libraries tend to be ignored in the process of planning and implementing the national information networks that are being activated in many countries.

Working hours

Daily hours of service to users range from 5.5 in Morocco, 6 in Jordan, 7 in Saudi Arabia, 9.5 in Tunisia, to 12 in Egypt and Syria.

The remaining eight countries all provide 8 hours.

Addresses of libraries included in the survey
1   Bibliothèque Nationale d'Alger,
     1 ave Frantz Fanon,
     Algiers
     Algeria,
     Tel. 630632

2   National Library of Bahrain,
     Manama
     Bahrain

3   National Library of Egypt,
     Nile Corniche,
     Ramlat Boulaq,
     Cairo,
     Egypt.
     Tel. 775649; 775000; Fax. 754213

4   National Library of Iraq,
     Bab al Muazzam,
     PO Box 14340,
     Baghdad
     Iraq
     Tel. 8849366; 8845043; 8845049

5   National Library of Jordan,
     PO Box 6070,
     Amman,
     Jordan
     Tel. 664549; 664985; 610311; Fax. 616832

6   Libyan National Library,
     PO Box 9127,
     Benghazi,
     Libya

7   Bibliothèque Nationale,
     BP 20,
     Nouakchott,
     Mauritania
     Tel. 24-35

8   Bibliothèque Générale et Archives,
     BP 1003,
     Rabat,
     Morocco
     Tel. 771890; 771252; 776062; Fax. 708318 (The Ministry)

9   Qatari National Library,
    PO Box 205,
    Doha,
    Qatar.
    Tel. 429955; Fax. 429976

10 King Fahd National Library,
    PO Box 7572,
    Riyadh 11472,
    Saudi Arabia
    Tel. 4653615; 4645197; 4624888; Fax. 4645341

11 Assad National Library,
    PO Box 3639,
    Damascus,
    Syria
    Tel. 338255; Fax 320804

12 Bibliothèque Nationale,
    BP 42,
    Tunis,
    Tunisia
    Tel. 256921; 245333; Fax 342700

13. National Library,
    PO Box 2380,
    Abu Dhabi,
    United Arab Emirates
    Tel. 215300; Fax 336059

Sources
(a) Questionnaire distributed to the selected sample of thirteen national libraries. Nine responses were received.
(b) Ibn Issa, Salah Eddin, *Directory of libraries in the Arab world*,Tunis, ALECSO, 1992.
(c) *World of learning*, London, Europa Publications, 1991.

Notes
1   Arab Maghreb, or Maghrib – Peoples and cultures of the north coastal region of Africa. Countries included in the region are Morocco, Algeria, Tunisia, and the western part of Libya. Bounded on the south by the Sahara. *New Encyclopaedia Britannica; micropaedia*, vol. 6, 1983, p. 482.
2   Arab Mashreq, or Mashriq – The cultural patterns prevailing in an area extending from the western border of Egypt to the western border of Iran. Modern countries included in the region, often

referred to as the Near or Middle East are: Egypt, Sudan, Saudi Arabia, the Yemens, Oman, Kuwait and the smaller Gulf States, Israel, Jordan, Lebanon, Syria, and Iraq. *New Encyclopedia Britannica; micropaedia*, vol. 6, 1983, p. 668.

3 A survey of education for library and information science in Egypt, the Maghreb countries, and Sudan

Mohammed Fathi Abdel-Hadi and Abdelmajid Bouazza

The objective of this survey is to give an account of the state of library science education in Egypt, the Maghreb countries, and Sudan, and therefore it deals with the topic as it applies to the entire African sector of the Arab world. Data has been collected by questionnaire, sent to 13 schools of library and information science in these countries. Only four responded, making a response rate of 30.76%, and the authors used recently published sources to supplement their information.

Egypt

Formal education for librarianship began in Egypt in 1951. It was the first new programme in Africa or the Middle East for almost half a century, and was established at the Higher Institute of Archives and Librarianship, Cairo University. It was intended to meet the need of the library profession for personnel capable of developing Egyptian libraries, many of which are the custodians of precious collections of manuscripts, papyrus documents and historic rare books. The Institute had a four-year academic programme and awarded a Diploma in Librarianship and Archives.[1] Three years later, in 1954, it was merged into the Faculty of Arts and became one of the university's academic departments; the Department of Librarianship of Cairo University.

Revisions of the programmes since then include the division of the department into two sections in 1976; Library Science and Archives, each with separate curricula, when it became the Department of Librarianship and Archives.[2]

In 1984, further programme development introduced major changes, and the most recent developments were due to start in the 1993–4 academic session. Henceforth the study of librarianship and archives will be generalized for three years, with specializations in the fourth, from which students will choose one of the following three sections: Library Science; Archives; Information Technology. Influenced by the changes in curriculum the department's latest name is the Department of Librarianship, Archives and Information.[3] This reflects the emphasis on information science and technology courses, to cope with current trends in the field.

The department was the first, and for three decades remained the only institution for librarianship and archive education in Egypt. The 1980s saw a boom in library education, and other departments were created in the face of growing enrolments, to meet the demand for places. These were:

1 Department of Library and Information Science, Faculty of Arts, Alexandria University, opened 1981–2.
2 Department of Librarianship and Archives, Faculty of Arts, Beni-Suef (affiliated with Cairo University), opened 1985–6.
3 Department of Librarianship and Archives, Tanta University, opened 1986–7.
4 Department of Librarianship, Faculty of Arts, El-Munifia University, opened 1991–2.[4]

There are at present five academic departments of library and information science, in addition to other departments that teach related courses.

The five (assuming output from the most recently started course at El-Munifia) major departments produce graduate professional librarians, information specialists, and archivists, who meet the needs of all kinds of libraries, archives institutions, and information centres. Their academic staff are actively involved in the affairs of the profession in Egypt and elsewhere. They offer consultancies on the establishment and development of information services, in addition to their personal research activities, teaching and supervision of training programmes in library and information work.

Study programmes
All Egyptian departments offer undergraduate (first degree) and graduate (postgraduate diploma, master's (MA) and PhD) programmes.

Undergraduate level
The bachelor's degree is awarded on completion of four years of study. Students are admitted to the programme on the result of the general secondary school examination. The BA course general is a mixture of library science and archives (except at Cairo University, where three years of general studies are followed by specialized study in the fourth).

The education system is a mix between institutions, of the formerly conventional academic year of terms in some, and the semester system in others. All the departments have generally similar programmes of taught courses.

Details set out below are of the courses at Cairo University, which is chosen as the senior Egyptian department. An undergraduate student here must take 44 courses during four academic years. Courses can be aggregated in two major areas: library and information science, and contributive courses. The former represents 68% of total marks, and the latter 32%. Contributive courses dominate in the first year and decrease gradually in successive years.

Library and information science
1   Introductory courses: introduction to information sciences, archives.
2   Information sources: audiovisual (AV) materials, general reference sources, Arabic manuscripts.
3   Technical services courses: collection development, descriptive cataloguing, classification, subject cataloguing, indexing and abstracting.
4   User services: library and information services.
5   Institutional courses: university libraries, special libraries, management of libraries and information centres.
6   Systems and technology courses: information retrieval systems, system design and analysis, new media for information storage and retrieval, information networks and communication technology.
7   Texts courses: specialized texts in a first foreign language (English or French)

Contributive courses
Includes: principles of statistics; introduction to humanities and social sciences; introduction to science and technology; first foreign language (English or French); Arabic language; public administration and linguistics.

Students receive practical training in some courses, like cataloguing and classification. In addition to theoretical classes in such subjects, they are divided into small groups for practice. This is in addition to a practicum in various libraries and information centres in the fourth year.[5]

Graduate level
The two channels of graduate studies in Egyptian universities are firstly, MA and PhD degrees.

MA study requires one year of advanced course work, prior to a second year working on a thesis. Admissions to these courses are BA in library science with a minimum C grade point average. For entry to a PhD course entrants must hold an MA in Library and Information Science (LIS), and prepare a dissertation on an original topic, during a period of not less than two years of registered work.

The secondary route is via the Diploma programme. This accepts as students those who have a BA in any other subject. The department in Cairo offers two diplomas: 1) Diploma of Library and Information Science; 2) Diploma of Archives. Each requires two years of study. A diploma holder may pursue graduate studies towards MA and PhD, subject to certain requirements.[6]

Academic staff
The department has 22 full-time academic staff, made up of PhD holders in the field who studied in Egypt, the United States and the United Kingdom. There are also some 15 assistant lecturers, MA holders who are working on their PhD. There are in addition ten demonstrators, who have BA degrees and are actively preparing their MA degrees. The department invites visiting professors to fill the gap in certain areas where expertise is needed. Contributive courses are taught by faculty members from other departments or colleges within the university.

The academic staff of the department carry heavy teaching loads. At the time of writing, five are teaching on secondment in the Arab Gulf States, and others are involved in teaching in other short-staffed departments in Egypt.

There is a total of 11 PhD holders among the academic staff of all the other departments in the country, and there are in addition an unspecified number of assistant lecturers and demonstrators.

Enrolment and alumni
Since the 1950–1 academic year, the numbers of students enrolled at Cairo have grown steadily, reaching 900 on the four-year programme in 1992–3. It has become the largest library science institution in Egypt, and also in the Arab world. There were, in the same academic year, 1992–3 a total of 750 undergraduate students in the other Egyptian departments. There were, in the same year some 200 postgraduate enrolments for diploma, MA and PhD studies in Cairo. The steady increase in numbers studying library science at all levels may be due, not only to opportunities at home for graduates, but also elsewhere in the Arab world.[7]

Output from all these departments is likely to rise dramatically, especially when the graduates of El-Munifia emerge in the middle of the 1990s. Cairo, which in 1992–3 had an undergraduate total of some 900, awarded a total of 3,500 degrees in its first 40 years. This impressive total is set to increase rapidly due to the success of present teaching methods. The other departments, which all date from the 1980s have graduated some 650 to date. This lesser, but significant contribution to the total output of library and information professionals is also making an impact in the market for personnel.

It may be assumed that the much lower proportion of graduate degrees is likely to rise in the future.

Facilities and services
All library science departments generally share teaching accommodation in affiliated colleges. There are, however, private rooms for certain staff. The following facilities exist for specialized use:

(a) Personal computer laboratories and AV rooms
(b) Bibliographic laboratories that comprise samples of reference books for practical training; sample titles for practical cataloguing, classification, and subject analysis.
(c) Special libraries' collections of books, periodicals, dissertations and reports in the field of specialization. It should be noted that students may generally make use of college and main university libraries.

Morocco
Formal education for library and information science started in Morocco in 1974, when L'Ecole des Sciences de l'Information (ESI) was set up with assistance from UNESCO/UNDP.[8] The school is under the authority of the Ministry of Planning, with a separate building and budget. Its main objectives are:

1 Meeting the country's needs for information specialists.
2 Promoting information science nationally, and encouraging research in this area.[9]

Training offered by the school is hybrid, both undergraduate and graduate. Graduates of the first level are awarded, after four years (three until the 1988–9 academic year), the diploma of 'informatiste' (Bachelor in Library and Information Science), and students on the graduate programme are awarded, after two years of course work and preparation of a thesis, the diploma of 'informatiste specialisé' (Master in Library and Information Science). Students in the first category are recruited, using an entrance examination, among baccalaureate holders, and government functionaries who are ranked at the 7th, 8th, and 9th grades of the administrative hierarchy. The graduate programme is open, also by entry examination, to bachelor or equivalent degree holders with at least four years' work experience in either the public or private sector. On average, 120 students are selected for the undergraduate course each year, and 10 to 15 for the post-graduate programme. The annual output is between 70 and 90 at undergraduate level, and up to 10 at graduate level.[10]

Curriculum

Undergraduate level
The curriculum at ESI is set out below:[11]

Library and information science
1 Foundations of information science.
2 Information technologies.
3 Information systems: analysis and design.
4 Computer information processing.
5 Strategies and techniques of database searching.
6 Research methods in library and information science.
7 Files processing and data structures.
8 Database management systems.
9 Office automation.
10 Historiography.
11 Introduction to diplomatic and Moroccan palaeography.
12 Oral sources.
13 Conservation and preservation.

Contributive disciplines components
1 History and classification of sciences.
2 Foundations of psychology and cognitive psychology.
3 Foundations of sociology and sociology of knowledge.
4 Logic/philosophy.
5 Law and Moroccan national institutions.
6 History of Morocco.
7 Economics of Morocco.
8 Communication techniques.
9 Management.
10 Computer programming: BASIC (Beginner's all-purpose symbolic instruction code).

Graduate level
Graduate courses are made up as follows:[12]

1 Libraries and information services in their social and

communication context.
2 Sources of information and bibliographic searching.
3 Organization of information for storage and retrieval.
4 Management of libraries and information services.
5 Particular types of libraries and information services.
6 Computer science.
7 Application of computer and other technologies.
8 Manuscripts and records management.
9 Quantitative and research methods.
10 English.

In addition, the graduate curriculum is in two parts: a first semester during which students holding BA and equivalent degrees in fields other than LIS take courses in library and information science. At the same time those with an undergraduate degree in LIS follow courses of equivalent credits in contributive and related fields. In either case, groups must take a two-credit course in statistics, and a four-credit course in English. For both categories of students the first semester offers the choice between a two-credit course in records management and its legal environment, or a two-credit course in computer science.[13] The academic system at ESI consists of a two-semester year.

Facilities, faculty and placement
There are 58 teaching staff at ESI, of whom 18 are full-time professors trained in the United States, Canada and Morocco. On average they have been teaching for 11 years.[14] French is the main teaching language.[15]

Facilities include two computer laboratories, equipped with 50 microcomputers, one audiovisual room, one language laboratory, and a library holding adequate collections of books and periodicals.

Regarding placement of its graduates, ESI has established direct co-ordination with government departments and agencies. A 1986 survey assessed the country's future manpower needs in the library and information professions.

Algeria
Library science education began in Algeria in 1975, when L'Institut de Bibliothéconomie was founded in the capital. There are now three library schools in the country; Institut de Bibliothéconomie d'Alger (founded in 1975), Institut de Bibliothéconomie de Constantine (1982), and Institut de Bibliothéconomie d'Oran (1984). In addition to these, there is the Centre d'Etudes et

de Recherche en Information Scientifique et Technique (CERIST), set up in 1989, which provides special training in scientific and technical information. These institutions all have independent buildings and budgets.[16] The three schools all have the common aim of training librarians, documentalists, and archivists. The objective of CERIST is the training of information specialists in the area of scientific and technical information.

Qualifications offered by the four institutions are:

(a) Institut de Bibliothéconomie, at Alger, Constantine, and Oran each offer DEUA (university diploma) on successful completion of three years of study.

(b) Alger, Constantine and Oran each offer license (bachelor's degree) on successful completion of two years of study.

(c) Alger and Constantine each offer DSB (postgraduate diploma) on successful completion of BSc in any subject plus two years.

(d) Alger and Constantine each offer a master's degree on successful completion of BSc in library science plus two years.

(e) CERIST offers DPGS (professional diploma) on successful completion of BSc in any field plus one year.

Totals of student enrolment in 1992 were:

- Alger: total enrolment 1060; average intake of 200 per annum.
- Constantine: total enrolment 280; average intake of 60 per annum.
- Oran: 460; average intake of 130 per annum.

Curriculum

DEUA cycle
The curriculum designed by Institut de Bibliothéconomie d'Alger for students following the DEUA cycle gives a representative impression of courses in the Algerian library schools. It divides into two sections:

Library science courses
Information sources and bibliographic searching; management of libraries and information services; information technology; archives management; organization of knowledge for information retrieval.

Contributive courses
Communication; statistics; languages; sociology of reading.

License cycle
The curriculum for this at the library school in Alger consists of:

Library science courses
Cataloguing and classification; information sources and bibliographic searching; bibliology; indexing; management of libraries
and information services; archives management; information
technology; information networks.

Contributive courses
Communication techniques; statistics; languages; linguistics;
information theory; social psychology.
Visits to libraries and information services; field-work; thesis.[18]

This programme emphasizes the importance attached to fieldwork. On the DEUA cycle it extends over 30 weeks, twice the
period allocated on the license cycle.[19]

Faculty, facilities and placement
The Algerian library schools are generously staffed. This is partly
due to the numbers of BA holders among full-time faculty. Of the
29 staff in Alger, one holds the degree of PhD, 10 have Master's
degrees, and the remaining 18 have BA. While tuition is in French
at Alger and Oran, Arabic is more generally used at Constantine.

Of the three schools, two suffer from a lack of necessary equipment; only Oran has a computer laboratory, equipped with eight
microcomputers;[20] the others are much worse off. There is only
one microcomputer at Alger. The libraries of all three schools
have inadequate collections of books and periodicals.

Total output of qualified personnel during two decades has
been around 2,000 assistant librarians (BA in LIS), 500 library assistants and technicians, and 140 information specialists (DSB or MA
in LIS). There is a continuing and unsatisfied demand for the latter.

Tunisia
Library education in Tunisia began in 1964 at the Institut Ali Bach
Hamba. It transferred in 1969 to L'Ecole Nationale d'Administration (ENA) and subsequently, in 1979, to L'Institut de Presse
et des Sciences de l'Information (IPSI). In 1981 L'Institut Supérieur de Documentation (ISD) was founded, and is at present the
only source of training in the country for information specialists.

Education programme
The undergraduate programme at ISD has two cycles, or parts.
The first cycle takes two years to complete and allows students to

graduate, after gaining 59 credits and a practicum of three weeks' duration, with a university Diploma in Documentation, Librarianship, and Archives Management (Library Assistant). The second cycle takes a further two years for the award of Bachelor in Documentation, Librarianship and Archives Management. For this it is necessary to score 66 credits in compulsory subjects, with a further 16 from options, as well as completing and defending a thesis.

In the first cycle, students are admitted in accordance with the orientation programme set up by the Ministry of Education and Sciences for students holding the high school diploma (baccalaureate). Admission to the second cycle entails having either the university diploma mentioned above, or having successfully completed the first cycle of a bachelor's programme in any other subject field. Diploma holders are considered acceptable for the second cycle according to their grade (10, 5 out of 20, or 52.5% overall as a minimum) if supported by a recommendation of the staff council of the school. Admission requirements for students entering librarianship from other subject fields are based on consideration of each candidate's transcript, and personal interview. Each year some 70 students enter the first cycle, and 35 are enrolled for the second cycle. The total enrolment in 1992–3 was 480.

Curriculum

First cycle
1 Information sources and bibliographic searching.
2 Information processing (cataloguing, classification and indexing).
3 Management of libraries and information services.
4 Archives management.
5 Information technology.
6 Information networks.
7 Communication techniques.
8 Sociology of reading.
9 Communication techniques in Arabic and French.
10 Analysis of historical texts.

Second cycle
In the first year, students entering from other subject fields follow a different programme from that of students with a background in LIS.[21]
1 Libraries and information services in their social and communication context.

2   Sources of information and bibliographic searching.
3   Organization of information for storage and retrieval.
4   Management of libraries and information services.
5   Applications of computer and other information technologies.
6   Manuscripts and records management.
7   Languages.

In addition to courses in the above subject areas, this category of students follows a two-week programme of fieldwork. Similarly with students having a background in library science, they must gain 29 credits in the first year of the second cycle.

In the second year, the formerly separate groups come together in following a common curriculum. The core of this is a two-month period of fieldwork, and courses in research methods; computer and information technology; user studies, and languages. They also select two options from:

(a)   Planning and evaluation of libraries.
(b)   Multimedia school centres and libraries.
(c)   Manuscripts and records management.
(d)   Information and business management.

They must also prepare and defend a thesis on an approved topic to gain their bachelor's degree.

Faculty, facilities, and placement

There are 56 teaching staff, including 17 full-time professors, who were trained variously in France, Canada, the United Kingdom, the United States, Morocco, and Tunisia. The professors' average length of teaching experience is three years. This surely indicates rapid growth in numbers by absorption of recently qualified personnel.[23] Tuition is in both Arabic and French.

ISD has two computer laboratories, equipped with 20 microcomputers, one audiovisual room, and a library of about 14,000 titles (mainly in French and Arabic), 300 journals, and 450 reference works.

Regarding placement of its graduates, ISD has established direct co-ordination with government departments and agencies, including employment offices. It also maintains close contact at personal level with heads of government and para-statal institutions. The demands of the job market are reflected in biannual changes in the content of elective courses.

Libya

Library science education in Libya dates from the founding of the

Department of Library and Information Science at Al Fatah University in 1976. Two other departments followed, at Garyounes University in 1985 and at Al-Jabal Al Gharbi University in 1993. All three are integrated in faculties, and have neither separate premises nor budgets.[24] For lack of detailed information this part of the survey will focus on the department at Al-Fatah University. Its objectives are stated to be:

1 Training information specialists who will be capable of managing all kinds of library and information services.
2 Providing continuing education for information professionals.
3 Promoting research and publications in library and information science.
4 Training researchers and faculty in library and information science.

Education programme

The department recruits its students among holders of the high school diploma. All candidates are interviewed, and priority for admission is given to individuals with appropriate work experience. In the academic year 1992–3, 400 students were enrolled.

Curriculum

The department's four-year programme leads to a BA in Librarianship in Information and Science. It consists of three sections:

Library and information science
1 Information processing (cataloguing and classification).
2 Information sources.
3 Information retrieval.
4 Management of library and information services.
5 Periodicals.
6 Publishing.
7 Information analysis.
8 Research methods.
9 Information technology.
10 English texts in library and information science.

Contributive fields
1 Statistics.
2 Audiovisual materials.
3 History of science.
4 Arabic language.
5 Foundations of education.

6   Psychology.
7   Political culture.

Fieldwork

Faculty, facilities and placement
There are 18 staff, of whom 13 are full-time professors, 2 part-time professors, and 3 lecturers.

The three departments in the country rely on shared teaching facilities at the institutions where they are located.

The government undertakes placement of graduates, of whom there has been a total output of between 700 and 800 from Al-Fatah alone, since its establishment.[26]

Sudan

The library school, at the Department of Archives and Librarianship of the College of Arts, Omdurman University was founded in 1966. A separate branch for library education for women was set up in the same university in 1972. During subsequent development the name changed, during the session 1990–1, when it became the Department of Information, Archives and Librarianship. Its programme has developed throughout to take account of current changes in professional activities. It aims to enable professionals to work in the various types of Sudanese libraries, archive institutions and information centres.

The sole programme of the department is the four year BA in Library and Information Science. Admissions are based on results achieved by entrants in the general secondary examination.[27]

Students are required to take 53 courses in a full academic year, of which 24 are non-specialized in Islamic and Arabic studies. There are two practicum courses in the second and third years, additional to practical training components in certain other courses.[28]

The department suffers from the lack of suitably qualified academic staff. At the time of writing faculty staff consist of two who have Master's degrees, and three demonstrators with BA Consequently the department relies to a large extent on part-time staff from other institutions.

The mixed student population totals 200, with an average annual output of 40 undergraduates.

Despite these severe problems it is thought that the department, by the dedication of its staff, may be meeting the immediate needs of the country.

Conclusions

1 Library education in these countries dates from the early 1950s, at the premier department in Cairo University. Most other departments were established during the 1970s and 1980s.

2 The most usual programme at undergraduate level extends over four years. Graduate studies are offered in three of the countries, Algeria, Egypt, and Morocco.

3 Shortage of qualified, full-time academic staff obliges most of the departments to employ part-time staff from other institutions.

4 Although reasonably good facilities are reported in Morocco and Tunisia, most of the others are handicapped by the absence of appropriate information technology resources.

5 The Arabic and French languages are used in teaching in Algeria, Morocco and Tunisia. Arabic predominates in Egypt, Libya and Sudan.

6 Despite the continuing need for staff in libraries and information centres, the job market cannot take up the total output of graduates in some countries in the region, for reasons both economic and social.

References

1 Al-Mahdi, Mohammed, *A Historical study of education for archives and librarianship in Egypt 1951–1964* (Translated title, Arabic text), Cairo, Cairo University Press, 1964, 4.

2 Abdel-Hadi, Mohammed Fathi, 'Education and training of librarians and information specialists in Egypt' (Translated title, Arabic text). In: Abdel-Hadi, *Librarianship and information*, Cairo, Maktbat Al Dar Al-Arabia Lel-Ketab, 1993, 30–2.

3 Halwagy, A. S., 'Recent changes in library education in Egypt', *Journal of education for library and information science*, **33** (3), summer 1992, 256.

4 Abdel-Hadi, op. cit., 33.

5 Cairo University, Faculty of Arts, *Internal statute of the Faculty of Arts*, (Translated title, Arabic text), Cairo, the Faculty, 1993, 35–7.

6 Abdel-Hadi, op. cit., 44–7.

7 Ibid., 51.

8 Mokhtari, Mimouni, *Library and information science education in Morocco: curriculum development and adaptation to change*, Rabat, Ecole des sciences de l'information, 1992, 2.

9 Ecole des sciences de l'information, *School brochure* (in Arabic), Rabat, ESI, 1990, 3.

10 Mokhtari, op. cit., 5.

11   Ibid., 12.
12   Miski, AbdelHamid, *Education of information specialists in the Arab region*, Paris, UNESCO, PGI, 1993, 13.
13   Ibid.
14   Ibid., 24.
15   Ibid., 15.
16   AbdelKader, Abdellilah, *La Formation des professionels de l'information en Algérie: quelques considérations générales*, Oran, Institut de Bibliothéconomie et des Sciences Documentaires, Université d'Oran, 1993, 5.
17   Ibid.
18   *Programme du cycle de Licence en Bibliothéconomie et des Sciences Documentaires, Université d'Alger, 1990*, Alger, l'Université, 1990.
19   Miski, op. cit., 15.
20   Ibid., 8.
21   Ibid., 19
22   Ibid.
23   Ibid., 24.
24   Sharif, Abdullah, *A Brief study on training of library professionals in Libya* (Translated title, Arabic text), Tripoli, Al-Fatah University, 1993, 6.
25   Ibid.
26   Ibid.
27   Miski, op. cit., 35.
28   Omdurman University, Faculty of Arts, *Program of study of Department of Information, Archives and Librarianship* (Translated title, Arabic text), Omdurman, the Faculty, 1990.

4 Education and training of librarians in the Maghreb (Algeria, Morocco, Tunisia)

Halima Semra

The need for training of librarians in the Maghreb made itself felt in the 1960s, following national independence.

The setting up of institutions of documentation such as: archives, National Library, university libraries, documentation centres, and others came up against the lack of trained personnel, capable of managing the different types of collection and service.

Teaching of library science was initially undertaken by institutions such as the Bibliothèque Nationale in Algeria (1963), or the Institut Ali Bach Hamba in Tunisia (1964), prior to the creation of specialized library science institutions, which have been created only in the last 20 years.

Although every community, developed and developing, is aware of the importance of documentation and information, the profession of librarian is not usually looked upon favourably in the Maghreb. No doubt because the profession is still young, but also because the means to ensure its development are still lacking, be they human, material or financial.

Algeria

From 1963 onwards, the formation of 'technical' personnel commenced in response to the lack of librarians who were able to manage existing library collections.

A decade later there was evidence of a need for 'scientific' personnel, with the creation and multiplication of national organs of documentation, and the first institute of librarianship was created in 1975 at the Université d'Alger. Other regions followed this example in the 1980s; the Institut de Bibliothéconomie at the Université de Constantine, 1982–83, and the Institut de Bibliothéconomie d'Oran, 1984–85.

Grades of training

There are different levels of training at the three institutes, as shown in Table 4.1 below.

Table 4.1

Level of training	Date started	Institute	Entry qualification	Duration of course (years)
DEUA	1990–91	Algiers, Constantine, Oran	Baccalaureate	3
Licenciate	1975 1982–3 1984–5 1982–3	Algiers, Constantine, Oran Constantine	Baccalaureate	4
DSB (2)	1982–3 1992–3	Algiers, Oran	Licenciate All Option	2
DESS (3)	1990–1	Algiers	Licenciate	2
Master	1982–83 1989–90	Algiers Constantine	Licenciate in Librarianship	2
DPGS (4)	1989–90	CERIST – Algiers	Licenciate or equivalent	1

Channels for training
1 Diplôme d'Etudes Universitaires Appliquées (DEUA). This
   course was provided initially by the National Library from
   1963 to 1969, and by the Ministry of Information and Culture
   from 1969 to 1985, under the title DTBA (Diplôme de
   Technicien de Bibliothèque et Archives).
2 Diplôme Supérieur de Bibliothécaires (DSB).
3 Diplôme d'Etudes Supérieures Spécialisées (DESS) – option
   Archives.
4 Diplôme de Post-graduation Spécialisé (DPGS).

Syllabuses
The initial syllabus for the licenciate and the DEUA (Annexes 1
and 2) underwent changes of content.

The licenciate syllabus in use from 1974 to 1984 contained
some awkward features. As an example, the modules for general
culture took up a sizeable proportion of total teaching hours
(about 700), by comparison with the technical modules (about
1,000). As a further example, in the final year of the original syllabus, concern was expressed with three options on documentation, library science, and archives, after problems arose where
final students found themselves blocked by the statement on their
diploma. Since the area of interest was not clearly defined, it was
not apparent that the qualification would be suitable for a particular post, such as that of documentalist in archives.

A new syllabus was drawn up in 1990–1 by the CPN (Comité
Pédagogique National), in response to certain findings. In view of
the development of the new information technologies, it became

necessary to place emphasis on these in teaching. Accordingly the general culture modules gave way to a large extent to others of professional character.

With regard to the other diplomas:

1 DSB (Annex 3)
The first postgraduate form of training, it was established in 1982 in response to the staffing needs of libraries, chief among these being the universities, where at this time there was a disastrous lack of trained staff.

The first year of the syllabus covers courses and classwork bearing on basic subjects such as: organization and management of libraries; bibliology; cataloguing; bibliography; archives; documentation techniques; and technology. The second year is devoted to practical work in a documentary institution, and the preparation of a thesis.

2 Master's (Annex 4)
This course is open to holders of degrees in library science, to provide library training institutions with teachers The syllabus is so arranged that repetition of work for the licenciate is avoided, while certain modules are covered in greater depth: for example, documentary research and data processing.

Theoretical instruction is given in the first year, together with a month's practical work experience. The second year is devoted to the preparation of a thesis.

These various forms of training are more or less permanently available (postgraduate degrees being run subject to ability and means). As a recent development, other forms of training are being geared to the needs of special institutions for qualified staff. Thus, the Institut de Bibliothéconomie d'Alger in 1990–1 started a DESS (Annex 5) for training archivists. 25 candidates were enrolled, more than half being staff of the Archives Nationales.

The Centre d'Etudes et de Recherche en Information Scientifique et Technique (CERIST) provides a one-year diploma course (DPGS), specializing in scientific and technical information. There have been 33 candidates since the start in 1988, 18 of whom were awarded diplomas.

Tables 4.2, 4.3 and 4.4 below show the number of enrolments and diplomas awarded in the three institutes since their creation.

Table 4.2   Algiers: 1975–1993

Level of training	Enrolments	Diplomas
Licenciate	1,201	658
DEUA	361	228
DSB	181	30
Masters	81	5
DESS	25	—

Table 4.3   Constantine: 1982–1993

Level of training	Enrolments	Diplomas
Licenciate	371	99
DEUA	158	67
DSB	30	16
Masters	9	—

Table 4.4   Oran: 1983–1993

Level of training	Enrolments	Diplomas
Licenciate	625	116
DEAU	863	191

Teaching staff

There are some 60 permanent teaching staff in the three institutes of library science; 40 in Algiers, 10 at Constantine and 10 in Oran. Their qualifications vary from State Doctorate, through Doctorate 3rd cycle, single thesis, master's (MA) degree to DSB. There are, of course, more holders of MAs and DSBs than there are holders of state doctorates.

Temporary posts are more common than permanent ones; 30 in Algiers, 20 at Constantine, and 14 in Oran.

Morocco

The concept of a professional training in information stems from the creation of the Centre National de Documentation (CND) and from the realization, following an enquiry in 1971, of the lack of specialist manpower in the field of documentation. The Ecole des Sciences de l'Information (ESI) was therefore brought into being in 1974, with the help of UNESCO.

Grades of training

At the start of 1974–5 teaching was provided at two levels.

Computer studies course
Open to holders of the baccalaureate or an equivalent diploma, the course takes three years. In the first 15 years, up to 1989, 3,124 students enrolled, of whom 746 were successful in gaining diplomas. The present intake is between 50 and 85 each year, a rise in numbers encouraged by improved facilities at the school.

Specialized computer studies course
Open to computer specialists and to holders of the licenciate or an equivalent diploma, the candidate must, in addition have four years of service in the public, semi-public or private sectors, in order to receive the diploma. In the same 15-year period, 300 were enrolled and 68 received the diploma.

Teaching staff
In 1989 there were 18 teaching staff holding permanent appointments, the majority with information science degrees from abroad (State Doctorate, Doctorate 3rd cycle or equivalent degree),and 35 in temporary posts.

Tunisia
Professional education began in 1964 at the Institut Ali Bach Hamba, with the aid and support of the West German Friedrich Neumann Foundation. Courses were open to candidates holding the baccalaureate, or those reaching a final acceptable standard, subject to an entrance examination, and with experience in institutions of documentation.

The syllabus, lasting six months, covered theory and technology, being based on that of the Institut des Etudes Sociales de l'Etat de Bruxelles. Practical training was received during a period of study in the former Federal Republic of Germany.

In 1969–70, training was transferred to the Ecole Nationale d'Administration (ENA), and was intended for candidates who had attained various levels of secondary education, were baccalaureates, or postgraduates. Three syllabuses were therefore envisaged, applicable to: Documentaliste-Bibliothécaire-Archiviste (DBA) assistants on the 1st grade – 15 months; DBA seniors on the 2nd grade – 2 years; DBA on the 3rd grade – 2 years.

When the Institut Supérieur de Bibliothécaire was established in 1981, with responsibility for training to higher levels of DBA, it carried on the development and administration of these courses.

Teaching staff
There were 28 in 1988, of whom only two were permanent.

Comparison of training in the three countries

While education for librarianship has been available from a single institution in Morocco, a proliferation of courses in Algeria and Tunisia led to a variety of possibilities for training which is now concentrated in university institutions.

Teaching syllabuses

Continuous evaluation of the syllabus, in the light of development in the three countries, has brought about some redefinition of content. A notable example is Algeria, where the courses of general culture have given way to the introduction of new modules such as: new information technologies; studies on users and information searching; evaluation of systems; management and marketing of information. The object of such innovations has been to adapt course material to the modern role of the librarian.

In general, training now consists of specialist theoretical instruction, and practical instruction through work experience and visits.

Teaching staff

Training immediately came up against the obstacle of a shortage of well-qualified teaching staff. At first, there was wide dependence on lecturers trained abroad, whose qualifications had been obtained mostly at European universities. Even now, despite increasing numbers of awards of postgraduate degrees, there are still not enough full-time lecturers in relation to the continual increase in students.

Thus the International Federation of Library Associations and Institutions' (IFLA) criterion, that there should be a (permanent) staff/student ratio 1:12, is far from being met. At the time of writing the ratios appear to be: Morocco, 1:18; Algeria, 1:25 or 30, Tunisia, not known.

To the general shortage of lecturers must be added the almost complete absence of certain specialisms among full-time teaching staff: computer-based information systems; archives; management and marketing of information systems. Also the lack of equipment, and the poor holdings of libraries in support of studies.

Although there are signs of a slight increase in numbers of full-time teaching staff who have a basic training in library science, the matter of their continuous education has yet to be tackled. The rapid and continuous evolution of the profession makes it imperative to update the lecturers. A beginning has been made, by means of what are usually brief overseas training secondments;

but a greater depth of retraining and exposure to techniques is needed to make the right impact.

Training and employment

Since their creation, teaching institutions in the Maghreb have worked towards the common objective of increasing the numbers of qualified staff in the existing institutes of documentation. However, results have varied in the three countries.

In Morocco, it would seem that graduates of the ESI find employment immediately they have obtained their degrees. In 1986, ESI carried out, with the CND, a 'National enquiry on staffing in information-documentation', in order to evaluate the need for information specialists.

In Algeria, it is often the case that graduates fail to find employment, despite the fact that the need for them is apparent in every sector. A paradoxical situation that has arisen because there have been no serious studies of manpower needs in specialist fields.

In Tunisia, the enquiry by Bouazza[1] into the training/employment ratio concluded that the training provided by the Institut Supérieur de Documentation (ISD) does not meet the expectations of employers.

In response to the urgency of the situation, a start has been made in Algeria, on holding a dialogue between training institutions and the socio-economic sectors, to determine the balance between content of courses and the needs of employers. The recommendations of the Tunisian survey mentioned above may be applicable to all three countries, with regard to the content of retraining provided for lecturers so that their courses may be more relevant to market needs:

1 Pay particular attention to the practical aspects and to periods of work experience in training.
2 Improvement in written and oral expression in Arabic, French, and English.
3 Pay more attention to instruction in the new technologies of information and telecommunications.
4 Introduce the student to information technology.
5 Proceed with regular revision of teaching syllabuses.
6 Take account of the interdisciplinary character of the information sciences.
7 Establish lines of co-operation and co-ordination with the socio-economic sector, and consult employers when drawing up syllabuses.
8 Enhance the quality of teaching staff, by making grants for

doctoral studies in information science to the best graduates and professionals.

9 Establish a pattern of updating training for lecturers.
10 Establish realistic criteria for admission of students into training institutions.
11 Transform the Institute's library into one of appropriate scope and develop its computers, audiovisual, and teaching facilities.
12 Develop in the teaching of information sciences a spirit of analysis, criticism, synthesis and creativity, by increasing the number of research projects, undertaken by both individuals and groups.

Scientific activities

Each teaching institution organizes seminars, study days, colloquia; at national level:

- ESI organizes annually a National Day of Information, in collaboration with the CND and the Association Nationale des Informatistes.
- ISD and the Instituts de Bibliothéconomie of Algiers, Oran, and Constantine, which hold annual seminars; or at international level, meetings between Maghrebian specialists allow for exchange of experience in the subject field. Recent gatherings have included:

    - The Colloque international de Bibliologie, the first bilateral Algero-French colloquium on library science, Algiers, 22–7 November 1992.
    - A meeting at ESI of experts in the teaching of information sciences in the Arab region, held with the collaboration of UNESCO, 10–13 May 1993.

In addition, the three countries maintain links with overseas institutions teaching library science in France, the United Kingdom, and Canada.

The following journals of library science should be noted, although the last has unfortunately ceased publication for the time being:

- Algeria: *Revue de l'information scientifique et technique* (*RIST*)
- Morocco: *Bulletin de l'informatiste* (monthly)
- *L'informatiste* (half-yearly)
- Tunisia: *La Revue maghrébine de documentation*

Conclusion

The teaching of information science in the Maghreb has undergone development in recent years, with varied approaches to staff training (at middle level in Tunisia, middle and senior levels in Algeria and Morocco).

However, there are many points of convergence which would benefit from the stimulus of effective co-operation between the three countries in drawing up common training projects.

Annex 1

Licenciate – 1st year

Subjects:

The living language; introduction to the information and communication sciences; cataloguing: author-title; introduction to data processing; introduction to bibliographical methods and bibliography in general; organization and management of documentation systems; documentation systems terminology; use of language; epistemology; Applied statistics in information sciences.

Licenciate – 2nd year

Living foreign language; cataloguing: title-author; special bibliography; information systems terminology; computer-based information; archives; bibliology; linguistics of documentation; visits to documentation centres.

Licenciate – 3rd year

Living foreign languages; computer-based information (computerization); information systems terminology; information and documentation technology; archive techniques; research methodology; information theory; psycho-sociology in the communication of information.

Licenciate – 4th year

Semester 7

Information science in the Arab world; evaluation of information systems; networks and information systems.

Note: the student also chooses three other modules from a common list drawn up for the Cours supérieur of the Institute.

Semester 8

A period of work experience of three months, comprising five half-days in each week, and an end-of-course dissertation.

Annex 2

DEUA – 1st year

Subjects:

Introduction to information methods; the living language;

terminology of documentation; cataloguing I; general bibliography; management and organization of documentation institutions; introduction to data processing; methodology and technique of research; archives.

DEUA – 2nd year
The living language; cataloguing II; special bibliography; terminology of documentation; bibliology; archives technique; computerization; cultural animation techniques; statistics.

DEUA – 3rd year
Seminar, 8 hours per week; practical work experience, 5-half days per week; cultural activities in seminar form, 8 hours per week.

Annex 3
Higher Diploma in librarianship [Diplôme supérieur des bibliothèques]

Subjects	No. of hours Course	No. of hours TD	Weighting Coefficient	Mark
1 Library science	60	60	2	40
2 Library administration and management	30	—	1	20
3 Description and analysis of documents	30	150	2	40
4 Bibliography	60	60	3	60
5 Information systems technology	60	60	2	40
6 Bibliology	60	60	2	40
7 Introduction to archives; visits to libraries; dissertation	30	—	1	20
			13	20

Note: Weighting coefficients: 1 = 20; 2 = 40; 3 = 60.

Annex 4
Master's
1   communication and society; 2   government publications; 3   terminology of documentation; 4   bibliology; 5   computer-based information and research; 6   English; 7   teaching methods; 8   bibliography; 9   communication and users.

Annex 5
DESS
Programme for archivists' training course and practical work:
legislation and organization of Algerian archives; management and care of archive material; Algerian history and institutions; organization and function of an archives centre; sit-

ing, facilities and protection of archives; business records; techniques related to archives; archives and data processing.

Annex 6
Centre d'Etudes de Recherche sur l'Information Scientifique et Technique (Algeria)
Teaching modules for DPGS
1st 4-month period:
Organization and management of documents; microcomputing; introduction to IST [Scientific and technological information]; English + information systems.
2nd 4-month period:
Documentation terminology; computer-based information; new information technology; networks + English.
3rd 4-month period
Algorhythmics; scientometry; communications; English.

Annex 7
1st year Information Sciences:
Basics of information sciences; introduction to library science; history and classification of science; basics of psychology and cognitive psychology; basics of sociology and sociology of learning; logic (philosophy); mathematics; economy; law and national institutions; Moroccan history; communications techniques; French; English.
2nd year Information Sciences:
Role and functions of information services; classification I; bibliographic description: monographs; archives: current records and care of files; reference services and general sources of information; practical work experience; introduction to data processing; statistics; Moroccan economy; computer programming (BASIC); French; English.
3rd year Information Sciences:
Classification II; bibliographic description: serials and official publications; indexing and making digests; information technology; audiovisual techniques and documentation; sources of information in technology, *or* sources of information in social sciences; computer processing of information; information systems: analysis and design; seminar on preparation for work experience; management; mass communication; English.

Options: History of the book and libraries; publishing and bibliology; *or* programming (PASCAL); information networks, *or* administration and management of non-current and completed archives; analysis of archives, arrangement, access, and research tools.

4th year Information Sciences

Information law; strategy and technique of database searching; planning and management of information services; computerization of documentary functions; research methods; work experience; follow-up to work experience; end-of-studies project.

Options: Children's books; school libraries; public libraries; research and special libraries, *or* file processing and data frames; DBMS [database management system]; office automation, *or* historiography; introduction to diplomatic and to Moroccan palaeography; oral sources; conservation and preservation.

Annex 8

Allocation of courses

1st–2nd year cycle:

Introduction to information science; cataloguing I; classification, analysis and indexing; general bibliography; research methods; administration documentation; information sociology; planning and management of information services; thesaurus building; cataloguing II; computer-based information I; audiovisual documentation; publishing and bibliology; Arabization and information sciences; information law; introduction to archives; Arab cultural heritage; linguistics; political economy; epistemology of science and technology; history of Arab-Moslem civilization; administrative law; statistics; data processing; English.

Each unit corresponds to 15 hours course work.

2nd year; 2nd cycle:

Seminar on research; comparative and international aspects of information sciences; bibliometry and special bibliography; computer-based information II; Moroccan archives and paleography; school and public libraries; national and university libraries; English.

The final award is conditional on acceptance of the end-of-studies thesis.

Annex 9

Institut Supérieur de Documentation (Tunisia)

First year

Special subjects:

Introduction to library science and documentation; introduction to archives; history of the manuscript and the book; modern bibliology; acquisition and conservation of documents; organization and function of SID [System of information documentation], I; bibliographic description: ISBD(M); documentation terminology, analysis and indexing, I; methodology of documentary research and general bibliographies; psycho-sociology of communication; introduction to general data processing.

Background subjects:

Modern history of the Arab world; history of civilization; administrative and political organization in Tunisia; general economic geography; English; Italian or other language; office management.

Practical work experience

2nd year

Special subjects:

Organization and function of SID [System of information documentation], II; Archives: collection, preservation and organisation; introduction to palaeography; bibliographic description: headings, authors, ISDS; documentation terminology, analysis and indexing, II; special bibliography; arrangement and typology of files; documentary sources for the Arab-Islamic world; typology, processing and conservation of non-book materials: maps, photographs, audiovisual etc.; library technology; data processing in documentation.

Background subjects:

English; Italian or other languages; typing, French and Arabic.

Practical work experience.

Bibliography

1 Bouazza, Abdelmajid, 'Adéquation formation/emploi dans le secteur documentaire en Tunisie', *Documentaliste – sciences de l'information*, **28** (4–5), 1991, 193–6.

2 Gharbi, Ibrahim, *La Formation des informatistes et informatistes spécialisés à l'Ecole des Sciences de l'Information (ESI) de Rabat*, Mémoire de fin de licence – Institut de Bibliothéconomie d'Alger, 1988-1989.

3 Hammou, Jaweher, *Présentation d'une institution de formation en Bibliothéconomie: cas de l'Institut Supérieur de Documentation en Tunis*, Mémoire de fin de licence – Institute de bibliothéconomie d'Alger, 1988.

4 Mansour, Ali, 'ISD – essai analytique du cycle court', *Revue maghrébine de documentation*, 1984, 161–91.

5   Semra, Halima, *Les Problèmes liées au transfert de l'information dans les pays du Maghreb (Algérie – Maroc – Tunisie)*, Mémoire de DEA, Paris, Ecole des Hautes Etudes en Sciences Sociales, 1980.
6   Semra, Halima, 'The Education and training of librarians in Algeria', *INSPEL*, 1987, 219–25.

5   Children's library services in Algeria

Azzedine Bouderbane

In order to analyse the subject of children's library services, we must deal with their practical situation and assess their contribution to the cultural and educational development of Algerian society. The country is still in the process of defining its cultural policy; much effort has so far produced modest results. The education system has encountered various obstacles and cannot stand as a strong supporting factor in development and innovation. Educators and their authorities have not yet realized the cultural potential of children's libraries. Parents and people generally speak more about food than about books. Reading is not yet recognized as a main priority.

Cultural policy in Algeria
Ever since independence, Algeria's leaders have dealt with culture as a changing phenomenon that is neither rigid nor static, but a permanent atom of national identity, continually receiving from and giving to other cultures. Its authenticity lies in the preservation of some key factors, such as the religion of Islam, the Arabic language, and all else that is integral to the national heritage. It must accept progress in respect to its origins.[1]

The Charter of Algiers (the National Charter of 1976) defines the country's culture as being national, revolutionary, and scientific and encourages all forms of cultural development. It emphasizes improvement of the individual's instructional level and technical competence. Its main objective is the promotion of instructional and cultural activities. This aspect is directed, above all, towards the young through the education system, and individual initiatives and productions, backed by exhibitions and artistic activities. The charter also underlines the means that help in disseminating culture, such as the press, radio, television, publishing houses, museums, schools of music, cinema, theatre, cultural centres, and public libraries.

The nation's leaders have consistently stated the necessity:

1   to explain the importance of the cultural and historical heritage;
2   to publish and explain Algeria's fundamental political and social options;
3   to consolidate and improve basic cultural infrastructures;
4   to train well-qualified cultural animators;
5   to clarify the role of cultural staff, so that they can be more effective in their activities.

Algeria has endeavoured to set up cultural institutions throughout the country, to fill the huge gap left after 132 years of colonization. The national culture had to be preserved, and executives in every field had to be trained. The Ministry of Information and Culture had a hard task. It had to establish the fundamental bases of cultural policy in the country through existing institutions such as:

- Algerian radio and television
- Cinemas and film-makers
- Publishing companies
- The Copyright Office
- The National Library
- The National School of Fine Arts
- Cultural centres throughout the country, and their libraries
- Theatres and the National Institute of Dramatists
- The National School of Music
- The National Archival Centre

To fulfil its objectives, the Ministry of Information and Culture has set up four departments; fine arts; fine arts and ruins; cinema and audiovisual aids; public reading and documentation.

State of children's libraries
Colonized by France from 1832 to 1962, Algeria, with a population of some 7,000,000 gained independence and a host of problems. Among the economic, political, and social problems of restructuring, it was faced with the inadequacies of its education system; the majority of the population was illiterate and many new schools had to be established.

More than 30 years later, though Algeria is still making great efforts to develop in every field, library service has not been accorded the priority that it merits as part of the development process. In 1962, the director of the National Library said that 'the library is now a school, a training, an educational and a cultural centre, and the librarian is an educator'. But what we notice now is that the whole education system is handicapped for lack of an efficient library service. Schools were built very rapidly in response to the incredible demand for education expressed by the people, but unfortunately this has not been supported by a similar programme of library provision.

Now, with a population of 26,000,000, including 7,000,000 who are illiterate, Algeria has to respond to the needs of a large young population throughout this very large country whose surface area is 2,382,000 km². Although the Ministry of Health launched a programme of birth-control instruction in 1986, population is still increasing tremendously.[2]

The United Nations Declaration of Children's Rights encourages parents, authorities and national governments to recognize the intellectual right of childhood, and it assures its application. UNESCO has consistently urged the introduction of libraries under national educational plans, and their continued backing, both morally and financially.

The objectives of children's libraries can be summarized as follows:

1 To facilitate access to books.
2 To provide children with a variety of documents that meet their needs and activities.
3 To guide children's choice of reading, and to enhance their reading habits.

They require staff with professional skills in library science and education. They need suitable buildings in which to provide efficient services and a welcoming atmosphere. Together with the various types of resources, they encourage the development of instructional skills, and the flourishing of national culture.

When considering types of library service we expect children's libraries to be included in pubic libraries and cultural centres, as well as in school libraries. In the first two there may be only a small section set aside for a children's library, but unfortunately even this modest provision seldom occurs in Algeria. The situation is so depressing that it is doubtful whether, in this country, children are really taken into account in public library legislation.

Public libraries
Public libraries are intended to serve all citizens located all over the country and to play a central role in the promotion of reading, with a varied and general stock of materials. Any citizen should have the opportunity to use a public library, whose main mission is to provide knowledge and leisure through reading, and to promote the national culture.

Algerian libraries do not yet fulfil this objective. Algiers, the capital, may be proud to possess some of the oldest libraries in Africa, but these institutions face a difficult situation.

The Municipal Library of Algiers was among the first of the early French cultural institutions. It was maintained for nearly a century by the colonizers, and was used exclusively by the Europeans. There were smaller libraries elsewhere, run by and for Algerians, but after the insurrection of 1871 the French closed them. The Municipal Library of Algiers was founded in 1872 and by 1914 had a book stock of 13,607 volumes. During the present century, smaller public libraries were founded in the capital and throughout the country. In 1933 the municipal library service, with its branches, had 63,661 volumes. Close to independence, 2,700 out of a population of 180,000 Europeans were registered public library users. In June 1962, a month before independence, the central Municipal Library building was subjected to bombing, and the greater part of the stock was burned.[3]

A law of 1977 decentralized Algiers into 14 communes, and branches of the municipal library were transferred accordingly. Existing libraries came under the authority of their respective communes, and new communes that moved quickly to set up libraries were: Bab El Oued, Casbah Oued Koriche, Algiers Town Centre, Sidi M'Hamed, El Madania, Kouba, Bir Mourad Rais, Hussein Dey. Their actions were followed by many of the *wilaya* (counties). This accelerated library development was largely prestigious, because they mostly had no guaranteed budget and were mismanaged by unqualified staff. Consequently they had a negative effect on the promotion of reading. According to the Sous Direction du Livre (Department of the Book) of the Ministry of Culture, 552 public library employees have now undertaken an elementary, but necessary training in library techniques: cataloguing, conservation, shelf arrangement, and preparation of book lists.

The major problem faced by public libraries staff is the lack of a statute setting out terms of service. Personnel are discouraged and demotivated by being considered as equivalent to office clerical staff. This affects their performance more than any other constraint on library services.

Between 1980 and 1989 the Ministry of Culture provided public libraries throughout the country, including the 48 *wilaya* with 938,066 books. Since then, because of financial cuts, book stocks have become static. Only the Municipal Library of Algiers receives a regular budget from the ministry. In its central library of 1143 m²; the children's section occupies 80 m²; there are in all

110 reader places for some 600 registered readers, who are served by a staff of six. There is no open access for readers to the stock of 4,488 books in Arabic and 4,512 mostly outdated books in French. The library's budget is 20,000 Dinars per annum.

Of the other libraries in the local communes, few receive more than 5,000 Dinars a year. Some are unable to acquire more than 20 books a year, while others, such as Hussein Dey have been obliged to close down.

Few of these libraries have suitable premises. They are usually housed in the administrative buildings of their commune. There is no legislation that defines their status, or puts communes under obligation to administer them to a given standard. No co-operation takes place. How is it possible then, to assure the promotion of reading? There is no children's section in 95% of them, and young children are allowed in the premises only when accompanied by an adult. However, few Algerian parents make time to accompany their children to libraries. They may take them to the stadium, a café or a restaurant, but seldom to the library. The habit has yet to take root. Loan of books to children is unlikely; audiovisual materials are seldom acquired, and when they do exist they are not used and exploited. Interior decor of the libraries, along with drab furniture and equipment are not attractive to users.

Cultural centres
Each *wilaya* has a cultural centre known as the House of Culture, containing a public library. They have financial autonomy but are linked administratively to the Ministry of Culture. The objectives of the centres are:

1 To promote a living culture through wide ranging cultural activities.
2 To create and publish artistic production.
3 To promote interaction nationally and internationally.
4 To encourage meetings and dialogue between artists.
5 To provide the practical means to enhance cultural and artistic activities.
6 To organize cultural activities, especially performances, films, conferences and exhibitions.
7 To promote public reading.
8 To publicize information about outstanding events.
9 To programme visits to natural, historical and cultural sites.
10 To establish clubs for artistic, didactic and recreational purposes.

11   To print and publish cultural periodicals.
12   To participate in cultural and artistic events at home and abroad.
13   To co-operate by exchange with similar institutions elsewhere.

The centres face problems in realizing their objectives:

1   Finance: inadequate budgets that constrain every kind of administrative and outgoing activity.
2   Staff: not enough qualified and experienced personnel.
3   Space: inadequate premises, especially the area allocated to the library.
4   Resources: inadequate technical equipment and support facilities for performances.
5   Social problems: lack of resources undermines staff motivation.

The first cultural centres were set up in Algiers, Constantine and Oran in 1974; others followed at Tizi Ouzou (1975), Batna (1976), Medea (1979), Tlemcen (1980), Saida (1981), Setif (1985), and at Annaba, Ouargla, El Oued and Tamanrasset in 1986.

The organization of and the dynamism exerted in each house of culture vary from one *wilaya* to another according to the competence of staff, their facilities, and the support received from local authorities.

Children may register at the centres on payment of an annual fee of 50 Dinars. They can then take part in the activities that interest them. Up to six years ago there were no children's sections in the libraries but some have developed following the engagement of suitably qualified professional staff. However, awareness of these emerging children's libraries is low, because of poor publicity by the centres where developments have actually taken place. The writer feels that Algeria's cultural centres operate more as business ventures than public services, taking 50 Dinars from members without due attention to providing better libraries.

Student use of libraries is high, and in the inadequate reading rooms in Algiers, Constantine and Oran there are some 50 readers for every reader place. Book stock varies between libraries, from about 7,000 to 20,000 volumes.

Table 5.1   Levels of education of staff in selected cultural
centres[4]

Centre	Graduate	Secondary	Middle	Primary	No schooling	Total	No.of library staff
Batna	1	8	3	8	10	30	2
T.Ouzou	2	5	4	7	24	42	0
Medea	5	4	3	4	10	27	1
Tlemcen	5	5	3	3	12	30	2
Saida	1	3	6	4	6	20	0
Setif	1	10	6	10	8	35	0
Ouargla	1	1	3	1	3	9	0
El Oued	1	3	4	3	5	16	0

Table 5.2   Statistics of selected cultural centre libraries

Centre	Seats	Members	Open access	Book stock/ Arabic	Book stock/ foreign languages
Batna	145	1,061	no	5,000	7,000
T. Ouzou	250	1,600	no	12,000	10,000
Medea	150	700	no	7,000	3,000
Tlemcen	100	300	no	7,000	6,000
Saida	30	—*	no	3,240	6,000
Setif	150	700	no	—*	5,000
Ouargla	—*	—*	no	5,000	2,000
El Oued	150	—*	no	2,000	1,500

* Information not available.

Foreign cultural centres
These centres were set up in connection with the signing of international conventions of Algeria and other countries wishing to enhance cultural co-operation.

The most popular foreign centres are the French one, which is rapidly expanding in Algiers, Annaba, Constantine and Oran; the British Council, which attracts many young people, especially through its diverse cultural activities in Algiers and Oran, and the American Cultural Centre, which operates only in the capital.

They provide language courses, and by their activities promote awareness of the documents about their respective societies. Many Algerian children and students register as members and consequently benefit from the library that is available in each centre. These libraries, with up-to-date book stock are much used by secondary school pupils, by students and even by school teachers and university lecturers.

School libraries
School libraries, which should be the basis for stimulating reading, face very crucial problems. They are often not to be found at

all in schools, and when they do exist their condition is lamentable. Much of the time, the school library is the mysterious cupboard whose keys are controlled by the headmaster. Whereas developed countries generally support school libraries as the reading laboratory for recreation, education and research, they are completely neglected as an input to children's education in Algeria. Elements in their 'non-existence' are:

1   There is no coherent national policy regarding libraries.
2   No effective library network has been developed.
3   School premises are overcrowded and libraries have no priority in allocating accommodation to school activities.
4   No legislation requiring school libraries.
5   Shortage of trained librarians.
6   Shortage of funds.
7   Children's books are not available in the market, and the range of instructional texts is limited.

School libraries should be in a position to provide recreation, information and support to learning throughout the child's school career. It should equip the pupil with basic skills for information searching, and exploitation of the results. It can also help teachers to improve their work through materials development and production. 'A school library is indispensable to the teaching in a school, and . . . a national library system without school libraries is a torso.'[5]

No specific budget is allocated to libraries in Algerian schools. The headmaster of a school may, however use the allocation for the school's cultural activities to buy books. School libraries are also supported, very modestly in most cases, by the public council of their *wilaya*, out of funds for the encouragement of cultural activities. For example, in 1992 the Public Council of Algiers allocated 135,000 Dinars to its primary schools. This amount, when shared among all the primary schools of that *wilaya*, resulted in 5 Dinars for each pupil. Other assistance is granted by the Ministry of Education, which in 1992 made available the sum of 580,000 Dinars for primary school cultural activities, of which 110,000 Dinars were for their libraries and other activities. Thus, 19% of the total allocation could have been spent on the libraries, assuming that the 'other activities' were also library related.[6] According to statistics from the Director of Cultural Activities at the Ministry of Education, there were in 1992, 2,355 school libraries in 38 out of 48 *wilaya* (the other ten had not responded to the request for information about library provision). Therefore there are on average some 62 libraries per *wilaya*, out of those that responded. This is a very small number of libraries in view of the numbers of schools. Figures for Algiers and six other *wilaya* show a total of 2,982 primary schools. It can therefore be estimated that the total number of primary schools nationwide, in 48 *wilaya*, is in excess of 20,000.

A visitor to an average primary school that has reported having a library will probably (in 95% of them) find that they are merely a cupboard in an office. So is it really possible to designate them as school libraries? The reading habit is rarely promoted at school, despite the ever increasing output of teachers. The library is most commonly the responsibility of the headmaster, or an aged or otherwise ailing teacher. Occasionally it will be organized by a teacher responsible for cultural animation.

Table 5.3   Increase in numbers of teachers in the 1980s

Period	Elementary school	Middle school
1980–1	87,241	26,778
1986–7	132,960	67,933

Source: Ministry of Education, Algiers

Table 5.4   Increase in numbers of teachers in cultural animation

	1984–5	1985–6	1986–7
Algerians	350	501	544
Expatriates	13	14	15
Total	363	515	559

Source: Ministry of Education, Algiers

The three Algerian institutes of library science organize regular meetings with headmasters, teachers, educators and others in charge of education, to emphasize the need for effective school libraries.

The school library standard of the British Library Association recommends that for each pupil aged from 5 to 11 there should be 11 items; 13 per pupil in the age group 11 to 16; and over 16 that there should be 19 items per head. The author's research has produced astonishing figures, in contrast to these norms, because the majority of primary and middle schools have a much lower ratio of stock per pupil. Statistics compiled in 1993 show what may be the best library provision in Algeria, at three highly regarded secondary schools in Constantine. It is not suggested that these show a general trend of provision in secondary schools throughout the country.

Table 5.5   Pupil/books ratio in three secondary schools in Constantine

School	Pupils	Book stock	Books per pupil
Fadila Saadane	889	4,157	4.6
El Houria	1,479	3,000	2.02
Youghourta	744	3,078	4.1

Children's literature

There are no specialist bookshops for children's literature. Worse still, few bookshops keep a section for children's reading. There is no publishing house that specializes in this field. The few Algerian authors of children's books are obliged to seek publication through the ENL (Entreprise National du Livre; National Enterprise of the Book). This is a state publishing house with an almost total monopoly of book production and importing.

Table 5.6   Children's book production, 1980-1985

Year	Titles
1980	14
1981	24
1982	31
1983	29
1984	46
1985	33

Source: ENL Editing Division

Table 5.7   Imports of children's books in Arabic, 1981–1985

Year	Titles	% of total book imports
1981	2,241	33.31
1982	3,014	32.29
1983	1,671	26.43
1984	3,136	36.49
1985	4,476	41.1

Source: ENL Division of the Arabic Book

Table 5.8   Imports of children's books (in Arabic and French, 1981–5)

Year	Copies	% of total book imports
1981	1,956,656	44.59
1982	1,934,800	48.07
1983	963,623	37.93
1984	1,614,760	51.29
1985	3,607,958	61.38

Source: ENL

There is no reliable, consistent information about Algerian writers of children's books, nor any listing of their books, or systematic advertisement of children's books and libraries.

Perspectives of development
A more efficient children's library service requires initiatives from parents, educators, and authorities concerned with the matter:

1 Children's and school libraries should be provided under legislation that decrees the provision of libraries and their staffing.
2 Their functions should be defined.
3 A unified management formula should be applied.
4 Librarians appointed should receive appropriate training.
5 Adequate annual finance should be allocated by governing bodies.
6 Government subsidies for publishing to encourage the production of more children's books.
7 Government support for research in the field of children's literature.
8 Cultural activities about children's libraries and their resources should be encouraged.
9 Specialist children's bookshops should be encouraged in centres of population.
10 Parents should be persuaded to encourage their children to read at home and in libraries.
11 UNESCO could initiate a pilot project in Algeria to provide a model for improving children's libraries.

Regarding their improvement, it is recommended that national objectives shall move towards:

1 A library in every school.
2 A department of school libraries be established under the Ministry of Education, and that it be represented in each *wilaya*.
3 Confirming the central role of the school library in educational programmes and the teaching process.
4 Education based on independent reading in libraries, instead of merely class teaching and examinations.
5 Establishment of an association of school libraries, which would interact professionally at international level.

Conclusion

Children have the right to flourish intellectually. In furtherance of this, their rights include access to reading materials, and the ability to use them. They should instinctively turn to the library, without being forced to do so. It has been shown that when a child begins to use libraries, he/she will continue to do so during the rest of his/her lifelong education. The development of children's literature is essential to the encouragement of reading and the use of libraries. Training of librarians for work with children must be a priority; it will add a welcome qualitative dimension to the librarian's role, and also help in creating the interactive environment that can transform a passive browser into an active learner. If society does not train its educators, they will fail in turn to train society. Children's librarians can equip the child with the basic library skills with which to exploit the library's resources independently, and further the process of self-development.

Our hope in Algeria is that our children will be good readers, getting the utmost from what they read. They have been neglected so far and there should now be a strong and positive impulse to reverse this state of affairs.

Algeria is now allowing more freedom and independence of action to private enterprise. This should have positive consequences for the development of reading and literature. Many people feel more optimistic about the future, as a fresh economic system emerges which encourages individual initiatives and competence. Energetic individuals, who were frustrated under the superseded system now have the opportunity to work, to innovate, and to improve the social situation. Optimists expect that the near future will see the emergence of children's book publishers, and a proliferation of children's bookshops throughout the country. The situation will then be ripe for our children to acquire, by encouragement, the reading habit. Their libraries are the key of any worthwhile progress. Much of the intellectual heritage that we have is conserved in libraries, to be explored by our children, the parents of the future. We must help them to appreciate their own past, as well as to develop under present circumstances.

References

1   Algiers Symposium on African Culture. Algiers, SNED, 1969, 178.
2   Berkani, M., *L'Enfant face aux livres et aux bibliothèques*, par M. Berkani et D. Alioua, Algiers, Institut de Bibliothéconomie, 1990, 21 (unpublished dissertation).
3   Bouchaib, H., 'La Lente dérive des bibliothèques', *El Watan* (676), 1992, 25.

4   Allam, M., *The Role of culture in Algeria*, Constantine, Institut de Bibliothéconomie, 1987, 70 (unpublished thesis).

5   Bredsdorff, A., 'Are children recognised in library legislation – practical aspects of school library legislation', *IFLA journal*, **6** (3), 1980, 266.

6   Bounadja, K., 'L'Etat des bibliothèques primaires algériennes', *RIST*, **2** (2), 1992, 81.

6 Library science programmes in the State of Bahrain

Robhi M. Alian

Libraries in this, the century of the information explosion are considered among the most important points of contact for individuals concerned with information on educational, social, cultural, economic and scientific activities. Libraries will be unable to achieve their objectives if certain essential requirements are not assured, of which the most important is qualified personnel. Although they also need suitable buildings, equipment, information resources and budgets to function, they need above all the professional staff through whom to realize their objectives.

The obvious deficiency at present, in most Arab libraries is the shortage of qualified librarians. Although, during their long past, libraries in the Arab world were managed by scientists, philosophers, and scholars in various disciplines,[1] their situation has changed completely in recent decades.

Developed countries have recognized, since the last century, the necessity of training specialized personnel who can work in different types of library. As a consequence, university departments and colleges developed multilevel training courses in library science.

The picture is very different in the Arab countries, as serious attention to this matter came rather late in countries such as Bahrain. Library science education in the Arab world dates from 1951, at Cairo University,[2] and followed at later dates in some other countries of the region, with variations in their courses that still prevail among the types and levels of education offered.[3]

Recognition of the importance of libraries in national development only began in many Arab countries towards the middle of the present century. Different types of library were established, and governments supported their development. The supply of trained librarians subsequently became a pressing need.

The first library in Bahrain was a school library, set up in 1919, and the modern library movement dates from 1945, with the opening of the first public library in the capital.[4] Today, the country has a developing library system with 175 school libraries, 10 public libraries, 4 academic libraries and some 40 special libraries. There are also a few children's libraries, several information and documentation centres, and one mobile public library.

In Bahrain, as in other developing countries, libraries face common problems that have been identified and recorded by Asheim,[5] Salman[6] and Al-Rumaihi:[7]

1 The concept of a library has different connotations in developing countries.
2 There are different perceptions of library service.
3 Lack of access to information sources.
4 Funds for library development have generally low priority.
5 Absence of new information technology.
6 Absence of library legislation, library co-operation, and planning at national level.
7 Not all countries have a national library, or a national library association.
8 Shortage of qualified nationals, and low status accorded to professional librarians.

Bahrain has adopted the following methods in the training of library personnel:

1 Sending staff to selected training courses, seminars, conferences and workshops in other Arab, and foreign countries.
2 Sending personnel on scholarships to other Arab countries with programmes of library science education, notably Egypt and Saudi Arabia, and also to non-Arab countries, especially the United Kingdom and the United States.
3 Engaging expatriate librarians from other Arab and foreign countries.

Unfortunately, these methods have not yet provided Bahrain's libraries with the required numbers or quality of professional staff. Therefore the country has also developed its own library education programmes at several levels.

What, therefore is the level of education available in Bahrain, and what problems are faced in developing this training?

Library science education programmes

1 *Training Directorate programmes (Ministry of Education)*
An Amiri decree, issued in 1983, reorganized the Ministry of

Education and established the Training Directorate,[8] which absorbed the body known previously as the Rehabilitation Education and Training Centre (RETC). It is the means of implementing the Ministry's policy on the training of all ministry staff. Its overall responsibilities are:

(a) Determining the training needs of the Ministry of Education.
(b) Planning the required training programmes.
(c) Implementing training, either alone or in co-operation with other educational institutions.
(d) Follow-up and evaluation of the results of training programmes, and subsequent documentation.
(e) Supervising continuing education activities organized for teachers, technicians, and other ministry staff.[9]

The Training Directorate currently provides all technical, managerial and financial facilities to implement training courses. It institutes follow-up procedures and evaluates the results. Since its establishment, the Directorate has implemented training courses for ministry staff in a number of different specialisms. It's activities for library science have been various, continuing the trend already established by the RETC.

Training commenced in 1978 when the RETC launched a course for participants drawn from schools and public libraries. The basic techniques taught included cataloguing, classification, and management of school and public libraries. The course lasted for two weeks and enrolled 24 librarians, 15 school librarians and 9 from public libraries. The principal lecturer and co-ordinator was Professor A.A. Anwar from Egypt.[10]

Two years later the Ministry of Education requested the RETC, which was then a unit of Bahrain University College, to start a rehabilitation programme for school librarians. This was to be operative within the next two years, 1981-2, and had as its objectives to teach participants to:

(a) Be aware of the importance of the school library as a cultural and education centre, enhancing the schools teaching.
(b) Organizing a library's stock to assist students in seeking information.
(c) Understand the principles of using information sources, and thus be capable of guiding students to their required information for study and research.
(d) Work on developing links between the school's objectives and its library's service.[11]

This programme has continued to run to date. Participants must be either headmasters or teachers, and must have passed the general secondary school certificate or its equivalent. They should have at least seven years to go before reaching retirement age, at the time of joining the programme, and on completion are awarded an in-service undergraduate diploma. The course has been conducted part time throughout , in evenings, as set out below:

First year
Introduction to library science
The book: its historical development and importance
Libraries in the Arab world
Library management
Technical services in libraries
    Cataloguing: theory and practice
    Classification: theory and practice
Arabic and foreign reference works

Second year
Introduction to information science
Library services
Research methodology: questionnaires
Human relationships
Children's literature
Production and use of audiovisual materials
Cataloguing and classification
Periodicals
Islamic references and sources
Documentation and information centres
Indexing and abstracting
Bibliography
Field visits to libraries[12]

Fifty-nine successful participants graduated from the first four programmes (see Table 6.1).

Table 6.1

Year	Females	Males	Total
1983	13	5	18
1986	7	1	8
1988	14	4	18
1990	11	4	15
Total	45	14	59

In 1982 the RETC held a one-week training course in cataloguing and classification, which was attended by personnel from school and public libraries. It should be noted that all such courses are open to public library staff, because the Training Directorate and public libraries are both controlled by the Ministry of Education.

In 1988 the Training Directorate organized an intensive course on children's libraries, attended by personnel from primary school and children's libraries. The lecturer was a Lebanese female specialist in the field.

2   *Learning and information resources programme (University of Bahrain)*

This arose in response to the project, adopted by the Ministry of Education in 1988, to transform school libraries into learning resource centres. A postgraduate diploma programme in learning and information resources was suggested. It was to be delivered at the College of Education of the University of Bahrain, commencing in the academic year 1990–1. Its objectives are:

1 Preparing graduates to work in libraries generally, and in school libraries and learning resource centres in particular.
2 Introducing students to the growth characteristics of individuals, their needs at different stages of learning, and how to help them.
3 To teach selection, production, and use of audiovisual aids.
4 Preparing the student to undertake technical service procedures (acquisition, cataloguing, classification).
5 Equipping students with research skills.
6 Training in user services, especially circulation and reference services to school pupils and their teachers, and training them in the use of available information sources.[13]

On completion of the programme, students are expected to have a broad understanding of information sources; of media technology; of the theoretical and practical approach to organization of information resources, and the operation of library and learning resource centres; and a commitment to providing user-oriented services. The programme is intended specifically for:

1 Undergraduates from various subject backgrounds wishing to follow a career as librarians or media specialists.
2 Experienced librarians and media specialists with a bachelor's degree other than library science, wishing to take a professional library qualification.

3 Experienced librarians and media specialists already qualified in library science who wish to upgrade their skills.[14]

Each year some 25 to 30 schoolteachers enrol, selected from an average of 120 applicants. Requirements for admission are: a bachelor's degree in an accredited university; passing examinations in Arabic, English, and general knowledge; passing a personal interview conducted by the Ministry of Education and the University of Bahrain. The Ministry's preference is in favour of candidates with the most commonly held specializations.

It should be noted that all those who are accepted then receive scholarships from the ministry, and study as full-time students. In the first year of its commencement, 1990–1, all students were required to take two non-credit courses; foundation of education, and introduction to psychology (each of three contact hours per week). Students without a library science qualification or previous experience were required to take two additional non-credit courses; foundation of librarianship, and role of the library in education (each of three contact hours per week).

By the following year, due to the ministry's expressed need for graduate output within one academic year, all students were exempt henceforth from these prerequisite courses. The current programme consists of 39 credit hours:

Education – 6 credits
Curriculum and teaching methods (3)
Research methods (3)
Educational technology – 6 credits
Educational technology (3)
Production and use of teaching materials (3)
Psychology – 6 credits
Psychology of children and adolescence (3)
Psychology of learning and reading (3)
Library science – 15 credits
Management of library resource centres (3)
Classification and cataloguing (3)
Information resources and services (3)
Microcomputers in libraries (3)
Practicum   (3)
English language – credits

Lectures are the principal teaching method in theoretical courses; practical training is used as much as possible on the library science and educational technology courses. Field visits to notable libraries are organized, and additionally each student is asked to work in a selected school library or resource centre, on Sunday and Tuesday of each week in the last term. The student's written report on the fieldwork and training is assessed as part of course work. By the end of the year 1992–3, three intakes had graduated from the programme (see Table 6.2).

Table 6.2

Academic year	Females	Males	Total
1990–1	16	8	24
1991–2	20	7	27
1992–3	26	5	31
Total	62	20	82

In 1992, the Continuous Education Programme at the College of Education began, with five courses in library science:

1 Dealing with information resources in libraries (20 hours)
2 Cataloguing of publications (25 hours)
3 Classification of library materials (25 hours)
4 Children's libraries (20 hours)
5 Management of special libraries (20 hours)

The first intake, of fifteen participants, commenced in mid-1992.[15]

3 Public Libraries Directorate programmes
In 1983, an Amiri decree established the Public Libraries Directorate, under the Ministry of Education. Its duties and objectives were set out as:

1 To formulate the general policy of the nation's public libraries, in accordance with the cultural and scientific requirements of its society.
2 Conducting research and studies into user needs.
3 Establishing public libraries and providing their resources.
4 Management of public libraries and their technical services.
5 Introducing programmes aimed at encouraging the public to use the libraries.
6 Providing mobile libraries, music libraries and film libraries.
7 Preparing the national bibliography of Bahrain.
8 Developing gift and exchange of publications with other libraries and information centres.
9 Organizing the procedures of legal deposit of Bahrain's publications.

The Directorate has, since its establishment, devoted its activities to staff development of Bahraini nationals working in public libraries, by assisting them to attend training courses in Bahrain and abroad, and also by developing in-service training programmes.

Initially, the Directorate was hampered in its training programmes by having to rely on external sources, for lack of suitable trainers in the country. This changed at the beginning of the 1990s, when the Directorate became more active internally, and has implemented more programmes at home:

(a)   A two-week public librarians' skills development course in 1990. It covered cataloguing, classification, documentation, reference work and public library management.

(b)   A series of training seminars for public librarians in 1991, to meet the objectives of:

1   Providing theoretical background on the latest developments in the subjects of the seminar

2   Training participants in all types of technical service, and the behavioural skills of the jobs

3   Developing new approaches by trainees to their work; public relations with both colleagues and library users.[16]

Each seminar was conducted in study days of five hours duration, from 8 a.m. to 1 p.m.:

1	Building library collections (acquisition)	5 hours
2	Cataloguing (descriptive and subject)	10 hours
3	Circulation: systems and services	5 hours
4	Dewey Decimal Classification	10 hours
5	Periodicals	5 hours
6	Indexing and abstracting	5 hours
7	Reference works and services	10 hours
8	Bibliographical services	5 hours
9	AV materials in libraries	5 hours
10	Library management	5 hours
11	Microforms in libraries	5 hours
12	Communication skills for librarians	5 hours
13	Children's libraries	5 hours
14	Documentation services	5 hours
15	Computers in libraries	15 hours
16	Library co-operation	5 hours
17	Advanced library services	5 hours
18	Revision, discusion, evaluation	5 hours

Total: 22 Seminars; 155 hours

The first series was conducted from January to March 1990; the second ran from April to June 1991. Altogether 27 librarians, the majority from public libraries, participated. The proportion of females to males, as in other courses, was approximately three to one.

(c)   The Directorate held a ten-day course, in January 1992 on practical application of DDC, for 12 public librarians. It aimed at providing the trainees with the technical skills for classifying according to Dewey, which is used in all Bahrain's public libraries.

It should be noted that in addition to training its staff, the Public Libraries Directorate also took a leading role in providing practical training and direct work experience for staff from other libraries in the country. This was done either through direct training, or by participation in the training seminars described above.

4   Library programmes of other institutions

British Council Library
This was the first in Bahrain to start training courses. Many of Bahrain's librarians took part in the first one-month course in 1974. Another course, organized jointly with the Public Education Directorate in 1977, gave an intensive basic training to participants.

Education Documentation Centre
Besides providing advanced library and information services for educationists, the centre offers in-service training to some government library staff, by special arrangement. It contributes to the practical training elements of the programme of the University of Bahrain. Staff of the centre act as consultants to libraries and in teaching on the various courses that take place.

Bahrain Studies and Research Centre
The centre's special library is considered to be the best in the country as regards its staff, collections, and services. It employs professionally qualified staff, and for this reason it normally offers in-service training to other government librarians. Its staff act as consultants and make inputs to teaching library science courses at other institutions.

Adult Education Directorate
This has responsibility for the eradication of illiteracy, and for

organizing adult education and continuing education programmes. Between 1991 and 1993 it implemented three library
science courses (see Table 6.3).

Table 6.3

Year	Course length (hrs)	Participants
1991 (1st)	40 hours	14
1992 (2nd)	40 hours	22
1993 (3rd)	30 hours	8
Total		44

The first was a general introduction to library science, the second dealt with cataloguing and classification, and the third concentrated on DDC.

Problems of library science education programmes in Bahrain
These educational programmes, as in other Arab and developing
countries, face many difficulties and obstacles to their development. Besides the expected problems, such as finance, there are
others:

Curriculum-related
1   Absence of pre-planning and feasibility studies before firming
    up curricula or the programme.s
2   Lack of clear objectives of the curricula and programmes.
3   Failure to co-ordinate recognition given to successive stages of
    qualification, from undergraduate through to higher degrees.
4   Current curricula do not match current developments in
    library and information science. They are too traditional.
5   Curricula have very similar content, regardless of their names,
    levels and duration. They are repetitive.
6   All courses are compulsory. They lack selective courses that
    give students the opportunity to concentrate on certain special
    interests.
7   Absence of any evaluation and assessment of the courses,
    which might lead to carefuly considered revision of their con-
    tent.

Lecturers
The scarcity of Bahraini lecturers in library science has led to
over-dependence on non-nationals in teaching.
    1   Most of the available lecturers are not educationally quali-

fied to teach according to current methods. On the other hand, not every local, practising librarian is abe to teach successfully.
2   The majority of lecturers employed for training programmes are not full time. Therefore their participation in planning and development is very limited.
3   Lecturers have little opportunity for in-service training, to develop themselves in their field. They are unable to interact and thus gain some professional refreshment and stimulation. This results in negative occupational attitudes.
4   Most of the courses or programmes offered depend mainly on one lecturer who teaches all subjects. This reduces the exposure of trainees to diverse points of view.

Teaching methods
1   The present teaching methods are very traditional, and depend heavily on the lecture as the main method of instruction.
2   Lack of laboratories, workshops and suitable libraries required for teaching and training.
3   Absence of audiovisual materials and equipment.
4   Shortage of the working tools needed for teaching and training in practical cataloguing, classification, reference work, and so forth.
5   The final evaluation of students depends on examinations in theoretical aspects of what has been taught.

Practice and fieldwork
1   The majority of courses focus on theoretical aspects of subjects taught; by comparison the practical and training aspects are neglected and receive much less time.
2   There too few suitable libraries and information centres for practical work experience.
3   Absence of direct supervision of fieldwork by lecturers responsible for student placements.

Students and graduates
1   The low average educational standard of students applying for library science courses.
2   Absence of a strong motivation among students, most of whom join library science programmes as a way of leaving teaching or other uncongenial jobs, thinking that librarianship will be less demanding.
3   High loss rate among female entrants to the profession.
4   Absence of follow-up of graduates from courses to check on

their professional progress; also the lack of inservice training programmes following their qualification. These are contributory factors to poor professional performance.

Other problems
1 The majority of people have no clear image of libraries or library science; some express surprise that there are degrees in library science.
2 There is no library association in Bahrain.
3 Library work is, in general, regarded negatively, and consequently libraries are under-regarded by the public and civil sevice. Therefore students who are interested in studying library science are unlikely to take much encouragement from other members of society.[17]

Conclusion
Despite the criticisms made earlier, Bahrain has a developing and promising library system. It does not have a national library, but all other types are operating in the country. The lack of specialized, trained or professional Bahraini librarians is the major deterrent to progress. Library science programmes at various levels have been offered, from short courses to postgraduate diploma. These originate mainly from the Ministry of Education, the Public Library Directorate, and the University of Bahrain. Factors that bear upon the success of library science programmes relate to curriculum content, lecturers and teaching methods, practical training and the students themselves. All of these must be assessed in the perspective of the short history of the library movement in twentieth-century Bahrain.

References
1 Nimer, R., 'History of the Arabic-Islamic libraries', *International library review*, **22** (2), 1990, 119–35.
2 Abdel-Hadi, M. F., *Studies in library and information science* (Translated title; Arabic text), Riyadh, Dar al-Marrikh, 1988, 181–2.
3 For more detailed information about library education in the Arab world see: Miski, Abdelhamid, *Education of information specialists in the Arab region*, Paris, Unesco, 1993, 1–35.
4 Sarhan, Mansour, *Cultural movement in Bahrain* (Translated title; Arabic text), Manama, Fakhrawi Library, 1993, 209–10.
5 Asheim, L., *Librarianship in the developing countries*, Chicago, University of Illinois Press, 1966, 11.
6 Salman, L., 'Information needs of the developing countries: analytical case studies', *Unesco journal of information science*, 3 (4), 1981, 241.

7   Al-Rumaihi, F.A., 'Libraries and information centres in the State of Bahrain' (Translated title, Arabic text), *Arab journal of information*, **10** (2), 1990, 21–6.

8   Bahrain, Ministry of Education, *Educational training system* (Translated title, Arabic text), Bahrain, the Ministry, 1991, 2.

9   Al-Saiegh, Abdullah, *The Achievements of the Ministry of Education in library training* (Translated title, Arabic text). Paper presented to the meeting on library science education in the Arab world, Riyadh, 7–12 November, 1981, 9.

10 Itayem, M. A, *Directory of library schools in the Arab world* (Translated title, Arabic text), Tunis, ALECSO, 1984, 41.

11 Ibid., 42–3.

12 University of Bahrain, *Programme of learning and information resources*, Bahrain, the University, 1990 (unpublished paper).

13 University of Bahrain, *Post-graduate diploma in learning and information resources* (Translated title, Arabic text), Bahrain, the University, 1990, 3.

14 University of Bahrain, College of Education, *Training courses at the College of Education*, Bahrain, the College, 1992, 8–10.

15 Bahrain, Ministry of Education, *Directory of the legislations and systems of the Ministry of Education* (Translated title, Arabic text), Bahrain, the Ministry, [199–].

16 Bahrain, Directorate of Public Libraries, 'A Series of training seminars in library and information science', Bahrain, the Directorate, 1990 (unpublished paper).

17 For further information about problems in library education in the Arab world see: Ballard, M., 'Library education problems in developing countries', *International library review*, **12** (1), 1980, 65–70; Namlah, A., 'Manpower deficiency in Saudi Arabia: its effect on the library profession', *International library review*, **14** (1), 1982, 3–20; Sharif, A., 'The Factors which affect the development of librarianship and library education in the Arab countries', *International library review*, **11** (3), 1979, 245–57.

7 Egyptian university libraries

Sandy Macmillen

Early history

The origins of academic libraries in Egypt cannot be dated precisely. Claims have been made for the library of the pharaoh Ramses II (c.1304–1237 BC) at Thebes, reputed to have contained 20,000 rolls of papyrus on religion and various other subjects. The tombs there of two librarian/archivists indicate a profession of some importance.

A better case may be made, perhaps, for the Alexandria library, founded by the Greeks in the third century BC It possessed at least half a million rolls during its heyday as the Mediterranean world's premier centre for research and information exchange, attracting the genius of Euclid, Ptolemy, Hippocrates, Archimedes, Eratosthenes, and many other Greek and Egyptian scholars. Ten large halls were devoted to the disciplines of physics, astronomy, mathematics, geometry, anatomy, biology, geography, literature, philosophy, and engineering. An aggressive acquisition policy was pursued, and much effort put into copying, translating and publishing works. The bulk of the library is thought to have been destroyed by the Romans in 47 BC, although other dates sometimes proposed are AD 391 (by the Coptic ecclesiastical authorities) and AD 641 (by the invading Arabs)

A number of Coptic monasteries maintained libraries of academic importance, albeit on a smaller scale. Some still exist, but many works perished or were taken to libraries and museums in Europe.

The Muslim era attached significance to books and learning, most obviously with respect to the Qur'an itself. By the ninth century some mosque libraries, known as 'madrasas' (schools) embraced mathematics, astronomy, medicine, and grammar, in addition to religion. Indeed, the Bait El-Alm (House of Learning, AD 988) has been viewed as the first secular university in Egypt. Al-Azhar, founded at the same time, claims to be one of the oldest universities in continuous use, but its interests remained confined to religion until the end of the nineteenth century.

These libraries were established by the ruling élite and wealthy individuals, particularly in the Shi'ite Fatimid period (AD 969–1171), so predating the first university libraries in medieval Europe by several centuries. Books were acquired by purchase, copying, and the deposit of copies by authors themselves; Al-Azhar owned about 50,000 volumes by AD 1100. The import of paper-making techniques from China around the ninth century was an important boost. Classified arrangements and catalogues were not unknown, with students being supported by public and private endowments. Access for the general public was permitted too.

Cairo, which overtook Alexandria as Egypt's political and cultural centre, rivalled Baghdad and Damascus as a seat of learning. Under the Ayyubids (AD 1171–1250) and Mamluks (AD 1250–1517) libraries flourished to an extent, but with the Ottoman era (AD 1517–1798) decline set in, and many precious books in Al-Azhar and other libraries were destroyed or stolen. For about 300 years Egypt remained on the sideline, uninformed about developments elsewhere, particularly in Europe.

Modern history

The French invasion of Egypt in 1798 marked the beginning of changes to a country and library system little altered in nearly a thousand years. Reform-minded Mohammed Ali, who ruled from 1805 to 1848, introduced European concepts of education, as well as the printing press. Other attempts to modernize the educational and library structure included the establishment of a national library in 1870, and the founding of Cairo University in 1908. But it was really only under Gamal Abdel Nasser (1954–70) and his successors, Presidents Anwar Sadat (1970–81) and Hosny Mubarak (1981 onwards), that the present network of state universities and libraries came into existence. The extremely rapid rate of construction in the 1970s and 1980s has tailed off, leaving Egypt with 12 universities. In addition, there is the private American University in Cairo (AUC), and Al-Hazar University which comes under the authority of Al-Azhar mosque.

Table 7.1   Egyptian University libraries

Name and location	Founded	Branches	Student numbers	Libraries
Cairo	1908	Beni Suef; Fayoum	95,000	1,000,000 vols; 7,400 serial titles
Alexandria	1942	—	92,000	1,100,000 vols.
Ain Shams (Cairo)	1950	—	104,000	not known
Assiut	1956	Sohag, Qena, Aswan	43,000	250,000 vols; 2,400 journal subscriptions
Tanta	1972	Kafr El Shaykh	36,000	not known
Mansoura	1973	—	43,000	not known
Zagazig	1974	—	95,000	not known
Helwan (Cairo)	1975	—	31,000	not known
Minya	1976	—	16,000	not known
El-Munifia (Shebine El Kom)	1976	—	18,000	not known
Suez Canal (Ismailiyya) (Arish)	1976	Suez, Port Said	10,300	not known
AUC (Cairo)	1919	—	3,900	225,000 vols; 2,130 serial titles
Al-Azhar (Cairo)	1961	—	100,000	80,000 vols; 30,000 MSS

Characteristics of Egyptian universities

Universities and their libraries are the responsibility of the Supreme Council of Universities (the regulating body) and, ultimately, the Ministry of Higher Education. Neither appear to have formulated any strategies for library development, although the former has an agreement with the British Council to implement a staff training programme.

The top post in universities is that of president, below whom are a number of vice-presidents, who may be responsible for a campus if the university is multi-site, or for undergraduates, or for postgraduate studies and libraries. Some universities also have a director of library services, usually an academic with library experience, who heads the library committee in cases where one exists. This is dominated by academics and administrators, particularly the deans of faculties, who control expenditure on and staffing of libraries, and their vice-deans who are meant to be responsible for the general supervision of library services.

In practice, university authorities are usually overwhelmed with paperwork generated by the simplest items, and made much worse because subordinates will not take responsibility, so everything is referred upwards. Certainly so far as libraries are concerned, quality hardly depends on the working or otherwise of official channels and mechanisms, but on the effort and initiative of individual deans and vice-deans in obtaining money for the library and finding competent staff.

University sites in Egypt

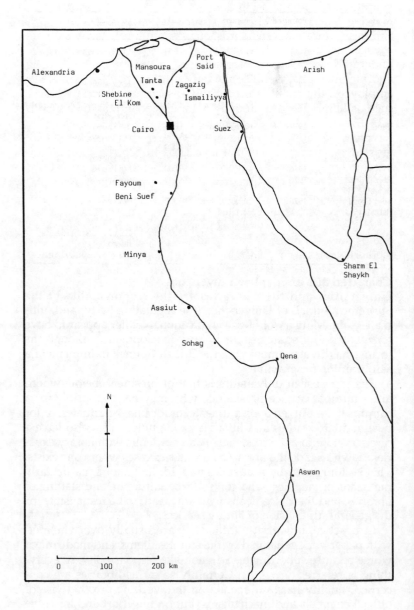

Serious problems face Egyptian universities. These are widely admitted, but little is being done to improve things. As part of a massive government effort to reduce illiteracy (still about 50%) and raise educational standards, quantity unfortunately took precedence over quality. Thus, student numbers are excessive (683,000 undergraduates, 90,000 postgraduates) in relation to the budgets and facilities provided. Combined with low pay for university employees, the result is predictably disastrous. Clerical workers such as librarians earn around 75–150 Egyptian pounds a month (£15–£30 sterling), and academics anything between 350 and 1,000 Egyptian pounds. The ranks of the former are characterized by gross overstaffing at minimal levels of competence, and stifling bureaucracy, with jobs regarded as little more than a form of unemployment benefit, except by the most conscientious workers.

Faculties struggle to attract high-quality teachers, especially outside of Cairo, and even then there is a good chance that a lecturer will depart at the earliest opportunity for a better paid job in one of the Gulf States. Many lecturers perpetuate the ineffective methods of learning that they endured as students, with heavy emphasis on theory and large amounts of rote-learning of texts. The teacher can force hapless students to buy the set books (often scandalously plagiarized from various sources) on pain of failing the examination. Even so, success is not guaranteed: students inexplicably fail, and exams are not properly marked; a few lecturers assign themselves the lucrative task of marking thousands of papers on subjects they may know little or nothing about.

Role and organization of libraries

With few exceptions, libraries do not play an important role in Egyptian universities. This is due to a number of factors, including: the faculty system, teaching and learning methods, poor quality of existing staff and services, ignorance of what could be provided and how to do it.

Central libraries have been introduced in a number of universities, but lack the powerful base of support that faculty libraries enjoy, and have not proved very successful in supplanting or improving upon them. Large faculties may be split into departments, each with a library. Arabic and foreign books are shelved separately. Closed access is less common these days, although books are not always within easy reach of readers. Reference material is kept out of the main sequence in most libraries.

Classified order is generally used, even if no catalogue actually exists. Most staffs find accurate classification difficult, particularly with foreign books. Dewey is the preferred scheme (except in the

AUC), although most libraries have only the 18th edition at best, either in English or translated into Arabic by the Jordanian Library Association.

Nominal divisions in sizeable libraries usually run to sections for acquisitions, cataloguing, periodicals, stacks, reference, borrowing, administration and accounts. Some large or multi-site universities have centralized certain procedures; for example, periodicals acquisition and administration at Assiut University, which helped reduce duplication of holdings and resulted in other benefits such as a union list of serials for the campuses. At Cairo University all acquisitions and cataloguing are centralized.

Library collections
'Library holdings of most Egyptian colleges and universities are very poor, and in many cases outdated.'[1]

This is certainly the case in comparison to economically advanced countries, or in relation to the huge numbers of students involved. The expansion of student numbers and university budgets has not been matched by a corresponding provision for library resources. Nonetheless, Egypt is fortunate in comparison with many developing countries since it possesses a large indigenous publishing industry, and consequently reasonable quantities of Arabic books and journals are usually to be found on the shelves. Acquisition of material in foreign languages is much more limited, especially in provincial universities and branches, and poses a particular problem in science, engineering, medicine, and foreign languages, where these publications (notably in English) are vital.

At Assiut University, faculty libraries typically contain between 5,000 and 20,000 volumes, and the proportion of foreign books varies between 20% and 90%, with a median of 27 current foreign journal subscriptions. Amounts basically depend on the size and prestige of the faculty, and its success in bidding for funds and utilising them appropriately: science, engineering and medical faculties on the main campus do best. Budgets are usually spent at the annual Cairo International Book Fair, although some libraries now order direct from publishers, bookshops or agents, notably Al-Ahram. The main gaps in collections are in periodicals, especially foreign ones, and other research material in the form of reference books, bibliographies, abstracts, and indexes. In their absence heavy use is made of secondary sources, particularly theses of former students. A number of libraries have audio and, occasionally, video cassettes, and often quantities of microfilmed journals from the 1960s and 1970s, donated by the

United States Agency for International Development (USAID).

Annual budgets are difficult to quantify, given a tradition of financial secrecy and the absence of systematic acquisitions programmes, but are in the region of 5,000–10,000 Egyptian pounds (£1,000–£2,000) for arts faculties and rather more on the science side; for example, 40,000 Egyptian pounds in the case of the science faculty at Sohag. Scientific journals may be expensive, but the science faculties tend to have much smaller student intakes and libraries that are consequently used less intensively than other faculties, so the differences in expenditure seem hard to justify. Gifts, primarily from the British Council and the Ranfurly Library Service, are an important supplement in libraries that have received assistance from Voluntary Service Overseas (VSO).

While some universities may be genuinely short of funds, often money is available but spent on more exciting areas than libraries. It is a common feature of many institutions that, for a variety of reasons, they must procure the latest hi-tech equipment, at considerable expense, while the basic necessities are neglected. Also, the lack of simple and effective purchasing procedures means book budgets are not always well spent. Librarians are usually not involved in selection at all, and lecturers are in the main ignorant of bibliographic aids for assisting in systematic acquisition, so collections grow haphazardly. There is no co-operative acquisition, despite the obvious advantages with foreign publications in terms of administrative simplicity and cost savings.

For practical purposes Al-Azhar can be considered in the same category as the state universities. Nasser's reforms of 1961 introduced faculties of engineering, agriculture, medicine, and business administration, in addition to the traditional staples: theology, Islamic law, Arabic. Gifts, including the transfer of manuscripts from other mosques, are an important source of accessions. In 1897, some of the books which had previously been scattered around the various teaching areas (leading to high rates of loss and damage), were collected together. Almost a hundred years on problems still remain; the library is largely uncatalogued and poorly organized, vulnerable to attack by the elements.

Many academics outside Cairo must travel there, time and cost permitting, in order to satisfy their information needs. The AUC is a popular destination, strong in humanities and social sciences, and containing a valuable rare books collection. It is organized along American lines, uses the DOBIS/LIBIS automated system, and its staff are well-trained. Other universities frequented are those of Cairo and Ain Shams, plus the National Library and a few specialist libraries. The British Council library is also well used, but mainly by Cairo students. Services, some of which are charged for, include CD-ROM and on-line searches, and document supply via the British Library Document Supply Centre (BLDSC).

Library staff

'Librarianship in Egypt is a depressed profession, suffering from low status, apparent irrelevance to academic and leisure needs, low wages and lack of professional cohesion . . . libraries are usually run by staff with little academic involvement, no career prospects, little motivation.'[2]

The question of low status seems to be a general problem in many developing nations, where modern information methods and resources have had little opportunity to demonstrate their value, and that of the staff employed in them. In Egypt personal contacts are the most immediate and important source of information.

Frequently staff lose interest in their job, and soon become alienated from the work environment. A number of negative features also result: most employees are school-leavers with no library skills, training, or experience. Staff are rarely given training, and all too easily acquire the bad habits of colleagues, which include smoking, reading the newspaper, idle chat, sleeping, eating breakfast, and continual tea-drinking. Juniors are often left to deal with the unfortunate readers, while their more qualified or experienced peers attend to cataloguing and classification duties. It is common practice for incompetent, lazy, or disruptive employees to be exiled to the library, from where it may be difficult to dislodge them, and certainly impossible to sack them.

The low level of English language ability displayed by most librarians is a further problem, given the importance of publications in English and the needs of postgraduates and lecturers in particular. It is extremely rare to find any graduates in English among staff.

A university graduate is usually in nominal charge of the library, but has no faculty rank and is unlikely to be involved in the organizational or managerial issues affecting the service for which he/she is supposedly responsible. Until senior librarians are made part of the academic establishment with a formal career structure, and until there is a mechanism for bringing librarians, academics, and administrators together, services will not improve greatly. At present, intelligent librarians see their main hope lying in further study and the prospect of thus rising above library employment.

Women occupy about a third of library posts. The vast majority have husbands and families to look after as their first priority, and work is sometimes just an escape from the pressures of domestic life. Their male counterparts invariably have a second (non-government) job in the afternoon or evening to help make ends meet, and for many this constitutes their real work.

Egyptian faculty libraries employ between three and fifteen people (seven or eight is typical), at staffing rates about twice those in the United Kingdom. If numbers were halved and rates of pay doubled, libraries would probably function far more effectively than they do now.

In such depressing circumstances one might be surprised to learn that Cairo University established a libraries and archives department as early as 1951, and before that training had been carried out by the Cairo Library Association. Latterly, departments have been founded at Alexandria (1981), Beni Suef (1985), Tanta (1986), and El-Munifia (1991), along similar lines to Cairo, and largely run by it as they are all small, and have only a few resident lecturers between them.

After a period of isolation from developments in the West, in the 1950s and 1960s, efforts at modernising both curricula and teaching methods have been made. Practical work and class assessments now count towards a quarter of the marks.

It would make an interesting study to trace the career paths of library school graduates. The author has met only one in Upper Egypt; the majority remain in Cairo, Alexandria and a few delta towns, while the brain drain stimulates continual migration to the Gulf.

Libraries staffed by qualified librarians are undoubtedly better off than those without, but languish, nevertheless under a system unsympathetic to their needs and aspirations. In this respect an active library association could make a big difference. However, with the Egyptian Library Association (ELA) currently in abeyance the department at Cairo University should play a larger role, as one of the few organized outlets for professional public relations.

Buildings and equipment

The AUC library is the only purpose-built academic library the author has come across in the country.[3] Modern concepts of library planning are not generally known about or considered important. Books have to be accommodated in whatever room is available. Warehouse-type metal shelving is standard, but poorly designed for book storage. Some libraries have wooden shelves made by local carpenters, which are usually better. Study space is rarely planned for the likely size of readership, and is simply what has been left over once all the stock has been put into place.

Microcomputers for cataloguing purposes have been introduced in go-ahead faculties, although not generally accessible by readers. CD-ROM technology has also attracted attention, although using ENSTINET (see below) would be more cost effective, as a university can have some 500 online searches per annum for the equivalent price. University authorities are often blindly convinced that automation is a panacea for all library ills, but most of the libraries require a great deal of basic work before computerization can become a viable priority.

It has been said that 'Arab librarianship . . . lacks the essential tools that librarians need',[4] and this is still the situation in Egypt, whether it be Arabic translations of the current editions of Dewey or AACR2, decent typewriters, pamphlet boxes, book supports, and even basic stationery such as book tape. With few mechanisms for information exchange it is difficult to know what is available or how to get it.

Library users and reader services
A typical Egyptian student is unlikely to have used a library before arriving at university, and with notions of independent learning still a novel concept he/she may well graduate without ever entering the library, having relied solely on memorising the lecturer's notes and whatever set books were required purchases. Outside the English department, and perhaps the medical faculty, library use is the exception rather than the rule, other than as a study area preceding exams. Even at postgraduate level and above the idea of a systematic search for information is a strange one. Preferred methods are to ask a friend, or meander along the shelves in the hope of coming across something useful. With luck there may be a catalogue, although not necessarily of great currency or reliability. Users are usually kept away on the grounds that they don't know how to use it and are prone to removing cards from the drawers. The fortunate reader, asking the right librarian at the right time, may receive assistance with his enquiry, but most librarians are regarded more as an impediment than an aide to library use.

For his part, the employee has little incentive to proffer help in view of his miserable pay, lack of training, and the absence of a strong public service ethos in society. Moreover, staff must pay annually for all book losses over and above 0.5% of the total stock. So it is hardly surprising that "library regulations . . . are the product of deeply rooted restrictions which greatly hinder library use'.[5]

These restrictions include limited opening hours (commonly 8.30 a.m. to 2 p.m., six days a week), and closure during the one to two months annual summer stocktake. Admittance for members of other faculties can be made very difficult, and certainly excludes borrowing rights. Undergraduates are usually allowed to take one book for a period of up to two weeks, although postgraduates and academic staff are treated more generously, especially if they wield power and influence. Expensive foreign books tend to be subject to greater restrictions.

Libraries are not always organized with users in mind: evidently so when they are closed access, whilst open access collections could benefit from much better signs, plans, and labels, not to mention basic accessories such as leaflets and guides to the catalogues and collections, and library tours. User instruction and reference services are in their infancy in the majority of institutions, although a few have undertaken more ambitious projects. Thus, Ain Shams is microfilming all Egyptian theses, the success of which depends on the standard of indexing as well as the quality of microfilm.

Co-operation

'The profession is organised vertically, with directives passed down from library director to employee . . . organised as it is, the profession has developed neither an active library association nor successful inter-institutional co-operation'.[6]

According to one school of thought[7] this simply reflects, on a small scale, prevailing modes of political and social organization in the Arab world. It is certainly true that participative forms of association and organization other than family and religion remain weak compared to Anglo-American and perhaps other traditions.

In the library context staff have little contact with anyone outside their faculty, and virtually no knowledge of the wider national or international scene. An Egyptian Library Association,[8] successor to the Cairo Library Association (1945–64), still exists on paper, but activities are confined to the Cairo University library school. Its journal, *Alam el maktabaat* (*Libraries world*) ceased publication in 1970. This is to be regretted, for it is the obvious body to encourage the process of opening lines of communication between libraries, which is essential if progress is to be nationwide. There is tremendous scope for all kinds of practical work to be carried out: translating more standard international tools of cataloguing and classification into Arabic; raising the profile of libraries and librarians with the Ministry of Higher Education, Supreme Council of Universities and other bodies; improving the equipment supply process; promoting good library practice and training for librarians; encouraging interest in co-operative projects with potential such as interlibrary loans and acquisition and processing of foreign publications; establishing contact with fellow Arab associations.

It is unfortunate then, both for librarians and library users, that co-operation appears to be 'an almost alien concept',[9] in view of the shared problems that need to be tackled. Within Cairo itself co-operation between the universities of Ain Shams, Helwan, Cairo, Al-Azhar, and the AUC could be most fruitful, not least by starting a van-delivered interlibrary loans service. At present readers are normally expected to travel to another library – not much consolation if one is in Upper Egypt, or to write direct to the author of a needed book. Yet there is a huge growth potential in document supply to satisfy research needs, based on the ENSTINET (Egyptian National Scientific and Technical Information Network) union list of foreign periodicals,[10] which includes the holdings of all universities in the country, albeit at varying degrees of accuracy. Requests can be made through ENSTINET, with photocopies usually supplied by the National Information and Documentation Centre (NIDOC) and AUC, but most librarians and users remain unaware of this system, and of the existence of the union list. However, the start that has been made has reduced dependency on BLDSC. A union catalogue of foreign publications would seem a logical extension of current efforts.

ENSTINET is basically a co-operative undertaking, depending upon some 18 nodes that contribute information to its several databases. Seven main nodes are specialist government libraries and documentation centres, led by NIDOC. Participating universities are Alexandria, Assiut, Mansoura, Suez Canal, Tanta, and Zagazig.

Apart from the union list of foreign periodicals. ENSTINET services include searches of CD-ROM and on-line databases, subsidized by USAID and the Egyptian Academy of Scientific Research and Technology (ASRT). About 3,000 searches are undertaken each year, MEDLINE being the most used. In-house databases comprise: details of theses, grey literature, reports and journal articles, available in printed form as *Egyptian scientific and technical abstracts* (in science and engineering); a who's who of scientific and technical workers and organizations; details of training courses; specialist files from the nodes.

ENSTINET is keen to encourage resource sharing and to reduce duplication of research effort; academics need to be more aware of what is being done, and the potential for achieving even more. Their institutions therefore need to participate more whole-heartedly, commencing with publicity by libraries about their resources and services. Otherwise universities will risk being marginalized, to an ever increasing extent, from the national science and technology effort.

So far as the National Library is concerned, it is not at present in a position to take a lead in promoting co-operation, and in addition its function under decree is confined to the organization of the public library network.

Foreign assistance

In financial terms, by far the largest project is the UNESCO sponsored Alexandria Library, which it is assumed will eventually be constructed. It should take the form of a type of academic library: one writer has described it as 'a public library for research'.[11]. Initially the emphasis of its collections will be on Egyptian (Pharaonic, Islamic, Coptic), Middle Eastern, and Greek civilization, with special prominence to the history of science and to works likely to have been contained in the ancient library.

The current (1993) estimated total cost for site preparation, building construction, equipment, and initial stock stands at $US152,000,000. The position of the National Library in relation to the new library is unclear. Such a sum would, in the opinion of many inside the country and abroad, be better spent on improving Egypt's existing academic libraries, for the more immediate benefit of their enormous reader populations, enumerated in table 7.1 on p. 83.

There is an annual American aid budget to Egypt of $US2 billion, but few signs of ongoing USAID assistance to academic libraries. In the past such aid has consisted mainly of equipment: furniture, microfilm readers (but not reader-printers), photocopiers, and back sets of journals on microfilm; also training abroad for staff. Some good libraries have resulted; for example, that of the Research and Planning Centre at Cairo University. However, as so often happens in the developing world, equipment that comes without back-up support for maintenance and supplies, and no training for staff who will be expected to use it in service to users is liable to end up unused and eventually unusable.

British assistance is effected through the British Council and

VSO. Council policy on aid to libraries has changed direction in recent years; away from indirect support in the form of free BLDSC coupons, and the popular Book Presentation Scheme, funded by the Overseas Development Administration. Current emphasis is on training librarians in Egypt, and courses are provided at a number of universities, under a two-year agreement with the Supreme Council of Universities.

The council continues to give valuable support to VSO librarians, of whom two were working in Upper Egypt in 1993. Since the library programme began in 1978 volunteers have worked in seven universities, always with the primary aim of training colleagues and library users in basic library techniques and procedures.

Conclusions

While there are definite success stories in the academic library field, improvement comes slowly, and in some instances resources and services are actually deteriorating. Egypt's resources are such that there is less excuse than in some other developing countries for offering library services that are so severely sub-standard. The country enjoys relative economic stability, and has a workforce that is better educated than in some neighbouring countries.

The solution may lie in reform of the enormous public sector, of which universities and their libraries are a small but important part.

References

1   Aman, Mohammed M., 'Egypt, Libraries'. In: *Encyclopedia of library and information science*, v. 7, 1972.

2   British Council, *Books, libraries and educational computing profile – Egypt 1985*, Cairo, British Council, 1985.

3   The prestigious Bibliotheca Alexandrina project is a notable exception to this statement, although the library has not yet (1993) been constructed.

4   Aman, op. cit.

5   Ibid.

6   Albin, Michael W., 'Touring Egyptian libraries', *Leads*, **22** (3), Fall 1980, 1–5.

7   Pryce-Jones, David, *The Closed circle: an interpretation of the Arabs*, London, Paladin, 1990.

8   Known in the 1970s as the Egyptian Library and Archives Association.

9   Lees, Nigel, 'Library and information work in Egypt: perspective

of a volunteer working in Assiut', *Journal of information science*, **16** (2), 1990, 99–105
10 *ENSTINET's union list of periodicals*, 2nd edn. Cairo, ENSTINET, 1989.
11 Tocatlian, Jacques, 'Bibliotheca Alexandrina: reviving a legacy of the past for a brighter common future', *International library review*, **23** (3), 1991, 255–269.

Bibliography

Aman, Mohammed M., 'Egyptian university libraries', *Library history review*, **2** (1), 1975, 1–9.

Arini, Mohsen El, 'Egyptian libraries', *Pakistan library bulletin*, **21** (2), 1990, 23–33.

Arini, Mohsen El, 'Al-Azhar university library', *Pakistan library bulletin*, **20** (1), 1989, 33–45.

Halwagy, A .S., 'Recent changes in library education in Egypt', *Journal of education for library and information science*, **33** (3), 1992, 255–259

Hyams, Peter, 'Egyptians move towards self-sufficiency', *Information world review*, Dec. 1990, 8–9.

Kabesh, Ahmad, 'Towards a national information policy for Egypt, by Ahmad Kabesh and Ahmad Bassit'. In: *Information, knowledge, evolution: proceedings of the forty-fourth FID congress*; ed. S. Koskiala and R. Launo, Amsterdam, Elsevier, 1989.

World of learning, 1992, London, Europa, 1991.

8 Libraries in Iraq: a short report

Amer I. Al-Kindilchie

Libraries existed in ancient Iraq (Mesopotamia), as early as 4,000 BC. The earliest written records of the Sumerians, Assyrians and Babylonians are the clay tablets recovered in the course of archaeological excavations. In the city of ancient Nippur, for example more than 60,000 tablets, which dated from the Sumerian period (c.4,000 BC) and from the Babylonian period (c.3,000 BC), were excavated at the end of the nineteenth century.

In the city of Nineveh, the Assyrian capital in the north of present day Iraq, many clay tablets were recovered that had been part of the royal library of King Assur-Banipal.

During the Middle Ages, the Arab-Islamic civilization of the Abbasids flourished. Their capital, Baghdad had 63 libraries that included some large collections of manuscripts and volumes, and were mostly opened for public use. There were, in addition, libraries at Basra and Kufa, among other cities of the period.

After the fall of Baghdad in AD 1458, and the mass destruction of buildings and material objects by the Mongol conquerors, thousands of manuscripts and volumes were thrown into the Tigris river, resulting in the permanent loss of a great treasure of mankind's recorded ideas and learning. According to folk-memory, people crossed the river by walking on the huge quantity of manuscripts that had been thrown into it.

Modern Iraq has a population of some 18,000,000, and an area of 435,052 sq. km. More than 4,000,000 people live in and around the capital, Baghdad.

Major political changes have taken place in the country during the second half of this century. The Republic of Iraq was declared on 14 July, 1958, when the monarchy, under King Faisal II was overthrown. There were several more changes to the political regime during the next two decades, prior to the commencement of the leadership of President Saddam Hussain, Head of State since 1979.

The Iraq–Iran war, commonly known as the first Gulf War

started in September 1980 and lasted for almost eight years. It greatly affected libraries and information centres in Iraq. The second Gulf War was launched in January 1991 and, led by the United States and other European countries, had even greater impact on the whole nation. Sanctions, which were imposed several months before the outbreak of war, affected all aspects of life, including libraries, publishing, and the book trade. They were deprived of many vital resources including paper and other printing materials, microforms, and computers and computer software.

Table 8.1   Variations in book publishing, 1968–1992

Year	Titles published
1968	473
1969	621
1970	851
1971	696
1972	859
1973	1131
1974	1411
1975	1043
1976	1515
1977	1751
1978	2384
1979	2532
1980	2484
1981	2569
1982	2354
1983	2330
1984	2245
1985	2447
1986	2374
1987	2081
1988	1461
1989	1294
1990	1399
1991	576
1992	540

Table 8.2   Titles published (000s), 1968–1992

Year	Under 500	500–1,000	1,000–1,500	1,500–2,000	2,000–2,500	Over 2,500
1968	+					
1969		+				
1970		+				
1971		+				
1972		+				
1973			+			
1974			+			
1975		+				
1976			+			
1977				+		
1978					+	

Year	Under 500	500–1,000	1,000–1,500	1,500–2,000	2,000–2,500	Over 2,500
1979					+	
1980					+	
1981						+
1982					+	
1983					+	
1984					+	
1985					+	
1986					+	
1987				+		
1988		+				
1989		+				
1990		+				
1990		+				
1991		+				
1992	+					

The National Library and National Centre for Archives

Although the National Library was established in 1920, its legal status as a depository library was designated only in 1961. Its building had become inadequate to house the growing collections as well as services to users, and a new building was inaugurated in 1976, in one of the most prominent positions in the centre of the capital. On July 1 1987 the National Library was amalgamated with the National Centre of Archives, which had been set up in 1963, forming a new centre called Dar Al-Kutub Wal-Watha'iq, the National House of Books and Archives; under the administrative supervision of the Ministry of Information, and with its own director. The centre has initiated joint activities, most notably computer networks and databases, and microfilming programmes.

Within the limitations imposed by the operation of import sanctions, and the regional conflict, coming so soon after the centre was formed, it has developed, quite substantially, its collections of books, periodicals, microforms, maps, and other materials.

Table 8.3   Growth of National Library collections (numbers of vols.), 1968–1992

1968–73	50,000+
1974–79	100,000
1980–85	200,000
1986–88	300,000
1989–91	540,000
1992	600,000

Its archives sector, the National Centre of Archives now houses more than 8,000,000 items of Iraq's archival materials, organized according to the National System for Iraqi Archives.

This was developed in Iraq, with more than 40,000 materials location categories, and action is in progress to develop a database for the recording and content searching of the materials.

The National Library sector of this joint centre has recently developed databases for a national bibliography; for recording Iraqi theses and dissertations; and the library's catalogue of holdings.

Out of the total staff of 181, 40 are professional librarians.

Table 8.4   Growth of National Archives collection (numbers of items) 1987–1992

1987	2,500,000
1988	3,000,000
1989	4,500,000
1990	5,000,000
1991	5,900,000
1992	7,750,000

Academic libraries

In general, academic libraries are regarded as the best developed among the libraries of Iraq, in respect of their buildings, professional staff, equipment, and services. There are some 90 libraries, serving 11 universities and institutes of technical higher education.

The library service of the University of Baghdad, with central library and 28 college libraries, is the oldest and largest. The collections total about 750,000 books, 5,700 periodical titles, and 50,000 other items (manuscripts, maps, films and other nonbook formats). The annual circulation figures for all library materials have been recorded in 1992 at close to 480,000.

The Central Library of Al-Musil University, which with its 14 constituent college libraries is the second largest in the country, has over 250,000 books, 2,850 periodical titles, and some 16,000 other items; circulation records show 152,057 issues in the last complete academic year. It is the best equipped among the country's university libraries, operating more advanced information services, especially CD-ROM and on-line searching. The library's audiovisual department offers a range of services to the university community, both individually and as groups.

From the late 1980s onwards, new universities and libraries have been in process of development; Tikrit, Al-Qadisiya; Al-Anbar; Al-Kufa, and Saddam University.

Table 8.5   Basic statistics of selected academic libraries

Institution	Population served	No. of libraries	Total collection	Reader places	Annual circulation	Staff Professionals	Others
University of Baghdad	53,575	29	807,222	6,047	1,280,820	112	154
Al-Mustan-siriya University	20,021	8	259,462	748	163,867	32	48
Al-Musil (Mosul) University	19,820	15	166,450	3,151	562,901	16	168
Al-Basrah (Basra) University	15,242	16	310,838	1,276	627,847	20	136
University of Technology, Baghdad	8,344	1	87,677	1,190	79,528	29	12
University of Salah Al-Din (Salahaddin)	8,308	8	201,789	1,364	132,433	6	86
Al-Kufa University	3,282	5	45,135	151	168,838	4	12
Al-Anbar University	1,063	2	5,268	637	1,601	2	9
University of Tikrit (Tikreet)	598	3	14,492	207	1,620	—	11
Technical Institutes Establishment *	49,209	30	374,826	5,186	625,276	25	81
Totals	180,519	117	2,273,159	19,957	3,674,731	246	717

* Eighteen institutes incorporated under the Foundation for Technical Institutes, Baghdad (*World of learning*, 1993, 764).

School libraries

There are 8,866 libraries serving the non-graduate levels of education, from kindergarten upwards. There are in all, 11,237 such educational establishments in Iraq, commonly referred to as schools; kindergarten; primary, high, and technical.

About 75% of secondary schools have libraries (1,925 out of 2,615). They have between them some 1,500,000 volumes; total annual circulation amounts to 1,270,810.

Only a small proportion (131) of the libraries up to secondary-school level is managed by professional librarians. The rest are managed part time by schoolteachers. That explains in part why students, at all levels of education are major users of public libraries, whose professional staffing is much better.

Starting in 1984–85, the Ministry of Education initiated a project to develop school libraries throughout the country. Its main aim has been to develop a number of resource centres in schools in Baghdad, with emphasis on audiovisual materials. The experiment was judged successful in respect of the 12 schools originally selected in the capital, and has been extended, since 1988–9 to take in a total of 35.

Table 8.6   School libraries in Iraq

Governorate	Kindergarten	Primary schools	High schools	Technical institutions	Total schools & institutions
Baghdad (Karkh)	79	574	269	47	1,014
Baghdad (Risafa)	74	659	315	3	1,051
Basra	57	516	161	6	740
Babylon	39	421	142	15	617
Anbar	4	520	247	7	778
Diala	26	645	181	15	877
Karbela	19	250	73	9	351
Maysan	18	219	48	9	294
Muthanna	4	221	45	7	287
Najaf	32	296	102	10	440
Nineveh	46	947	228	24	1,245
Qadisiya	4	397	85	12	528
Salah Al-Deen	25	451	170	15	661
Ta'meem	34	499	149	12	694
Thi-Qar	28	561	165	15	769
Wasit	25	435	92	16	568
Total	554	7,611	2,472	222	10,879

Source: Data from Ministry of Education statistics, concerning the schools (the majority of all in the country) that are under its control, 1992–3.

Public libraries
There are more than 70 public libraries, with collections that total over 1,000,000 volumes. They are distributed throughout the 18 governorates of Iraq.

Eighteen of the libraries are in Baghdad, having close on 250,000 volumes between them. There are 267,065 registered users, and annual circulation records of use of 142,550 items. Of 170 staff, 29 are professionally qualified, or else have undergone some formal training course.

There are two children's libraries in the capital, one on each side of the River Tigris; the one on the east bank was set up in 1964; that on the west bank started in 1985. They serve children between the ages of five and fourteen years.

Table 8.7   Public library authorities: basic statistics

Governorate	Population served	No. of libraries	Total stock	Reader places	Staff Professionals	Others
Baghdad	4,053,740	178	2,989,331	11,829	488	475
Nineveh	1,580,508	43	586,066	4,139	97	141
Salah Al-Deen	780,942	14	75,308	520	22	41
Al-Tameem	607,779	19	94,345	1,134	26	25
Diala	1,016,235	16	95,485	1,156	35	60
Al-Anbar	888,826	24	144,213	1,105	38	51
Babylon	1,194,848	25	113,791	1,423	43	49
Kerbela	521,767	8	57,767	382	17	28
Najaf	629,107	16	*—	1,341	28	53
Al-Qadisiya	588,557	14	—	800	19	21
Al-Muthanna	338,529	6	—	336	5	22
Thi-Qar	987,923	22	—	1,347	29	58
Wasit	582,522	12	51,206	560	17	28
Maysan	513,644	17	—	1,305	32	48
Al-Basrah	912,012	30	—	2,493	107	143
Duhook	300,298	6	16,667	295	8	17
Arbil	812,843	22	282,747	1,817	27	104
Sulaimaniya	1,002,975	17	104,464	520	46	48
Total	17,322,055	489	4,611,395	32,502	1084	1412

* Figures not available

Note: Statistics for use of materials are not available

Special libraries
All ministries, and most other governmental and non-governmental establishments have their own collections of information materials. As an outstanding example, the Ministry of Planning, in existence since 1960, has a collection in excess of 145,000 items, with circulation (restricted to ministry staff) over 10,000 per annum.

Iraqi National Network for Libraries and Information Centres
A number of libraries and information centres in Iraq use computers and CD-ROM in their systems and services, most especially college and university libraries, and special libraries serving ministries and other official bodies.

Between them, they have co-operated to form an information network in Baghdad and certain other cities, sharing information that is available on CD-ROM databases. This project has become the Iraqi National Network for Libraries and Information Centres. The central libraries of all universities in the country are members, as well as the National Library and National Centre for Archives. The network operates with the aim of increasing access to information held on CD-ROM throughout the country.

The Profession
Courses in library and information science are taught, or sponsored by several academic and other recognized sponsoring bodies; for example, Al-Mustansiriya University, Al-Basra University, the Iraqi Library Association, and the Central Library of the University of Baghdad.

Professional education in Iraq began with the establishment of the Central Library at the University of Baghdad in 1958, when it was requested to organize training courses for staff working in all types of library.

Al-Mustansiriya University opened the first library science department in Iraq in 1970, offering a two-year diploma course to secondary-school leavers. This was followed shortly after by a similar programme at the University of Baghdad, which in 1972 offered a graduate, higher diploma programme from the Higher Institute of Library Science and Documentation. Al-Mustansiriya extended its own programme in 1980, offering a BA in library science, and by the mid-1980s changed the name of its department, as well as the programme to reflect the trend towards library and information science. Both Al-Mustansiriya and Basra universities are currently offering bachelor's degrees in library and information science; the former having ceased its higher diploma course, in favour of a master's degree in library science. A doctoral programme in library science (the first in Iraq) started at Al-Mustansiriya in the academic year 1992–3.

These programmes have attracted a certain number of students from abroad, Algeria, Bahrain, Jordan and Morocco.

Sources
1   Al-Kindilchie, Amer I., 'Libraries and documentation centers in Iraq' (Translated title; Arabic text), *Arabic journal for information science*, **5** (1), 1984, 42–53.

2   Al-Kindilchie, Amer I., 'National network for libraries and information centers in Iraq: problems and selected solutions'. Paper presented to the Symposium on information systems of the 21st century, Yarmouk University, Irbid (Jordan), 28–30 June, 1993.

3   Iraq, Ministry of Planning, *Statistical yearbook, 1991*, Baghdad, the Ministry, 1992.

4   Iraq, Ministry of Education, *Some statistical data*, 1993 (unpublished materials).

5   The author acknowledges assistance received to gain access to statistics prepared in the Ministry of Education.

9 Library and information services in Jordan

Najeeb Al-Shorbaji

The issues of library and information services in Jordan should be addressed within the general framework of Jordan as a developing country, with its special features and characteristics. These services have to be seen as part of the general scene and not in isolation from their physical and human environment. Traditionally, libraries have constituted a major facet of the cultural life of the country. Other facets include theatre, music, arts, folklore, poetry, and storytelling. In common with many other areas in the world, this has changed during the present century. Libraries are no longer merely part of the humanistic cultural life of a country; they are as well, part of its scientific movement, and of economic and social development. The status of development of libraries reflects the state of development of the country itself. One can argue that a country with well-developed library and information services is a developed country. Poor library and information services are characteristics of developing or underdeveloped countries.

Jordan: geography, history, and development
Jordan is situated near the south-eastern coast of the Mediterranean and is part of the Arabian Desert. The total area of Jordan (East Bank) is 92,300 square kilometres.[1]. Officially known as the Hashemite Kingdom of Jordan, it is bounded to the south by Saudi Arabia, north by the Syrian Arab Republic, east by Saudi Arabia and Iraq, and west by Occupied Palestine. Arabic is the national language. In 1922, the area east of the River Jordan was named Transjordan, and was recognized in 1923 as a state under the British Mandate, within the Mandate System of the League of Nations. In March 1946, it was designated a kingdom, to become a member of the Arab League and the United Nations. In 1948, a new state, Israel was created from part of Palestine, after the British Army's withdrawal, and the rest of Palestine (West Bank) was linked with Jordan in 1952. In 1967 the West Bank was occu-

pied by Israel, and as a result of these wars, conflicts, and political changes, about two million refugees went to neighbouring countries, particularly Jordan. The description of the state of libraries and information services will be confined to (East) Jordan.

As a result of the series of wars and political instability in the Middle East, the social and cultural life of Jordan is formulated in a way that reflects the changes taking place all the time. Jordanian society is built on the family concept and families try hard to stay together as long as they can, but economic constraints and the new facts of life make it more difficult for people from rural areas not to migrate to urban areas. Four major sections can be distinguished in the structure of Jordanian society:

1   Urban population: consists mainly of people living in cities and large towns; they are the more educated, they work in the industries and government central services.
2   Rural population: consists mainly of people living in the villages and the agricultural areas; the main trade is agriculture and its related activities. This category is in constant decrease as a result of migration to urban areas.
3   Bedouin population: people who live in the desert areas of Jordan. They depend on the herds and what they produce. They tend to move in search of water resources. The government has developed pilot projects to encourage settlement of these communities.
4   The refugee camps: as a result of the 1948 and the 1967 wars with Israel, and the Gulf War in 1991, over 1.5 million, mostly Palestinians, fled into Jordan.

The total population of Jordan by the end of 1991 was 3,888,000. (2,005,400 male and 1,882,600 female); 3,029,000 in urban areas and 858,000 in rural areas.[2] Amman, the capital, contains over 61% of the total population. Other major cities in Jordan are Zarqa, Irbid, Mafraq, Salt, Karak, Ajloun, Aqaba, Tafileh, and Maan. A majority (51%) of the population are under 15 years old and 25% are of working age (20–60 years old).

As part of the social and economic development in Jordan, education has been considered a priority by successive governments. Investment in people has been seen as the best mechanism to achieve sustainable development. The number of students enrolled at all educational levels in 1952–3 was 101,763, distributed at 487 schools and taught by 2,378 teachers. In 1992–3, the total was 1,214,064 students distributed at 3,780 schools and taught by 51,948 teachers. In higher education, the first university was opened in Jordan in 1963 with 167 students; in 1974–5 there

were 4,085 students at the University of Jordan, the only university at that time. By 1981–2 there were 20,653 students registered in
the country's four universities. This has grown by the current academic year, 1992–3 to a total of 44,026, of whom 20,325 are female
students. Additional to these are the estimated 4,072[3] students
enrolled in the private universities that have been established
during the last four years. The total number of full-time professors working in the four government universities was estimated
in 1991–2 to be 1,795.[4]

Health care in Jordan forms part of the strategy for sustainable
development. The first Ministry of Health was established in 1950
under which 52 physicians worked all over the country. By the
end of 1991, there were 4,762 physicians in all specialities registered in Jordan, about 49% of them working in the public sector.[5]
Primary health care constituted the mechanism for realization of
Health For All 2000, an indicator of the improvement in health
services is reduction of infant mortality, from 216 per 1000 in 1950
to 36 per 1000 in the present decade.[6] The estimated size of the
labour force at the end of 1991 was 552,000.[7]

Library and information services: history and development

The two chapters on 'Libraries in Jordan' that appeared in the
Encyclopedia of Library and Information Science, by Asali[8] and
Younis[9] provided a historical background on libraries in the area
known as the Fertile Crescent, which includes Iraq, Jordan, Syria
and Palestine. This area while governed under three consecutive
empires; Ommayad, Abbassid and Ottoman, shared the same history and cultural life, including libraries. The mosque was the
centre of religious and educational life of Islamic countries, therefore libraries that belonged to mosques flourished and prospered.
Al-Aqsa Mosque, in Jerusalem, had become in the seventh century an academy in its own right that provided religious and linguistic studies. It had a remarkable library comprising several
thousand volumes. The influence of the Crusaders in the twelfth
century and the French occupation of Egypt and part of Syria
under Napoleon Bonaparte at the close of the eighteenth century
was also felt. In the nineteenth century and during the first half of
the twentieth century, the Christian missionaries in the Holy
Land established several libraries. Most notable of these were the
Orthodox Patriarchate Library (500 volumes in 1865); the Library
of the American School of Oriental Research (7,000 volumes in
1907); the Library of the Palestine Archaeological Museum (30,000
volumes in 1928); and the Young Men's Christian Association
Library in Jerusalem (25,000 volumes in 1933). The first published

library catalogue, in 1847, was that of the library of the Greek Orthodox Patriarchate which comprised 400 manuscripts and 10,000 printed volumes. The first printing in Palestine was started in 1847 by the Franciscan Fathers, whose example was soon followed by many others.

During the British Mandate of Palestine and Jordan (1917–48) little progress was made as far as the development of modern libraries was concerned. There was no public library prior to 1948. Some social clubs were established during this period, with little more than token libraries. Many schools in 1920 were actually without reference works, and the building up of a modest library in each school was a very slow process. The library of the largest academic institution, the Government Arab College, contained 7,122 books in 1946. In Transjordan, where the development of public education was much slower, school libraries were still poorer. In most cases they did not exist at all.

Library and information legislation
Comprehensive legislation, covering all aspects of information work does not exist in Jordan. Fragmented bits and pieces of library and information legislation are included in some of the laws and regulations of government agencies. Specific reference will be made to regulations covering the library and information services in school libraries, college and university libraries, public libraries, the national library, special libraries, the national archives and the National Information Centre.

School libraries
The Education Law does not make any specific reference to the development of school libraries, although it emphasizes the importance of access to information, reading, and other cultural activities. The Ministry of Education's 1960 guidelines for school libraries defined the functions of the school library. In 1966, guidelines for book selection and acquisition for school libraries were implemented. Guidelines No. 11 of 1981 included a paragraph specifying the functions of the school librarian.

College and university libraries
Higher education institutions are supervized by the Ministry of Higher Education. The Higher Education Law does not include specific reference to libraries in higher education institutions in Jordan. However, in 1987 a regulation was introduced regarding the accreditation of community colleges belonging either to government or the private sector. The regulation stated that a college

should have a library, and specified the number of staff and their desired qualifications, standards for library buildings and for furniture, and size of book collection and its organization.

Universities that are run by the Government of Jordan have been established by specific laws and regulations. None of the legislation has included any recognition of the library as an institution within the university. It was left to each university to deal with this matter individually. Private universities are regulated by a temporary law passed in 1989, which makes no specific reference to their libraries. However, the licensing regulations of private universities put the availability of a library as a precondition for licensing; specifying the number of books per student and the minimum number of books in the library and library buildings.

Public libraries

Two laws have been introduced regarding public libraries. The Law of Municipalities, passed in 1955, included the provision that the 'Municipal Council should establish museums, public libraries, schools, cultural, sports and social clubs and their supervision.' No specific reference was made in the law as to the size, staffing, collection, services, or budgeting of public libraries. The second law, that of 1961, is specific for the Amman Municipality Library, and includes items regarding the status, management, budget, and services of the library.

National Library

At present the National Library is part of the Ministry of Culture, under a law of 1990. The same applies to the National Documentation (Archives) Centre. Two new laws, specific for the National Library and the National Archives were being considered in 1993.

Special libraries

Such libraries belong to government ministries, departments and agencies, and exist because each ministry's legal statute includes an item regarding organization of documents, archives, and files, although not specifying that they be administered as a library. Some government departments have a section in their regulations regarding development of libraries, or they may have included a library in the structure of the department, without specifying its functions, staff, or budget.

Library and information services: present status

National Library

The National Archives Centre was established in 1975 with the aim of preserving the public records and archives of government and the public administration. Soon after, in 1977 the Directorate of Libraries and National Documents was established as part of the Ministry of Culture and Youth. The Law setting up the Directorate defined its objectives as being to:

*   Establish and develop the National Library.
*   Develop the sections that are responsible for national archives, documents, documentation and information, and their catalogues and bibliographic control.
*   Supervise the public libraries, co-ordinate them, and develop the technical basis for their development.
*   Propose and apply standards and criteria for libraries and documentation services.
*   Act as a deposit centre for all types of documents.
*   Revive the national heritage.
*   Co-ordinate and collaborate with special libraries.

In July 1990 a new law for the Ministry of Culture was passed, which dismantled the Directorate of Libraries and National Documents and created three units in the Ministry: The National Library, The National Documentation Centre, and The Royal Cultural Centre.

A draft law on the organization of the work of the National Library and the National Documentation Centre is, at the time of writing, being considered by the Cabinet before proceeding to Parliament for approval. A major development related to the work of the National Library is the issuing of Legal Deposit, and the Copyright Law that was passed in November 1992.

The National Library as it stands now employs 32 technical staff of whom 13 are qualified librarians, and in addition 14 support staff.

The library's book collection has over 50,000 titles, most of them published in Jordan. The journals collection includes all journals published in Jordan, including back sets.

The library catalogue is being converted from card to a machine readable catalogue. The UNESCO CDS/ISIS system is used in the library. It is planned to introduce MINISIS in the near future.

A recent agreement was made between the Governments of Jordan and China by which the latter would grant Jordan a total of $US6,000,000 to build the National Library and National Documentation Centre. It is expected that work on the project will start in early 1994.

The National Library has implemented the recently introduced Copyright Law which designated it the country's legal deposit library. Copies of all published materials in Jordan are being deposited and registered in the library. The Law covers both printed and non-printed materials such as musical works, art works, and computer programs.

The Library provides the Cataloguing-in-Publication data (CIP) for all newly published books, as part of its services, along with registration of materials sent for legal deposit. Every published book in Jordan includes the CIP data in addition to the deposit number.

The Library has taken steps to adopt the international and Arab documentation and information standards as Jordanian standards. ISO 521–1984: International Standard Book Numbering (ISBN) and IS0 581–1984: International Standard Serial Numbering (ISSN) have been adopted, so that ISBN has become JS 919–1992, and ISSN is JS 918–1992. Other relevant standards will be adopted in the near future.

Library services are open to researchers, with a minimum of formalities. Services include photocopying, reference services, and reading rooms. Lending is not allowed except in very special cases.

National Documentation Centre

The National Documentation Centre is located within the National Library at present and is run by the same staff, although it is legally considered as a different body from the National Library. The Centre has taken steps to act in accordance with its constitution, which requires it to be responsible for government records, from their creation until they are archived, or destroyed.

Public libraries

The only public libraries in East Jordan prior to the First World War were attached to mosques and churches. They contained mostly holy books and religious information materials. There was no indigenous publishing at that time, but access to publishers in Turkey, Egypt, and Lebanon meant that books were made available for those who could read. After the establishment of the Emirate in 1921, Prince, then King Abdullah, paid attention to the cultural life in general and to libraries in particular. He established a library at the palace which included reference books, poetry and history in Arabic, English, and Turkish.[10]

Between 1949 and 1957 three public libraries were developed; the library of the British Council, late 1949, the library of the American Cultural Centre in 1953 and Irbid Public Library in 1957. During the 1960s 10 more libraries were established and a further 12 in the 1970s; while the 1980s saw a great expansion, when more than 60 libraries were opened.

The responsibility for establishing public libraries lies with the Ministry of Municipalities, Rural Affairs and the Environment. Development of library services in municipalities and local authorities has the same standing, under legislation governing their provision, as other public services such as roads, water supply, sanitation, and electricity.

In a report on public libraries in Jordan in 1964, *Rissalat Al-Maktaba* indicated that there were seven libraries in East Jordan and four in the West Bank.[11] The directory of libraries in Jordan, which was compiled and published by the Jordan Library Association (JLA) in 1976 showed that there were 17 public libraries in the country.[12] An unpublished report compiled by the JLA in 1984 recorded 36 public libraries, of which 25 were members of the Association. Public libraries in Jordan are attached to institutions as follows:

- Municipalities and local authorities.
- Government ministries (Ministry of Culture, Ministry of Interior).
- Cultural centres of foreign diplomatic missions.
- Private sector.

In 1989, Zash,[13] quoting the Department of Libraries and National Documents, listed 39 public libraries attached to municipalities as of November 1988, and noted that the first public library had been inaugurated in Irbid in 1957.

A comprehensive study conducted by Al-Amad,[14] collected information from 86 public libraries concerning their buildings, facilities, budget, staffing, collection, organization, and services. A number of serious problems were identified in the study including:

Buildings
Most of the libraries surveyed occupy one floor and less than 500 square metres. In fact there were libraries that occupy 20 square metres only.

Facilities
Most libraries suffer from lack of furniture: shelves, chairs, tables,

audiovisual materials, photocopiers, and other facilities. As an example the numbers of reading tables range from 1 in a minor municipality library to about 38 in Greater Amman Municipality Public Library. One library, which belongs to the private sector, has a machine-readable catalogue and a computerized serials control system.

Staffing

The study showed that a total of 210 staff work in the public libraries included in the survey; 79 male and 131 female. One library has 22 staff, while there are four libraries with no full-time staff. Qualifications held range from high school certificate to university degrees.

Budget

The study showed that very limited financial resources are allocated for the libraries, especially in the case of municipal libraries. Libraries that belong to the private sector or diplomatic missions and other ministries are in a better position as far as funding is concerned.

Library collections

The study showed that over 35% of library stocks have less than 2,000 titles. A grand total of 476,667 titles is available in the 86 libraries under study. Periodicals subscriptions are very limited in most of the libraries.

Organization

The majority of public libraries are classified and catalogued. The Anglo-American Cataloguing Rules (AACR2) are used for descriptive cataloguing, standard Arabic and English subject headings lists are used for subject cataloguing, and Dewey Decimal Classification is used to classify the collections.

Services

Traditional library services are provided by most libraries including lending, reference, children's services, and photocopying in a few places. The number of users ranges from less than 1,000 per month to over 1,500 a day.

General observations on public libraries in Jordan are characterized as:

- Lack of awareness of the role of public libraries in education and culture.
- The status of the public library is very low in the organiza-

tional structure of municipalities and local authorities.
- Lack of resources to support public libraries including human and financial resources.
- Lack of co-operation and co-ordination between public libraries, even among those belonging to the same authority. This situation created problems in staffing, collection development, organization, and services.

Special libraries and documentation and information centres
Special libraries and documentation and information centres belong to government ministries, industrial and commercial institutions, research centres, and regional and international organizations.

The JLA Data Base includes profiles of 73 special libraries in Jordan that are members of the Association. It should be stated that the actual number of special libraries is more than this figure due to the fact that each of the type of institutions mentioned above has its own library, but not all are members of the JLA.

The following general observations on special libraries are based on a survey in press at the time of writing:[15]

1 The majority of these libraries are run by one staff member, who is usually a qualified librarian.
2 Very few special libraries employ what can be called 'a subject specialist'.
3 Most of the special libraries have collections of less than 10,000 volumes and under 50 journal subscriptions.
4 Libraries attached to ministries and government agencies have the least staff, poorest collections, and are generally the least developed of all types of library in Jordan.
5 Libraries attached to research centres and regional and international organizations are adequately staffed, with better collections, more journals, and provide better and more information services than other libraries in the country.
6 Library automation began in special libraries. Younis indicated that out of the ten libraries that were computerized in 1986, six of them were special libraries.[16] Records of the CDS/ISIS User Group in Jordan show that there are 30 computerized special libraries.[17] The systems that are used include CDS/ISIS (24 libraries), FoxBase or DBase (3 libraries), Cardbox (1 library), and ULTRA (2 libraries) database management systems. Examples of the computerized special libraries are:
   - Government: Ministry of Planning, Ministry of Agriculture, Vocational Training Centre and Water Authority of Jordan;

- Private: Arab Bank, the Housing Bank and the Union of Chambers of Commerce;
- Regional: the Arab Mining Company and the Arab Organization for Administrative Development;
- Research: the Royal Scientific Society and the National Centre for Transfer of Technology;
- International: Centre for Environmental Health Activities, UNESCO and ESCWA.

7 Current awareness services, selective dissemination of information, special bibliographies, accessions lists, abstracting and indexing are among the most frequently provided services by these special libraries.

8 Most of the library buildings were not purpose-designed; they have usually been converted from some other purpose, with consequent effects on the operation of each library.

9 There is no specific legislation for special libraries in Jordan, which has meant that library collections are considered the same as any other stock kept in the organization, and therefore the librarian is an administrative officer.

Academic libraries

Presentation of academic libraries in this section will cover libraries that belong to the two types of higher education institutions in Jordan; community colleges, and universities. The JLA Data Base includes profiles of 37 academic libraries, 12 of which are university libraries.

Community colleges

Two higher education institutions were established in Jordan in 1952, as teacher training institutes. One of them was in Amman (for men), the other in Ramallah (for women) in the West Bank. They started with the specific aim of preparing school teachers to support the educational process in elementary and secondary schools. Since then their aims have become increasingly diversified, and teacher training has become one among many programmes covered. Other programmes include training of assistant librarians and documentation officers, school librarians, paramedical education, laboratory technicians, assistant engineers, and religious studies. By the year 1979 there were 32 such colleges In 1979–80 the name for these colleges or institutes was changed to 'community college'. In 1985 the Ministry of Higher Education was established and its Higher Education Law defined community colleges as 'Any educational institution that provides any type of educational programme and skill after Secondary Education for a duration of no more than three years.'[18] The criteria for accreditation of community colleges in Jordan include standards for the library in the college; personnel, book collection, furniture, and building.

In a recent study by M. Al-Qawasmeh,[19] he surveyed the community college libraries to assess their status and to identify problem areas related to personnel, library buildings, collections, equipment, furniture, organization, services, budget, and interlibrary co-operation. The survey covered 53 libraries that are run by the following bodies:

- Colleges of the Ministry of Higher Education, 11 libraries.
- Colleges of the private sector, 22 libraries.
- Colleges of UNRWA, 2 libraries.
- Colleges of other ministries and government agencies, 18 libraries.

The study showed that 109 full-time librarians are employed in these libraries, of whom 58 are professionally qualified librarians. The total number of titles available in the 53 libraries was 557,721, an average of 10,523 titles per library, and an average of 13.23 titles per student. A total of 1,574 journal subscriptions was shown in the survey in addition to 117 newspaper subscriptions. Out of the 53 libraries surveyed, 47 have their collections catalogued and classified using AACR2 and DDC. Library services including lending, reference services, photocopying, bibliographic services and user education are provided by all community college libraries. Co-operation is very weak among these libraries as the study showed that only 28 of them have some kind of co-operation.

A general observation that can be made here is that the libraries attached to United Nations Relief and Works Agency (UNRWA) colleges have the largest collections, best staffing, and best equipment, followed in second place by the government colleges, while the libraries in private colleges are least well provided with staff, stock, and equipment.

University libraries

The first university in Jordan was established in Amman in 1962, under the name University of Jordan; its library dates from the same time. In 1976, Yarmouk University and its library opened in Irbid in the northern part of the country. Muta University and its library were founded in 1984, in Karak in the southern part of the country. Jordan University of Science and Technology and its library were set up in 1986. In 1989 the first private university was given a licence to take students and opened in 1990. Since then seven more universities have been opened in Amman, and two more are getting under way in KJarash and Zarka. There is also another government-funded university at Mafraq. Each university's library is part of the facilities provided in support of teaching and research.

Comparison of numbers of students and academic staff in private universities, and in government universities shows that the vast majority is in the latter. Private universities place more emphasis on teaching, while the research component occupies an important part of the activities of the government universities. Libraries in the private universities are characterized by the following:

1 Library buildings are relatively small. Although in most cases they were designed as libraries, there was not enough forward planning for take-up by growth of stock and users, and therefore no adequate projections of future expansion.

2 Since all these libraries are new, their library collections are relatively small (less than 30,000 titles).

3 They employ fewer staff by comparison with the government universities.

Table 9.1 shows some of the characteristics of the university libraries in Jordan.[20]

University	Date	Collection	Classification	Staff
University of Jordan	1963	500,000	DDC	120
Yarmouk University	1976	240,000	LC	84
Muta University	1984	197,000	DDC	60
al Quds Open University	1987	5,000	DDC	3
Amman Applied Engineering University	1989	22,000	DDC	8
Jordan University of Science & Technology	1986	73,000	LC	26
Jordan University for Women	1991	18,000	DDC	7
Amman Private University	1990	34,000	DDC	18
Philadelphia University	1991	13,000	DDC	6
Al-Isra University	1991	15,000	DDC	9
University of Applied Science	1991	50,000	DDC	14
Zaitona University	1993	15,000	DDC	8
Zarka University	In process of establishment			
Jarash University	In process of establishment			
Al Albeit University	In process of establishment			
Beir Zeit University's Liaison Office in Amman				

Formal programmes of co-operation or interlibrary loan do not operate between university libraries in Jordan, despite the existence of some bilateral agreements on interlibrary loan.

Library automation has reached an advanced stage in some of the libraries although others are still run by manual systems. As an example, Yarmouk University has recently computerized its library system by using MINISIS to produce its machine-readable catalogue, and has introduced Open Access Catalogue for students and academic staff. The catalogue is also open for remote access by outside users. The circulation system has also been computerized, and a further extension of automation in general has been the use of microcomputers, mostly in the private universities' libraries.

Library services are provided everywhere on a centralized basis, so that users need to come to the library to search for materials and to borrow them. The University of Jordan Library has branches distributed in some faculties, with specialized collections and full-time librarians. University libraries in Jordan are similar in their organizational structure. In most cases they are organized in two divisions: Technical Services and Public (User) Services. Within that there are units for classification and cataloguing, periodicals, acquisitions, circulation, reference services, and photocopying. Most libraries have some special subject collections, to which access may be more restricted.

The University of Jordan Library has the unique Hashemite Collection, which includes books and other materials published on the subject of Jordan and the Royal Family. Another unique collection comprises manuscripts in both paper and microforms. The Library has been designated by the Federation of Arab Universities to be a depository library for theses accepted by Arab universities

School libraries
The 1990–1 statistics[21] showed that there were 3,623 schools in Jordan of which 2,457 were the basic education stage, 579 were academic secondary stage, 41 were vocational, and 546 were kindergartens run by four authorities: Ministry of Education, Armed Forces, private sector and UNRWA.

Development has followed the general pattern of educational development and in particular that of schools. Ellayan[22] notes that at least 13 school libraries were established between 1930 and 1950. Asali,[23] in his description of the school library situation said that until 1958 school libraries in Jordan were small collections of books without effective organization. They were run on traditional lines. Financial allocations were very small and mainly consisted of contributions from students. No clear acquisition procedures, classification systems, or loan regulations existed. In 1958, the Department of School Libraries was established as part of the Ministry of Education. It is responsible for:

1   Providing school libraries with bibliographic tools and lists of books suitable for school libraries;
2   Supplying school libraries with books and other library materials;
3   Co-operation with other departments to provide training to school librarians.

In 1965, the Ministry of Education issued its regulations for school libraries. These included definitions of school library, library committee, duties of school librarians, library sessions, library services, selection and acquisition procedures, financial regulations and stock control. The Ministry of Education decided that a full-time school librarian should be assigned in any secondary school having a furnished library room and a book collection of not less than 2,000; in other cases a teacher/librarian should be assigned.

The first survey of school libraries was that by El-Akhras[24] in 1975, in which he analysed the status of school libraries, with a full description of their situation in Jordan. In 1987, the First National Conference for Educational Development was held, whose recommendations are now considered as the basis for action. The eighth major recommendation[25] of the conference, on educational technology, included the following:

(a) establishment of resource centres which include specialized laboratories, workshops and a comprehensive library, with the support of the necessary staff and equipment, to satisfy the needs of schools in a specific geographical area;
(b) building of a library in schools with old buildings if land is available. The library's size should be according to the number of students at the school;
(c) build a library in schools, designed according to established criteria, so that at least 10% of the pupils should be able to read at any time;
(d) make available in every educational directorate a centre to be used as audiovisual library and production centre.

One paper presented at the conference, regarding educational technology and facilities, made specific recommendations for school libraries. These were adopted by the conference and made specific reference as to the size and location of the school library, furniture, staff, services and activities, library collections, management and organization; also the development of the school libraries department in the ministry, development of central libraries to serve local communities, relocation of qualified librarians in the ministry, and acquisition policies.[26]

A comprehensive study was conducted in 1986 by Al-Sheikh[27] in which he surveyed libraries in all 493 secondary schools, 438 of which are run by the Ministry of Education, seven by the Armed Forces and 48 are private. The study concluded that:

1   412 schools (83.5%) have a special room used as a library.
2   The average space allocated for the library is 61.09 square meters.
3   All libraries have a room which is used as a reading room and stack at the same time, nine have an office for the librarian, and two have separate rooms for audiovisual materials.
4   352 libraries have enough natural light, 373 have ease of access, 142 have heating facilities, 299 are located in a quiet environment and the premises of 125 libraries are capable of expansion.
5   Adequacy of furniture varies from library to library but all have, at minimum, shelves, reading tables, chairs, and a desk.
6   The total number of books in all libraries is 135,776, an average of 5,6 per student.
7   493 staff work for these libraries, of whom 305 are full-time, 9 are qualified librarians (at university level), while a further 100 hold the intermediate diploma in librarianship.
8   75 libraries still have closed stacks, 108 are catalogued, 233 use a classification scheme, and all libraries have a circulation system.

At the basic school level, the situation of libraries is less good. Ministry of Education statistics[28] showed that only 28% of schools have library rooms, compared with 94% of secondary schools. It showed also that 90% of basic schools do not have qualified librarians (67% in secondary schools). In the basic schools 89% of the libraries do not have suitable furniture, compared with 17% of the secondary schools.

According to Ministry of Education statistics[29] for 1992–3 there are 611 secondary schools and 1,577 basic schools run by government, which employ a total of 752 full-time librarians and 1,436 part-time (teacher/librarians). Among these 2,188 librarians, 14 hold a postgraduate diploma, 2 have a bachelor's degree, 327 have an intermediate diploma and 473 have attended a training course. No distinction is made in available data between qualifications in librarianship and teaching.

National Information Centre

The idea of developing a national information system in Jordan goes back to the early 1970s when a plan was put forward to develop what was then called 'The National Central Bank of Information'. It aimed at creating a central unit to compile sets of data and information that had been collected by other institutions using the telecommunication network. Centralization was seen to be the solution for information access at the time. After realizing that the national information system cannot function in a centralized way, the prime minister took a decision in March 1987 to establish the National Information System (NIS). It comprised two existing information systems: the Socio-economic Information Centre at the Ministry of Planning, and the Science and Technology Information Centre at the Royal Scientific Society. The aim in setting up the NIS was to prepare and provide information as an aid to the formulation of policies, and to conduct economic and social studies, and scientific research. Its basic objectives were to:[30]

- Co-ordinate and regulate the process of acquiring economic, social, scientific and technical information.
- Study the needs of officials for various types of information, to designate the institutions that are qualified to prepare the information, to reach agreement with beneficiaries on the form and content of the required data to the extent that they are available at potential sources of information, and to help prepare the required preliminary information and data in agreement with branch administrations.
- Provide information services to beneficiaries.
- Provide advanced scientific techniques enabling beneficiaries to easily define the sources of information needed as well as the methods of obtaining the information.

The NIS functioned with difficulty for about four years, during which it faced a lot of problems. These related mainly to data collection, updating, lack of compatibility among its participants, and the absence of the library and information sector. NIS put more emphasis on statistical than upon documentary and archival data. Libraries and information centres were not considered part of the NIS.

Affiliation of the NIS was not clear, either to its users or its operators; whether it was part of the Ministry of Planning or of the Royal Scientific Society. This made it a body with two heads, which meant difficulties in planning, finance, data collection, communication with other centres, development of systems and tools, and provision of information services.

In 1992 a bye-law was passed to create what is now called the National Information Centre (NIC).[31] Taking into consideration the experience gained through the development of the NIS, the new NIC has been affiliated to the Higher Council of Science and Technology, which was established in 1987. NIC is designated one of the research and development units of the council.

The aim of the Centre is to:

1 Develop and manage an integrated information system at the national level. It aims to link, in a national information network, all those centres that generate or collect information in the public and private sectors. It will co-ordinate between them to make available economic, social, and technological information.
2 Process and develop this information to ensure its flow to users in the public and the private sectors.

The NIC started its work, after staff recruitment, by forming a technical committee with four subcommittees: information subcommittee; technical facilities subcommittee; evaluation subcommittee; standards and specifications subcommittee.

As a co-ordinating centre for the National Information Network, the NIC will not be responsible for data collection or management as such. It will facilitate information management and dissemination through the development of systems and tools, training, development of referral databases, development of telecommunication facilities, selection and development of software. The NIC will work closely with concerned government agencies, especially with regard to software and hardware development and telecommunication.

The NIC has, jointly with the Jordan Library Association, convened a national symposium for the development of a Jordan Communication Format. As an immediate outcome, the NIC has decided to develop the format, which will be published and distributed to libraries and information centres. It is to be the only bibliographic format used to develop bibliographic data bases in Jordan.

Library and information science education

Library and information science education started in Jordan in the mid-1950s, when the Ministry of Education sent the first Jordanian to study librarianship in Great Britain. Since then different forms of library education have been in operation. Jordanian librarians and information specialists have received their professional training from two sources:

Library education abroad
This category includes professionals who were trained abroad, either by attending short training courses or by acquiring academic degrees in library and information science. The records of the Jordan Library Association show that the following countries have contributed to the training of Jordanian librarians: Egypt, India, Iraq, Lebanon, Libya, Pakistan, Russia, Saudi Arabia, Sudan, the United Kingdom and the United States. Most of the qualified librarians from Arab countries hold bachelor's degrees in library science, while all the graduates from other countries hold postgraduate degrees (diploma, masters or PhD). It is only natural to have a full range of quality and diversity of content in terms of the degrees awarded by these countries. This diversity has to some extent enriched the professional experience of librarians in Jordan.

Library education in Jordan
It can be categorized by a number of types: formal and informal, undergraduate and postgraduate, degree courses and non-degree courses. In this account it will be considered at three levels:

1   *Short training courses*   The leading institution in running short training courses has been the JLA, from 1965 onwards. Training courses offered by the Association include a three-month introductory course, covering cataloguing, classification, collection development, library management, and library services. Since 1982 it has mounted occasional one-week courses in library automation, indexing, abstracting, CDS/ISIS and library management. Over 2,500 librarians have taken a JLA course. Other organizations offering short courses are the University of Jordan's Consulting Services Centre, Yarmouk University's Community Services Centre, UNRWA, community colleges, Abdul Hamid Shoman Foundation (AHSF) and the Ministry of Education especially for its own staff.

2   *Intermediate diploma*   A number of community colleges (teacher training institutes prior to 1980) have been offering library education at the post-secondary level since 1966. The year 1980 witnessed a real revolution in the number of community colleges offering library education. Prior to 1989 nine colleges used to run two types of programme: one was designed for school librarians, covering all aspects of librarianship and general education through 48 credit hours, 32 on librarianship and the rest on educational methods and technology. The other programme was for assistant librarians, to be trained to work in any type of library

or information service on a 48 credit hour course with emphasis on librarianship, documentation, and social sciences.

In 1989 a new programme emerged by the name of 'Diploma in Educational Resources', which supposedly covers librarianship, newer media, educational technology, and educational methods. It is a two-year course of 76 credit hours. All courses are accredited by the Ministry of Education.

3 *Postgraduate diploma* The University of Jordan, launched its Postgraduate Diploma Programme as part of the work of the Faculty of Education in 1977. Originally called the Librarianship and Documentation Programme, it was later renamed Library and Information Science. Having started as a two-year part-time study programme of 33 credit hours, plus a graduation project, it was altered in 1992 and became a one-year course leading to the award of a 'Vocational Diploma' of the University of Jordan. Holding a bachelor's degree in any discipline is a prerequisite for entrance to the Programme, and by the end of 1992 over 200 professional librarians had been awarded the postgraduate diploma.[32]

Information technology
The term 'information technology' is used here to coin the use of computer systems and telecommunication facilities in library and information services. Computerization is a fairly recent development in Jordan. The first computer was installed in the Department of Statistics in 1969. The Royal Scientific Society followed suit in 1972, and the Royal Air Force in 1973. In the private sector the Arab Bank was the first to introduce computers in its operations, in 1972. The Computer Centre of the University of Jordan was established in 1975. Nusseir[33] stated that in 1985 computers were used in 552 systems, of which 28 were mainframe, 166 minicomputers and 358 microcomputers, and in addition it was estimated that over 2,000 microcomputers were owned and/or used by individuals in Jordan.[34]

Prior to 1986, library automation in Jordan was characterized by developing machine-readable lists of library collections, using the computer resources of the mother institutions. This in effect meant that an inventory of books and other library materials was made without any reference to standard formats like MARC, or any of the bibliographic description standards of the time. Computer specialists had responsibility for this task, due to lack of expertise among existing library and information staff.

Most library applications were made either by home-made

programmes in one of the programming languages, or by using a relational data base management system, namely, DBASE III. In a survey that covered 255 libraries, to study their use of computers, Younis[35] showed that ten libraries (3.9%) used computers in some aspect of their library and information services. He identified the problems of library automation or obstacles as:

- lack of technically trained staff, both on the computer side (understanding library systems) and on the library side (understanding computer systems);
- lack of sufficient funds;
- insufficient physical facilities in the libraries;
- insufficient number of users to justify automation;
- resistance of administrators to the need for change;
- lack of suitable software designed to serve Arab libraries' needs.

In a survey to study the criteria for selection of computer-based library systems, which covered a sample of 18 computerized libraries, Al-Shorbaji[36] found that the first library computerization was in 1980, one in 1983, six from 1983 to 1988 and another nine between 1989 and 1991.

The year 1986 may be considered as the turning point in the history of library automation in Jordan. That year witnessed the introduction of the UNESCO Mini-Micro CDS/ISIS and the International Development Research Centre's (IDRC) MINISIS into the country. Each package provided a suitable environment for computerization of library procedures and information services in libraries. In the same survey Al-Shorbaji[37] indicated that there are two categories of computerized library systems in Jordan:

1   Libraries that use minicomputers, in particular Hewlett-Packard 3000 and DEC-VAX computers. These libraries are AHSF, Arab Mining Company, Arab Organization for Administrative Development, Yarmouk University, University of Jordan, Jordan Academy for Arabic Language and Beir Zeit University Liaison Office.
2   Libraries that use microcomputers that are either IBM compatible, or Apple Macintosh. Applications include development of machine-readable catalogues, text processing, spreadsheets, factual databases, desktop publishing, statistical databases, online searches and circulation.

Factors in the introduction of microcomputers in libraries in Jordan are:

1 Most libraries can be described as small, with less than 10,000 titles.
2 Most libraries are run by a single librarian and in some cases an assistant librarian or a clerk.
3 Microcomputers are more cost-effective to use with regard to their price, operation, maintenance, working environment, and so on.
4 Microcomputers and the uses of their software packages are easy to learn. There is no need for computer specialists to supervise their operation after installation and set up of systems, and the initial careful training of staff in their operation.
5 Many of the microcomputer applications start on an experimental basis such as text processing, spreadsheets, simple statistics, and the use of off-the-shelf database management systems. After the initial experimentation to overcome some of the information technology barriers, the true library applications come on stream. This serves as a training period for librarians at a low cost.

A CDS/ISIS user group was formed in 1990 that includes in its membership all librarians and computer specialists who use the package. The group publishes a newsletter and meets monthly to discuss technical issues related to the package. A MINISIS user group was also formed which has in its membership users of the package both in-house and as remote users.

The year 1993 has witnessed a further revolution in library automation in Jordan. Six leading libraries that use CDS/ISIS have decided, through the International Development Research Centre (IDRC), to upgrade to MINISIS. They are the National Library, Jordan University of Science and Technology, Amman Private University, Jordan University for Women, Al-Isra University and Zarka University. Four others are also considering the same system for their automation.

At present there are over 120 libraries that use microcomputers. With four exceptions, the majority use CDS/ISIS, while the other packages used in isolation are FoxBase, DBase and Cardbox.

Al-Shorbaji's survey[38] showed that the great majority of the libraries surveyed use either CDS/ISIS or MINISIS. Criteria that influence the selection of software packages include the Arabization options that are available, the backing of international organizations, the memory required, the data structure, the retrieval language, and the printing facilities of the package.

Computer applications in Jordanian libraries include:

1 *Cataloguing* The vast majority of libraries have developed machine-readable catalogues, to enable searching and retrieval of bibliographic data and production of printed bibliographies and catalogues.

2 *Indexing and abstracting* A limited number of information and documentation centres have developed databases with indexing and abstracting services,

3 *Circulation control* The major circulation control system is that used in Yarmouk University Library, on MINISIS. Other small-scale systems are in use on microcomputers.

4 *Acquisition systems* A very limited number of libraries use computerized control of acquisition procedures. AHSF Library is the only one that has active acquisition procedures as part of its integrated system on MINISIS.

5 *Statistical and other non-bibliographic databases* A number of libraries and information centres have developed applications in the form of data banks, which include statistical data on commodities, persons or other units. Directory databases have also been developed for projects, professionals and institutions.

6 *Other applications* These include text processing, spreadsheets, desktop publishing, electronic mail, and graphical presentations.

An important aspect of library automation in Jordan is having access to international information networks and databases. The first library to have a subscription to DIALOG and Bibliographic Retrieval Services (BRS) was the Royal Scientific Society in 1982, followed shortly after by Yarmouk University and University of Jordan. At the present moment there are seven libraries that have access to international information systems in North America and Europe. With the advent of CD-ROM, more libraries have found this type of data base searching to be a viable alternative to online services. The estimated number of CD-ROM databases available in Jordan is 150, in use among university and special libraries. Yarmouk University has taken the lead role in developing a CD-ROM network within the university, and has organized a national seminar to discuss issues related to CD-ROM subscriptions, co-operation between libraries, and exchange of services. A directory of databases on CD-ROM available in Jordan is being compiled.

Jordan Library Association
The Jordan Library Association (JLA) has been mentioned in the preceding sections. JLA may be considered as a major component

of the library movement in Jordan. All those who have written about any of the library and information science activities in Jordan have given credit to JLA, whether it is training of librarians and information specialists, development of systems and tools, bibliographic control, development of libraries, publishing, or awareness creation among professionals and decision makers. The Association has played a leading part in the nation's library movement, and also in the Arab region.

The Association was established in 1963 as a professional society. Starting with 25 members, none of them qualified librarians, but all enthusiastic for the future of the library movement in Jordan. By the end of 1992 it had 1,716 individual and institutional memberships. Out of this number 1,143 are qualified librarians (having library training; certificate, diploma, bachelor, master or PhD degree).[39]

JLA aims and objectives
The JLA constitution and bye-laws[40] specify its aims and objectives as follows:
1　Unification of efforts of all working in the library and information fields to advance library and information services, especially;

　(a) development of library management procedures, standards and services
　(b) development of necessary means to improve the professional status of librarians and their qualifications
　(c) initiation and proposal of library legislation
　(d) establishment of libraries, and information and documentation centres to serve all types of users
　(f) urge government to develop library services
　(g) develop and encourage bibliographic studies
　(h) compile and publish library research and other types of publication which serve the aims and objectives of JLA
　(i) provide training to librarians through training courses and any other means.

2　Contribute to the development of library and information services in the Arab countries and elsewhere.
3　Perform all duties that lead to the realization of the above aims and objectives.

Objective '1h' above has been implemented by JLA in the following ways:

1 Publishing monographs that can be used as text books, guidelines, and case-studies. Examples are:

- Introduction to library and information science, 1981
- Technical processing of information, 1986
- Introduction to UNESCO Mini–Micro CDS/ISIS, 1991
- Practical guide to classification, 1986.

2 Development, adaptation and publishing of systems and tools. Examples are:

- Anglo-American Cataloguing Rules, second edition, first Arabic edition
- Dewey Decimal Classification, 17th edition, Arabic version.

3 Compilation and publishing of bibliographies. Examples are:

- *Jordan National bibliography*, since 1979
- Jordan Palestine bibliography, pre-1979
- Special bibliographies.

4 Publication of *Rissalat Al-Maktaba (The Message of the Library)* which has been published without interruption since 1965.

One major project which JLA has undertaken with the co-operation of municipalities and local authorities is 'Contribute a Book to Establish a Library'. The intention is to encourage municipalities to provide a library building and a full-time librarian, and then to lead a national campaign to donate books and library materials to that particular library. Since 1982 six public libraries have been established and have been maintained in this way.

The part played by JLA in the training and professional development of librarians in Jordan was described earlier.

References
1 Jordan, Ministry of Information, *Facts about Jordan: people, land and climate*, Amman, Ministry of Information, 1992.
2 Jordan, Department of Statistics, *Statistical yearbook 1991*, Amman,The Department, 1992, 19–23.
3 *Al-Dastour*, **27** (9229), 2 May 1993.
4 Jordan, Department of Statistics, op. cit., 253.
5 Ibid., 381.
6 *Al-Dastour*, op. cit.
7 Jordan, Department of Statistics, op. cit., 82.
8 Asali, K., 'Jordan libraries'. In: *Encyclopedia of library and information science*, vol. 13, 1975. 300–10.

9   Younis, A. R., 'Jordan libraries'. In: *Encyclopedia of library and information science*, vol. 42, supplement 7, 1987, 339–362.

10 de Trazi, Philip, *Khazain Al-Kutub Al-Arabiya fi Al-Khafiqain*, Beirut, Dar Al-Kutub Allubnanieh, 19–, vol. 1, 141–5.

11 'Public Libraries in Jordan', *Rissalat Al-Maktaba*, 1 (4), 1966, 40–5.

12 Dahbour, S. and Shbitah, F., *Directory of libraries in Jordan*, Amman, Jordan Library Association, 1976.

13 Zash, Amal, *Libraries in Jordan: status and prospects*, 2nd edn, Amman, Zash, 1989, 33.

14 Al-Amad, Hani, 'Public Libraries in Jordan: the present status', *Rissalat Al-Maktaba*, 25 (4), 1990 (special issue).

15 Al-Shorbaji, N. and Abu Ajamiyeh, Y., *Special libraries in Jordan: a survey* (in press).

16 Younis, A. R., 'The use of computers in libraries and information centres in Jordan: a survey', *Program*, 22 (2), 1988, 268–74.

17 Jordan Library Association. CDS/ISIS User Group files.

18 Jordan, Ministry of Higher Education Law number 28 of 1985, Amman, The Ministry, 1985, 4.

19 Al-Qawasmeh, M., 'Library situation at community colleges in Jordan', *Rissalat Al-Maktaba*, 26 (4), 1991 (special issue).

20 Information was gathered through telephone contacts with responsible officers in the libraries.

21 Jordan, Department of Statistics, op. cit., 232.

22 Ellayan, R., 'Library movement in Jordan', *Al-Maktaba Al-Arabiya (Arab Library)*, 1 (2), 1982, 137–48.

23 Asali, op. cit.

24 El-Akhras, M., *Development of school libraries*, London, Library Association, 1975 (Fellowship thesis).

25 *First National Conference for Educational Development: final report and recommendations*, Amman, Ministry of Education, 1988, 78

26 'Educational technology, school facilities and laboratories'. A paper presented at the First National Conference for Educational Development. (Amman, 6–7 September 1987), Amman, Ministry of Education.

27 Al-Sheikh, M. S., *Status of secondary school libraries in Jordan*, Amman, University of Jordan, 1986 (MA thesis), published as a special issue of *Rissalat Al-Maktaba*, 24 (2), 1989

28 'Educational technology, school facilities and laboratories', op. cit.

29 Jordan, Ministry of Education, *School libraries statistics, 1992/1993*.

30 *National Information System: a brochure*, Amman, Royal Scientific Society, 1988.

31 Law Number 50 of 1990, National Information Centre, According to item 11 of the Higher Council of Science and Technology, Law Number 30 of 1987.

32   Jaradat, O. and Kharoof, Y., 'Library education in Jordan', *Second Jordanian Librarians Conference (Amman: 6–8 October 1991)*, 41pp.

33   Nusseir, Y., 'Status of computers and their applications in Jordan'. Regional Meeting of Computer Experts in the Arab World to Develop a Co-operation and Co-ordination Informatics Network (Amman, 6–8 May 1985), p. 5–7.

34   Nusseir, Y., *A report on the policy of uses of computers in Jordan*, Amman, Royal Scientific Society, 1986.

35   Younis, A. R., 1988, op. cit.

36   Al-Shorbaji, Najeeb, 'Criteria for selection of data base management software in libraries in Jordan', *Second Jordanian Librarians Conference (Amman, 6–8 October 1991)*, 30pp.

37   Ibid., 2.

38   Ibid., 16.

39   Jordan Library Association membership data base, Amman, JLA, 1993.

40   Jordan Library Association, *Laws and bylaws*, Amman, JLA, 1992.

10 School libraries in Kuwait: before and after the Gulf War

Mohamed H. Zehery

The development of school libraries in Kuwait can be traced to the beginning of public education in the early 1900s, and to the development of the country's first elementary school, the Al-Mubarakiyah School (Al-Madrasah Al-Mubarakiyah) in 1912, and Al-Madiyah School in 1921, although they had no formal libraries until 1936.

From 1955 onwards there was very rapid growth in the number of new schools, due to the massive rise in oil revenues and the sharp increase in government expenditure on public education. Fifty-two schools were established in that year, and accommodation for a library designated in each school in the country.[1]

School library organization and distribution

The school library system of Kuwait was established in 1954, under a separate School Libraries Department within the Ministry of Education. It was reorganized twice, in 1965 and 1981 to meet the needs of providing adequate library resources and services to students and teachers. The department's responsibilities grew to include the development and implementation of service programmes, recommending policies and procedures for acquisition and collection development, and the organization of library materials. Other responsibilities included participation in selection and training of new staff, supervising and evaluating staff performance, administering the annual school library inventory, and reporting on libraries' progress to the Ministry and to school district authorities.[2]

The Director of the School Libraries Department is responsible for managing, supervising, co-ordinating, and monitoring departmental functions and school library activities, so as to ensure the provision of library services that will meet the educational and instructional needs of students and teachers. The director reports, and is accountable to the Assistant Under Secretary for Educational Services of the Ministry of Education. The department has three main sections: School Library Services; Research and Programme Development; and Library Instruction.[3]

School Library Services, which is the major element of the three sections, is responsible for collection development, and directly organizes all acquisitions. It selects audiovisual materials in co-operation with the Department of Educational Media Technology of the Ministry of Education. The section has so far been engaged mainly in acquisition functions, including ordering, receiving and processing, and distributing materials to every school library in the system. Although it takes part in book selection, final decisions on this rest with one among several book selection committees.

The cataloguing and classification unit of the section organizes cataloguing and classification of the library materials, in accordance with the Arabic version of AACR2 (Anglo-American Cataloguing Rules), a modified Arabic edition of Dewey Decimal Classification, and Ibrahim Al-Khazindar's *List of Arabic subject headings*. The unit also produces catalogue cards, and maintains the union catalogue of school library holdings.

The Research and Programme Development section is concerned with the preparation of annual budget requests for the department and school libraries. It conducts library studies, collects statistics, and prepares periodic, special, and annual reports on school library activities and progress.

The Library Instruction section develops, co-ordinates, and monitors implementation of library service programmes and activities. It is also accountable for supervision and training of librarians and library assistants, staff evaluation, and identification and assessment of future needs in library services.

The School Libraries Department is supported by an administrative and secretarial office for collection preservation and maintenance, purchase of equipment and supplies, inventories and other related functions.[4]

There were 465 public school libraries in 1991–2; a 50% increase in the 15 years since 1978, when there were 330. The surge in numbers of new schools is due in part to the absence of co-education in Kuwait, except at kindergarten level. This has required the construction of separate schools for boys and girls at elementary, intermediate, and secondary levels, and also schools of special education.

Table 10.1   Schools (and their libraries), 1988–1989

Type of school	Male	Female	Total no. of schools	Students
Kindergarten	—	—	120	24,150
Special education	5	5	10	1,928
Elementary	64	54	118	126,441
Intermediate	64	66	130	119,037
Secondary	45	42	87	77,626
Total	178	167	465	349,182

Resources

In 1988–9, the total number of books in school libraries was 1,550,272 volumes, of which 783,871 were in the 87 secondary schools, 482,122 were in the 130 intermediate schools, 151,449 in the 118 elementary schools, and 28,430 in the 120 kindergartens. Over half a million volumes were lost during the Iraqi occupation, and many of the libraries were pillaged or vandalized. In a report issued by the School Libraries Department in 1991 it was estimated that $15,000,000 worth of library materials was lost during the occupation. School library collections had lost more than 900,000 volumes. 99% of books in elementary schools had been destroyed; 50% in intermediate, and 36% in secondary schools.

Table 10. 2   School library collections before and after the Iraqi occupation of Kuwait[6]

Type of school	1988–9	1992–3	% of books lost
Kindergarten	28,430	22,293	22%
Elementary	151,449	789	99%
Intermediate	564,662	358,875	55%
Secondary	783,871	504,832	36%
Special education	22,517	21,860	3%
Total	1,550,272	909,306	

Since their early development, school libraries have not been guided by clear policies for developing basic core collections, and formulating criteria for reviewing and evaluating collections, thus determining their adequacy, coverage, and validity. The usually small collections in kindergarten and elementary schools are mainly Arabic. This is due to the absence of public support for writers and publishers of children's and juvenile literature, and to government restrictions, not only in Kuwait but in most Arab countries, making it difficult for publishers to market their books.

Because Arabic is the language of instruction in public schools, Arabic materials constitute 80% of their library collections. Standard tools for selection do not exist and there are no effective substitutes for the lack of reading lists, national bibliographies, lists of Arabic books in print and reliable publishers' catalogues. Consequently, sporadic selection of books at exhibits and fairs is common practice among many librarians in Kuwait, although not school librarians, for whom the final decision on what is selected rests with several book selection committees. There is a committee designated for each level from kindergarten upwards. As a rule, members of the committees are drawn from curriculum specialists, senior teachers and library supervisors.[7]

When selecting a book, a committee assigns one of its members to evaluate that book. The evaluator reports back, recommending its acquisition or rejection. Several hundred copies will be bought of approved titles, which are distributed to all the libraries in a given level of school.

In intermediate and secondary school libraries, the best provision is in the areas of Arabic literature, fiction, and history. The sciences, technology, and social science are less well provided.

Selection of periodicals and popular magazines is also the responsibility of these selection committees, which have the final decision about rejecting or approving requests for subscriptions by any library, for any journal title. Criteria applied in journal selection are more rigid than for books, especially on sensitive issues of a social nature. In 1988–9, the School Libraries Department subscribed to 200 different periodical titles. They were mainly Arabic, acquired in large numbers of multiple copies. School librarians have authority to order popular magazines and newspapers direct from local sellers if they appear on the list of journals that have been approved by their book selection committee.[8]

Finance

No separate budget is allocated specifically for the School Libraries Department, or for school libraries as such. Budget figures mentioned here are based on estimated expenditures in previous years. At present, budget preparation requires the department to submit annual budget requests to the educational services. It is estimated that expenditure on books and magazines in 1989–9, in the region of half a million dollars, acquired about 30,000 volumes, mostly in Arabic. Although library materials expenditure is low, the School Libraries Department tends to order large numbers of multiple copies, and consequently a single library may receive between five and ten copies of a book.

Budget allocations for salaries and other expenditure on personnel are determined by the Personnel and Finance Department of the ministry. In general, school libraries need better financial support to develop their collections in all formats; to strengthen and upgrade staff development and training programmes; procure new equipment, and to introduce automation.[9]

Personnel

Well-trained professional, para-professional and clerical staff are essential for libraries to provide the services that will support the country's education system. Kuwait's school library system suffers because of a shortage of qualified staff. The librarians in many schools were inadequately trained, and are poorly motivated to provide the professional leadership and skills needed to plan and implement strong service programmes.

In 1988–9, more than 1,200 people were employed in the school library system, of whom only 60 held a bachelor's degree in library science. They worked in secondary school libraries, in technical services, or as school library supervisors. The majority of them are Egyptians, who had acquired their library education at the Department of Library Science of Cairo University. All secondary and intermediate school libraries were staffed by graduate personnel who had received some training in librarianship, organized by the School Libraries Department. The libraries of most kindergarten, elementary, and intermediate schools had Kuwaitis who have two-year post-secondary school diplomas from the Library Assistant Programme of the College of Basic Education. Several hundred Kuwaitis with qualifications up to the level of secondary school diploma held posts in clerical and support services.[10]

The Library Assistant Programme of the College of Basic Education (formerly the Teacher's Institute) was started in 1978, to train and develop Kuwaiti personnel at para-professional level, for all types of library. During the last ten years, many library educators and professional librarians have criticized the programme for its casual admission requirements, lack of qualified teaching staff, and the inadequacy of its training, especially in technical services, language, and computer skills. It has been noted that the majority of those coming out of this programme sought school library jobs because they offer job security, good pay, relaxed work atmosphere, and a long summer vacation.

Two salary scales have been observed for many years by the Ministry of Education; one for Kuwaitis and another for expatriates. A Kuwaiti graduate of the Library Assistant Programme earns in the region of $1,500 a month, while a non-Kuwaiti with a bachelor's degree in library science, plus several years working experience, is likely to be paid half that amount. These factors lead to apathy and low morale among expatriates, who do not enjoy the same benefits as their Kuwaiti colleagues.[11]

School library services

At present, school library services do give adequate support to the learning process. They are ineffective and do not strengthen the library's role as a dynamic factor in the advancement of public education in the country. Students need to read a variety of printed media, to review and listen to different non-print materials, to develop personal skills in using computers, and to have access to information related to the curriculum.

The libraries serving schools open 40 hours a week; there are scheduled weekly classes, and designated hours for free reading at all levels. Regular library service includes reference, circulation, library instruction, training 'Friends of the Library' groups, and indexing journals. Many repetitive and routine tasks are performed on a monotonously regular basis, and inhibit staff from responding effectively to the needs and requirements of students and teachers.

The effectiveness of these libraries might be enhanced if more emphases were to be placed on individualized, student-directed strategies that use media resources more fully. Semi-obsolete routines that are maintained by the School Libraries Department, and in the libraries include outdated manual methods of processing, filing, verifying, and registering stock. An exception to this is the centralized organization of cataloguing and classification. Although clerical tasks are assigned to library assistants, librarians are still preoccupied with processing materials, making lists and conducting annual inventories, at the expense of closer work with students and teachers to ensure their access to information resources and services.[12]

Library facilities

Library accommodation varies in size between schools. In many cases the size of library premises is influenced by the date the school was founded. In new buildings, a kindergarten library varies between 800 and 1,000 sq. ft.; in elementary schools, approximately 1,200 sq. ft. with 30 reading places; intermediate schools get 1,500 sq. ft. and 40 places. The largest allocation goes to secondary schools, with more than 2,000 sq. ft. and 50 reader places.

The average library in older schools was not originally planned as such, and may still be based in one room, which will vary in

size according to type of school and size of classes. The layout of
most of these is cramped, thus limiting reading, shelf provision,
and staff activities.

When planning modern school library media centres, space
and layouts are usually the outcome of teamwork by architect,
interior designer, and library consultant, working to agreed standards. The floor plans of such centres normally allocate functional
areas for reference, circulation, reading, book collections, audiovisual media, listening and reviewing stations, multi-purpose
rooms, and staff work areas.

Standards and specifications for library furniture and equipment do not exist in Kuwait, and minimum standards should be
established, to ensure functionality, safety, durability, and opti-
mal utilization.[14]

Conclusion

The Kuwait school library system has made remarkable progress
in support of the country's educational system. It has exceeded
the achievements of public libraries, but in spite of this, school
libraries still need to undergo fundamental changes, in order to
develop a system capable of supporting and enhancing the educational process. To attain this goal, library objectives must be
reviewed, services upgraded, and the system of library provision
reorganized.

The concept of the school library should be based upon:

1 A new collection development policy that will provide standard core collections for all grades of school.
2 Selection and implementation of an automated library system
   to facilitate access to information, enhance communication,
   improve processing and the organization of record keeping,
   and to support major library functions.

Long-term commitment of adequate finance is needed to fund
services, to attain targets that have been agreed under strategic
and operational plans, with specified results that must be
achieved.

Programme budgeting techniques and cost analyses should be
applied, to justify appropriation requests, and guide the expenditure of funds for development. Print and non-print materials
should be integral to the resources of media centres, as well as a
good core collection of materials for each type of school, in support of the curriculum and of the needs of students and teachers.
Book selection should be more extended in subject coverage, and
be more flexible in responding to individual needs of the library's

users.

The preoccupation of the School Libraries Department with the annual inventory of libraries should be minimized, and limited to only once in three years. This would give more time for librarians and their staff to concentrate on issues such as user services, and weeding the collections of unwanted and obsolete materials.

Library standards, policies and procedures should be established, specifying the minimum professional qualifications and basic certifications required of librarians and library assistants, as well as upgrading training and staff development programmes so that they take account of the continuous changes in librarianship and information technology.

Special attention should be given to the development of a staff organization plan, to include policy for recruitment and appointments, job descriptions, performance plans and evaluations, and salary scales.

Librarians, teachers and media specialists should co-operate in developing services that do serve the true needs of users, rather than merely perpetuate outdated activities. As a media centre, a school library, at least at secondary level, should offer reference and referral services, instructional and orientation programmes, interlibrary loan, library research and computer use skills, circulation and photocopying.

The School Libraries Department is in a strong position to provide the leadership needed to attract young, dedicated, and serious candidates to a promising career in the library profession. It could transform the libraries under its control from a standstill situation to dynamic media learning centres. This would enhance curriculum development and implementation, enrich the students' learning experience, and encourage teachers' personal and professional maturity.

Standards are yet to be developed for both new and remodelled library quarters, that would in each case meet minimum requirements for provision of service. They should also be made the means for re-equipping with more appropriate and functional library furniture and fittings.

By such means the emerging school library media centre can become the catalyst for change in Kuwait's public school system, and be a major force for improving traditional methods of learning, instruction, and education in general.

References

1   Zehery, M.H., *Library service in Kuwait: a survey and analysis, with recommendations for public library development,* University of North

Texas, 1975. (PhD dissertation).
2 Kuwait, Ministry of Education. School Libraries Department, *School libraries: definitions and instructions,* 2nd edn. (Translated title; Arabic text), Kuwait, 1992, 26.
3 Kuwait, op. cit., 27
4 Ibid., 32–3
5 *Unesco statistical yearook, 1988,* Paris, 1989, 161–2.
6 Kuwait, Ministry of Education, School Libraries Department, *Report on school and public library conditions in Kuwait before and after the Iraqi invasion* (Translated title; Arabic text of unpublished paper). Kuwait, 1991.
7 *School libraries,* op. cit., 71.
8 Ibid., 54–5.
9 Kuwait., op. cit., 3–14.
10 Prostano, E. T. and Joyce S., *The School library media center,* 3rd edn., Littleton, Colo., Libraries Unlimited, 1982, 21–8.
11 Urbank, Mary Kay, *Curriculum planning and teaching using the library media centre,* Metuchen, NJ, Scarecrow, 1989, 72–3.
12 *School libraries,* op. cit., 85.
13 Zehery, op.cit., 85
14 Luskay, Jack R., 'Current trends in school library media centers', *Library trends,* **31** (Winter 1983), 426–6.

11 Public libraries in Saudi Arabia

Hisham A. Abbas

In order to understand the development of public libraries and librarianship, it is important to describe briefly the basic features of the country. The Kingdom of Saudi Arabia in south-western Asia is the largest country on the Arabian Peninsula, being some 2,150,000 square kilometres in extent. In 1990 it was estimated that 1,178,000 people inhabit this vast area,[1] resulting in the low average of 4 persons per square kilometre. Only 26% of the total population live in urban areas.[2]

Saudi Arabia is well-known as one of the largest oil-producing countries of the world, and this has maintained the highly accelerated growth of the economy and national wealth in recent years. Saudi Arabia is a constitutional monarchy headed by King Fahd, who is a member of the Al-Saud family.

Education is free and available to all students through the network of primary, secondary, vocational and technical schools, universities and institutions of higher training. Education is neither compulsory nor co-educational; separate facilities are maintained for men and women. Literacy training is an important adjunct to the overall educational process, and in 1978 25% of the population could read and write.

While a traditional universal respect exists among Saudi Arabians towards education, students are conditioned to memorizing as the major process of learning. The dependence of students on textbooks and the use of memorizing as the best methods of transmitting knowledge have minimized recognition of the need and use of libraries in the country.

Naturally Arab culture prevails among Saudi residents, the majority of whom are Muslims. Arabic is the country's official language, although many Saudis have acquired a knowledge of English and other languages through education, pilgrimage, and commercial contacts abroad.

Today, public library systems, especially in developing nations such as Saudi Arabia are in a state of evolution. Growth, distribution and composition of population; advanced communication, industrialization and rapid urbanization; occupational changes, and restructuring of educational programmes, are all factors that bring changes to the library scene.

Historical development of Saudi Arabian public libraries

In general, public libraries can be divided into two categories according to date of establishment and the nature of their collections and development. The first comprises libraries founded before the establishment of the Kingdom of Saudi Arabia, located in Makkah and Al-Madinah (Medina), and noted for their collections of manuscripts and rare books dating from the early Islamic period. The other category comprises all libraries that have been established since the ending of Dual Monarchy and the establishment of the Kingdom of Saudi Arabia in 1932.

Thus the earliest libraries in Saudi Arabia, as in most of the Islamic world, were the mosques. Since the time of the Prophet Mohammad in the seventh century, mosques have served as repositories of human knowledge, and have played important cultural and educational roles similar to that of schools and public libraries. For that reason most of the libraries in Saudi Arabia were established in the two holy cities of Makkah and Al-Madinah. The Al-Haram Mosque of Makkah and the Prophet's Mosque in Al-Madinah were for long the sole cultural and educational centres, each with a heavy emphasis on theological education. Set up in or adjacent to mosque premises, the rich collections at Makkah and Al-Madinah developed through donations and endowments from scholars, caliphs, sultans, and distinguished pilgrims.

The trend for each mosque to have a library, however small has continued to the present time. New mosque complexes include separate and purpose-built library accommodation. In anticipation of the way that Andrew Carnegie used his wealth to establish public libraries in the United Kingdom, some early philanthropists set up public libraries in the Kingdom of Saudi Arabia. For instance Sheikh Mohammad Ibn Futuh Al-Mikhnasi founded a very small collection inside the Holy Mosque of Makkah in AD 1085[3] that was subsequently enriched by continuing donations of significant materials from various individuals. The other famous ancient library is the Arif Hikmat Library in Al-Madinah, which owns unique archives and manuscripts.

The actual development, in the modern sense, of public libraries goes back to the founding of the General Directorate of Public Libraries under the Ministry of Education in 1959,[4] which has primary responsibility for the spread of public libraries throughout the country. The directorate controls 59 libraries, and is also responsible for the centralized selection, acquisition, and processing of books and other reading materials, which it then distributes to the libraries under its administration. In rural areas the public library service is rendered through schools, although many schools themselves have inadequate libraries.

Division of responsibility for the provision of libraries serving the public has arisen because of the allocation of certain functions to the Ministry of Pilgrimage and Endowment, the Directorate General Judiciary Decree, Propagation and Guidance (DGJDPGO), and the General Directorate of Holy Mosque Supervision (GDHMS). This has had adverse effects upon overall public library development, a point that was emphasized as early as 1979 in the MLS thesis of Ali S. Sowanie.[5]

Successive development plans; First Five-Year Plan 1970–5,[6] Second Five-Year Plan 1975–80,[7] Third Five-Year Plan 1980–5,[8] Fourth Five-Year Plan 1985–90[m] have certainly played a prominent part in the development and improvement of libraries. The ongoing Fifth Five-Year Development Plan, 1990–5 has equally focused attention on the expansion of public libraries, and the quality of library services to their communities.

Present state of public libraries
This part of the study attempts to analyse and interpret data collected in the light of functions and requirements considered relevant in the examination and evaluation of existing libraries in a country. These are: administration resources, finance, physical facilities, services, and personnel.

Distribution of public libraries in Saudi Arabia
It is clear from Table 11.1 that the Central Region has more libraries than other regions. It leads with 33, followed by the Western Region which has 14, of which 8 are historical collections.

Also, it should be noted that there are no equalities regarding the distribution of libraries in the different regions. For example, the population of Jeddah is only slightly less than that of Riyadh, but the latter (see Table 11.2) has five public libraries while there is only one in Jeddah. Also, the number of public libraries nationally is far short of the centres of population; 102 towns and more than 10,000 villages.[10]

Table11.1 Distribution of public libraries according to regions

Region	Libraries controlled by:				Total	%
	Min. of Ed.	Min of Pilgrimage	DGJDPGO	GDHMS		
Central	32	—	1	—	33	48.52
Southern	9	—	—	—	9	13.23
Eastern	7	—	—	—	7	10.29
Western	6	6	—	2	14	20.58
Northern	5	—	—	—	5	7.38
Total	59	6	1	2	68	100

Table 11.2 Distribution of public libraries in main centres of population

Towns	Libraries controlled by:				Total
	Min. of Ed.	Min of Pilgrimage	DGJDPGO	GDHMS	
Riyadh	Dar ul Kutub + 3	—	1	—	5
Makkah	1	—	—	1	2
al-Madinah	1	5	—	1	7
Jeddah	1	—	—	—	—
Taif	1	1	—	—	2

Table 11.3 highlights the inconsistency in the number of public libraries and shows also a decrease in their number, especially in recent years.

Table 11.3 Date of establishment of public libraries controlled by the Ministry of Education, by five-year development plans

Years	No. of libraries	%
Before 1970	12	20.33
1970–5	11	18.64
1975–80	16	27.15
1980–5	8	13.55
1985–90	11	18.64
1990–5	1	1.69
Total	59	

As shown in Table 11.3, many public libraries existed prior to the first of the sequence of five-year plans. Established and sponsored by private citizens, they subsequently came under the control of the Ministry of Education.[11] The Ministry also worked in this field prior to the implementation of development plans, and its pioneer public library at Bureida, begun in 1955 was expected to act as a pilot scheme for development and expansion of library and information services to the general public.[12]

At the time of writing, the library in Ar'ar was the latest to be established, in 1989.[13] One might be inclined to conclude that over the period from 1955 to 1989, at least some of these libraries must have improved and responded to the needs of users and their interests. However this is not the case since they do not have the necessary materials to provide the required services.

Administrative organizations

Most public libraries are administered by the General Directorate of Public Libraries of the Ministry of Education, which was established in 1959. This was responsible for setting up modern libraries and drawing up specifications for the necessary buildings and furniture, in addition to procuring library materials, organising centralized cataloguing, and the recruitment of personnel. The directorate has ten departments; national book, cataloguing, procurement and registration, microfilms, periodicals, reading rooms, administrative affairs, and storage.[14] Other public libraries not under the control of the Ministry of Education, are the important historical collections which include the Library of Haram in Makkah, and the Library of A'rif Hikmat in Al-Madinah. They are controlled variously by the Ministry of Pilgrimage and Religious Endowments, DGJDPGO, and GDHMS.

In addition to the fact that public libraries suffer drastically from control by many different ministries and government departments that are not closely related in their activities, some of them suffer from duality in administrative supervision and inefficiency of administrative procedures. For example, those controlled by the Ministry of Education fall under the administrative control of two independent departments of that ministry. The first is the General Directorate of Public Libraries in Riyadh, which supplies a wide range of resources to libraries under its jurisdiction. The second is the Administration of Education in different regions of the Kingdom, charged with the responsibility of providing libraries with furniture, equipment, and other requirements, in addition to exercising administrative supervision.

Other libraries suffer because they do not have independent administrative bodies; this is the case with those that come under ministries and other government bodies. Routine procedures, and preoccupation of the Ministry of Religious Endowments with numerous activities, have diversified and distracted the degree of attention needed for consistent improvement of public libraries.

The budgets for public libraries are not independent, because they are not identifiable separate from the general ministry budget. With regard to buildings, the picture is not encouraging since most public libraries, especially those under the Ministry of Education have limited provision of halls and sections for common functions such as administration, reading rooms and periodicals rooms; they may even be without any provision for reference and separate children's rooms. A few of the libraries that come under other governmental bodies, contain reasonable accommodation for administration, periodicals, catalogues, binding, and printing.

Goals and objectives
None of the public libraries in the Kingdom has any clearly written statement of goals and objectives, although their senior staff usually claim in general terms that they aim to serve society in areas of education, culture, and entertainment.
Taking these three goals into account, libraries need to have long- and short-term aims. There should be clearly defined objectives that contribute overall to national progress. The main objectives for a public library therefore should be:[15]

- To provide service to all (emphasis upon reaching the unserved).
- To provide information services.
- To provide adult and continuing education.
- To collect and disseminate all kinds of informational, educational and cultural materials, including non-print resources.
- To support education – formal and informal.
- To serve as a cultural centre.

The National Advisory Commission on Libraries also developed and recommended the following objectives:[16]

- To provide adequate library and informational services for formal education at all levels.
- To provide adequate library and informational services for the public at large.
- To provide materials to support research in all fields and at all levels.
- To provide adequate bibliographic access to the nation's research and informational resources
- To provide adequate physical access to required materials or their texts throughout the nation.
- To provide adequate trained personnel for the varied and changing demands of librarianship.

Library personnel
By the end of the Fourth Five-Year Plan, the number of employ-

ees in public libraries was 262. Out of these, only 45 are professional librarians and the rest, 217, are non-professionals.[17] Most of the professional librarians are secondary school and university graduates with a background in the library field, or who have completed a short training course. The average number of employees in public libraries is 4.5. Some libraries have no professional staff, with the consequent effect on services.

An example of this is the public library in Oneiza. Although this has the largest number of employees who have gained work experience, especially in other libraries, a fair proportion have no previous experience prior to taking up their position, and after some years in post have received no formal training. Personnel are discouraged by lack of incentives, poor working conditions and obligations to undertake tasks unrelated to their proper library work.

Public library staffs deserve better incentives in the way of deserved promotion, and the chance to work in a more professional environment. They should not be preoccupied with matters that eventually affect their performance, such as equating them scientifically or financially with staff in other educational or even non-educational organizations.[18] They should feel more like valued professionals and not as storekeepers.

Library collections
Many public libraries have not fulfilled users' expectations, even though many of them have 25 years of existence. The prosperous social and economic circumstances that accompanied their inception did nothing to boost their development, and the subsequent years of their existence have not, on the whole, benefited development of the collection, except for a few isolated examples.

Until now, these assets have never been subjected to assessment by statistical analysis, either to investigate their suitability to the needs of society, or to investigate the balance of the library resources for such a study. There is little specific statistical data and therefore no reliable measures and standards for evaluation. The basic information and data available to the author about the size of collections in public libraries is summarized in Table 11.4.

Table 11.4   Size of collections in Ministry of Education public
libraries[19]

Library Collection	No. of Libraries	%
5,000–10,000	17	10.03
10,000–20,000	19	11.21
20,000–30,000	15	8.85
30,000–40,000	4	2.36
40,000–50,000	3	1.77
Over 50,000	1	0.59

Thus it appears that the majority of public library collections are between 5,000 and 30,000 volumes, and only a few rise to 50,000 or above. Table 11.5 shows that the public library in King Faisal Street in Riyadh has the largest stock, with over 63,000 volumes. It was established in 1968. At the opposite end of the scale, the public libraries of Aloyaynah and Arar have the lowest resources, each with slightly more than 4,000 volumes. They were set up in 1987 and 1989 respectively. Taking their local populations into consideration, they do not conform to international standards of stock provision in meeting the aspirations and fundamental needs of readers.

Table 11.5   Distribution of public libraries

A. Controlled by the Ministry of Education

	Library	Established	Personnel	Holdings	Population in thousands
1	Buraydah	1944	15	40,207	254
2	Hariq	1953	5	14,632	3.6
3	Hutat Bani Tamim	1956	5	20,017	15
4	Hutat Sedair	1957	6	9,205	9
5	Unaizah	1959	16	25,050	50
6	Hafuf	1961	4	30,751	250
7	Dammam	1962	7	49,625	418.5
8	Delum	1964	6	8,522	14
9	Muzahimiyah	1965	4	20,017	10
10	Huraymila	1968	6	20,048	5.5
11	King Faisal St., Riyadh	1968	5	63,150	1,417
12	al-Madinah	1969	4	25,070	500
13	Russ	1970	3	1,646	30
14	Mudannab	1971	3	18,726	15
15	Rodat Sedair	1971	7	5,057	5
16	Tabouk	1972	3	22,117	150
17	Zulfi	1972	7	25,076	29
18	Bukairiyah	1973	5	20,067	15
19	Shagraa	1973	4	23,171	18
20	Mujma	1973	5	21,514	21
21	Kubar	1974	3	21,085	00
22	Jizan	1974	2	19,517	79
23	Abha	1974	2	10,117	60
24	Quwayah	1975	3	20,047	9.4
25	Oshaygir	1975	3	15,033	— *(cont.)*

	Library	Established	Personnel	Holdings	Population in thousands
26	Baha	1975	3	7,032	50
27	Taif	1976	12	41,518	283
28	Hail	1976	11	12,217	101
29	Najran	1976	3	8,017	53
30	Bisha	1977	5	19,075	22
31	Yanbu	1977	4	25,082	52
32	Layla	1977	3	32,195	—
33	Dawadmi	1977	2	8,020	32
34	Jeddah	1977	6	31,975	1,312
35	Makkah	1977	8	34,322	742
36	Karj	1977	8	17,097	97
37	Mizal	1978	1	5,027	—
38	Sakaka	1978	4	22,074	55
39	Kamis Mushait	1979	4	12,018	164
40	Qunfuda	1980	1	13,017	11
41	Qurayat	1980	3	10,539	43
42	Durma	1980	3	11,567	6
43	Kamaseen	1981	2	12,017	—
44	Daumat al-Jandal	1981	2	11,017	14
45	Qusb	1981	2	5,018	—
46	Mirat	1982	5	5,017	4
47	Tamir	1982	6	4,065	4.8
48	Muhayal	1983	3	10,587	9
49	Riyadh at Madur	1987	3	39,518	1,417
50	Oaynah	1987	2	4,020	2.5
51	Masim at Riyadh	1987	2	10,067	1,410
52	Qatif	1987	4	5,018	167.5
53	Hafur al-Badin	1988	1	15, 023	52
54	Al-Qaysumah	1988	1	16,023	—
55	Al-Oun	1988	3	7,130	—
56	Silyl	1988	4	6,028	7.28
57	Jubail	1988	4	11,856	28
58	Sharura	1988	3	6,028	15
59	Arar	1989	2	4,041	65
60	Thadik	Recently	—	—	3.7

B. Controlled by the Ministry of Pilgrimage & Endowment

	Library	Established	Personnel	Holdings	Population in thousands
1	Mahamudyah al-Madinah	1821		7,075	500
2	Arif Hikmat al Madinah	1853		7,997	500
3	Al-Elmiyah Al-Saliyah	1953		10,100	
4	Abdullah ibne Abbas at Taif	1958			283
5	King Abdul-Aziz Library	1960		16,304	
6	Makkah	1971		12,000	
7	Mushaf	1980		1,744	

C. Controlled by the General Directorate of Holy Mosque Supervision

	Library	Established	Personnel	Holdings	Population in thousands
1	Al-Haram al-Maki	1850		31,000	742
2	Al-Haram al-Madni	1923		6,345	

D. Controlled by the Directorate General Judiciary Decree, Propagation & Guidance

	Library	Established	Personnel	Holdings	Population in thousands
1	Al-Saudia at Riyadh	1950		19,850	

Table 11.6   Types and languages of materials in Ministry of Education public libraries[20]

Materials	Arabic language	Other languages	Total
Books	997,246	132,352	1,129,598
Periodicals	1,087	12	1,099
Manuscripts	294	—	294
Total	998,627	132,364	1,130,991

This shows that books form the great majority of the collections, 99.98% of the total overall. Audiovisual materials are not available, despite their importance in teaching illiterates and groups of elderly people. Popular magazines are also neglected; many do not even subscribe to daily newspapers. It is known that the General Directorate of Public Libraries has placed subscriptions, for general distribution to its libraries for some 32 Arabic periodicals.[21]

Libraries of Endowments and Al-Haram Library are outstanding for their collections of rare books and manuscripts.[22]

It is notable that children's materials are poorly provided; these collections are markedly inadequate and are usually characterized, as in the adult sections, by a preponderance of religious, literary and social subjects.

All public libraries depend primarily on the ministry or governmental departments for finance and supply, and to a lesser extent on exchange and endowments from individuals, groups, or establishments. The General Directorate of Public Libraries usually undertakes all the procedures of choosing, checking, and purchasing books. It buys 150 copies of each title selected and each library receives at least one copy. This system does not take account of known needs and preferences of readers in individual libraries, and selection tends to be based on personal preferences of the selectors, who in turn are constrained by having to operate within the general concept that library stocks shall not contradict traditions and norms considered essential for the stability of Saudi society. For this reason their stocks are not vivid.[24] Consequently their usefulness and utilization are limited, and they are unable to achieve their goals. Furthermore, the lack of various modern materials, and dearth of exchange and co-operation programs, combined with manpower shortage have negative impact on libraries' activities.[25]

It is notable that public libraries lack balanced collections, and are out of date and little used. Therefore they are regarded as useless and stagnant, because they do not even have the administrative system by which to discard burdensome and unwanted materials. Small as stocks are, their overcrowded shelves make it difficult to accommodate new items, when they are supplied, and there is damage and deterioration due to exposure to light, heat, humidity and insects. Few libraries have been planned to provide suitable accommodation for manuscripts and rare books.

Classification and cataloguing

The procedures of classification, cataloguing, and the distribution of cards are centralized by the Ministry of Education, with the exception only of materials that have come to libraries by gift or exchange. These are processed by individual libraries. Libraries controlled by the other government departments named previously perform the classification of stock themselves, using the Dewey Decimal Classification, but shortage of professionally qualified staff leaves some items unattended to.[25]

Catalogues still use the typewritten sheaf form; some are handwritten, without co-ordination, consistency or discipline. In an attempt to improve catalogue presentation, some have been replaced by card catalogues under authors' names, but copied without correction from earlier sheaf catalogues.[26]

The Ministry of Education libraries use three-part card catalogues, under names of authors, titles, and in classified arrangement, but the subject approach is most usually neglected. They use the descriptive cataloguing rules of Mahmood Shoniati and Ahmed Kalbash, but libraries under the control of other government departments do not follow any recognized standard rules. Only a handful of libraries is known to follow Anglo-American cataloguing rules.

Location and space (distance)

Public libraries in the Kingdom do not usually occupy more than two floors, and most are away from heavily populated districts, adjacent to main city centres. Their space capacity varies greatly. For example, most of them have between 100 and 800 sq. m., rising for some more fortunate few upwards to 2,000 sq. m. The library at Hafoof is the largest with approximately 2,820 sq. m. Surprisingly few of the buildings provide the required environment for resources and readers, i.e. air-conditioning, heating, or controlled ventilation. Adult areas are not separated from children's sections.

Furniture and equipment

Library furniture in most of the public libraries is designed exclusively for use by adults, without any concessions in size for children. It does not reflect required standards to make them more suitable for providing library service, and for storage and maintenance of resources. Equipment for normally common formats such as microfilms, slides, overhead transparencies, audiocassettes, Xerox copies and other audiovisual formats is not usually provided.

Opening hours
In general, opening hours are inadequate. They mostly follow the working pattern of government offices; they start formally from 8 a.m. to 2.30 p.m., with the exception of a few libraries that work an afternoon shift. The great majority remain closed at weekends. In the case of those that do offer extended hours, staff are not punctual and their libraries frequently fail to open for service.

As a consequence the opening hours of most public libraries are not suitable for the majority of potential users because they correspond too closely with readers' own working hours. This undoubtedly minimizes their efficiency and explains their inadequate provision per capita of population.

Users' services
Public library services are limited to reading facilities within their premises, as regulations do not permit external borrowing. The Ministry of Education libraries permit open access to stock, but those controlled by other ministries maintain closed access, requiring a librarian to fetch books for the readers. In other words, the concept of browsing, which is taken for granted in western countries does not yet prevail in Saudi public libraries.

Apart from reference services, advice and guidance, and occasional Xerox copying or other reprography, few other services are available. Some manuscripts have been microfilmed by the General Directorate of Public Libraries. The administration has also issued occasional bibliographies such as:[27]

- Bibliography of Saudi publications, 1972.
- Bibliography of Islamic jurisprudence books located in the National Book House, 1976 (for the Conference of Islamic Jurisprudence, Riyadh).
- Bibliography of the most important books about the Arab Peninsula and the Middle East, 1976 (for the Conference on the Arab Peninsula, Riyadh).

Many public libraries attempt to organize seasonal activities such as holding sessions, seminars, lectures, and book exhibitions, or visiting schools to publicize their services. Some derive benefits by establishing good relations and extending co-operation to other libraries through interlibrary loans, gifts and exchange.

With regard to numbers of readers and their use of libraries, little record-keeping takes place. In the absence of reliable statistics they have provided rough estimates of numbers, but it is not possible to quote exact figures. However it is estimated that the reader use in most of these libraries is between 5 and 30 persons monthly; few attract as many as 30–50 people in any monthly period. The library in King Faisal Street, Riyadh comes highest, serving 83 persons monthly. Most readers are secondary school students, a few are university students or research workers. The so-called peaks of use occur prior to examinations for serious study, and during summer vacations for recreational reading of newspapers and magazines.

Thus, public libraries attract so little attention that they get no publicity from external information media. They do not attempt to cultivate public relations with media houses, and thus escape the notice of the general public. This state of affairs only emphasizes the need to enlighten Saudi society about the role that should be played by public libraries as an educational and cultural instrument.

To sum up, while some progress has been made since the beginning, public library service in Saudi Arabia is still limited in scope, and uneven in availability. Some corrective measures can be anticipated, but in general, the General Directorate of Public Libraries of the Ministry of Education has not yet formulated an overall policy, or instigated programmes to bring about substantial improvements in this regard. Consequently, the presently small and poorly equipped public libraries, which try to serve large areas and increasing populations, will continue to offer substandard services, the short- and long-term effects of which are clearly undesirable.

References

1   Al-Shoshan, Ahmad A., 'Saudi Arabia: the country nutrition profile'. In: *FAO/WHO Conference on Nutrition, Rome, December, 1992*, Rome, FAO, 1993, 28.

2   Nyrop, Richard F., *Area handbook for Saudi Arabia*, 3rd edn. Washington, DC, Government Printing Office, 1977, 66.

3   Tashkandy, Abbas S., Saudi Arabia, Libraries. In: *Encyclopedia of library and information science*, 1979, 26, 317.

4   Abbas, Hisham, A., *A Plan for public library system development in Saudi Arabia*, Graduate School of Library & Information Science, University of Pittsburgh, 1982, 8 (PhD dissertation).

5   Sowaine, Ali S., *Public library and community development in Saudi Arabia*, University of Denver Graduate School of Librarianship, 1979, 13 (MLS thesis).

6   Saudi Arabia, Central Planning Organization, *First five year development plan, 1970–1975*, Dammam, Al-Mutawa Press Co., 1970, 100.

7   Saudi Arabia, Ministry of Planning, *Second five year development plan, 1975–1980*, Jeddah, Okaz House for Publishing and Printing, 1975, 107.

8   Saudi Arabia, Ministry of Planning, *Third five year development plan, 1980–1985*, Riyadh, the Ministry, 1980, 250.

9   Saudi Arabia, Ministry of Planning, *Fourth five year development plan, 1985–1990*, Riyadh, the Ministry, 1985, 154, 367–8, 373.

10 Al-Siryani, Mohammed M., 'Aspects of urbanization in the Kingdom of Saudi Arabia', *Gulf & Arab Peninsula studies journal*, **16** (63), Thu-Al Hijja, 1410 AH, 25–9.

11 Halawah, Mustafa M., 'Planning for extending library service in Saudi Arabia', *Faculty of Arabic Language journal of Imam Mohammad Ibn Saud Islamic University* (7), 1397 AH, 529.

12 Saudi Arabia, Ministry of Education, General Directorate of Public Libraries, *A List of public libraries in Saudi Arabia*, Riyadh, 1413 AH, 9 (unpublished report).

13 Ibid.

14 Al-Hadi, Mohammad M., *Report on the development of the General Directorate of Public Libraries in Saudi Arabia.* Riyadh, General Directorate of Public Libraries, Ministry of Education (12 Dec. 1980–Jan. 1981), 10.

15 Public Library Association, *A Strategy for public library change: proposed public library goals feasibility study*, Chicago, American Library Association, 1972, 46.

16 'Library services for the nation's needs: the report of the National Advisory Commission on libraries'. In: *Libraries at large: traditions, innovation, and the national interest*, eds Douglas M. Knight and E. Sheply Nourse, New York, Bowker, 1969, 497.

17 Saudi Arabia, Ministry of Education, op. cit., 10.

18 Namlah, Ali I., 'Shortage of manpower and their effectiveness on books services', *Alam Al-Kutub journalI*, **5** (3), Muharram, 1405 AH, 490.

19 Saudi Arabia, Ministry of Education, op. cit., 10.

20 Ibid.

21 Ibid.

22 Tunisi, Hamadi A. M., *Public libraries in the Holy City of Madinah, its present and past*, Department of Library and Information Science, King Abdulaziz University, 1401 AH, 229 (MLS thesis).

23 Saudi Arabia, Ministry of Education, op. cit., 12.

24 Tashkandy, Anas S., *Library profession in Saudi Arabia: survey*, Department of Library and Information Science, King Abdulaziz University, 1982, 77 (MLS thesis).
25 Ibid.
26 Tunisi, op. cit., 231.
27 Saudi Arabia, Ministry of Education, op. cit., 16.

12 LIS consultancy in the Arab world: the Sudanese experience

Alhaj Salim Mustafa

The recruitment of librarians and other information specialists as international consultants[1] to advise on library and information science in developing countries is not an entirely new phenomenon. More than six decades ago the Carnegie Corporation of New York sent a number of British and American librarians on advisory missions to East, West, and southern Africa, to the West Indies, to Australia and New Zealand in connection with its programme of aid to overseas library development.[2] Consultancy in library and information science became more popular and widely practised in developing countries after the Second World War, especially with the establishment of UNESCO, and the involvement of organizations such as the British Council, and other specialized UN agencies.

Definitions of what constitutes a library and information consultant are various, such as those by James Lockwood[3] and Duane E. Webster and John G. Lorenz.[4] However the most relevant definition in the context of this paper is perhaps that by Marta L. Dosa:

> The International consultant . . . is a technical expert from an industrialized country who advises and assists less-industrialised countries in a particular aspect of development. Whether working individually or as a member of a team . . . assigned to a short-term task or a long-term mission, the consultant is a carrier of specialised information and technological knowledge from one culture to another.[5]

David Clow extended this definition by adding another three aspects: payment for the services of the consultant, the consultant's independence of the employer and the consultant's active participation in implementing the consultancy report.[6] He further identified three principal players in the process of consultancy by suggesting that in most cases it includes the client or the host; the aid agency, which is often the main funder of the consultancy;

and the consultant. He noted that: 'there is a tripartite relationship and the consultant is bound to feel some responsibility to all three partners: to the host employer, to the aid agency, and to himself. If all three partners' goals coincide, of course, there is no problem, but they rarely do'.[7]

In the Arab world library and information science (LIS) consultancies started as early as 1951, when UNESCO sent its first expert mission to Syria.[8] Up to 1982 it was reported that UNESCO alone had sent 162 missions to these countries.[9] Other specialized agencies and individuals were also involved in this work. The region is still receiving quite a number of consultancies every year, either as part of technical aid from international organizations or because consultants are invited direct by the countries concerned.

Despite the proliferation and popularity of consultancy in the Arab world, the results of these missions and their achievements were questioned by many librarians and other information workers in the region. Although some consultancies achieved a degree of success, there have been more failures than successes. A closer look at the projects initiated by those consultants will bear testimony to this argument.

This paper discusses LIS missions to the Sudan during the period 1960-86, with the aim of finding out the general trends of their advice, and to offer a critique of their findings and recommendations. The Sudan shares many characteristics with other Arab countries and it can offer a better understanding of the benefits derived from consultancies, which other Arab countries may find helpful in future planning.

Consultancy in the colonial period

In contrast to the interest shown by the British government in library development in some parts of Africa during the colonial era, library development in the Sudan was completely neglected. This could partly explain the reasons for not sending library advisers to the country, whereas the eastern, western and southern African colonial territories were enjoying the services and advice of many British library advisers in the closing years of that period of their history.

The first library consultancy in the Sudan took place in 1951 and was initiated by The Inter-University Council for Higher Education Overseas (IUC) which was set up by British universities in 1946 to 'help develop university education in developing countries overseas'.[10]

With financial assistance from the Carnegie Corporation of New York, IUC established the post of library adviser in 1947, and the first appointee was Dr. Richard Offor, who had nearly half a century of experience in the library profession at University College, London and later as librarian of the University of Leeds.[11] The work of the library adviser involved 'planning of buildings; the appointment of librarians and the provision of books either by purchase, by gift or by locating articles in periodicals and their reproduction'.[12]

In a tour which took him to Malta, Kenya, and Uganda in his capacity as IUC library adviser, Dr Offor visited the then newly established University College of Khartoum in 1951. Although his visit was not strictly a library consultancy per se for its main intention was to: 'establish intimate and friendly relations with those who have to create and develop great libraries under special difficulties, not only by correspondence but by . . . visiting them as far as practicable'.[13] Nevertheless he made some general observations and offered advice to these libraries, including the University College of Khartoum on such matters as the status of the library in the academic hierarchy of the university, librarians and their qualifications, the planning of library buildings and collection development. His accounts of the libraries he visited were recorded in two articles published in 1954.[14]

Consultancy after independence

P. H. Sewell's mission (1960)
Library development in the Sudan in the early years of Independence was less than satisfactory and almost non-existent in many areas. However, it was generally felt at the time that conditions in the Sudan were:

> favourable to the development of library service on sound lines . . . There is a wide desire for education and cultural advancement . . . a pattern for urban library provision already exists in embryo . . . [and] further, the economy of the country would appear to be sufficiently stable to justify the immediate creation of a realistically planned national library service.[15]

The Sudanese Government approached UNESCO in 1960 for a consultant to advise on the nation's library development. The request could not have come at a better time. In 1959 UNESCO had organized a regional seminar on library development in Arabic speaking states, in Beirut, which emphasized *inter alia* that 'sound planning on a nation-wide scale was the essential condition of library development; . . . its aim should be the establishment of a national system including provision of adequate library services at various levels: national, university, special, public and school libraries . . . '[16] These recommendations were still fresh in the minds of the UNESCO officials when the Sudan made its request for a library consultant, and consequently P. H. Sewell was contracted for a six-month mission to the Sudan, in January 1960. He undoubtedly had appropriate qualifications, professional experience and the ability to undertake the consultancy mission as a 'UNESCO Library Expert'. He was at that time Head of the School of Librarianship at the North-West London Polytechnic, and subsequently became Senior Library Adviser in the Department of Education and Science (UK).

His terms of reference were:

(a) giving a course for librarians;
(b) advising the government on the future organization of a school for librarians;
(c) completing the survey of the libraries of the country, which had been started by the university librarian; and
(d) drawing up a plan for the development of libraries on a nationwide basis.[17]

After surveying the existing LIS provision in the country, making visits to various libraries in and around Khartoum, undertaking itineraries to some ten major towns across the Sudan and establishing contacts with provincial and municipal officials, Sewell concluded that there was wide scope for the establishment of school libraries with trained teacher-librarians, to facilitate the integration of libraries into formal education programmes in primary, intermediate and secondary schools. He stressed the need to develop the central library of Bakht er Ruda Institute of Education with its postal library services as a centre for national school library provision and development.

In line with UNESCO's approach to library development in the 1950s and early 1960s. i.e. the establishment of 'pilot' or model public libraries in developing countries, as a means of promoting library services in those countries, Sewell proposed that the Omdurman Central Library should be developed into a model public library and be designated as a centre for public library provision at national level. It would support provincial libraries working as branches in the areas of book selection and acquisition; centralized cataloguing and classification; centralized book binding; loans administration and general supervision.[18] Provincial libraries in turn would supply book boxes to villages via rural district councils. In view of this, rural library services were anticipated as being performed through book box services, or where possible by mobile libraries similar to those developed by the Ghana Library Board.

With regard to special and public libraries, it was recommended that these be co-ordinated and integrated into the proposed national library system. The University of Khartoum Library, being the most developed library in the country, was to be the base on which the whole national library system would be built. In his final report to UNESCO, Sewell produced a 12-point list of recommendations, (in summary):

(a) The Library of the University of Khartoum be designated the National Library and enabled to act as a centre for research libraries;

(b) A central libraries board be established with a duty to promote the development and co-ordination of libraries and reporting to the Minister of Education.

(c) The Ministry of Education's Central Library in Omdurman be developed as a model public library, and the centre of public libraries provision in the Sudan, providing some centralized services to other municipal libraries.

(d) The provision of public libraries of an adequate standard be mandatory on town councils.

(e) The provision of library service in rural areas, using schools or other premises and where feasible, the establishment of mobile libraries.

(f) The cost of public library services be allocated by provinces to districts and town councils.

(g) The provision of school library services.

(h) The development of special libraries be encouraged by the Central Libraries Board with support service from the National Library.

(j) Library staff be given proper status and better career prospects.

(k) Education and training facilities for library staff be given at various levels.

(l) Steps be taken to improve the supply of reading materials for new literates.[19]

Although the recommendations were sound in the main and mostly applicable, there were weaknesses in its applicability to the actualities of the country's administrative processes.

The first was perhaps the over-emphasis given in the report to the development of public libraries as the basis for overall library development in the country, at the expense of other types, especially special libraries, which had been given a low priority. Second was the total concentration on books as the medium for information provision, in a country where more than 80% of the population were illiterate. Such emphasis seemed to have been deliberate and was biased towards urban and metropolitan areas, at the expense of rural communities. A third weakness was the omission of any mention of the development of archives service; this being an integral part of library and information development.

Because of disturbances and political instability in southern Sudan at the time, Sewell was not able to visit the three southern provinces.[20] Although LIS in the south is not very different from the situation in the rest of the country, nevertheless the mission can only be considered as partial in this context.

Although Sewell had identified the importance of library services in national development, together with the need for national co-ordination of such services, his report did not include any detailed recommendations towards their planning or costing. This in effect left the Sudanese authorities without a clear methodology or financial guidelines as to how to go about implementing the report's recommendations.

Unfortunately, as the result of inherent cultural, administrative, and political problems in the Sudan at the time, the report has never been implemented. When J. S. Parker visited the Sudan in 1971 on a similar mission he found that: 'little effort seemed to have been made to implement any of the recommendations made by Sewell, and that any developments which correspond with Sewell's recommendations did so by accident'.[21] He also noted that the overall picture of the state of library services in the Sudan was one of stagnation and even deterioration since Sewell's visit.[22]

Ironically the Sewell report had been published by UNESCO and made available to the Sudanese authorities only in 1963, almost three years after the completion of the mission. The irony of ironies still is that the report 'has never been generally available in the Sudan'.[23] Parker reported that he could not even find an official copy of the report at the time of his visit in 1971.[24]

Failure to implement Sewell's recommendations can be attributed to several factors. The following are some which we are able to identify:

1 the failure to establish the Central Libraries Board or any national agency with overall responsibilities for LIS development;
2 lack of commitment and absence of any guidelines and policies on LIS development, resulting in a total failure to provide the funds necessary for implementing the Sewell report;

3 lack of qualified Sudanese librarians of the right professional calibre. This is a very important factor in the success of any library development programme. In addition to carrying out the implementation of the recommendations, such librarians should play an important part in convincing disinterested and sometimes suspicious decision makers and planners of the importance of LIS in national development. At the time of Sewell's visit not a single Sudanese was trained as a fully qualified professional librarian. The first qualified Sudanese librarian had obtained his qualification from London and returned to the Sudan in 1961 – a year after the mission;

4 the separation between the recommendations made and their actual implementation. It is often the case that UNESCO leaves the implementation of its missions' recommendations to the authorities in the recipient countries without any attempt to undertake follow-up or evaluative exercises. This will not only delay the implementation process, but may also kill the enthusiasm and the momentum for action that has been built-up by the consultants. That was exactly what happened in the Sudan, as far as the Sewell recommendations were concerned.

In spite of the apparent weaknesses and failure of the Sewell mission, for reasons not entirely of his making, it had been successful in that it made recommendations at a time when the concept of library development planning was in the embryonic stage. Furthermore it laid a solid foundation for subsequent missions in the same field.

J. S. Parker's mission (1971)
The Parker mission could not have come at a better time than 1971, in both national and international terms. At national level the political climate in the Sudan was undergoing a tremendous change, with the formation of a new political system after the May 1969 military coup, and the establishment of new administrative structures that introduced decentralization. A five-Year development plan for 1970–1 to 1974–5 was also under way. The fortunes of libraries appeared to have turned when a librarian was appointed as Minister for Culture and Information.

At international level, more sophisticated development planning techniques and methodologies had been developed at UNESCO's regional meetings on national planning of library services in Quito (1966) Colombo (1967) and Kampala (1970). These meetings, and in particular the Kampala meeting, recognized the overlapping areas of responsibility of different types of library – a fact which emphasized the need for co-ordinated planning of all publicly funded library and documentation services. At the same time UNESCO was preparing for its fourth meeting in the series of regional conferences, scheduled to be held in Cairo (for the Arab states) in 1972.

As in previous regional meetings, model national library plans were prepared, for use as case-studies, along with discussion guidelines for the country in which the meeting was to take place; but for the Cairo meeting a decision was taken to prepare the model plan for the Sudan rather than Egypt because the Sudanese authorities had already asked UNESCO to provide an expert to advise on library development in their country.[25]

UNESCO had appointed J. S. Parker to undertake a three-month mission to the Sudan in late 1971. Like Sewell before him, Parker appeared to have the qualifications and experience, and therefore the competence to carry out the consultancy mission. He arrived in the Sudan in October 1971 with the following terms of reference:

(a) to make a study of the present state of the documentation and library services and evaluate the future needs of the country; and

(b) draw up a national plan for the development of documentation and library services with short-, medium-, and long-term objectives, including statistical data and cost estimates for the target period.[26]

Interestingly, these were almost identical to those given to Sewell in 1960. This indicates clearly that nothing significant had been done over the 11 years that had elapsed since Sewell's report. The survey carried out by Parker on his arrival revealed that:

whilst some progress had been made in one or two isolated areas, and small numbers of libraries had developed and improved their services and stocks during the past ten years, . . . the overall conclusion was that the existing library and documentation services in the Sudan were quite inadequate for the needs of the country.[27]

He noted in particular that there was no central library board and therefore no co-ordination of library services in the country, that school libraries had declined considerably, as had public libraries, and that special and academic libraries continued in their uncoordinated manner. The only library in the country that reported considerable progress was the University of Khartoum Library.

Lack of co-ordination, money, equipment, personnel, and of

any general appreciation by the authorities, of the cost and complexity of a national library development plan, were factors correctly identified by Parker as the main hindrance to library development in the Sudan.

Following his survey, and consultation with Sudanese librarians and government officials, Parker concluded that the most urgent need [was] for a national body, established under proper legislation, with responsibility for co-ordinating and directing library development in all its aspects.[28]

His main points were for the most part a reflection of and in line with the thinking current at that time in UNESCO circles; that there was need for:

(a) Integrated provision of library and documentation services for the whole country.

(b) A network of conventional library services loosely linked with national development needs.

(c) Co-ordination of various library and documentation services through the establishment of statutory bodies.

(d) Library education and training through the establishment of proper educational and training institutions.

In addressing these issues, Parker prepared a detailed, fully costed, and programmed ten-year library development plan, requiring the establishment of the following elements:

1 A National Council for Library Development, under the chairmanship of the Minister of Culture and Information and representative of the bodies chiefly interested in the provision of library services, charged with various duties in respect of library development.

2 Provincial library councils.

3 A National Library Network consisting mainly but not exclusively of school, public and joint school/public libraries.

4 A National Documentation Centre with responsibilities for co-ordinating and improving the services of special libraries and documentation centres.

5 A school of librarianship at the University of Khartoum to run sub-professional, professional and postgraduate courses.

6 A National Central Library.

Detailed forecasts and projections for the establishment and development of the various elements of the services outlined above, including provision for book acquisition, staff requirements, buildings, and other recurrent and capital expenditure were prepared in the course of the mission. It was established that a total capital cost of LS 8,594,000 and a total recurrent expenditure in the final year of the plan period of LS 3,189,000, representing 4.78% of estimated gross educational expenditure would be needed to execute the plan.[29] All such proposals were, for the most part, approved by the appropriate authorities before the final plan was submitted. Furthermore a draft for a National Library Development Act was prepared by the consultant and discussed at ministerial level and revised during the course of the mission.

For the implementing of this plan, Parker recommended in his final report the following 'practical' steps:[30]

1 Adopt the National Library Development Act.
2 Establish the National Council for Library Development.
3 Appoint the director of the National Library Network.
4 Appoint the director of the Library Development Council.
5 Appoint the Director of the National Documentation Centre.
6 Appoint the Head of the School of Librarianship.
7 Make provision in the ordinary recurrent budget for estimated recurrent expenditure required for the first year of the plan.
8 Make financial provision from Development Budget contingency funds for the necessary capital expenditure during the remaining period of the five-year development plan.
9 Establish the advisory committees as well as the supporting services and posts as laid down by the National Library Development Act.
10 Pending the establishment of the School of Librarianship, provide facilities for suitably qualified candidates to be sent to library schools abroad for full professional training.

The overwhelming enthusiasm shown to Parker by ministers and senior government officials at the end of his mission had led him to believe, prematurely and a little unrealistically perhaps, that 'the widespread awareness of the importance of better library services which the writer found in the Sudan during his visit was most encouraging'.[31] and that: 'there [was] good reason to hope that there would be real progress in library development in the Sudan . . . and that the value of detailed national development planning would be demonstrated'.[32] Such high hopes remain largely unfulfilled to the present day.

The Parker plan was probably one of the first fully costed and programmed LIS development plans to be mounted in an Arab state. Therefore it was in many ways a pioneering and innovative mission, even by UNESCO's standard of achievement.

Considering the short duration of the mission and the effort on the part of the consultant to collect hard-to-find data and statistics, one must admire the tremendous task undertaken by Parker to formulate such a development plan, which still appears to be sound and largely applicable. There were defects, however, which can be summarized:

1 It appears that Parker had to depend overmuch on unreliable sources and hearsay, when surveying the situation and assessing the exact needs of the country. By his own admission he said that: 'finding out about library services in the Sudan is so difficult . . . because . . . there is no central source of statistical or other information about libraries, and such data as can be obtained is often incomplete or unreliable'.[33] This led him to make some false assumptions and misleading projections of, for example, the number of public libraries in the country, and the level of expenditure in some college libraries. This state of affairs was largely due to the fact that the three months he spent in the Sudan was too short a period to enable him to acquaint himself fully with the real situation there.

2 Originally, it had been proposed by UNESCO that the phasing of the proposed development plan should be expressed in terms of short-, medium-, and long-term objectives covering periods of two, five, and ten years. However Parker was of the opinion that it was not desirable to establish long-term objectives, arguing that: 'it would be impossible to do so without introducing elements into the plan which would have no other purpose than to establish such targets'.[34] Therefore he suggested the establishment of short-term objectives up to 1975. As the Sudanese experience of development planning would suggest, Parker was right to offer only short-term objectives in his plan, as these are generally easier to implement. However, the nature of the mission and the plan objectives as laid by Parker would certainly indicate the need for the establishment of long-term objectives, because most of infrastructure for library services would have to be established from nothing. In this case it would have been more appropriate, from a development planning point of view, to establish such long-term objectives and attempt to phase their implementation, in order to maintain the continuity of the planning process and its validity.

3 Parker recommended that 4.87% of the educational expenditure in the Sudan should be allocated to the development of library services by the plan's terminal year (1983). This may

have been a short-sighted suggestion because he did not take into account the need to identify the priorities in the education system itself. If it had been perceived for example that library services are of major importance, then the plan could have considered allocating more than the fixed percentage at the initial stages of library development, and with compensatory adjustments when the services had become well-established, relative to the adjusted target expenditure.

4 because of the absence of Sudanese librarians experienced in LIS development planning, and the unfamiliarity of existing development planners with concepts of library service, the plan was seen as complicated and difficult to understand. This had led the Minister of Education to appoint a committee of senior librarians and development planners 'to discuss, review and report on Parker's plan'.[35]

In the interest of simplicity and economy, the committee made a comprehensive summary of the entire report, and recommended modifications in structure and finance, the establishment of public libraries, and on library education.[36] Like Sewell's recommendations, the elaborate plan by Parker has never been implemented. Thirteen years on from its completion, he noted that: 'as is often the case with short term missions . . . with the expert's departure the impetus largely disappeared; and although valiant efforts were made by a few Sudanese librarians to persuade the authorities to proceed with the implementation of the development plan, they had met with very limited success'.[37]

The factors that contributed to the failure of the Parker plan do not differ much from those that affected the Sewell mission, discussed earlier. In addition there were:

(a) The transfer of personnel in the top government hierarchy who had shown interest in the plan and were keen on implementing it. As is frequently the case in the Sudan, plans are scrapped when a new administration is installed, irrespective of the validity and usefulness of what has been initiated during the previous administration.

(b) The absence of experienced librarians with strong personalities and qualitative leadership style, to persuade the government to carry on with the implementation of the plan.

(c) The plan coincided with a period of intense political propaganda, internal civil service conflicts and ambitious but unfulfilled development aspirations. Because libraries do not lend themselves to immediate and tangible cost-benefit analyses, nor are they perceived as being politically rewarding as means by which to increase government popularity, the plan has been completely ignored.

(d) It is also possible to suggest that the proposals represented too great a leap from the situation Parker found during his survey, and that he underestimated the reaction to such expenditure at a time when the country's economy was weak and struggling to build momentum. He may also have over-estimated the availability of outside aid.

P. H. Sewell's second mission (1978)

At the time of Sewell's second mission in late 1978, there were major new developments in UNESCO's LIS programmes. These included the merger of UNISIST and NATIS programmes into PGI, which recognized the need to develop a co-ordinated infrastructure of LIS, and to ensure the provision of information services in furtherance of all aspects of national development.

It was along the lines of the PGI concept that the Sudanese authorities approached the United Nations Development Programme (UNDP) for a consultant to 'advise on the co-ordination of library, documentation and other services, based on a survey of these as components of a national information system for development'.[38] The second Sewell mission also coincided with the launching of the Sudanese government's six-year development plan 1977-8 to 1982-3 which included recognition that the lack of an adequate information system severely handicapped government and institutional decision making, and stressed the need to secure adequate information as a basis for proper planning and effective follow-up.

Against this background, UNDP/UNESCO sent Sewell to the Sudan on a four-month mission with the following terms of reference:

(a) carry out a survey of the existing library services, documentation centres and other relevant components of the national information system;

(b) prepare recommendations for the co-ordination of the work of different libraries, documentation centres, and other information services, in order to make the most efficient use of the information services; and

(c) advise on the establishment of a co-ordinated national acquisition policy.[39]

As can be seen, they were very similar to those of his 1960 mission, and of Parker's, except perhaps for the greater emphasis now placed on the practical development of library services, documentation centres, other information services, and archives. The tendency to repeat the same terms of reference in subsequent consultancies is not really surprising because no effective action had been taken to implement most earlier recommendations; only one from the report by Parker had borne fruit in that the National Documentation Centre (NDC) was established in 1974. Neither the National and Provincial Library Boards or Councils, nor the provision of a National Library network as envisaged in the two previous missions had materialized.

Bearing in mind the failure of his first encounter with library development problems in the Sudan in 1960 and the normally unconstructive attitude of the Sudanese authorities with regard to implementing consultancy reports, Sewell arrived this time a wiser and perhaps more realistic man. Instead of attempting to produce an elaborate overall development plan, with complicated budgeting and costing methodologies, that librarians might not easily understand, and which were probably unworkable in a country like the Sudan at that time, he opted for an approach which was to 'produce recommendations which both recognised the realities of the local situation and were acceptable to local librarians and officials'.[40]

Sewell first identified the main areas of emphasis. They were:

(a) stimulating awareness of the importance of having information services in support of national development;
(b) involving local librarians and officials as closely as possible in formulating plans for developing a national information system; and
(c) reflecting the financial constraints that affected all aspects of the Sudanese economy.

The thrust of his thinking, which was generally in line with the objectives of PGI objectives were:

(a) To gain general acceptance of the principles of sharing library and information resources and of the importance of so organizing services that local research findings could be exploited, and international information services tapped.
(b) To create an official framework within which the details of a co-ordinated information structure could be worked out.
(c) To link short- and medium-term programmes for co-ordinating services in and around Khartoum with a long-term programme for creating a country-wide series of provincial library networks, in line with the proposals

made in the earlier consultancy reports.

(d) To establish a national accession policy and ensure that essential information materials were acquired by the most appropriate institutions, avoiding unnecessary duplication.[41]

After meetings with librarians, ministers, and senior government officials, visiting libraries in Khartoum, Medani, Port Sudan, and Juba and conducting a survey of LIS resources in the country, Sewell had been able to assess the current situation. He identified the major determinants affecting library service, which include the size of this huge country (2,505,813 sq. km), the inadequate internal communication facilities, high concentration of research and information facilities in the Khartoum area, the pressing economic difficulties, and the absence of systematic information provision.[42]

To tackle such problems and establish a national information system capable of providing the country's developmental information needs he made fresh recommendations for the co-ordination of libraries, documentation centres, and other information services. These included:

(a) Establishing a National Committee for Information (documentation, library and archive) services, with wide responsibilities:

- to set up networks as found necessary, by level and type of materials or information e.g. groupings by subject;
- to assist and promote the establishment of the provincial and regional committees for information; and
- to establish the technical basis for enabling the Sudan to make use of and to contribute to international information networks.

(b) The services initiated by the National Committee for Information to be co-ordinated through advisory committees for:

- special libraries and scientific and technological information (STI);
- academic libraries – university and other higher education institutions;
- general libraries – public, school and youth and community groups;
- archive services.

(c) Establishing a National Central Library such as that suggested in the two earlier reports.

(d) Public library networks be established to provide essential local links with the national information system, headed by the National Central Library and co-ordinated at the provincial level by provincial central public libraries.
(e) launching a series of programmes for user education.
(f) production of more and competent librarians.
(g) the setting up of a postgraduate facility for library and information science.
(h) manpower planning to implement national LIS development plans.

Sewell's report stressed the need to provide information for institutional and individual requirements, on the one hand, and to furnish a base for international links and co-operation, on the other. He also drew attention to the role of the NDC in co-ordinating the work of information services in the country.

Concerning the establishment of a nationally co-ordinated acquisition policy, he recognized the limited chances of success of such objectives because of the size of the country and its poor internal communication systems. However, he made a contribution to this objective by providing a survey of existing LIS services in the form of a directory of information resources, along the lines of Walford's *Guide to Libraries of Government Departments*.

Sewell did not commit himself to producing detailed programming for implementation of his proposals. He wisely left this task to be performed by local librarians through the proposed National Committee for Information, and instead provided practical and easy to implement suggestions, such as the setting up of an interlibrary transport system to facilitate the exchange of library materials, along with the start of union lists of periodicals. In addition, he actively participated, before his departure, in implementing one of the objectives of his report, by compiling the directory of information resources mentioned earlier.

This second report by Sewell was much more realistic than its predecessors in that it stressed the importance of drawing short-term objectives and then attempting to implement them, rather than drawing long-term and largely unrealistic objectives. The recommendations and blueprint were simple and easy to grasp by the local librarians and development planners alike. An important feature of the report was the greater emphasis placed on the role of local librarians in the library service planning process. However, one of its weaknesses was the failure to address such crucial aspects as the categorization of information users, and the identification of their actual needs and how those needs could be met.

However, in common with short-term consultancies of this type, its recommendations were never fully implemented. Although a National Committee for Information was created in 1979, it met only once before it was dissolved and to date no tangible progress has been achieved in implementing Sewell's recommendations, or to plan for a national information system.

Other consultancies

J. A. Dagher's mission (1976)

The high focus of attention on documentation services in the mid-1960s, evident in the literature emanating from the International Federation for Documentation (FID) and other organizations had influenced UNESCO to accept and encourage the establishment of specialized and general documentation services in the developing countries.

It was in this spirit that, at the request of the Sudanese Ministry of Education, UNESCO sent J. A. Dagher, Librarian of the National Library of Lebanon on a five month mission to the Sudan in 1967 to 'advise the government on the establishment of a National Educational Documentation Centre attached to the Ministry of Education'.[43]

The main objectives of the centre as envisaged by UNESCO were:

(a) to act as a centre from which school libraries in the country could obtain their required library materials; and

(b) to provide government officials, educationalists and all those interested in the educational process with up-to-date and accurate information on educational matters.

Dagher produced very practical recommendations on the establishment of the centre covering the centre's buildings, administration, the establishment of the collection, and its rules and procedures. Because UNESCO provided enough funding for the project to be set up, the centre was duly established in 1968. It functioned well in its first two years, but deteriorated rapidly after the 1969 military coup, in common with many other institutions. The centre could still make a useful contribution to the development of school libraries if it were to be reviewed and the recommendations made in that report carried out.

T. S. Rajagopalan's mission (1972)

At the request of the Sudanese Ministry of Foreign Affairs, which was undergoing a major reorganization process at the time, UNDP and UNESCO sent a documentation consultant, T. S.

Rajagopalan, on a six-month investigation in 1972 with the following terms of reference:

(a) to set up a documentation centre in the Ministry of Foreign Affairs;
(b) to establish a procedure for the processing of documents procured for the centre;
(c) to prepare bibliographies, indexes, etc., where required;
(d) to train local personnel and establish training programmes for those who are sent abroad for training;
(e) to establish contacts with documentation centres abroad; and
(f) to advise on the establishment and organizing of sub-centres.[44]

After studying the situation the consultant concluded that the Ministry of Foreign Affairs had an unusually high concentration of top level, able, experienced and well-qualified personnel, for whom a high standard of information service was essential. He noted that the library service provided by the Ministry's existing library was inadequate for the information needs of diplomats and other officials, and that a documentation centre was required. Rajagopalan drew up a very good and comprehensive plan for the establishment of such a centre, including its administration, physical facilities, printing equipment, budget, technical services, and training of personnel.

The report was accepted by the ministry with a view to immediate implementation, but nevertheless nothing has happened. The consultant wrote later that: 'the objectives of the mission have been fulfilled only in parts. The period of the mission has been too short, especially in the absence of staff and budget to implement all the proposals drawn for setting up the documentation centre in full operation'.[45]

R. Munn's mission (1978)

At the request of the then newly established University of Gezira, the Ford Foundation sent Dr R. Munn, Dean, Library Services of the West Virginia University, USA on a 20-day mission to advise on the issues of organization and administration, staff, faculty libraries, technical services, size and nature of the collection, photocopying and other matters needing immediate attention.[46] His report is a generalized one which could be applied to any one of a number of universities. A closer reading of the report confirms the danger of employing a consultant who had no adequate foreknowledge of the realities of LIS in developing countries.

Although Munn's qualifications can never be in doubt, his report should have been written for a large American university library and not for that of a new university in one of the poorest countries in the world. He recommended, for example setting up large faculty and departmental libraries, in this country where main university libraries are struggling to survive as viable central service departments. Munn's proposed standard of library staff, with basic qualifications at master's level, and the sizes of library collections were possibly in excess of those attained in many so-called developed countries.

D. K. Lindley's mission (1986)
In 1986, UNESCO funded a two-week mission to the Sudan under its regular programme for 1986-7. The terms of reference of the mission which was undertaken by D. K. Lindley were:

(a) to advise the national authorities on the establishment of a national environmental data and information system involving the co-ordination, integration and development of factual and bibliographic databases and associated information services, with particular reference to the problem of desertification;

(b) to prepare, in collaboration with the National Research Council, taking into account the already completed survey of environmental databases in Sudan, a working document on needs and strategies for access to environmental data and information, to be discussed at a national symposium; and

(c) to present the document and help moderate the discussions at the above national symposium.[47]

There was a new approach in this mission in that the consultant was not required to draw a plan for an information system or make specific recommendations to that effect, but rather to prepare a working document for the National Conference on an Environmental Information System, take part in its deliberation, and provide some additional support for the survey of the databases in science and technology in the Sudan which had already been started by the National Documentation Centre (NDC).

The approach taken this time to the investigation was a series of meetings with key officials of national institutions and in international agencies concerned with environmental issues, as well as with academics, research workers, librarians, and other information specialists. The summary conclusions of these meetings were incorporated in the final report, which acknowledges the difficulties of establishing an information system in the Sudan but identified some possible methods of introducing limited applications of modern information technology. Much of the report was devoted to discussing the choice of computer systems, software programs and training of operators. It recommended that 'the NDC should act as a growth point and be provided with sufficient funds to enable it to benefit from the use of modern technology so that it can develop a more effective information system'.[48] Fortunately, the help received by NDC from the Ford Foundation and the International Development Research Centre (IDRC), along with the dedication of its present director has enabled it to implement this recommendation. The national database project started in 1988 and was due for completion by 1991.

In addition to the major consultancies discussed previously there were a number of other specific purpose missions. By way of a summary of these, a checklist of all missions to the Sudan that could be traced is provided in Table 12.1. Its starting-point is J.S. Parker's 'Index to UNESCO consultants 1946–1982' which appeared in his Unesco and Library Development Planning as Appendix A.

Conclusions

After more than 20 LIS consultancy missions to the Sudan, spread over some 30 years, one can safely conclude that there were more failures than successes in their outcome.

J. S. Parker, from his wide exerience, assessed the results of consultancies in LIS up to 1978 and concluded that 'it seemed clear that more is required for successful library development than a mere production of a development plan, however detailed'.[49] This raises questions as to the relevance, usefulness and even the need for the consultancies in the first place.

By no means all LIS consultancies were worthwhile and relevant to the Sudan. There are valuable lessons to be learned from them, however because more often than not, they may have enhanced dependency, or worse may serve to transfer unrealistic and unworkable solutions to the country's problems. This view should not however be read as a biased judgement, or an argument against consultancy work. In view of the current state of LIS in the Sudan, consultancies will be urgently needed for the incorporation of appropriate systems and methods, drawn from elsewhere in the service of development. A pressing need at present is to develop clear guidelines for consultancy work in developing countries, to ensure the success of future consultancies in these countries and in particular, the Arab world.

Table 12.1 LIS consultants in the Sudan 1951–1986: a checklist

Consultant	Country of	Purpose of mission	Report	Duration	Dates	Sponsor
Nazir Ahmed	India	National Documentation Centre		1 year	1974/1975	Unesco
Anon	Unspecified	National Documentation Centre		—	1983	PADIS (OAU)
H.K. Asplund	Sweden	Cultural Centre & Library Buildings		—	1958	Unesco
Brown & Kelly	Ireland	Library & Information Development & Training		10 days	1977	Irish Gov.
J. C. Creasy	UK	Information Services		2 weeks	10–24/2/82	Unesco
J. A. Dagher	Lebanon	Educational Documentation Centre		5 months	8/1–8/5/67	Unesco
E. Dudley	UK	Establishing Library School		—	1979	IUC*
R. F. Eatwell	UK	University Libraries		—	May 1982	B.C.**
D. K. Lindley	UK	National Information System		2 weeks	15–30/6/86	Unesco
R. Munn	USA	University Library		20 days	1978	Ford F.
A. Neelameghan	India	Information Services		3 weeks	8/88	UNDP
R. Offor	UK	University Library		—	1951	IUC
J. S. Parker	UK	Library & Documentation Services		3 months	14/10/71–5/1/72	Unesco
T. S. Rajagopalan	India	Ministry of Foreign Affairs Documentation Centre		6 months	6/72–3/73	UNDP
M. Roper	UK	Archives Service		2 weeks	1988	Unesco
K. M. Saiful Islam	Unspecified	Abstracting & Indexing Services		—	1980	Unesco
K. Servomaa	Unspecified	Library Services		—	1972	—
P. H. Sewell	UK	Library Services		6 months	3/1/60–2/6/60	Unesco
P. H. Sewell	UK	Library & Information System		4 months	11/78–2/79	UNDP

* Inter-University Council
** British Council

In an attempt to formulate such criteria, IFLA's Standing Committee on Theory and Research Panel discussion at the IFLA general conference held in Manila (1980) developed a list of important factors to be considered for the success of consultancies in developing countries.[50] They were the outcome of discussion between experienced consultants in developing and developed countries, and they set out the essence of a wealth of practical experience in consultancy work, from the perspectives of both donors and recipients.

In the light of the results of past consultancies in the Sudan, we shall attempt to develop some criteria to be considered for the success of future consultancies in the Sudan and other parts of the Arab world. Criteria listed below are largely based on the Manila guidelines, which in our opinion are relevant and applicable:

(a) The consultant should have an adequate knowledge of the politics, culture, history, manners, customs, and preferably the language of the host country, in addition to a thorough knowledge of the role there of library services and their administrative problems.

(b) The consultant must also have good public relations skills to enable him to deal with high ranking officials in the host country, thereby winning their confidence. This can be crucial in implementing the consultant's recommendations because, as D. K. Berninghausen noted: 'the key to changing or developing an overseas library is not in the library. It is in the Prime Minister's or the General's office, the Ministry of Education, the office of the Rector or the Dean or the Faculty or other committee meetings'.[51]

(c) A clear definition of the problems and realistic expectations as to the goals and objectives of the project, before the consultant is chosen, may contribute positively to the success of consultancies. It will be useless to recommend a service which advocates for example, the use of the latest information technology in a country lacking the basic requirement. A prior agreement between the consultant and the host country on the objectives of the consultancy is therefore deemed necessary.

(d) Involvement of local librarians at all levels of activity, with emphasis on project continuation beyond the term of the consultant's tenure.

(e) There is a need for more contacts between the consultants and librarians and other information specialists in the host country, rather than concentrating too much on their meetings with government officials, however influential they may be in the final stages. As R. Adam observed:

> for these consultants it is enough to discuss with officials (never professional librarians) their reports which are often ambiguous and full of jargon and high technical phrases. The officials are not going to declare their ignorance before experts and in a party of nodding heads and shaking hands, projects are accepted and recommended for urgent implementation without being understood.[52]

This in a way explains why consultancy reports are full of praise for the 'overwhelming support and enthusiasm of government officials to the consultant's missions'. A sentiment that often has no foundation in action and may mislead a consultant to assume that the level of LIS in a given country is sufficiently developed to warrant recommending sophisticated and consequently unworkable systems.

(f) The need for multi- and interdisciplinary consultancy schemes should be stressed in future consultancies. Such an approach may be more productive and successful than those undertaken by specialist consultants, working alone.

(g) Consultants should participate in the implementation of the mission's recommendations. As is often the case in developing countries, governments seem to be more favourably disposed towards implementing recommendations from consultants funded by an aid agency than they are to the proposals from their own staff; especially if there is the prospect of more donor aid to implement them.[53] More use could be made, more economically of local consultants. The breadth of appropriate experience that has become available in developing countries during the last two decades must surely be a strong recommendation for using those who will be closely, and instinctively attuned to the needs and potentials of a given country.

(h) Aid agencies should take more active roles in the implementation of consultancy recommendations, rather than leaving this aspect of the outcome to the recipient countries. They should also be alert to co-ordinating consultancy missions, to avoid duplication of effort and to ensure follow-up reviews of recommendations. This is a very important step because, not infrequently different aid agencies send consultants to the same country for much the same purpose.

References

1   The use of the term 'international consultants' in this paper is favoured to the less comprehensive terms used in the literature such as 'foreign experts' or 'overseas consultants'.

2   Parker, J. S., 'The overseas library consultant', *Library review*, **28** (winter), 1979, 214.

3   Lockwood, J., 'Involving consultants in library change', *College and research libraries*, **38** (6), 1977, 498.

4   Webster, D. E. and Lorenz, J., 'Effective use of library consultants', *Library trends*, **28** (3), 1980, 346–7.

5   Dosa, M., 'The consultant as information intermediary'. *Information services and use*, **3**, 1983, 301.

6   Clow, D., 'Consultancy roles in library development', *International library review*, **16** (1) 1984, 9.

7   Ibid.

8   Parker, J. S., *Unesco and library development planning*, London, Library Association, 1985, 178.

9   Ibid., 398–408.

10   Inter-University Council, Chairman's report to the Council for the Academic Year 1976–77. Quoted in Harry Fairhurst, 'Twenty Eight Years: The Inter-University Council . . . '. In: *Middle East and libraries: a felicitation volume for J. D. Pearson*, ed. B. C. Bloomfield, London, Mansell, 1980, 35.

11   Offor, R, 'University libraries in the British Colonies and the Sudan', *Libri*, **5**, 1954, 55.

12   Offor, R., 'The development of university libraries in the British overseas territories', *Aslib proceedings*, **6**, 1954, 151.

13   —— 'University libraries in the British Colonies and the Sudan', op. cit., 56.

14   See references 11 and 12.

15   Sewell, P. H., 'The development of library services in Sudan', *Unesco bulletin for libraries*, **15**, 1961, 87.

16   'Summary report of the regional seminar on library development in Arabic speaking states', *Unesco bulletin for libraries*, **15** (2), 1961, 117.

17   Sewell, P. H., *Report and survey on library services in the Sudan 1960*, Paris, Unesco, 1963, 2.

18   —— 'The development of library services in Sudan', op. cit., 20–1.

19   —— Ibid., 17–18.

20   —— Ibid., 2.

21   Parker, J. S., *Unesco and library development planning*, op. cit., 181.

22   —— *Development of library and documentation services* - Democratic Republic of Sudan, Paris, Unesco, 1972, 30.

23   —— Ibid., 30.

24 —— Ibid., 30.
25 Parker, J.S., *Unesco and library development planning*, op. cit., 231.
26 —— *Development of library and documentation services – Democratic Republic of Sudan*, op. cit., 2.
27 —— Ibid., 31.
28 —— 'Library development in the Sudan', *Unesco bulletin for libraries*, **27** (2), 1973, 81.
29 —— Ibid., 89.
30 —— *Development of library and documentation services – Democratic Republic of Sudan*, op. cit., 48.
31 —— 'Library development in the Sudan', *Pakistan library bulletin*, **7** (3 & 4), 1975, 14.
32 —— *Unesco and library development planning*, op. cit., 234.
33 —— *Development of library and documentation services – Democratic Republic of Sudan*, op. cit., 17.
34 —— Ibid., 32.
35 Mamoun, I., 'Libraries and documentation service in the Sudan'. In: Sudan, *Libraries, documentation, Budapest*, FID, 1974, 31.
36 —— Ibid.
37 Parker, J. S., *Unesco and library development planning*, op. cit., 234–5.
38 Sewell, P. H., *A National information system for Sudan*, interim report 1978, 1 (unpublished).
39 —— *Developing an information system for the Sudan*, Paris, Unesco, 1979, 1.
40 —— 'The Co-ordination of library and information services in Sudan 1978-79', *Focus on international and comparative librarianship*, **10** (2), 1979, 16.
41 —— Ibid., 16.
42 —— *Developing an information system for the Sudan*, op. cit., 2, 3.
43 Dagher, J., Sudan, *Educational documentation*, Paris, Unesco, 1967, 2.
44 Rajagopalan, T., *Sudan: Documentation Centre of the Ministry of Foreign Affairs*, Paris, Unesco, 1973, 1.
45 —— Ibid., 37.
46 Munn, R. *The University of Gezira*, a planning report 1978, 1 (unpublished).
47 Lindley, D., *Developing a national environmental data and information system for the Sudan*, Paris, Unesco, 1988, ii.
48 —— Ibid., 8.
49 Parker, J. S., *Unesco and library development planning*, op. cit., 181.
50 For more details on these factors see: Dyer, E. and Layzell Ward, P., 'The International role of library consultants', *International library review*, **14** (2), 1982, 379-90.
51 D. K. Berninghausen. Quoted in Marta Dosa, 'The consultant as information intermediary', op. cit., 303.

52   Adam, R., *The role of Governments in planning and developing library and information services in the Sudan and the region of East Africa,* University College, London University, 1986, 442 (PhD Thesis).
53   Shimmon, R., 'Consultancies: on the receiving end', *Information development,* **2,** 1986, 6.

13 Library and information services in the Sudan

Cecile Wesley

The Sudan is the largest country in Africa and one of the poorest in the world. It has an area of 2.5 million sq. km., the size of Germany, France and Spain combined. Its eight neighbours are, clockwise from the east, Ethiopia, then Kenya, Uganda and Zaire to the south, Central African Republic and Chad to the West, and Libya and Egypt to the north. Since 1956, the year of independence, Sudan has witnessed three parliamentary and three military regimes.

There are a variety of ecological zones which range from desert in the north (approximately 30% of the land) to tropical forests in the south. The White and Blue Nile rivers link the country longitudinally, and form the oases around which the towns and villages are strung like beads on a thread. Almost a third of the population occupies less than 7% of the land, and about half live on 15%, mostly along the two rivers.[1]

The total population of 25,000,000 is growing at the rate of 3.1% – the third fastest in the world. Almost half the population is under 15 years of age. There are some 600 tribal groups, speaking 100 different languages. Arabic is the official language, and the most widely used in the country. The cultural and social heritage is Islam in the north, and indigenous African traditions in the south.

Sudan has experienced economic disaster in recent years, brought about by man-made and natural causes. These have included most notably the results of increasing desertification, drought, and famine (mostly between 1983 and 1987); influx of refugees from neighbouring countries (some 3% of aggregate population); civil war in the south; and critical shortage of foreign exchange income. Their implications have been colossal: raging inflation, deterioration of GDP and per capita income, and huge external debt.

Education and research
According to government statements, education is regarded as a

basic right of every citizen, and universal basic education as a national goal. In 1988–9 gross enrolment was nearly 49% of eligible population. It is estimated that 28% of the total population are literate.

The government's policy, consistently has been to discourage students from studying abroad, in order to conserve foreign currency reserves. Therefore a revolution in higher education is under way; intakes have increased tremendously, and several new universities have been established.

Scientific research, in the modern sense, dates from the early twentieth century. The Wellcome Tropical Laboratory was set up in 1922, to work mainly on the control of diseases and pests that affect humans, animals, and plants, and other institutions have extended the range of specialist research into improvement of crop quality as the century has progressed. The amounts allocated to research in the 1980s, equal to nearly US$20,000,000,[2] has diminished in real terms under the impact of devaluation and inflation. Consequently, with the expenditure of a much greater percentage of research funds on salaries each year, inadequate amounts are left to finance research.

Many research reports remain buried in the files of the administrators to whom they are delivered. Some studies and reports, especially those prepared for or commissioned by donors and UN agencies, are reproduced in only small numbers and are seldom accessible. A high percentage of scientific research papers is published outside the country. There is, in the Sudan, an absence of bibliographical aids and sales outlets by which to draw attention to the existence and distribution of published materials.

Communication

Efforts are under way to revive parts of the country's deteriorating infrastructure through large-scale aid projects.[3] Despite its size, the Sudan has only 16,000 km. of roads, of which 3,000 km. are paved. They run mostly between cash crop producing areas, the larger Nile towns, and Port Sudan. There are 4,800 km. of railways, which mostly duplicate existing road routes. Little use is made of the potential for cheap river transport.

As regards telecommunication, it is estimated that only about a third of telephones in the capital are operative. Telexes are frequently out of order, for various reasons, technical and financial, such as Sudan's periodic inability to settle international accounts because of lack of foreign exchange.

Parts of the country are served by electricity, the rural areas being the most deprived in this respect. Even in urban areas, the lack of maintenance of generating stations, and shortages of spare parts result in erratic power supply.

Libraries, documentation and information services
Library and information services, in the modern sense are new and still developing in Sudan. Scientific libraries were established in the first half of the twentieth century, with the establishment of higher education and research institutes. The library of the University of Khartoum, established in 1945 was the leading library until the early 1980s. Its budget in 1972 represented well over half of the total estimated expenditure of libraries in the Sudan.[4] The library is a depository for United Nations publications. With its four branches serving faculties of medicine, engineering, law, and agriculture and veterinary science, it continues to be the largest in the country, but remains, with one exception, traditional in its systems, little influenced by information technology.

With the proliferation of libraries and documentation centres, there are some outstanding examples of good practice and efficient service. Among these are the Agricultural Research Corporation, which is the focal point for AGRIS (the FAO Agricultural Information System); the Documentation and Information Department of the Industrial Research and Consultancy Centre, which is the focal point for INTIB (UNIDO International Technical Information Bank); the Documentation Department of the Commissioner for Refugees; Faculty of Medicine of the University of Khartoum; and Ahfad University College for Women.

The Committee for Sudan Archives was created in 1948. This developed and became the Central Records Office in 1965, and under a law of 1982 was designated the National Records Office, having a national council as its governing and policy-making body.

There is no national library, nor a current national bibliography or any general trade list of Sudanese publications. Least attention of all is given to public and school libraries.

Libraries exist in isolation. This situation perpetuates weaknesses such as the omission of certain subject areas, fragmentation of resources, inadequate service nationwide, and wasteful duplication of materials. Parker observed the uncoordinated state of library service in the 1970s, and little has changed up to the present. 'Libraries are not linked in any kind of administrative structure, and examples of wasteful duplication of effort and overlapping responsibilities are numerous'.[5]

Several attempts have been made to promote development and co-ordination of libraries at national level. In 1960, Sewell, a UNESCO consultant, recommended the establishment of a Central Libraries Board. In 1971 Parker, also acting as a UNESCO consultant, recommended the creation of a National Council for Library Development. Later still, in 1979 a third UNESCO mission, in collaboration with the National Documentation Centre, recommended[6] a co-ordinated library and information system, and the creation of a National Committee for Information Services, with four advisory committees to cover special libraries and scientific information, university and higher education, general libraries and archives services.[7] These and other consultancies are covered in more detail by A.S. Mustafa, in Chapter 12.

Although some of the consultants' recommendations were implemented in part, the interest and enthusiasm they created was not sustained in subsequent follow-up action. Several other attempts have been made, the latest being a presidential decree of June 1992, which convened a conference a month later, whose main objective was to draw up and propose the structure for a national information network. This was linked with the preparation of a national plan for statistical information, in anticipation of recommendations from a forthcoming Conference on National Strategy. This conference was to draw contributions from librarians, documentalists, information specialists, statisticians, and computer and telecommunications specialists, but had not, at the time of writing yet taken place. However, a further UNESCO consultancy took place in mid-1993, in the framework of the national information network and the recently established National Information Centre.

On the whole, the present state of library and information services shows that existing organizations and their resourcing are inadequate for the country's needs, specifically those of research, education, extension services, and economic and social development.

Libraries in the 1990s have fewer resources than 20 years earlier. At present, most have no funds to renew journal subscriptions, and for the past decade there have been only meagre funds for local book purchases.

Along with pressure on shrinking resources there seems to be little perception that timely and reliable information is a vital input, not only to planning and decision making, but to the development of a positive response to change, to research, and to practical know-how. Without such perception it is not surprising that library and information services generally receive low priority.[8]

Obstacles to development of libraries and the national information system

1 Serious shortage of funds. This problem is aggravated by the fact that the national treasury may be unable to release even the agreed and appropriated budgets when required. Foreign exchange is severely constrained, and a series of exchange rate crises and devaluations have dramatically decreased the budget's dollar value.

2 The brain drain of qualified and experienced manpower has now extended over two decades, thus making the recruitment and retention of qualified personnel one of the most serious difficulties facing libraries. In a manpower survey[9] carried out in 1985, the response to a question on the numbers of staff leaving the service during a 12-month period, was tabulated as: professionals, 40%, para-professionals, 13.5%, clerical, 23.5%, non-librarianship graduates, 11.75%, others (library attendants, binders), 11.75%. As a consequence of this trend, many libraries and documentation centres do not have a critical mass of human resources, while others have serious shortages at middle management level.

3 Lack of opportunities for continuing education and human resource development, such as exchange programmes, study tours, internship schemes, and twinning of programmes and services in selected centres with those in developed or other developing countries.

4 Libraries are not integrated in the educational and learning process. The education system depends on memorizing and is not oriented towards information seeking, information use, and information sharing.

5 Few people use a library regularly. Information is not sought and followed-up as a matter of everyday living, but more usually because of the need to pass an exam, or fulfil the requirements of a degree course. Even educated people, including university faculty and research workers, do not naturally engage in information seeking to acquire new knowledge or update themselves.

6 Lack of an information policy to guide the systematic development of the information sector, along with the absence of a national co-ordinating mechanism for the overall development of library and information services. There is no body that looks after, or offers assistance in the form of centralized services, financial aid or technical advice.

7 Lack of a unified personnel classification scheme in the library and information sector, to stipulate types and levels of

responsibilities, the necessary qualifications, salary ranges, and performance standards for each category.

8 The shifting interests of changing governments and the frequent changes of top officials, which bear greatly upon the understanding by government and its officials of libraries, and therefore the allocation of funds for their development.

9 The overlooking, by both professionals and funding agencies pursuing their own narrow interests, of the overall development of the national information system, when planning for the development of their sectional information units.

The Documentation and Information Centre
This, which was known originally as the National Documentation Centre, is a unit of the National Centre for Research (formerly National Council for Research). It was set up in 1974 with assistance from UNDP/UNESCO, and was maintained more recently by the Ford Foundation and the International Development Research Centre (IDRC). Its activities are:

1 Collecting, processing, and disseminating information on publications relating to Sudan, and on current research. In addition to following conventional procedures for acquiring local source materials, foreign located sources relevant to Sudan, and documents that exist as single copies elsewhere are copied in microform and added to the centre's Sudan Collection.

2 Several national databases have been created and are maintained, using CDS/ISIS. One is a bibliographic database; another is of ongoing research projects; another of specialists in environmental health and institutions working on environmental matters; and another a union list of serials.

3 Two publications are produced regularly using database contents. The *National register of current research* gives information on active research projects, research workers, research institutes and funding agencies. It also provides statistical analysis of information collected, including the percentage distribution of projects, by sector, field of activity, region, duration, and source of finance.[10] The second of these publications, *Sudan science abstracts*, which currently appears twice a year, abstracts and indexes studies, findings and journal articles relating to Sudan, which may originate anywhere in the world. Its coverage includes the pure, applied and social sciences, and economics. Publications abstracted are available for use in the Sudan Collection.

4 Information services offered are based on the library's resources, which include the national databases generated

there, and CD-ROM versions of MEDLINE, CABI, AGRI-COLA, AGRIS, TROPAG and RURAL, POPLINE, and ERIC.

5 Links with international and regional information networks. The centre is the Sudanese focal point of INFOTERRA (International Information System for the Environment), PADIS (Pan-African Development Information System), CEHANET (Centre for Environmental Health Activities Network), INIS (International Nuclear Information System) and UNISIST.

6 Contributing towards the development of a national information system. Activities towards this include surveys of special libraries, information centres, and databases; initiating conferences to promote awareness and use of information services, and conducting training courses on the use of CDS/ISIS and CD-ROM services.

Library education

The first organized training in librarianship was a six-week course given by Sewell in 1960, during his UNESCO consultancy. He also conducted a ten-day seminar for senior librarians.

At present, educational programmes in librarianship include certificate and middle diploma courses by the Extra-Mural Studies Institute of the University of Khartoum. The university's Centre for Information, Libraries and Archives has offered a postgraduate diploma course since 1987. BA degree programmes are offered by Omdurman Islamic University (started 1966), Ahlia College (1986), and most recently (1992) by El-Neelen University, which was formerly the Khartoum branch of Cairo University.

The curricula of most of these conform to traditional concepts and practices of librarianship. Teaching in the main depends heavily on part-time input from practising librarians. The main constraints on their development are:

1 Scarcity of qualified staff to teach courses in newly developing topics and practices.

2 Poor library collections and scarcity of publications and teaching materials in Arabic, especially in the field of information provision.

3 Non-availability of laboratory facilities for using book selection tools, reference publications, audiovisual aids and computers, all of which are essential for providing hands-on experience.

4 Poor state of development of the national information infrastructure, which both affects, and is affected by the inadequacy of education and training programmes.

Without doubt, the products of these educational programmes are old-fashioned professionals, narrowly occupied with cataloguing and classification of books, and giving little attention to information services that will attract attention to the merits of libraries. They continue to act as custodians rather than information providers. Much more imaginative effort will be needed to create educational programmes and service-oriented libraries that can realistically operate on continuing modest resources, yet try to set higher standards.

Future development
Major improvements are needed in the quality of library and information services. In order to improve those areas in need of attention it will be necessary to:

1 Strengthen the present information infrastructure with better financial, human, material, physical, and working resources, and increase their ability to provide the input needed for the country's development.
2 Develop an information conscious society with the support of an educational system that will teach citizens to seek and then use relevant information in furtherance of their respective tasks.
3 Create institutions such as information analysis centres, which will supplement bibliographic information by analysing, transforming, and providing appropriate information, in readily usable form to decision makers, planners, extension workers and thence the masses.
4 Learn and practise methods of transforming and disseminating technical information, and thus have a more direct impact on information transfer and its utilization.
5 Emphasize outreach rather than storage of information, and improve communication between those who need and those who provide it.[11]
6 Strengthen links between libraries, research, education, economic, and social sectors in order to improve the processes of information transfer and feedback.
7 Ensure relative financial and administrative autonomy of national information structures.
8 Propose and endorse legislation that will specify the mandate of the various components of the national information system.
9 Find ways and means of creating conditions to alleviate the constraints that hinder the development of the information sector.

Conclusion
It is a truism that the state and level of any country's develop-

ment influence the progress of its libraries. Equally so do these services contribute by their effectiveness to the nation's scientific, social, and economic development. International experience shows that the provision of relevant information in appropriate forms is important in accelerating human development. Therefore information specialists, by their vision, active interest, and ability, have the responsibility to demonstrate, and by result to convince policy makers and providers of finance that library and information services are major inputs for development.

References

1 Abu Shama Faisal Tag-el-din, 'Scientific research policies'. Paper presented at the First Scientific Conference, 25–28 January 1993, Khartoum, National Centre for Research, 1993, 1.

2 UNICEF, Sudan Country Office, *Children and women in the Sudan: situation analysis*, compiled by the UNICEF Sudan Country Office and the National Economic and Social Research Institute, Khartoum, UNICEF, 1990, 1–1.

3 Ibid., 1–6, 7.

4 Parker, J. S., 'Library development in the Sudan', *Unesco bulletin for libraries*, **27** (2), 1973, 80.

5 Parker, J. S., *Development of library and documentation services – Democratic Republic of Sudan*, Paris, Unesco, 1972, 18.

6 Sewell, P. H., *Developing an information system for the Sudan*, Paris: Unesco, 1979.

7 Wesley, Cecile, 'National information policies and networks in Morocco, Tunisia, Egypt and Sudan: a comparative study', *Alexandria*, **2** (3) 1990, 32.

8 Sewell, P. H., 'The Development of library and information services in Republic of Sudan in relation to international developments', by P.H. Sewell and Cecile Wesley. In: *Information consultants in action*; ed. J. S. Parker. London, Mansell, 1986, 249.

9 Wesley, Cecile, 'Library/information manpower survey in the Sudan'. In: *Librarianship and information studies: a handbook of teaching and learning materials, vol .2*; ed. L. Huttemann, Bonn, German Foundation for International Development, 1986, 75.

10 Wesley, Cecile, 'Information on current research in the Sudan', *Information development*, **1** (4) 1985, 217–22.

11 Wesley, Cecile, 'Appropriate information systems in under developed countries: the case of Sudan', by Cecile Wesley and Richard Weyers. International Symposium on the Future of Scientific, Technological and Industrial Information Services, Leningrad, 28–31 May 1990. (IAEA-SM–317/38)

14 The Assad National Library, Syria

Ghassan Al-Lahham

Libraries in Syria were formerly to be found only in schools, mosques, and the houses of some scholars and distinguished individuals whose interests lay in collecting books and manuscripts. The school and mosque libraries, which often contained rare and valuable manuscripts were made available for use by learned persons

During the nineteenth century, many collections were damaged or lost through various causes. For this reason, it was thought necessary to establish a public library where surviving manuscripts from different sources could be collected and preserved, and made available to the public. In 1880 a library was founded, housed in the school building of King Al-Zaher Bebers in Damascus. The collection quickly grew to some 2,165 manuscripts, transferred from the libraries of ten different schools.

When the Arab Academy was established in Damascus, in 1919, it was charged with the supervision of this library, by then named the Al-Zaherieh Library. The administrators of the academy placed great emphasis on increasing the collection of manuscripts, and also acquiring books. The collection numbered 2,465 manuscripts in 1919, and by 1945 the total of manuscripts and books was 22,389. It was regarded as the Syrian National Library during this period, because it was the largest library open to the public, but was, in fact more a conventional public than a national library, because there was no legal deposit of new publications. It also lacked the range of functions and services that are essential components of a national library's activities.

With the beginning of the independence era in 1946, the need for a modern national library was felt more strongly; the expansion of education, realization of the cultural heritage, and the growing output of national publishing houses, all helped to engender a feeling for the importance of collecting Syrian materials. There was, in addition increasing interest in collecting materials about development throughout the Arab world, and internationally.

The necessary formalities began with the establishment of the Ministry of Culture under Law no.197 of 1958. In 1968, the Ministry of Culture issued Decision no.52, which placed responsibility for establishing a National Library onto the Cultural Centres Directorate. However, lack of funds delayed implementation at that time.

By the early 1970s the project to build a National Library in Damascus had worked slowly through more bureaucratic procedures, with the issue of the Decision of the Prime Minister no.145 in 1972. This set up a committee whose function was to formulate specifications for the National Library, and to supervize construction of its building. The committee consulted UNESCO to determine the final specifications and then commissioned the International Federation of Architectural Engineers, in Paris to set up an international competition for the building design. An arbitration committee was convened to select from the projects that had been submitted, and the winner was J.-J. Maysner, a Polish architect.

The foundation stone of the library was laid in 1978 and construction was carried out, over a period of five years, by the Syrian Military House. Legislative Decree no.17 of 1983 , which was issued a few months before completion of the building, legally established the Assad National Library, defining its functions and administration. The library was officially inaugurated in November 1984.

Assad National Library

The Assad National Library is situated on the western side of Damascus, adjoining a large public square and surrounded by gardens. It covers 6,000 sq. m. and forms a natural extension to the gardens of the square, which front the building. Total floor area of the premises is 22,000 sq. m., distributed through nine floors, two of which are below ground level:

- Second basement: houses printing, stores, and maintenance workshops.
- First basement: on the same level as a side street, includes blind and handicapped services, receiving bay for delivery of publications and supplies, parking lot, employees' rest area, and certain offices.
- Ground floor: at main street level, it comprises two halls, separated by an exhibition area. One hall includes a lecture room used for symposia, film shows, and music recitals; the other houses administrative offices, and cloakrooms for readers.

- First floor: includes manuscripts, preservation section, documentation section and a small area for display of new books.
- Second floor: includes work areas for classification and cataloguing, and acquisitions; also public catalogues, a reading area for newly arrived periodicals, computing, cultural activities, and a buffet for use by readers.
- Third floor: has three reading rooms, an audiovisual room, information services, individual study carrels and a small seminar room.
- Fourth floor: has three readings rooms, documents photography, and manuscripts.
- Fifth and sixth floors: comprise the book stacks. These are placed at the top of the building because of the rivers that flow close to the site, and the effect they have on humidity in the basements. They have a limited capacity, because of the fairly restricted area of each floor, but future planned extension into the gardens could accommodate collections up to 5,000,000 volumes. Present stock amounts to around a quarter of a million items, housed in good atmospheric conditions.

Directorates and Sections
The library performs its functions through 11 directorates and sections:

1   *Acquisitions directorate*   Responsible for the selection of books, and for gifts and exchanges. It also administers the legal deposit of materials by Syrian publishing houses and authors.

2   *Classification and cataloguing directorate*   Responsible for the preparation of card catalogues and indexes. The following are maintained: catalogues under names of authors, titles, and subjects; indexes of publishers, and special catalogues of private libraries that are now part of the collections. They are maintained as card catalogues, according to traditional methods, but are in process of being entered in the library's computerized database. It is expected that computerized catalogues will be operative in 1996.

3   *Lending directorate*   Responsible for the movement of books between stacks and reading rooms; organizes the main reference materials in reading rooms; issues subscription cards to readers, and undertakes the annual inventory.

4   *Documentation and information directorate*   Prepares material for the library's publications: *Syrian national bibliography; Analytical index to Syrian newspapers and periodicals; List of dissertations*, and indexes of manuscripts housed in the library.

5 *Manuscripts directorate* Locates and acquires manuscripts through purchase, exchange or donation. Is responsible also for their documentation, and storage under suitable conditions. It co-operates with the Preservation Section to ensure effective conservation of these materials. The Directorate also co-ordinates the preparation of indexes of manuscripts by other libraries.

6 *Printing, preservation and photography directorate* Has four main sections:
   (a) *Document photography*
   Its function is to respond to requests for reprography, either photocopies or microforms, by readers or other libraries
   (b) *Preservation section*
   Is responsible for preservation of documents in the library, and to provide technical advice to private owners of manuscripts and other nationally important documents
   (c) *Printing section*
   Prints the library's publications
   (d) *Binding section*
   Binds books and journals in the library's collections

7 *Cultural activities directorate* Initiates and supervises the holding of symposia, lectures, music recitals, and exhibitions, in co-operation with outside cultural associations.

8 *Administration directorate* Oversees employees' affairs in accordance with prevailing terms of service. Also organizes library staff training courses, and compiles annual statistics of the directorates' and sections' activities.

9 *Finance directorate* Responsible for financial administration.

10 *Technical maintenance directorate* All maintenance of the building and equipment.

11 *Office of the Director General* Supervises activities that are not the sole responsibility of any of the above mentioned directorates and sections. It is currently initiating the library's databases; organizes the annual book fair held in the library; maintains a special archive of materials relating to President Hafez Assad, and an archival collection of library publications.

Library use
The library is open to users daily, from 8 a.m. to 8 p.m. There are some 650 reader places in the various reading rooms. Loans for reading outside are not permitted, and use of materials is confined to the library premises. Reader cards, on subscription, can be applied for by all who are over 18 years of age. A total of 102,000 readers used the library during 1992.

Each reading room is subject specialized, and materials on the specializations are available on open access in the appropriate reading areas. Other materials are available from stacks on request to reading room supervisors. The main movement of books is vertical, carried out in six book lifts. There are, on the third and fourth floors, employees whose task is to deliver books from lifts to reading rooms using small handcarts.

There are, in the catalogue section, staff advisors on catalogue use, as well as others who advise readers on information sources. Library users are guided between sections by prominent blue posters, which explain the sequence of sections and their purpose.

Personnel
The total number of personnel is 302, 14 of whom are specialists in librarianship. Eighty-five hold non-librarianship university degrees and received orientation for library work, by attending special training courses. There are 123 clerks, 33 professionals (technical cadre) and 47 service workers. In preparation for the opening of the library in 1984, staff who were to comprise its technical cadre attended a special, six-months' intensive training course in documentation, photography, preservation, and cataloguing. This was necessary because of the shortage of such specialisms among library personnel in Syria. The first school of librarianship opened the following year.

Library activities
1   Collect and document the Syrian cultural heritage, and make them available to research workers. These materials include books, periodicals, manuscripts, dissertations, written music; cultural, scientific and movie films; copies of selected plastic art works; complete sets of Syrian postage stamps and currency; also non-commercial posters. Implementation of legal deposit assists the collection of many of these items.
2   Selects and acquires important works published outside the country, especially in the Arab world. Apart from Arabic language materials, emphasis is placed on acquiring materials in English and French. Co-operation and exchanges assist in obtaining books from abroad, and also help to spread awareness of Syrian publications outside the country.
3   Symposia, lectures, music recitals, and film shows are organized in co-operation with local, and other nations' cultural organizations.
4   Training courses in documentation, preservation, photography, and general library management. These courses are

designed primarily for workers in the National Library, and open also to those in other libraries and government archives.

In addition to the above, occasional special courses are held for trainees from other Arab countries, coming under established cultural agreements.

5 Regular publications:

(a) *The Syrian national bibliography.* Compiled and published annually since 1984. There are also retrospective issues for Syrian publications prior to 1984.

(b) *Analytical index to Syrian periodicals and newspapers* A detailed guide to the contents of 70 periodicals and newspapers. Issued quarterly since 1985.

(c) *List of dissertations* Includes documentation about Masters and Doctoral degrees awarded in Syrian universities, or to Syrian students abroad. It is an occasional publication.

(d) Manuscripts index, records the library's holdings. A first volume was published in 1993.

(e) Arabic Book Fair index. Is a subject index of items displayed at the annual fair, which takes place at the library.

7 *Data bases* In 1990 the library compiled its first database, the Syrian Legislations database, which is a record of the country's legislation since 1918. Some government departments are linked in, thus extending availabilty of the service to lawyers, judges, and legal research workers. The library compiled a second database, of speeches by President Hafez Assad, in 1992.

Other databases in process of implementation at the time of writing include indexes to the collections; Arab publishers; Arabic periodicals and newspapers; Syrian information centres and libraries; Syrian men of intellect, art, and managers (by specialization). The library connects to major international databases, as part of its service to research. More economically, the introduction of selected CD-ROM databases has widened the scope for personal research based on microcomputers.

15 Infrastructure of information and libraries in Tunisia

Souheil Houissa

Tunisia, a country of North Africa in the east of the Maghreb, is bounded by a coast of 1,300 km on the Mediterranean Sea, north and east, on the south by Libya, and on the west by Algeria. It covers an area of 164,150 km², with a population estimated in 1990 at 8,095,000 of whom 61% are urban dwellers, and some 60% are under the age of 25. The climate is warm temperate in the north, hot and dry in the desert south.

Islam is the religion, but there are small communities of Jews and Christians, in which Roman Catholics, the Greek Church, French Protestants and the Church of England are represented. The official language is Arabic, and French is widely used. Education is free at all levels, and illiteracy among those under the age of 35 is between 10 and 15%.

History of libraries

Before the coming of Islam, Tunisia had been the seat of several cultures. Carthage, the capital of the Phoenician colony was famous, not only as a commercial centre; the Carthaginians engaged in intellectual activities, and one of their libraries, the Senate Library was praised in the *Florida* of Apuleius in the second century BC. The Roman conquerors also founded libraries, such as that at Timgad, in the west of their North African province.[2]

There was an active intellectual life during the early Islamic era, especially in the Aghlabide period. The first known library of Tunisia was in the great mosque of Kairouan. It contained works on parchment in the fields of religion, linguistics, and literature, and numerous copies of the Qur'ān. The library was sacked by the Hilalian Bedouins in 1057.

A bibliophile Emir, Ibrahim II, founded the academy and library of Beit-el-Hikma (House of Knowledge) at Rakkada in 878. The library was furnished with carved wooden cabinets, and students and scholars sat on carpets and cushions to consult works written by scribes on parchment. The collections included translations from Greek, Persian, and Latin. Knowledge was disseminated from this library by means of translations into Latin of Arabic works on science, philosophy, and medicine. Al Muliz, of the Fatimide dynasty further enriched the library with versions of the Qur'ān, philosophical and literary works, and maps on silk, embroidered with gold thread.

The Zeituna mosque, as the first university in Africa had a library, founded in the eighth century. This, the Abdellia library was a great public library that served teachers and students. It was pillaged by the army of Charles V of Spain in the sixteenth century.[3]

During the Beylical era, 1574–1881 there were the outstanding Ahmadia and Sadikia libraries, the former included rich collections gathered from various countries by Ahmed Bey, Khaznadar, and the minister historian Ibn Abi-Dhiaf.

During the nineteenth century, the minister Kheireddine founded several establishments of higher education with affiliated libraries, such as the Military Academy of Bardo, in 1838, which contained works in Turkish, French, and Arabic.

Surviving parts, which are considerable, of these collections are now housed in the National Library of Tunisia.

Following the French occupation in 1881, garrison libraries began to be implemented. These 'institutions of instruction and studies' were considered as vital and 'a duty for the Republic'.[4] By 1905 there were 203 military libraries in metropolitan France, Algeria, and Tunisia.

The 'French Library' was established in 1885 and contained works by European writers on geography, history, ancient Africa, and Tunisia. In 1910 it became the 'popular library of Tunis', and later in the century became part of the foundation collection of the National Library.

Some outstanding foreign libraries were set up. That of the Institut des Belles Lettres Arabes (IBLA), of the White Fathers Catholic missionary society dates from 1937, and has a collection of 22,000 volumes in several languages. Others of note are the British Council (1943) and the American Cultural Centre (1948).

Information infrastructure
Several approaches have been suggested as methods for establishing the feasibility of safe and successful transfer of technology to less-developed countries. Two studies have been made to date which use an evaluation of one of these approaches to a case study of Tunisia.

The indicators approach
Hasni[5] used microeconomic indicators to assess information related activities in Tunisia. She utilized 195 indicators from the Information Utilization Potential (IUP) project of Borko and Menou, which was subsequently reviewed and published.[6] They were examined in terms of their availability, accuracy, reliability and international compatibility. Because the statistical data was neither complete nor current, the indicators seem to be indicative but are not positive. She concluded that the IUP measures were compatible with other information measures, and likely to generate a successful and comprehensible multi-informational system.

The systems approach
Kuesters-Schah[7] used the systems analysis approach of Eres[8] in assessing factors that inhibit information technology transfer to developing countries, based on the case of a small agricultural library in Tunisia. The approach proposed six general factors in which conditions in developing countries are checked. First, the economic factor, including labour intensity, capital availability, recurring costs absorption, and expenses of information technology (IT). Second, the manpower factor, its availability, the quality and prestige of trained personnel, their problems and experience of team work. The psychological element includes limitation of resources, geographical situation, cultural, demographic and social factors, unemployment, language barriers, and acceptance of new technology. Finally, the political factor. This comprises stability of government, administrative constraints, centralization of decision makers, and impact of scientific research and development at the highest level of government.

Kuesters-Schah studied the existing information infrastructure and identified the quality of telephone service as a potential, there being in 1987 one telephone for every 24 people. The network is cable connected to Marseilles in France. In broadcasting, there were 1,693,527 radios (1:4.7 persons) in 1988 and one TV for every 15 people.

She found a generally positive picture and concluded that 'What is needed to encourage success is the means to promote and implement what is planned.'

Linguistic background
Tunisians learn Arabic and French at primary school and start English or another third language at college. At university level, there are special departments for different languages. However, French is still the major language, especially in teaching sciences,

technology and economics. Experimental pilot English language teaching of science in selected secondary schools, with a view to getting higher education in English speaking countries has been abandoned, because of the difficulties experienced in getting sponsorship for candidates to take up places abroad.

Tunisian National Radio and Television, and the four regional radio stations broadcast in Arabic. Its international channel broadcasts in French , and also carries Italian, Spanish, and English programmes. Most TV sets in the country can pick up France 2 TV programmes, but its news broadcasts are not included. Instead, the French language version of Tunisia's official news is presented. Some French documentaries are liable also to be censored.

Satellite dishes have spread rapidly in recent years, but have not had much impact on people's linguistic abilities. They merely have access to additional French channels. The French Canal Horizons has set up a Tunisian branch. Apart from the special subscription for decoder programmes, it has an open period of largely Arabic broadcasts. There is no news, and most items are films, sports, or music.

Although Tunisians regard English as important and useful, French is still the dominant language in schools, administration, and the media, and remains in competition with the national language.

Information technology

National Centre of Informatics (CNI)

A National Commission of Information Technology was established in 1974. Its objectives were the promotion of information technology and related fields, telecommunications, their legal aspects, and introduction of these media into administration, industry, and public establishments.

The CNI (Centre National de l'Informatique) was founded in 1976. Its function since then has been to serve as a secretariat to the commission. Purchases of IT materials have to be scrutinized by the centre to ensure better co-ordination and control of expenditure and supplies. The CNI mainframe computer is the host of databases of government departments and other companies. Its specialist staff offer services in systems analysis and design programming, staff development, and training in IT.

Education and training for IT

According to a forecast of 1991, Tunisia currently needs 2,680 information specialists and technicians. There are several institutions responsible for education and training. The University of Science, Technology and Medicine (Tunis II) has a school of computer engineering, a department of computer science in the Faculty of Science, and the El-Khawarizmi computer centre. These, between them offer a range of computing courses. In addition, many private institutes offer courses in programming, systems analysis and data processing; while computing is entering into the syllabus for secondary education.

Computer applications in Tunisia
In terms of production, there are numerous active computer applications, especially in the fields of economics and administration:

- Databases of national centres of specialized information
- Database of standards and industrial property
- Management of the Customs
- Civil service personnel management
- Court management (Ministry of Justice)
- Tunis-Air reservation system
- Invoicing (National Electricity and Gas Company)
- Accounts management (banks, post office)

A number of projects in the 7th national development plan (1987–91) have been achieved, such as the land use database of the Ministry of the Interior; database of research and other activities of Tunisian experts and university research workers; statistics, administration of production units and teaching in agriculture.

The market for computer sales is growing noticeably, with 83% of sales being new equipment. There are 300 importers of hardware and software products from the United States, France, the United Kingdom, Germany, and Italy. Tunisia does not assemble IT equipment.

International activities
Tunisia is a member of the International Bureau of Informatics (II) in Rome. The National Library and several other institutions are members of IFLA, and thus from time to time, supply members to serve on the organising committees of sections and divisions. The special committees of the National Institute of Standardization are involved in the preparation of standards in documentation, information and micrography. They represent the country on ISO (international), ORAN (African), and ASMO (Arab).[9] The

National Library is the national co-ordinating centre for ISSN and ISBN, and the National Information Centre for Agriculture (CNDA) is a national centre of AGRIS, the leading worldwide agricultural information system.

Regional Institute of Informatics Sciences and Telecommunications (IRSIT)
IRSIT (Institut Régional des Sciences Informatiques et des Télécommunications) was founded in 1986, and operates under the supervision of the state secretariat for scientific research. It is becoming active in the Arab/African region through conventions with governments, and is linked to the rest of the world via the European Academic Research Network. Its objectives are:

1 To encourage projects, and their implementation, for computerized systems in government institutions.
2 To develop standards for new materials, new programming and retrieval languages, and promote Arabized information products.
3 To promote the information technology industry.
4 To supervize the selection and collection of information for special databases, and their diffusion via networks.
5 To organize meetings, conferences, exhibitions, and exchange of specialists and technicians in IT and telecommunications.
6 To assure post-university education, and to work for the development of fundamental and applied research in the fields of IT.
7 To undertake initiatives for international co-operation and responsibility by Africa and the Arab world.

Arab League Educational, Cultural and Scientific Organization (ALECSO)
Tunisia has been a member of ALECSO since 1975 and has been its base since 1980. Co-operation between the two has produced significant results in construction of Arabic databases, notably the statistical SAEB and financial SAFA, within the frame of ALECSO's FARABI system. The National Library contributes to the elaboration of the computerized *Arab bulletin of publications*, a union catalogue of the publications of 21 Arab countries.

Arab League Documentation and Information Centre (ALDOC)
ALDOC was created in 1979 in Tunis, and moved to Cairo in 1991. It is the most sophisticated information centre in the Arab world, completely automated and a pilot and training centre for

Arab professionals. It was responsible for Arabising the programming language MINISIS. CNDA co-operated in the unification of Arab standards of information and informatics with ASMO, which is the equivalent for ASCII for the Arab countries. Tests of multiscript data processing have been conducted on keyboards and terminals, to verify conformity of the unified Arab standards. ALDOC also generated ALIT, a statistical database, and ARIS-NET, which were promoted by the United Nations Development Programme.

The Tunisian information system

National Committee for Documentation (CND)
CND was created in 1977 as a response to UNESCO's recommendations at the intergovernmental conference on national documentation, library and archives infrastructures. The committee's remit has been to prepare the general policy for documentation, to arrange co-ordination between documentation units, and to contribute towards developing international co-operation. A higher council was proposed in order to direct the broad outline of Tunisian information policy. There was to be a structure of co-ordination by which to implement the national information system, with sectional committees to develop documentation. The main objectives of the national committee are to achieve national coverage by sectional information, adherence to standards, and specifications on the use of advanced technology. Twelve sectors were planned: health, agriculture, education, economics and finance, industry and technology, administration, law, communications, culture, defence, the National Library, and the governmental National Archives. The last two already existed, and most other sectors were partially covered. The most important are the National Documentation Centre (CDN, Centre de Documentation Nationale); the National Centre of Agricultural Documentation (CNDA, Centre National de Documentation Agricole), and the National University Centre for Scientific and Technical Documentation (CNUDST, Centre National Universitaire de Documentation Scientifique et Technique).

National Documentation Centre (CDN)
CDN was created in 1957 and is the first and oldest documentation unit of the Ministry of Information. Its main duty is to collect all documents relating to Tunisia, wherever they originate. The centre covers the sector of information and communications, and is responsible for the selection, acquisition, utilization and dis-

semination of national and international documents relating to political, economic, social and cultural matters. With the backing of UNESCO, the centre has been automated. TANIT (Traitement Automatisé National de l'Automation Tunisienne), is a data bank made up from three existing databases:

1 TANIT-CHRONO; Tunisian incidents since 1964. 25,000 documents had been handled in the first stage in 1984.
2 TANIT-POLECO; political and economic. Textual database of the speeches of the president and prime minister, and cabinet reports.
3 TANIT-BIBLIO; bibliographic database of the book and periodical collections of CDN.

A local thesaurus, TUNIS (Thesaurus Usuel National Informatisé et Selectionné) has also been constructed.

Ghannouchi[10] described some problems in the centre's experience of automation. Apart from lack of financial support and specialist staff, translation into Arabic and poor communication between librarians and specialists led to the failure of some systems. She believed that 'the systems designer should be a member of the library staff and aware of the different systems' capabilities'.

CDN uses the CNI Mistral mainframe to store its large databases, using magnetic tapes for back-up and transfer, and a dedicated telephone line for communication. In spite of their importance, the databases are not fully exploited by users.

National Centre for Agricultural Documentation (CNDA)
CNDA was established in 1975 by the Ministry of Agriculture, with financial and technical support from UNDP and FAO. It has launched two databases:

1 TUNAGRI; retrospective database of 20,000 documents dating back to the nineteenth century.
2 CARIST; current agricultural research.

About 80,000 known agricultural documents are to be sorted, at present at the rate of 11,000 each year, but more human and financial resources are need to accomplish this large and increasing quantity of material.

CNDA's main mission is the collection and treatment of all current and retrospective agricultural documents, but it also performs other tasks. The JORTAGRI database of agricultural legislation, other databases related to the offices, credits, property affairs, and 18,000 ministry personnel occupy considerable resources of personnel and time. Abdeljaoued wondered whether these extra jobs were the cause of CNDA's problems, in that they undermine the performance of the project. Although the service they provide may justify the centre's existence in the eyes of authority, it implies also that no recognition is given to the importance of the main task.[11]

Centre National Universitaire de Documentation Scientifique et Technique (CNUDST)
Founded in August 1980 CNUDST offers online services via the French vendor Questel Databases. It has also created Tunisian databases:

1   TUNIDOC; Tunisian non-serial documents since 1973.
2   ARCHIVE; archival documents from the nineteenth century.
3   EXPERT; details of Tunisian university specialists.

The centre also collects copies of Tunisian documents from outside the country, located by on-line searches.

In 1981 a UNESCO consultant, G. Thirion examined university libraries and the role that CNUDST should have in their development. He proposed that it should act as a central university library (CUL). Its objectives, as described in the law that set it up are acquisitions, communication, interlibrary loans, a national co-operative acquisition programme, and a union catalogue of academic library holdings.

Co-operation remains the most fundamental activity for the role of a Central University Library. Its organising committee should comprise representatives drawn from CNUDST and university libraries. Thirion's report set out a detailed programme for the services and objectives of CUL, but apart from certain co-ordinating of university library practices, it has merely developed closely along the lines of established academic libraries. It is therefore, a newer library, better equipped and staffed than others, but has not taken the central role that was required by its establishing law. Tasks are being wastefully duplicated between libraries and there has been mounting dissatisfaction with its service, and therefore with CNUDST to the community of academic libraries.

Present infrastructure of libraries
There are a variety of libraries throughout the country. The oldest and largest, such as the National Library, university libraries, and specialized information units are in the capital. There is also a

nationwide network of regional and public libraries, and a number of school libraries.

The National Library

Its official name is Dar al-kutub al-wataniya (National House of Books), but it is usually known as the National Library. Since 1910 it has been based in the souk El-Attarin, the perfumers' market. Its origins lay in the French Library, started in 1885, when collecting proceeded spasmodically, mostly from private donations such as the library of Charles Tisot, a former French consul in Tunis. The library has been regarded as the national collection since 1910, and its functions and organization were confirmed by law in 1967. It had long operated as a public library and this function was discontinued only in 1974, when its responsibility as the public reading office (Direction de la Lecture Publique, DLP) ceased.[12]

The library has the richest collection of any in the country. It grew from 240,000 items in 1955 to reach 345,000 in 1970. The additional materials were largely Arabic works and manuscripts acquired from 1965 onwards, especially from the mosque of Kairawan. The latest estimated total available is 830,000 (1985), including 25,000 manuscripts and about 200,000 volumes of current and discontinued periodicals.

The library is responsible for copyright collection of all printed or published documents of any type in Tunisia. Commercial publications under copyright deposit date from 1956, and official publications from 1976. It also receives donations from foreign embassies, international organizations, and other national institutions located in the country. There are three main departments: manuscripts, periodicals, and printed materials.

Budget is well below the real needs of a national library. At TND193,000[13] of which an average of TND80,000 can be spared for acquisitions, it compares sadly with the Faculty of Arts and Humanities of Tunis University, which has TND150,000 for book acquisition.

Personnel totalled 28 in 1970 and 180 in 1985. Apart from 78 domestic workers, only 46 of the remaining 102 are professionally qualified. Consequently the library cannot meet its obligations to provide the range of services that it should.

The *Tunisian national bibliography* has been published three times a year, accumulated annually, since 1976. It lists new items received on deposit, and includes university theses and periodical titles, in addition to monographs from commercial and government sources. The library also compiles special subject bibliographies.

The library uses ISBD(M) and ISBD(S) entry rules, and is one of the few functioning African national centres of the International Serials Data System. It is also the national bibliographic agency of Universal Bibliographic Control. Approximately 25,000 users were recorded in 1986, of whom 30% were academics. 40,000 documents were consulted, of which 40% were in literature and linguistics.

The library's premises, in three separate buildings amount to 2,280 sq. m. They are crammed to capacity with the stock of more than 800,000 items. These are unacceptable service conditions, and the situation does not permit it to play its proper role as the leading library of research and study, or even to conserve the nation's heritage effectively. A new building was funded in 1984, but is not yet ready. Automation of its catalogues would help with some of the current problems. Automation was recommended in 1977, in the UNESCO mission of Jeffreys,[14] but has not been taken up. It is hoped that the Maghrebine information database, which is in process of implementation in 1993 will become functional. It will have a starting-point of 40,000 records and will bring together and unify varying original catalogue entries written or typed in different calligraphic styles.

Public libraries

Since independence, and following the promotion of education, the number of public libraries has increased, from 9 libraries in 1962 to 261 units (including 21 mobile libraries) in 1993. A unit can include a branch for adults and young people and another for children. This network of libraries is managed by the DLP (Direction de la Lecture Publique) of the Ministry of Culture. Total reader places are 16,161 throughout, which averages at one for every 509 of the population. No region has reached the required minimum standard of one seat to every hundred people.

There is a great shortage of books in public libraries, which can offer only one for every three of population. Few books are bought and distributed by the DLP, and others are acquired mostly by gift. The overall total of collections is recorded as approximately 2,492,957. Of these, 1,865,336 are in Arabic and 627,621 in French and other languages. Literature is the most represented subject with 58% of the total; science and technology have 7% and the remaining 35% for the humanities. Most library operations, such as acquisitions and cataloguing are performed by the central services of DLP.[15]

Few qualified librarians work in public libraries. There are 130 professionals (3 senior librarians, 32 librarians, 82 assistant librarians, and 13 library assistants), and the remaining 460 staff have no library education or training.

Students and school pupils are the majority of users. Most of them use libraries as a place to study rather than to use the collections.

School libraries

More than 96% of Tunisian children go to school at the age of six. There are 1,500,000 pupils attending school throughout the country, of whom about 250,000 are in secondary schools. However, only 199 secondary schools have libraries. Statistics record a total stock in the system of 1,036,000 items, of which 377,000 are considered to be for personal reading, and the rest are manuals and novels required for the curricula. Two-thirds of the novels are in Arabic, the remainder in French. Many libraries have a small collection of slides, cards to illustrate geography, history, and biology, and recordings of speeches by the president. Most of the periodicals are the official daily newspapers, acquired at a cost of TND200 a year, out of an average budget of TND670. There are few scientific periodicals out of the total of 28 titles recorded.

Collections are usually kept in a separate room with an average area of 90 sq. m., but seating areas occupy between 10 and 20 sq. m., and provide between 15 and 30 reader places.[16]

School libraries provide textbooks to poor pupils, and sufficient copies of required novels for reading comprehension classes. Loan is permitted for final year students, teachers, and school officials. Libraries usually open for 37 hours a week, according to the hours observed by the administration.

Management of school libraries is performed by 203 members of school staffs, of whom only eight have received any professional training, while a few others have had some short practical training. However, these libraries mostly predate the establishment of public libraries, and have played their part in the encouragement of reading and learning.

Since the establishment of the Ministry of Culture in 1962, school and university libraries have remained under the control of the Ministry of Education. This caused organizational problems and has delayed the setting up of a rational library infrastructure. 'There are almost no school libraries' states a work paper of a National Library seminar on UAP in Tunisia.[17]

Library education and training

Library education began in 1964, but progressed slowly. The Institut Ali Bach Hamba was the first to offer training courses, with financial help and input from the Friedrich Neumann Foundation. Six training sessions, each lasting six months were conducted between 1966 and 1971. An international team of lecturers from the Netherlands, Belgium, France and Germany delivered the courses, under the auspices of FID. The students, who were mostly from the French-speaking countries of Africa, were already working in the information sector. Scholarships were paid in part by UNESCO, governments and the foundation. Certificates were delivered to successful students after final examinations. Elsewhere, two groups of library assistants and clerical secretaries benefited from programmes offered by the National Library.

In 1977, training was transferred to the Ecole Nationale d'Administration (ENA), the school responsible for training administrative staff of government departments. The Friedrich Neumann Foundation continued the finance and recruitment of foreign lecturers, whose numbers reduced by two-thirds after the return of Tunisian professionals from training abroad.

Library education moved again in 1979, to IPSI, and for the first time came under the jurisdiction of the Ministry of Education. In following the recommendations of Vaughan, another UNESCO consultant, reforms were achieved.[18] The existing four-year programme was replaced by one of two years for entrants who passed an entrance exam, and then proceeded to a two-year bachelor's degree course. A postgraduate programme, introduced in 1985 was cancelled a few years later. It had attracted 100 students a year, but was totally reliant for teaching on 24 professional librarians who lectured part time.

The Institut Supérieur de Documentation (ISD) was started in 1981 to provide an undergraduate programme. By 1985 it had 150 students and only one full-time lecturer out of a total of ten. This has improved up to the present, when there are ten full-time lecturers, and a number of part-timers who provide needed specialisms.

In 1990, ISD took full responsibility for training librarians, archivists, and documentalists. Some reforms have been implemented, and final year options added to meet the needs of employers. However, many of its graduates no longer work in the field of information provision. At the time of writing surveys are being made to draw recommendations for better performance in library education.[19]

Library automation courses
Instruction in automation began at the Institut Ali Bach Hamba.

ENA later taught a two-year course in automated documentation. At IPSI a two-year programme, which still runs has not become sufficiently established to help students cope with new technologies. There is a pressing need for more time for IT courses, free of unnecessary theoretical detail, with emphasis on practical work, visits, and hands-on training. The librarian or the information specialist as a packager and agent of transfer of information, should be trained accordingly to realize this role. Reforms have been suggested to introduce computer applications in libraries through courses on the application of technology to routine methods.[20]

University libraries

It is, of course, the purpose of university libraries to provide extensive and extended service to their academic communities. However, they need the financial, human and technical means to achieve this, working co-operatively with their peer institutions across the country in order to maximize the pool of resources they all hold. Are Tunisian university libraries ready to play their role in terms of structural organization, leadership, personnel, funds, and techniques?

The sole modern university, founded in 1957, replaced the former French Institute of Higher Studies of Tunis, which had been founded in 1878. After the unification programme of general education and Zeituna education, it became the Faculty of Theology. The university extended from the 1960s into many institutions and faculties of a variety of disciplines throughout the country. In 1986 it was divided into three universities, North (Tunis), Centre and South, and in 1988 the North University was reformed into four distinct universities; Tunis I (arts and humanities), Tunis II (science, technology and medicine), Tunis III (law, economics and management), and Zeituna University (Islamic studies). There are no central libraries but each institute or department has its own library. They are administered as a department under the control of an administrative officer. Overall supervision of many of these institutions is shared by other ministries such as health, agriculture, culture, communications, and so on.

Present state of university libraries

As the university sector has developed, the number of students has increased more than three times in 15 years, from 20,500 in 1975 to over 63,000 in 1992. The total of full-time teaching staff rose to almost 4,000 in the same period.[21] Unfortunately the libraries were not allocated the means or opportunities to cope with such growth.

University libraries have not previously been mentioned in legislation, apart from general phrases about purchase of books and periodicals, or charging subscription fees. A new law of 1989, on university organization stated clearly that each university should have its central library, or a department of library services to control and co-ordinate institutional libraries. However, neither has been implemented so far, and libraries remain without any autonomy, and reliant on their host institution for all financial allocation and organization of administration.

Until 1977, the purchase of books was included in the institutional funds for stationery. This placed the library at the end of the queue. Fortunately this has been changed in subsequent legislation, but the mentality and behaviour of administrators remain unaltered.[22] Funds that are nominally reserved for book purchase are often raided when other monies run out.

Expenditure on libraries is contained in the amounts provided by government to institutions of higher education and research. In 1992, out of a total library allocation of TND4,276,000, TND1,376,000 were spent on book acquisitions, TND839,000 on periodicals, and TND61,000 for binding and stationery. This was a 40% increase over two years, and represents 12.6% of the whole institutional budget. It does show that some effort is being made to improve the state of university libraries, but there is a tremendous leeway to make up. This improved budget does not yet meet the needs of the increase in users by two-thirds in a decade and a half, or with the high rate of price inflation (225% over a ten-year period), which set back collection development so disastrously. 65% of the acquisitions budget was spent on the arts, law and social sciences. Technology and science received 25%, and 10% went to medicine and pharmacy. Supply of books from abroad, even for those in Arabic is very slow. Orders for English books usually take 18 months to be supplied, and even French publications take eight months to arrive.

The position of university librarian is regarded as optional and complimentary. Libraries do not recruit their own staff; recruitment and payment are handled centrally by the ministry, according to vacancies and the availability of finance.

Statistics show a low number of professionals working in these libraries. Some have no qualified personnel at all. Thirion[23] commented that: 'This limitation is very dangerous and explains, to a high extent, the difficulties of Tunisian university libraries.'

There are 412 members of staff in 42 university libraries (421 in 1990); 4 senior librarians and 11 librarians have left for a better situation. Ninety professionals (20%) have had a library education of at least one year's duration. This is an improvement on the 1980s when the figures were 14% in 1984 and 16% in 1986. The continuing turn over of professional staff is attributable to typical government salary scales, which cause librarians to seek better opportunities as library school lecturers, working in industry and business, or in the Gulf states.

There are no library committees, nor any co-operation between libraries to control and define acquisition policies, and thus try to avoid wasteful duplication through unawareness of collection development elsewhere. The position of acquisitions librarian is not commonly designated.

When selection of items has been decided upon, ordering is not a simple task. Librarians are usually obliged to find a supplier who offers good payment facilities under the financial limitations that prevail. Working in such a manner a library cannot meet the users' real needs for speedy supply of the most appropriate materials. Ordering by a local supplier is slow and delays delivery, but must continue as long as Central Bank licenses for currency transfer remain difficult to obtain.[24] UNESCO vouchers are the best way around these problems, but are difficult to obtain in the large amounts that librarians would like to have.

Open access to the contents of libraries is not usually granted to all users. The classification is sometimes non-standard and in-house, but some libraries use UDC or DDC, and 25% have subject catalogues. Effective serials control is unusual.

Use of university libraries has increased 8% in two years; 95% of users are undergraduates. The larger libraries have special-use rooms (periodicals, theses, reference) where access may be restricted to final year students, postgraduates, research workers and lecturers. Loans are usually restricted to lecturers, but some libraries allow students to borrow on payment of a refundable deposit.

Conclusions

Tunisia is neither very rich nor remarkably poor. It has a reasonable information and communication infrastructure, able to back-up technology transfer. Despite a high rate of expenditure on education, libraries are still seen as low priority, and have no effective financial support. Shortage of books, especially in science and technology is a continuing barrier to the country's development. Librarians have yet to attain recognition and social status. When comparing themselves to other professionals they feel necessary, yet despised at the same time. Therefore the profession does not attract young professionals, or students in their choice of career or field of study. This state of affairs has a considerable impact on quality of service, because of the quite small proportion of qualified staff in most libraries. Availability of funds is important for the success of any institution, but other factors cannot be ignored. Rational and careful management, along with sensible planning based on consultancy may improve the overall situation. Decision makers must become more thoroughly convinced of the primary importance of libraries in the development process.

A comparison with the experience of other developing countries[25] shows that the state of libraries in Tunisia is not especially critical. However, reforms should be considered with the aim of promoting libraries and librarianship. Librarians deserve more equal opportunities, comparable with other professionals, so that they may do better, professionally and personally. With such motivation and encouragement, more professionals will enter the service. It is widely expected that wider application of automation would improve the position. Equally, co-operation with other Arab and African countries is vital. This will be a large part of the process of generating solutions on a regional scale, and thus move towards the concept of appropriate librarianship practices. Cross-continental exchange of experience may be the most suitable approach for Tunisia to take its place in the international community of proactive libraries and information providers.

References

1   *Statesman's year-book . . . 1991–1992*, London, Macmillan, 1991, 1205.
2   Abid, Abdelaziz, 'Libraries in Tunisia'. In: *Encyclopedia of library and information science*, vol. 31, 204.
3   Ibid, 206.
4   Turlan, Patrick, 'Les Bibliothèques militaires'. In: *L'Histoire des bibliothèques françaises: les bibliothèques de la révolution du xix ième siècle: 1789–1914*, Promodis, Cercle de la Librairie, 1991, 408.
5   Hasni, Najia, *The Indicators to information activity: the IUP in Tunisia*, City University, London, 1982, 100p. (MSc thesis).
6   Borko, H., *Index of Information Utilisation Potential (IUP): final report . . . by H. Borko and M. Menou*, Paris, Unesco, 1983. 200pp.
7   Kuesters-Schah, Ursula, *Determination of the potential effectiveness of the automation of library services*, University College of Wales, Aberystwyth, 1991, 138 (MPhil dissertation).
8   Eres, Beth-Krevitt, 'Transfer of information technology to less developed countries: a systems approach', *Journal of the American Society for Information Science*, **32**, 1981, 99.
9   Hadhri, K., 'La Documentation et la normalisation en Tunisie',

Revue maghrebine de documentation, **3** (Mars) 1984, 110; and 'Arab standard specifications in documentation and data processing', *Arab magazine of information science: special issue*, **8** (2) 1987.

10 Ghannouchi, Latifa, 'Informatics and documentation, advantages and problems: the experience of the CDN' (Translated title, Arabic text), *Rassid*, (3–4), Dec 1985, 5.

11 Abdeljaoued, Mohammed, *Les Bibliothèques en Tunisie (Bibliothèque Nationale, bibliothèques publiques et universitaires): introduction . . . la mise en place d'un réseau nationale de bibliothèques*, Tunis, Imprimerie TIAG, 1988, 151–2.

12 Habaili, H., 'Tunisia', In: *ALA world encyclopedia of libraries and information services*, 2nd edn., Chicago, ALA, 1986, 805.

13 Tunisian Dinar (TND) 1.64 = £1. (March 1991). See: *Statesman's yearbook*, op. cit., 1206.

14 Jeffreys, A. E., *L'Automatisation du catalogue de la Bibliothèque Nationale [Tunisia]: report of a consultancy*, Paris, Unesco, 1977, 42.

15 Tunisia, Ministry of Culture, 'Direction de la Lecture Publique', *La Lecture Publique en Tunisie*, Tunis, the Ministry, 1993. 9p.

16 Abdeljaoued, Mohammed, *Les Bibliothèques en Tunisie: les bibliothèques scolaires: situation insertion dans le réseau, guide de fonctionnement*, Tunis, Publications de l'ISD, 1989, 30–45.

17 Kuesters-Schah, op. cit., 355.

18 Vaughan, A., *La Formation de documentalistes, de bibliothècaires et d'archivistes . . . l'Institut de Presse et des Sciences de l'Information (IPSI)*, Paris, Unesco, 1981, 49.

19 Bouazza, A. et W. Gdoura, 'Le Comportement informationnel des enseignants-chercheurs tunisiens en sciences exactes', *L'Ecluse*, **4** (1), Janvier–Mars 1992, 14–15; 'Adéquation formation/emploi dans le secteur documentaire en Tunisie', *Documentaliste*, **28** (4–5), 1991, 193–6.

20 Adda, Gladys, 'L'Enseignement de la DBA face au développement des technologies nouvelles', *Rassid*, (1–2), 1985, 15–16.

21 Abdeljaoued, Mohammed, 'Situation des bibliothèques universitaires en Tunisie en 1992', *BUER informations*, **9** (1), 1993, 5–10.

22 Abdeljaoued, Mohammed, *Les Bibliothèques en Tunisie . . . op. cit.*, 106.

23 Thirion, Gérard, *Tunisie: Bibliothèque centrale universitaire (rapport)*, Paris, Unesco, 1981, 6.

24 Cooper, D. W., 'Libraries of Tunisia', *Wilson library bulletin*, **53** (10), June 1979, 699.

25 Houissa, Souheil, *The Needs and the barriers of the automation of university libraries in developing countries, with special reference to Tunisia*, University of Wales, Aberystwyth, 1992, 93 (MLib thesis).

16 Medical libraries and their services to the health sector in the United Arab Emirates (1971-1993)

Mohamed Sadiq Jaffer

Introduction

The history of medical libraries and their services in the Arab world dates from the period when early writings by Muslim scholars were translated from Arabic into Latin. The influence of these translations was immense and imparted knowledge of Arabic and Greek learning throughout medieval Europe. Among these distinguished figures was Ibn Sina (980–1034, known as Avicenna), whose famous work *Qanun al-tibb, (the law of medicine)* for example, was studied in the universities of Europe for over four centuries and is probably one of the most influential textbooks ever produced.[1] Ibn al-Nadim compiled the first comprehensive Arabic bibliography in 1528 (*Al-Fihrist*, which means *the Catalogue*). Hajji Khalifa is another scholar whose book *Kashf Al-Zunun* was introduced in the seventeenth century. One of the first Muslim philosophers, Al Kindi, was a librarian and like many Arab librarians and philosophers of his period, his major preoccupation was the classification of knowledge. For them, epistemology was the theoretical half of librarianship. For Al-Kindi, who produced the first Muslim classification of knowledge, the organization of information, the arrangement of books on a shelf, reflected the ideology of the organiser.[2] Paper was first introduced by Al-Fadul Ibn Yahayah Al-Barmaki, who established a paper factory in Baghdad during the Rasheed regime.[3]

Arabs, in modern times, take pride in their intellectual past, while making their own contributions to science and culture, despite colonialists' efforts to shatter that identity. The Arabization of medicine is of one of the main objectives of the Arab Centre for Medical Literature (ACML), which was established in 1981 in Kuwait. The centre encourages physicians and pharmacists to write in Arabic, since 'it is the language of one hundred and forty-two million people.[4] It assists research and authorship through translation services and standardization of terminology as part of its programmes of service to medicine.

Despite these efforts, aimed at helping Arabs to play a significant role in one of the major areas of modern science, most medical schools throughout the Arab world conduct their studies in English. Medical and other academic libraries in the United Arab Emirates (UAE) are still at an early stage of development. Lack of professional, qualified librarians and their own unawareness of their role is the reason underlying the poor services provided by all types of libraries in the country. Most of the librarians have been recruited from other Arab countries, a high proportion being graduates of library schools in Egypt and the Sudan. As elsewhere in the Arab world, there has been no national scheme for developing library services, no systematized bibliographic control, nor a national library association.

Writing about the Gulf States generally, Shearer observed:

> There are now two kinds of library education training programs: professional library education level and sub-professional level. The sub-professional library education courses are organised by associations, universities, UNESCO and ALESCO (The Arab League of Education, Scientific and Cultural Organisation, 1945) institutions and in-service training. The professional library education programs are attached to the universities (Egypt, Libya, Sudan, Oman, Qatar and Saudi Arabia) except for the School of Information Science in Morocco, which is attached to the National Documentation Centre. There are no training facilities in Syria, Yemen, United Arab Emirates, Qatar, Oman and Bahrain.[5]

In 1988, the Arab Centre for Medical Literature (ACML) in Kuwait published the scientific papers presented at the training seminar held in Kuwait in February 1987, which was attended by 28 trainees from different Arab countries.[6] The centre's activities are augmented by the National Scientific and Technical Information Centre (NSTIC) of the Kuwait Institute for Scientific Research (KISR), which seeks the co-ordination of scientific and technical information services, and the determining of a national information policy.

There are few publications that deal with medical libraries, or even libraries in general in the UAE. Several UNESCO reports in the 1970s explained the background of intended development in the country; A.W. Bartram's *Investigatory mission to Abu Dhabi in respect of the establishment of an audio-visual centre, 23 July–3 August 1974*; A. H. Helal's *Outline for a national documentation and information centre: UAE mission 15 December 1974–2 January 1975*; and J. C.

Gordon's *Circulation of the printed media: Arab States mission, 29 May–24 June 1977*. In 1988, Al-Nuaimi, the previous Director of the UAE University Libraries, wrote about the importance of the library service and its role in the learning process.[7] More recently, in 1992 L.B. Kalburgi, the Librarian of the General Industry Corporation in Abu Dhabi, wrote about the development of libraries and information services in the UAE.[8] These and similar studies about libraries in other Gulf countries reflect the status of libraries in general in the UAE.

A high proportion of enquires in medical libraries come via telephone or fax, since the country has an excellent and efficient communication service. Increasingly, attention has been paid to automation, especially in the university, which currently uses a built-in system in co-ordination between the Deanship of University Libraries and the University Computer Centre. New developments are occurring in different academic library activities, such as interlibrary loans and interlibrary document delivery services, and co-operative acquisitions and cataloguing schemes that help to avoid unnecessary duplication of information materials.

The United Arab Emirates: background
On 2nd December 1971 the United Arab Emirates was formed, a federation of seven individual emirates, occupying the southeastern coastline of the Arabian Gulf. It has a population of 1.68 million at present in an area of 32,300 square miles. During the nineteenth and early twentieth century, the emirates depended primarily upon fishing, trading and farming, the main occupations being pearl diving, herding and fishing, all of which date back to ancient times.

After independence, the great wealth derived from the oil exports, initially from Abu Dhabi and later from Dubai as well, has given the country one of the highest per capita incomes in the world. Efforts are being made to develop agriculture and industry in order to be less dependent on a single resource, and to achieve national self-sufficiency in the near future. Massive sums have been invested to develop health and other social services, to ensure that the people of the UAE can make the best use of the country's wealth. Etisalat, the national telephone company provides excellent and most up-to-date telecommunication facilities. International telephone calls are relatively cheap during holidays, weekends and off-peak hours. Internal calls within each emirate are 24 hours free of charge. International courier companies offer a comprehensive range of services locally and internationally.

Excellent international airports serve Abu Dhabi, Dubai and Sharjah. Al Ain International Airport is expected to be completed in December 1993. A very good road network has been built and signposted bilingually in Arabic and English. Satellite stations serve the country in the provision of telephone and telex lines as well as TV and radio programmes.

Arabic is the main and official language, although English, Hindi and Urdu are also widely spoken. Camel racing and falconry are traditional and popular sports. The weather is hot in summer (June–October, 35–50 degrees centigrade) and warm in winter (November–April, 25–35 degrees centigrade). Humidity is more than 90% near the coast in summer. Local newspapers are published in Arabic and English. There are five daily Arabic newspapers: *Al Khaleej, Al Itihad, Al Bayan, Al Wihda and Al Fajer*. English newspapers are *Khaleej Times, Gulf News, Emirates News and Gulf Mirror*.

The Ministry of Education was established in 1972, along with the introduction of compulsory free education for children aged six to twelve.

The university was established in 1977 at Al Ain, an oasis town 160 kilometres from Abu Dhabi, the capital city. Al Ain is famous for its date palms and flower gardens. The university has eight faculties and enrolment in 1993 was more than 8,000 students. The government provides free higher education at all levels, wherever it is taken, either in the country or abroad. There are two separate campuses, one each for male and female students. Thursday and Friday are the weekend in the university although Fridays only constitute the weekend in the UAE.

The Ministry of Health hospitals are modern and well equipped, and emergency care is free. There are 33 hospitals in 10 medical districts throughout the county and the government has adopted the campaign by the World Health Organisation, 'Health for All by the year 2000'. A number of private clinics are available, as well as herbal medicine centres to meet the people's needs for medical services.

The two most important libraries in the country are the University Central Library (Zayed Central Library) in Al Ain, and the Cultural Foundation Library, which serves as the UAE National Library, in Abu Dhabi.

Medical libraries in UAE fall into four categories:

- Academic health sciences libraries (affiliated to university/college/MOH)
- Ministry of Health hospital libraries (affiliated to hospitals)
- Ministry of Defence hospital libraries (affiliated to Zayed

Military Hospital)
• Private hospital libraries

Academic health sciences libraries

These include the University Faculty of Medicine and Health Sciences (FMHS); Dubai Private Medical College; the School of Nursing at Abu Dhabi and the Institute of Nursing at Dubai. Al Mafraq Institute for Medical Research and the Emirates Medical Association (EMA) in Dubai have been active in dissemination of medical information. The EMA publishes a regular medical journal in English, *Emirates medical journal* and the *EMA bulletin*, for its members.

Faculty of Medicine and Health Sciences

The Faculty of Medicine and Health Sciences (FMHS), of the United Arab Emirates University was established in March 1986, and the first intake of students was admitted in August of that year. Between 1987 and 1993 the faculty grew to comprise five basic science departments, five para-clinical departments and seven clinical departments. It has semi-autonomous status within the university, to make it competitive with other international medical schools worldwide. The mission statement of the FMHS is to produce medical and paramedical graduates and postgraduates of internationally recognized quality, specifically attuned to the needs and aspirations of the UAE and its culture. The curriculum is one of problem-based learning, along with oriented and independent study. This approach encourages students to develop a desire to go on learning. It requires exposure to various materials in a variety of formats, and a high standard of library and resource centre collections and services. A major curriculum review was implemented in 1991.[9] The course of study is eight years and English is the medium of instruction in FMHS. At the present time there are 113 faculty members, 168 non-faculty staff and 157 students, of whom 110 are female and 47 male; a ratio of 2:1.

The National Medical Library (NML)

The only medical library of any significance in the country is the National Medical Library (NML). It was established in May 1987 to serve the educational and clinical needs of the FMHS, Ministry of Health hospitals, and other institutions in the country. It is the largest English language health sciences library in the UAE, and serves as a national focal point in providing health sciences literature and medical information services to international standards. For the FMHS, the library constitutes the cornerstone of its programmes and is expected to cater for the needs of the entirety of health sciences professionals in the UAE in the near future. Therefore, the library facilities and staff are organized as an integral part of the total educational process of FMHS. The NML is not a branch library of the Central University Library, which was established earlier in 1977 but does not hold health sciences materials, although the two work closely together. The NML is located in a central position, to reflect the interrelationship between the library and the other 17 departments of the faculty, which are located on eight dispersed sites around Al-Ain. Administratively it is under the Dean of the Faculty of Medicine and Health Sciences and its annual budget is prepared and approved by the administration of FMHS.

One of the obvious features in this library, as noticed by Mr. Philip Thomas of the International Group of The Library Association of the United Kingdom during a visit in 1992, is the separation of facilities for male and female students. Segregation is maintained between students in classrooms and in the library, but not between faculty/staff and students, in accordance with tradition and custom. Therefore, book collections are duplicated between the male and female libraries. In cases where there is only one copy, which is normally shelved on the male side, the circulation staff have to serve it to the other side of the library. However, journals are not duplicated but divided by title between the two sides of the library; A–J are shelved on the male side and L–Z are on the female side, and circulation staff have to serve each side from their central service point.

In order to avoid unnecessary duplication of the library staff the building is designed to accommodate most of the staff in a central core area having two separate circulation desks as explained by the following map. However, the situation in this building is now different after a fire in the library, caused by an electrical fault, which occurred on the first day of the summer vacation in 1992.

Fire crisis
On the day after the end of the 1991–2 academic year a fire caused substantial damage to the NML building and the teaching facilities at the FMHS. There were no injuries to staff or students, who were out at the time of the fire, just before closing time.

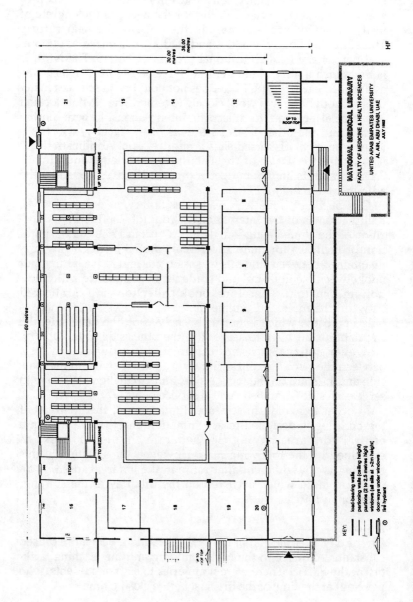

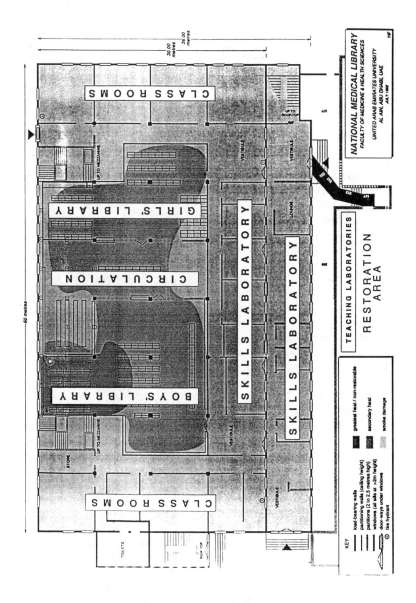

The building was damaged by intense heat, smoke, and water. Massive rescue efforts took place and within 24 hours the loss adjuster began to make regular visits, since the library fortunately was fully insured. An international recovery team of three was requested by the university to come from the Data and Archival Damage Control Centre (DADCC), in London. Plans were made for teams to work to get the library functioning by the beginning of the new academic year in September 1992. Approximately 48%, i.e. 5,351 books and 5.8%, i.e. 1,197 journal issues were lost in the fire, which had also destroyed 50%, i.e. 257 journal titles of the holdings on microfiche from 1976–86, and some audiovisuals. Equipment lost included a microfiche reader/printer, 2 photocopiers, 13 computers, and 9 laser printers. The estimated cost of restoring the building is 2 million Dirhams (US$542,299) and of recovery or replacement of stock is 5.7 million Dirhams (US$1,545,553).

The library reopened exactly four weeks after the devastating fire, dispersed on three temporary out-house sites, and restoration of losses has been completed. The main and male students' library is temporarily located at the Islamic Institute Campus, sharing the main hall of the Shari'ah and Law library. A female branch library is on the Medical Education Facilities Campus and the Technical Services Department is at the Jimi Mosque Campus. The library staff put in a tremendous amount of time, energy and commitment towards this priority. Helene Donnelly, DADCC managing director, said, 'she was impressed by the spirit of the team that emerged within a very short time and the unity on the campus'.

Library collections are now growing rapidly and new and improved services have been introduced since the fire. Stock, post-fire totalled 8,121 volumes of books in stacks, reference, and reserve, 750 international journal title subscriptions and 250 journals on microfiche backfiles. Special collections on reserve (short loan) consist of multiple copies of books of curriculum-specific materials, the FMHS faculty reprints collection, examination resources collection, audiovisual materials and UAE leisure reading collection. However, the reference collection is incomplete and consists of old editions that need to be replaced.

Journal shipments are received weekly on a regular basis, and new book orders are prioritized by faculty and the library committee. More than 1,800 book replacements have been received since June 1992. They are mainly those recommended on core lists by Brandon and Hill, and the WHO Regional Office for the Eastern Mediterranean (EMRO).[10]

There are 21 members of professional and para-professional library staff, of various nationalities; 15 budgeted permanently contracted positions, 5 daily basis positions, and one lump sum non-permanent. During the initial years, 1987–9, the library was organized by only two professional librarians. It was very difficult at that time to find or hire a local professional librarian, and much useful support was given by volunteers such as professors' wives and children

It was expected, at the time of writing, that the NML would operate from the three temporary locations for the reminder of the semester and move back to the reinstated building before the beginning of the new academic year in September 1993.

NML systems and services

In the Reference Department, using printed bibliographies such as the *Index medicus*, can be time-consuming and tedious. By contrast, online searching enables the user to select from and scan thousands of references very quickly. Therefore, on-site database services include new and enhanced MEDLINE on CD-ROM, networked for remote multi-user access at three stations, with one additional CD 120 stand-alone station. Online time limit was set to 30 minutes to prevent remote users blocking the line for a very long time. After 30 minutes, the host system will notify the remote user about time expiry and then disconnect. After dialling in, if a remote user does not have any data transfer or other recorded activity for five minutes, the host will automatically disconnect. MEDLINE (1966–date); CINAHL (1987–date) and CURRENT CONTENTS: life sciences (1990–date) were first introduced in NML in 1991. All registered users are requested to make an appointment with the Reference Librarian to utilize this service. Diskette and CD-ROM software for a variety of databases can also be accessed through the new system. The library provides interlibrary document delivery services through several methods, post, fax, and hold shelf, for faculty members and students free of charge. It has maintained a deposit account with the British Library Document Supply Centre, Boston Spa, UK since 1988. Only items that are not available in local libraries or Arabian Gulf libraries will be requested on interlibrary loan. Photocopying is also provided but solely as a service by library staff to users, who submit free photocopy request forms at the circulation desk, along with the material to be photocopied. The Copyright Act (No. 40 for 1992) must be consulted before submitting the material. Copies of requested material will be ready for picking-up from the hold shelf within 24 hours and urgent requests can be handled more rapidly. There is a limit of 50 pages per user per week, while bulk copying of material such as handouts should be done at departmental locations or co-ordinated with the Department of Medical Education. Since the library opens for 14.5 hours per day, Saturday to Tuesday, 11.5 hours on Wednesdays, and for 6 hours at weekends (Thursday and Friday), borrowing privileges are limited to a maximum of three books. Journal issues and audio-visual materials may not be circulated.

International textbooks of high academic repute are distributed to students. Their ordering and distribution are part of the library's responsibilities. Each student is entitled to a free copy of each textbook to be taught during the module, and three copies are allocated to instructors of the module. The NML continued throughout to support and co-operate with the Ministry of Health hospital libraries in Al-Ain, which are considered as the FMHS teaching hospitals (Tawam and Al-Jimi), and to provide training and half-time staff coverage to the Al-Jimi Hospital library. Current awareness and bibliographic verification services are provided regularly from the Technical Services Department on Al-Jimi Mosque Campus. The American National Library of Medicine classification scheme is used because it is convenient for library staff and users, by its gathering of like materials in one place under specific entry heading for given topics. The addition of new automated cataloguing via an overseas vendor, Marcive-US, produced good quality full catalogue card sets to international MARC standards, acquisitions lists, and computer tapes for loading into the proposed university-wide automated library system. A journal table of contents service was implemented to faculty members interested in receiving Current Contents service (Life Sciences and Clinical Medicine) which is available also on diskette. The serials check-in, of 750 journal subscriptions, is computerized using Mircolinx software. *Index Medicus* for the Eastern Mediterranean Region (IMEMR) is received regularly. The compilation of this index for the region constitutes an effort to bring to light more relevant information on the region's health problems and plans. A total of 108 health science periodicals has been identified as suitable input to IMEMR.[11] The library also provides a service of health information newspaper cuttings, which is appreciated, most especially by medical students. Because it is time-consuming, the library hopes to be able to access this service through the new database of the Arab Information Bank (AIB) in Dubai that has now accumulated more than 90,000 articles from English language local daily newspapers on different subjects, including health sciences. The AIB host computer in Dubai is connected to the international telecommunications data networks, to facilitate access by subscribers. Education and training of all library users of NML are of great importance. It is regarded as a primary responsibility of the professional library staff, and a formal course on integrated library skills instruction is offered to new students. From the director down, the librarians are involved in students' introductory sessions on library bibliographic instruction. It differs from traditional types of bibliographic instruction along the lines of 'how to use the library'. The main objective of the course is to familiarize the students with the available resources, and ease of access to services in NML, and to encourage their optimum use, such as finding books and references in specific subjects, use of microforms, and 'hands-on' computerized bibliographic databases. The library skills instruction is in line with the basic philosophy of the FMHS, to produce lifelong independent problem-solvers who have learned how to learn, rather than being passive recipients of information. Knowledge of these skills is important, not only for study but because it prepares students for subsequent semesters, when they will be introduced to research. Therefore, 'permitting users to find reliable information more easily is the immediate rationale for teaching library use.'[12]

Library orientation and a guided tour are regular activities arranged for new users, individually or in groups, on their first visit to NML. They are introduced to the physical layout of facilities, the services and the library staff. This motivates new users to come back and imparts an atmosphere of helpfulness and friendliness about the library systems and services. However, this orientation is often judged by students as 'too much information in too short period of time'. The library formerly published a monthly newsletter, *The Lamp of learning*, which introduced new materials and services but unfortunately it had to cease due to the workload of staff.

The library subscribes to five international library and information science journal titles and other professional literature to update staff on current developments. Professional librarians in NML contribute to local hospital libraries in terms of effort and support. These contacts continue to be important in the development of co-operative collections, systems and services. The detailed statistics of NML departmental activities that follow can indicate to some extent the quantity, quality and use made of the services, which were set up on the model in IFLA's statement on university library standards.[13] While statistics of routine activities are valuable as baseline measures, they are sometimes misleading as they do not guarantee any improvement, and 'future services on the basis of needs require access to wider range of information than routine statistical information'.[14]

nmls stats, accessioned/non-accessioned volumes, post-fire recovery

national medical library collection	status	english nml volumes	english dewey volumes	arabic nlm volumes	arabic dewey volumes	totals	dadcc recovered
accessioned	circulating @time of fire	446	0	0	0	446	0
	recovered/stacks	948	482	129	423	1,982	1,982
	recovered/reference	513	47	37	1	598	598
	recovered/reserve	1,185	22	4	1	1,212	1,212
	sub-total	3,092	551	170	425	4,238	3,792
	recovered/in-cataloguing	799	0	344	0	1,143	1,143
		208				208	208
		239				239	239
52%	*sub-total recovered*	4,338	551	514	425	5,828	5,382
	unrecoverable						0
	destroyed/missing						0
48%	*sub-total unrecovered*	3,711	617	782	241	5,351	0
100%	*original total accessioned*	8,049	1,168	1,296	666	11,179	0
not accessioned								0
	circulating @time of fire	0	0	0	0	0	0
	recovered/in-cataloguing	1,244	0	94	0	1,338	1,338
	sub-total recovered	1,244	0	94	0	1,338	1,338
	unrecoverable destroyed/missing						
	sub-total unrecovered						
	original total not accessioned						
(grand total recovered)							6,720

accessioned volumes include books, some audiovisuals for cataloguing
non-accessioned volumes include books and some audiovisuals not yet
processed or donations/exchange volumes

prepared by m sadiq/revised11august92

CIRCULATION DEPARTMENT ACTIVITY
NATIONAL MEDICAL LIBRARY, FMHS, UAEU
July 1988 - April 1993

Registered Users (cumulative)	Academic Year 1992/1993 July-April 1993	Academic Year 1991/1992**	Academic Year 1990/1991	Academic Year 1989/1990	Academic Year 1988/1989
FMHS	375	226	144	74	37
UAEU	204	56	29	8	4
MOH (Al Ain District)	189	90	73	24	8
Others (MOH, etc.)	170	121	88	37	24
total	938	493	334	143	73

Items Circulated by User:					
FMHS	626	1,413	1,570		
UAEU	58	35	63		
MOH (Al Ain District only)	66	405	238		
Others (MOH, etc)	14	234	188		
total	764	2,087	2,059	1,298	*

Items Circulated by Date Due:					
2 days	159	171	337		
2 weeks	485	1,580	1,487		
renewals/others	120	334	198		
total	764	2,085	2,022	2,705	524
2 hour (Reserve)	588	989	932		
In House Use (Room Pick-up)	11,698	10,454	13,978	*	*
Grand Total	13,050	13,528	16,932	*	*

Photocopy Services					
FMHS Students Self-Service	25,505	54,596	123,331		
FMHS & ILDD	97,848	119,789	276,374		
UAEU	4,684	908	1,190		
MOH (Al Ain District only)	4,631	5,391	10,022		
Others (MOH, etc)	2,829	5,881	4,129		
total	135,497	186,565	415,046	374,273	101,497

Average Weekly Users	Female	Male				
FMHS	104	170	223			
UAEU	0	85	3			
MOH (Al Ain District only)	0	78	17			
Others (MOH, etc)	0	83	24			
total	104	416	267	*	*	*

Average Weekend Users					
FMHS	2	8			
UAEU	1	0			
MOH (Al Ain District only)	2	1			
Others (MOH, etc)	2	1			
total	7	10	*	*	*

Key:
*Data not available during this time period   ** data for May-June missing due to 22 June fire
prepared by circulation department/april 1993

INTER-LIBRARY DOCUMENT DELIVERY DEPARTMENT ACTIVITY (UNTIL April 1993)
NATIONAL MEDICAL LIBRARY, FMHS, UAEU

NUMBER OF ARTICLES THE NML BORROWED FROM	Academic Year 1992/1993		Academic Year 1991/1992		Academic Year 1990/1991		Academic Year 1989/1990		Academic Year 1988/1989	
	ordered	filled	ordered	filled	ordered	filled	ordered	filled	ordered	filled
UAE Libraries: medical	160	139	33	24	0	0	0	0	0	0
UAE Libraries: non medical	27	20	32	17	0	0	0	0	0	0
sub total	187	159	65	41	0	0	0	0	0	0
East Med Region/WHO Libraries	496	375	572	414	244	132			8	8
WHO Alexandria Library:	1	0	5	2						
sub total	497	375	577	416	244	132	0	0	8	8
sub total (reciprocal)	684	534	642	457	244	132	0	0	8	8
British Library Document Supply Centre	595	501	590	497	490	446	130	79	0	0
sub total (paid)	595	501	590	497	490	446	130	79	0	0
GRAND TOTAL BORROWED	1279	1035 81%	1232	954 77%	734	578 79%	130	70 61%	8	8 100%

NUMBER OF ARTICLES THE NML DELIVERD TO:	Academic Year 1992/1993		Academic Year 1991/1992		Academic Year 1990/1991		Academic Year 1989/1990		Academic Year 1988/1989	
	requests	supplied	requests	supplied	requests	supplied	requests	supplied	requests	supplied
UAE Libraries: medical	265	222	202	178	47	37	0	0	0	0
UAE Libraries: non-medical	48	40	9	0	15	9	0	0	0	0
sub total	313	262	211	178	62	46	0	0	0	0
East Med Region/WHO Libraries:	68	53	30	25	5	4	0	0	0	0
WHO Alexandria Library	0	0	0	0	0	0	0	0	0	0
sub total	68	53	30	25	5	4	0	0	0	0
GRAND TOTAL DELIVERD	381	315 83%	241	203 85%	67	50 78%	0	0	0	0

key:
ordered=number of articles ordered by NML from other libraries
filled=number of articles rec'd from number ordered
requests=number of article requests rec'd from other libraries
supplied=number of articles supplied for requests rec'd from other libraries

REFERENCE DEPARTMENT
ANNUAL REPORT OVERVIEW
NATIONAL MEDICAL LIBRARY, FMHS, UAEU
July1988 - April 1993

Reference Activity by Type of Question	Academic Year 1992/1993**	Academic Year 1991/1992	Academic Year 1990/1991	Academic Year 1989/1990	Academic Year 1988/1989
Direction	204	323	697		
Instruction	164	246	644		
Publication	283	257	445		
Biography	125	106	261		
General Subject	162	102	173		
Extended Subject	81	74	87		
Verification	1,616	1,300	1,165		
total	2,635	2,408	3,472	*	*

Number of Questions asked by User Status:					
Faculty	1,420	1,267	1,242		
Staff	188	266	481		
Student	494	381	771		
Others (MOH, etc)	533	494	978		
total	2,635	2,408	3,472	*	*

Number of Questions asked by User Affiliation:					
FMHS	6% 1,919	-21% 1,807	2,280		
UAEU	18% 122	100% 103	0		
MOH (Al Ain District only)	3% 247	-61% 239	616		
Others (MOH, etc)	34% 347	-55% 259	576		
total	9% 2,635	-31% 2,408	3,472	*	*

MEDLINE Activity by Years Searched	Academic Year 1992/1993	Academic Year 1991/1992	Academic Year 1990/1991	Academic Year 1989/1990	Academic Year 1988/1989
1989 - 1993	-2% 461	-2% 471	483	20	16
1984 - 1988	-26% 95	-48% 129	67	13	13
1976 - 1983	-41% 41	73% 69	40	8	8
1966 - 1975	0% 30	-6% 30	32	8	6
total	-10% 627	9% 699	642	49	43

MEDLINE Activity by User Affiliation:					
FMHS	-34% 236	30% 360	277	17	17
UAEU	-17% 15	-53% 18	38	0	1
MOH (Al Ain District only)	-37% 52	100% 82	0	0	0
Others (MOH, etc)	29% 192	-23% 149	194	4	0
total	-19% 495	20% 609	509	21	18

Orientation/Tours					
by total No. of Persons	445	440	237	150	200

Bibliographic instructions	55	50	15	30	70

total number of persons	500	490	252	180	270

**May-June forthcoming   *not available

Future plans
Priorities include binding the journal collections and implementation of a library security system, to protect valuable resources of prime importance. Library automation, co-ordinated with the Central University Library is due for completion before the end of 1994, with the aim of transferring all library functions from paper to machine-readable systems. It will then be possible to offer dial-up services and electronic indexes, and to encourage library users to attend more extensive sessions of hands-on bibliographic instruction in online databases. Further progress should also be made towards establishing the NML as a key resource centre for journal articles within the Emirates, Gulf, and the Eastern Mediterranean Region of WHO

It is planned also to improve clinical, research, and multimedia resources in the library and to encourage library users to utilize them, while expressing more precisely their real needs and opinions about current systems and services.

The Female Private Medical College Library, Dubai
Started in 1988, to serve the medical education of females who cannot, for social reasons, go abroad to study, the first intake graduated in 1992.

The library is still embryonic in terms of establishing itself as an academic medical library. Currently supervised by the secretary of the college, it has very limited facilities and services. The collection consists of few major medical works and there is no library committee or annual budget for collection development.

The schools of nursing libraries
The information needs of nurses are quite similar to those of physicians. Regardless of level and kind, both need continually to update their professional knowledge with the latest information relevant to their practice. Therefore, nurses are provided with a variety of training courses, procedure books, and motivation from tutors to encourage the use of the library. Relatively little is known in detail about their information needs. It depends on tutors and librarians to pay attention and for the latter to provide the required relevant service.

There are three Nursing Schools in the UAE, located in Abu Dhabi, Dubai, and Sharjah. The School of Nursing in Abu Dhabi was the first, established in 1974. Its library lacks many communication facilities, including even telephone/fax and photocopier. It has a limited book stock and an erratic collection of old journals. An up-to-date collection is needed to cater to the needs of the staff and the nursing students. However, the school publishes a regular quarterly newsletter, *The Nursing Forum*, which serves the purposes of continuing education for the nursing staff in Abu Dhabi and circulates widely in the other emirates.

The School of Nursing at Dubai has a small collection of books, journals and audiovisuals but needs to increase and develop them. The School at Sharjah is recently established (1987) and has only limited library service.

Ministry of Health hospital libraries

The progress of both national development and urbanization has brought into being a number of new hospitals of international standard, which have associated library facilities. The libraries were set up to serve physicians, nurses, technicians, and administrators of the Ministry of Health with print and non-print medical materials or with 'clinical tools', as they have been described by an American physician. Administratively they come under the hospital's control. Currently there are 24 hospital libraries located in major centres of population. They support the delivery of patient care by providing health care professionals with library services, to meet their informational, educational and research-related needs. The concept of library service as qualified by international standards does not exist in UAE. Most of them are staffed by one person who is not often a qualified librarian. As mentioned earlier, most of the libraries lack the right number of qualified staff to run them efficiently. At present they need the impetus derived from a spirit for team work:

> An active medical librarian usually builds up a network
> of personal associations with other medical librarians in
> the world, and from their resources he is able to satisfy
> the requests of his patrons. Therefore, the provision of
> health literature services by competent librarians can
> make the difference between good and poor health ser-
> vices, a difference between life and death.[15]

In order to gather information, a questionnaire was mailed to all 24 libraries. Twenty of those who received the questionnaire responded, representing an 83.3 % response rate. An important point to note is that seven indicated that they are waiting for a qualified Medical Librarian to be appointed. Data collected from the questionnaire is presented in a short directory at the end of this article.

Physicians and practitioners require information that will enable them to determine the state of health of the patient, to identify appropriate ways of improving the patients' state of health and to deliver an efficient service. As Anne Wilkin, of the Central Information Services, University of London, commented:

> there is widespread agreement that medical libraries can play a part in lessening the gap between medical knowledge and its application to medical practice, but only if they provide services which are convenient, prompt, and particularly relevant to clinical needs. Otherwise services will not be used by busy clinicians who have more patients than they can adequately handle, and who may lack the time to go to a library, assuming that an adequate one is nearby. As a result, they are frequently forced back on their own sources which may be inadequate in scope and out-of date.

Physicians, as the potential users of UAE hospital libraries, have been reported to be well-informed about the literature in their speciality, and it was recognized that online searching and interlibrary loan for articles from abroad, must have priority among services to be provided to them. Hospital librarians have to be active as information brokers, to link practitioners to powerful sources of information. Some of these libraries are described and discussed below.

The Directory

Abu Dhabi

The Jezira and Central Hospitals Library is served by one professionally qualified medical librarian, supported by only one library assistant. The library committee, which has ten members including the librarian, takes responsibility for policy and procedure. The collections, which are up to date, include medical texts, 1,063 volumes, regular journal subscriptions to 96 titles, and some audiovisual materials, 137 videos and 76 audiocassettes.

The library serves 173 physicians, 525 nurses, and 316 technicians during 13 opening hours per day, in two shifts. The collections are rather small, but relevant and well used. The library offers most of the usual services, such as interlibrary loan, free photocopy, current awareness and literature searches. It publishes an acquisitions list of books, and a journal holdings list. These two are the first fruits from using the newly received library computers. Future plans include computerization of all other library activities.

Al Mafraq Hospital Library is another good example, where a qualified medical librarian works without any other support staff. The library committee, of six members, is there to give support to the library's operation and budget expenditure. Funds are divided into two equal parts for books, 100 volumes a year, and journals, 116 subscriptions. It has a few video cassettes and 100 floppy diskettes. The library opens for one shift of 6 hours per day, and provides interlibrary loan as well as free photocopy and literature search. Acquisitions lists, the journal holdings list and the library bulletin/newsletter are computerized and distributed occasionally. Its budget amounts to Dhs 200,000 per year, but due to difficulties in the purchasing procedure, the whole sum is not often fully utilized and there are gaps in the continuity of journal subscriptions.

In Al-Ain city, Tawam Hospital library and Al-Jimi Hospital library also contribute to health information services. The Tawam Medical Library is affiliated to the Medical Records Department in the hospital. A reasonable standard library service is provided, with the addition of a recreational library of audiovisuals. The collection is up to date and new materials are received regularly, thanks to the direct purchasing policy. The growing collections at present stand at 1,500 volumes of books and 325 journal subscriptions. This library has the most extensive audiovisual collection in the country. It is well organized, with a printed catalogue that encourages use. The collections are heavily used by medical staff of the hospital, and clinical medical students of the FMHS, who spend most of their time in the hospitals and have little time to go to other libraries. At present, the problem of space is pressing and the collections are dispersed among small separate rooms. Most of the other hospital facilities occupy good and appropriate premises.

Dubai

There are seven health sciences libraries in Dubai, including the Medical College and the Institute of Nursing libraries. The establishment of a new central health sciences library is expected to introduce new and better library services in the near future.

Rashid Hospital Library has the largest book and journal collections, with a qualified librarian in charge. The purchasing committee takes responsibility for collection development. There is a book stock of 3,250 volumes and subscriptions to 282 journal titles. It opens for 8 hours a day and provides interlibrary loan services, free photocopy service, and literature search via NML. The library is not automated at present but that is a priority.

Al Wasl Hospital is newly built and specializes in maternity and child health care. The library is affiliated to the Department of Health and Medical Services and has a library committee of six There is no regular annual budget and the occasional purchase of materials is done through foreign agents. It currently, in 1993, has a book collection of about 1,000 volumes, and 103 journal subscriptions. There are some audiovisual materials; videotapes, audiotapes, floppy disks, slides, and films. Most of the usual library services are offered to users, and some, such as acquisitions and serials control are being automated, although in cramped accommodation.

Al Maktoum Health Centre Library was established in 1988 and is supervised by a part-time health services officer. Part of his duty is to establish a library for primary health care, and to look for a qualified medical librarian. There is no annual budget and the average of new additions is less than 100 books per year. The total book collection is 694 and there are 44 journal subscriptions.

Sharjah
The New Al-Qassemi Hospital Library in Sharjah is a small one with 340 books and only five current journals. The library's users have taken to subscribing individually to journals, which they circulate between each other, to make up for some of the deficiencies of the library. The other medical library in Sharjah is at the Kuwaiti Hospital with no librarian and only about 100 books. Here also, medical staff of the hospital take out and share the results of personal subscriptions.

Ministry of Defense hospital libraries

Zayed Military Hospital, Abu Dhabi
This is the only medical library for the Armed Forces. It is a small reference library run by a well-qualified librarian with the support of a four person library committee. Its ultimate goal is to provide medical staff in the hospital with needed in-house information. The collections include reference books, journals, and audiovisual materials.

The hospital's Directorate of Medical Services publishes a valuable medical journal the *Emirates Armed Forces medical journal* in English and Arabic, which is distributed free of charge to individuals in the ministry.

Private hospital libraries

Oasis Hospital Library, Al Ain

It is a small private hospital library organized recently by one of the NML volunteers. It is supervised by the Medical Director, for lack of a medical librarian to take on this responsibility. The library remains open for 24 hours for the benefit of medical staff working in shifts.

Conclusions

A strong medical library system should be recognized as an essential component of medical information transfer, so as to be able to manage effectively the rapid growth of medical information during the third wave of the information explosion. The system has to promote and facilitate effective use of recorded information in different formats. It is recognized that printed materials still remain as essential keys in searching medical literature in most of the Arab world. The library's place in national planning, and the future of library education and library manpower planning in the UAE is not promising. A school of information and library studies is needed, preferably in the university, to meet the heavy demand for professional librarians and information scientists. There should also be regular short courses and training seminars, to help semi-professional library staff. UAE personnel would have to be encouraged to join these courses and to go for further studies outside the country.

There is a need to develop an indexing and abstracting service of UAE medical journals, and to evaluate international foreign journals through citation analysis and international core lists. There is an urgent need also for co-ordination and delivery of materials through the optimum sharing of available resources in the country, because no library can be self-sufficient. To achieve this, academic and hospital libraries must support each other and should be linked through advanced telecommunication systems at national, regional, and international level. The National Medical Library should take on this responsibility, as part of its role as the national focal point health sciences library. Facsimile transmission in some libraries now supports this work by getting material requested from NML. Other materials, especially printed volumes need further consideration, and the devising of a system of delivery such as utilizing the post-office mail services at a privileged rate, or hiring a mobile librarian to travel regularly between hospitals, delivering and receiving materials.

Directory of Health Sciences Libraries in UAE

Places City/Library	Collections Books Vols	Jour sub 1993	V/C	A/C	SL	CD	FD	MF	Ref	ILL	Photo	OnlineCD	Open hrs p/w	No. of seats	No.of lib Staff	Librarian	POB	Tel	Fax
Abu Dhabi																			
Al-Jazira Hospital Library	1063	94	137	76	0	0	15	0	✓		✓		71	36	1	Mr Mohan	2427	02-214900	02-216007
Corniche Hospital Library	153	25	0	0	0	0	0	0			✓		48	10	0	0	3788	02-724900	02-720782
Mafraq Hospital Library	394	116	7	0	0	0	100	0	✓	✓	✓		36	18	1	Mrs Tasneem	2951	051-23100	051-21549
School of Nursing Library	1560	0	10	0	0	0	0	0					63.5	35	3	Mrs Olga	233	02-465474	0
Zayed Military Hospital Libr	30	3	10	7	55	0	0	0					42	20	1	Mrs Khalidah	3740	02-448100	02-448414
Ajman																			
Ajman Hospital Library	100	1	20	0	0	0	0	0	✓		✓		36	20	0	0	402	06-422227	06-441144
Al-Ain																			
Al-Jimi Hospital Library	1534	0	42	29	0	0	0	0	✓		✓		46.5	22	1	Mr Babu	1006	03-635688	03-634322
National Medical Library	8121	750	10	15	4906	15	10	6675					80	60	21	Mr. sadiq	17666	03-511715	03-511036
Oasis Hospital Library	500	8	30	0	0	0	0	0		✓	✓		144	4	0	0	1016	03-641251	03-666007
Tawam Hospital Library	1500	190	264	200	0	0	0	0	✓	✓	✓		48	12	1	Mrs Wafa	15258	03-677444	03-677274
Dubai																			
Al Maktoum Hospital Library	694	44	114	12	12	0	0	0	✓		✓		48	6	1	Mr Salah	1899	04-221211	04-277921
Al-Wasl Hospital Library	1000	108	0	0	0	0	0	0	✓	✓	✓		48	10	1	Mr. Salim	9115	04-372939	04-369756
Institute of Nursing Library	4000	17	0	0	9	0	0	0					36	30	0	Ms Zahia	4545	04-541117	04-368152
Medical College Library	457	0	1	0	0	0	0	0					12	30	0	0	19964	04-886465	04-887271
New Hospital Library	1818	86	12	3	95	0	0	0	✓		✓		48	24	1	Mrs Rukiya	7272	04-229171	04-236295
Rashid Hospital Library	3250	282	0	0	0	0	0	0	✓		✓		48	18	1	Mrs Sughra	4545	04-371111	04-368152
Fujairah																			
Fujairah Hospital Library	300	20	0	0	0	0	0	0	✓				72	10	0	0	10	09-224611	09-229077
Sharjah																			
Institute of Nursing Library	45	10	0	0	0	0	0	0			✓		36	10	0	0	3500	06-386444	06-387200
Kuwaiti Hospital Library	100	0	0	0	0	0	0	0			✓		36	6	0	0	2072	06-242111	06-242100
New al Qassimi Hospital Libr	340	6	0	0	0	0	0	0	✓	✓	✓		36	10	1	Mrs Mona	3500	06-386444	06-387200

Prepared by M. Sadiq, Asst Director, NML on 15 Dec 1990, revised 02 Oct 1991, revised 16 June 1993
to update contact: Mr. M. Sadiq Jaffer
National Medical Library (NML)
Faculty of Medicine & Health Sciences (FMHS)
United Arab Emirates University, Al Ain, POB 17666
τ: 03-511715, 03-634717
Fax: 03-511036, 03-631405

Key:
V/C   Video Cassette
A/C   Audio Cassette
SL   Slides
CD   Compact Disk
FD   Floppy Disk
MF   Microfilm/Microfiche

Book trade and distribution are still in their infancy. The lack of a national book development plan, and the absence of satisfactory academic health science bookshops are results of the weak links between local and international publishers, and local booksellers, who have little experience of supplying libraries. They have not previously had to develop such skills, because the bulk of local booksellers' trade at present is in stationery and magazines. Book demands are also very low because of the free distribution of textbooks in schools and colleges, and also teaching methods that do little to promote library usage.

The problem of space is an ongoing constraint on the development of many health sciences libraries in UAE. Professional planners, working in co-ordination with librarians, should give closer consideration, at the planning stage, to future growth of library collections, increase in potential users, and the requirements of new systems and services that are likely to be implemented.

References

1 Auchterlonie, Paul, 'The development of Arabic studies in Britain from the Middle Ages to the present day'. In: *Arabic resources: acquisitions and management in British libraries,* ed. D. Burnett, London, Mansell, 1986, 1–10.

2 Sardar, Ziauddin, *Information and the Muslim world: a strategy for the 21st century,* London, Mansell, 1988, 147–8.

3 Muraqi, M. A., *Dirasat fi al-muktabah al-Arabia,* Beruit, Dar al-Aulum, 1991, 59–65.

4 Shearer, K., 'The Arabian Gulf plans its library future', *International library.review,* **13** (3), 1981, 259–73.

5 Sharif, A., 'The development of professional library education in the Arab countries', *International library review,* **13** (1), 1981, 87–101

6 Salem, Shawky, *Medical information systems and services* (Translated title, Arabic text), Kuwait, Arab Centre for Medical Literature (ACML), 1988, 5–26.

7 Al-Nuaimi, A. N., *An Evaluation study of the educational role of the library service in UAE University* (Translated title, Arabic text), Cairo, Maktabat Al-Falah, 1988 (PhD thesis).

8 Kalburgi, L. B., *An In-depth evaluation of development of libraries and information services in the UAE after its independence: possibilities, problems and current boundaries of building up an effective library and information service system,* Dharwad, Karnatak University, Department of Library and Information Science, 1992 (PhD thesis).

9 Lanphear, J. H., 'The evolution of medical education in the United Arab Emirates University: a new curriculum for a new era', *Emirates medical journal,* **9** (3), 1991, 214–24.

10   World Health Organisation, *List of basic sources in English for a medical faculty library.* 6th ed. Alexandria: WHO/EMRO, 1992

11   Guirguis, G. A., 'Health literature and information services in the WHO Eastern Mediterranean Region', In: *Medical libraries: keys to health information.* Proceedings of the 6th International congress on medical librarianship, and pre-congress seminar on 'Health information: Impact of technology development on its production, analysis, distribution and consumption', New Delhi, Medical Library Association of India , 1990, vol. 2, 509–12.

12   Farber, E. I., 'Reflections on library instruction', In: *The LIRT library instruction handbook,* ed. M. Brottman and M. Loe. Englewood, Colo., Libraries Unlimited, 1990, 3–4.

13   Lynch, B., 'Standards for university libraries', *IFLA journal,* **13** (2), 1987, 120–5.

14   Hepworth, J. B., 'Staffing intelligence services: a survivor's guide', *Health libraries review,* **9** (2) 1992, 52–61.

15   Okwuowulu, A., 'The role of libraries in the health service in Nigeria', *International library review,* **11** (1), 1979, 163–74

Further materials consulted

1   Picken, F and Khan, A., *Medical librarianship in the eighties and beyond,* London, Mansell, 1986.

2   Birnhack, J., *Audio-visual resources in a hospital medical library: their organisation and management,* London, Mansell, 1987.

3   Pantelidis, V., *The Arab world: libraries and librarianship 1960–1976: a bibliography,* London, Mansell, 1979.

4   Al-Nahari, A., *The role of national libraries in developing countries: with special reference to Saudi Arabia,* London, Mansell, 1984.

5   Bin Daa'ir, S., *Educational change in the United Arab Emirates,* Abu Dhabi, The Cultural Foundation, 198?

6   Burnett, D., *Arabic resources: acquisition and management in British libraries,* London, Mansell, 1986.

7   Anwar, M., *Information services in Muslim countries: an annotated bibliography of expert studies and reports on library, information and archive services,* London, Mansell, 1988.

8   Fairservice, I., *Dubai: gateway to the Gulf,* Dubai, Motivate, 1987.

9   Bakewell, K., *Managing user-centred libraries and information services,* London, Mansell, 1990.

10   Roper, F. and Boorkman, J., *Introduction to reference sources in the health sciences,* Chicago, Medical Library Association, 1984.

11   Darling, L., *Handbook of medical library practice,* 4th edn., Chicago, Medical Library Association, 1982, 2v.

12   Ludwig, L. T., '1991 survey of recent health sciences library building projects', *Bulletin of the Medical Library Association,* **80** (2), 1992, 115–23.

13 Swanson, D. R., 'Medical literature as a potential source of new knowledge', *Bulletin of the Medical Library Association,* **78** (1), 1990, 29–37.

14 Namlah, A. I., 'Manpower deficiency in Saudi Arabia: Its effect on the library and information profession', *International library review,* **14** (1), 1982, 3–20.

17 Economic and social change in the Emirates: is the information provision adequate?

Bakri Musa Abdul Karim

The United Arab Emirates is a federation of seven states (each known as an emirate) which was formed in 1971. They are: Abu Dhabi, Dubai, Sharjah, Ajman, Ras Al Khaima, Um Al Quwain, and Fujaira; located around the north-eastern side of the Arabian Peninsula, with a combined area of about 80,000 sq. km. They were British protectorates from 1822 until 1971. The country is ruled by a federal supreme council, which has absolute power in decision making. The provisional constitution gives the federal government jurisdiction over foreign policy, defence, economic planning, education, health and information services, although governors of individual emirates retain wide-ranging legislative powers over local affairs and municipal services. UAE is a member of the Gulf Co-operation Council (GCC), which also includes the states of Bahrain, Kuwait, Qatar, Saudi Arabia, and Oman.

Economy and business environment

Prior to the discovery of oil in 1962, the seven emirates were regarded as some of the poorest areas in the world. Their main economic activities were fishing, spear diving, livestock grazing, and subsistence farming. Following the commercial production of oil, the economy has undergone drastic changes, increasing most dramatically after independence in 1971. Today, the country produces around 3% of the world's total oil output and has reserves to maintain present levels of production for the next 200 years.[1]

Economic growth was almost 18% per annum between 1972 and 1988. According to figures released in 1992 by the Ministry of Planning, the country's GDP increased by 26% between 1986 and 1991. Per capita income in 1992 was approximately US$19,300, with estimated per capita expenditure of US$8,967. Although the oil and gas industries remain the dominant sectors of the economy, there is now a coherent government policy to diversify economic activity in favour of other sectors.[2]

The government adopted a *laissez-faire* attitude towards attracting foreign investment and technology, in seeking to create a free and diversified market economy. This policy has also helped create a modern and sophisticated infrastructure of roads, telecommunications, and health and education services.

The strategic position of UAE makes it an important regional centre of global flows of finance and trade, and it has become a gateway to the Gulf for onward distribution of trade. In 1992 the volume of re-export trade amounted to 49% of its total non-oil exports. Even before the oil boom of the 1970s, Dubai had developed as a major trading centre, catering to the demand of the early Gulf oil producers, namely Saudi Arabia, Kuwait, Bahrain and Iran. During the past few years there have been predictions that Dubai may rival Hong Kong by the time of the latter's merger with China in 1997.

Demographic changes

Change in the political structure, and rapid economic growth have also been accompanied by changes, in both composition and size of the population. According to official censuses, the population has increased from under 200,000 in 1968 to more than 1,900,000 in 1990, and is projected to reach 2,000,000 by the beginning of the twenty-first century. This increase is attributed largely to the influx of expatriate labour, as a consequence of expansion in the various sectors of the economy during the same period. About one-third of population is aged between 5 and 19. This youthful majority therefore poses considerable implications for public policy and social strategy.

Cultural background

The UAE has been described, justifiably, as a cosmopolitan society. This is a relatively new aspect of the country, which until recently was characterized by its cultural isolation. Rapid economic growth necessitated communication with the outside world and brought about closer regional and international cultural contacts. The influx of expatriate workers, particularly from south Asia, and other Arab countries, has created a multilingual and multifarious society. Thus, while Arabic continues to be the official language, English, Urdu, and Hindi are widely understood. English, however, remains the main business language and the common medium of communication between the different ethnic groups. Cultural ties have also been fostered by expatriate teachers and lecturers, coming to teach in the newly opened schools and colleges. Increasing numbers of UAE nationals have been given opportunities to travel for study abroad, and these in turn contributed to cultural exchange between UAE and the rest of the world. Islam is the official religion and, along with Arab traditions, acts as the major spiritual and social force. Despite its outward features of a cosmopolitan society, the country is still committed to its cultural heritage. Its society appears quick to adopt modern technological products such as expensive cars, and the latest communication devices, but remains somewhat reluctant to compromise on traditions and social customs. There is much concern among local people that traditional culture will be overwhelmed by foreign influences.[3]

Education and training
The UAE, with its small population and massive wealth, has recognized the need to develop its human resources. Therefore, education and training at all levels have been given high priority in the government's development plans. The history of formal education can be traced back only to the early 1950s, when there were about six schools between all the emirates. There are at present more than 800 government and private schools in the country.

The United Arab Emirates University is at present the main source of supply of graduates, and the authorities are extending the base for tertiary education, with special emphasis on the technical and scientific fields. During the past five years 14 higher education colleges have been established, by government, and in the private sector. Training opportunities have also increased as a result of the recent availability of corporate-sponsored local training in fields such as banking, oil industry, telecommunications and management studies.

Distance education (external study) appears increasingly to be chosen as a means of continuing education. It is especially preferred by female students. About 95% of the students registered in external study courses of the university between 1986 and 1990 were women.

Information services in developing countries
Without doubt, the role of information in economic and social development is well recognized in modern information societies. Masuda[4] defines the information society as 'a society that grows and develops around information, and brings about a generally flourishing state of human intellectual activity, instead of affluent material consumption'. This applies also to most of the world's advanced countries. On the other hand, recognition of the role of information appears to be lacking in the majority of developing countries although, fortunately it is beginning to emerge in some of them. The problems hindering the development of library and

information services in the Third World have been well documented in the literature of this topic. The following factors are widely cited as the major constraints that apply:

- Insufficient financial resources for information services
- Shortages of skilled staff in areas of information
- Under-utilization of existing information resources because of difficulty of access
- Lack of co-operation, co-ordination, and networked systems
- Lack of support for information services from policy makers, planners and political leadership
- Low reading habit among the literate public and consequent low use of information in the decision-making process

It was noted by Sliney that even in other oil-rich countries, like Saudi Arabia, Kuwait, Libya and Nigeria financial problems still hamper development of library and information services.[5] It is a fact that information provision in a country is shaped, not solely by that nation's economic resources. There are cultural and historic factors, as well as the pragmatic necessities for making a successful transition into a modern society. Therefore, it appears important to evaluate the library and information services of developing countries in a multi-faceted approach; one that takes into consideration cultural, historical, and political, as well as economic factors.

Library and information services in the UAE: the present status
Kalburgi's evaluative survey reported that the usual range of library services is to be found throughout the country; school, academic, public, and special, and differing widely in size, coverage, technical standards, staffing levels, and quality of service to users.[6] Most government departments and public corporations have libraries or information centres tacked to them, but they have yet to be linked into an integrated national information network system. This is largely due to the absence of a national policy on information. As will be shown later, the sources, technology and funds are available. An important missing element appears to be any clear vision and direction regarding the role of information in society.

Public libraries
Although the Federal Ministry of Information and Culture assumes complete responsibility over public library services throughout the country, each of the seven emirates has set up its own library organization and policies.[7] In Dubai, for instance,

public libraries are under the jurisdiction of the municipality, while in neighbouring Sharjah they are administered by the Information and Culture Directorate, which is a department of the regional government of that emirate. In the other emirates, they are under direct control of the Federal Ministry of Information and Culture.

The first organized public library was established in 1963, and still exists as the nucleus of the system in Dubai. In Sharjah and Abu Dhabi, the central library exits as part of a larger organization, which acts as a cultural centre and provides a wide spectrum of activities such as seminars, book fairs, and arts and folklore exhibitions. In addition, each of these public libraries has a small number of branches in other towns and residential areas.

The Cultural Foundation of Abu Dhabi is the largest of all such complexes. It has a public library with around 90,000 volumes, and is housed in purpose-built premises in the centre of the capital. Because of its location in the country's political centre, and its funding by the Federal Ministry of Information and Culture, it is the designated National Library of UAE. Although it performs some conventional national library functions, it is closer in its activities to being a public library. It does not, for instance, perform the role of lender of last resort, nor does it provide photocopy services to remote users. There is no legal deposit law in UAE, and therefore the national library has to purchase books and collect local publications using ordinary acquisitions' procedures. It does not seem to have fulfilled the national library mission as a leader of other libraries in the country, but has, however, recently become active in bibliographical control, by compiling a union catalogue of periodicals in the country, and the start of a national bibliography. Each of these is far from comprehensive in coverage, due perhaps to non-cooperation by other libraries about supplying information on their holdings. The national bibliography is, therefore based only on the collection held in the National Library.

The library complex also houses a children's library, the National Archives and a library of manuscripts. The latter contains about 5,000 rare manuscripts, which are well maintained and preserved.

About 80% to 90% of all public library collections are in Arabic. Public library collections are mostly Arabic literature and Islamic books, with smaller sections on technical and specialized subjects. They cannot therefore help the majority of non-Arabic speaking expatriates, who comprise more than half the total population. Many non-Arabic readers turn to the British Council library in Dubai, with its stock of about 15,000 books, and also to the American and French cultural centres, which maintain small public libraries.

Another characteristic of public libraries is their lack of information and reference services. Apart from the British Council library, few reference facilities are readily available to the public. The concept of public libraries as a source of public information does not exist. Borrowing facilities are very restricted. Libraries that allow books to be checked out do so only after a rather complicated membership procedure. A non-citizen who wishes to join a library is usually required to produce documentation that must include a copy of his/her passport and an employer's letter of endorsement, in addition to a deposit of about US$50, as a safeguard against the loss of books. Librarians frequently complain about the high loss rate through non-return of borrowed materials.

All public libraries are in purpose-built and well-maintained buildings, which have separate reading areas (and sometimes different opening hours) for men, women, and children. Technical services are most usually organized centrally in each authority; books are classified according to the Dewey Decimal scheme, and catalogued by the Arabized version of AACR2. This has not come about as the result of a deliberate standardization of practice, but merely by fortunate coincidence. Unfortunately, however, there is no form of co-operation or co-ordination between public libraries in the different emirates.

Academic libraries
These include the libraries in the national university and other colleges of higher education. They are found to be fairly well organized and are striving to enhance their services. They are reasonably well staffed by professional librarians. The largest and oldest academic library in the country is that of the United Arab Emirates University at Al-Ain. The university was established in 1977 and currently has some 8,000 students and 750 teaching staff. The library service consists of a central library and five branches, one of which is for female students. As the only institution of its kind in the country, the university is generously funded by government, and the library does not appear to have very severe budgetary constraints. Its current stock is around 300,000 titles, with more than 2,000 periodical subscriptions. In addition to serving students and staff, the University libraries extend their services to outside readers, especially professionals and technical

staff in government and other academic institutions.

The library of the Faculty of Medicine and Health Sciences is designated as the National Medical Library. It is the most important source of medical literature, serving medical and health workers throughout the country.

Another outstanding library is that of the Etisalat College of Engineering, which specializes in telecommunications engineering. There are libraries also in the recently established technical colleges. The most important of these is in the Higher College of Technology, based in Abu Dhabi and with a campus in each of the other emirates.

Most academic libraries in the UAE are staffed by professionally qualified personnel. This is another area where they have the advantage over other types of library in the country; public libraries, for example are always short of qualified staff. There is no local training for information work, and so all professional jobs have to be filled by expatriates. As far as it has been possible to ascertain, there is as yet no native born professional librarian in the country. Librarianship seems not to be an attractive career in many of the rich Arab countries, whose graduates prefer more socially attractive jobs in government and business.

School libraries

Libraries are to be found only in secondary schools, and are supervized by the Ministry of Education. According to current official statistics.[8] there are 440 secondary schools, of which 357 have libraries. Although the majority of them are in the charge of trained librarians, these libraries are still undeveloped. They have small funds, and therefore have poor book stocks. In fact, a typical school library is only a collection of 500 to 1,000 books, kept in a single room and issued to pupils during weekly library periods. They do not provide much reference and other curriculum support material. These defects are exacerbated by the difficulty of access by children to public libraries. Where a public library has no separate children's library, children are likely to be refused the use of any other books.

Special libraries

Most government departments and public corporations have libraries or information centres attached to them, which normally keep official reports and publications of the parent ministry or department. In most cases the library is intended mainly for the internal needs of its own ministry, without regard to external users. As there is no one with overall responsibility to collect official publications, it is usually difficult to locate government information in the UAE. The Government's undeclared policy seems to be of restricting the free flow of information, apparently to ensure privacy or security of state secrets, although in contradiction of its *laissez-faire* policy in encouraging business activity. Consequently, the role of government libraries in dissemination of government information is rather limited, and restricts them to being mere information warehouses. However, it is frequently argued that in the UAE, as well as in other Arab oil-producing countries, the public has no interest in pursuing public information because there are no channels for expressing opinion it.[9]

Chambers of commerce as sources of business information

Chambers of commerce and other trade associations have a long tradition of business information services in advanced countries.[10] In the UAE, the most developed special libraries in the field of business information are those of the chambers of commerce and industry. Each of the seven emirates has set up its own chamber. They are all affiliated to the Union of Chambers of Commerce and Industry (UCCI), which acts as a co-ordinating body. The Dubai Chamber of Commerce and Industry is rated as the best organized, and its library has proved to be a most useful source of business information throughout the UAE. It serves, in addition to it own members, investors from all over the world. At the present time, an international data bank is being set up and is expected to serve as a business information bank that can be accessed online by remote users over the Emirates Data Network. UCCI plays another important part in business information by publishing a monthly magazine of business statistics, new regulations and company news. Individual chambers also publish their own information bulletins, which have a similar function. Because of the liberal economic policies of the country, privatization has emerged as a strong economic and social force in certain sectors, but the private sector's support of individual special information services is yet to be developed. Writing in 1987, V. N. Misra felt that because of the failure of government in this respect, the role of the private sector should not be ignored.[11] Among the library and information centres currently operating, only 12 belong to the private sector.

Other business information providers include the Statistical Centre of the Dubai Municipality, the Industrial Data and Information Bank at the General Industry Corporation in Abu Dhabi, and the Trade Data Bank at the British Embassy. The latter is particularly for businessmen when locating information on

British Standards. There are also information services from foreign trade missions such as the Information Centre at the American Trade Mission, and the Japanese Information Bank at the Embassy of Japan. These mainly provide trade information about commodities and services produced by their respective countries, as well as advice and consultation services about investment opportunities in UAE to investors from those countries.

The place of UAE as an expanding regional and international business centre has been discussed earlier. Indeed, information is an essential input in international trading activity, and is emerging as an important competitive factor in business and marketing.[13] The information infrastructure will, therefore need to be expanded for the country to maintain its economic relationship with the rapidly advancing information technologies of its trading partners, Western Europe, North America and Japan. In 1992 imports from these countries amounted to more than 55% of its total imports, and they in turn took some 50% of its exports.

An online database: the Arab Information Bank
The Dubai-based Arab Information Bank (AIB) merits special attention because it is the first online information service in the country. Since its establishment in 1983, the AIB database has developed to become the world's only English language database on Arab affairs. It is owned by a local Arabic newspaper, *Al Bayan*, but is managed independently. It holds more than 100,000 citations of news items covering wide-ranging topics relating to the Arab countries and the Middle East, in more than 18 subject fields. Information is drawn from Arab world newspapers, and specialist publications elsewhere.[14]

Unfortunately, local demand for AIB services is not encouraging. Only a few of the institutions that would be presumed to make intensive use of information are currently logged on to the database. Others, such as the USE University, and chambers of commerce are conspicuously absent from the list of subscribers. Demand from foreign users is moderate but encouraging. AIB is connected to several international databases, including GENIOS in Germany and INFOCHECK in the United Kingdom. In 1989 agreement was reached with DIALOG to load the AIB database for searching worldwide. Data traffic statistics from DIALOG show that from 1989 to 1990, net connect hours to AIB files were 170, during which 9,850 abstracts were printed online, and 17,000 were requested off-line. In addition, GLOBAL SCAN database has become available on AIB and covers other geographical areas in Europe, North America and the Far East.

Policies affecting information provision in the UAE

The information society, already well established in advanced countries, is now reaching the thresholds of some developing countries, and presents new challenges to them.[15] They therefore must respond positively in order to reap the benefits to be had from the emergent information society. They urgently need to broaden their concepts of national information policy by taking into account all the facets that make up information society; libraries, information centres, databases, publishers, telecommunication networks and information technology, as well as their users. The need for a coherent policy therefore, is pressing. Hernon and McClure defined information policy as: 'a set of interrelated principles, laws, guidelines, rules, regulations, procedures, and judicial interpretations that guide the oversight and management of the information life-cycle: the production, collection, distribution/dissemination, retrieval and retirement of information . . . [It] also embraces access to, and use of, information'.[16]

The need to formulate national information policies may be more evident now, but it is not a new phenomenon. Ever since the 1970s, UNESCO's General Information Programme has persistently advocated that: 'The formulation and implementation of a national information policy is the only way to ensure that all who engage in administrative, educational, scientific, and cultural activities have access to the information they need.'

Telecommunication policies

The number of telephones per inhabitant is widely believed to relate to the level of information provision in a country. The Gulf Arab States are reported to be the largest importers of telecommunications technology and equipment. Their combined investment over the next eight years is forecast to be around US$2,000 million a year. In the UAE expenditure on telecommunications equipment and development was US$152.3 million in 1986, and is likely to reach US$202 million and US$307 million in 1995 and 2000 respectively.

Since its establishment in 1976, as the country's sole supplier of telecommunications services, the Emirates Telecommunications Corporation (Etisalat) has grown steadily. In a report on communications in the UAE, the journal *Communication Middle East/Africa* (June 1992), gave the following interesting comparisons: 'The UAE currently have more mobile telephone user subscribers than Belgium, more exchange lines per 100 inhabitants than any other Middle East or African country, more public telephones than New Zealand and more telex lines than the Republic of Ireland – and a smaller population than any of these states.' One of Etisalat's most ambitious strategies is to place UAE in the central node for global telecommunications, and the country may have set up the technological infrastructure to achieve this goal.

Telephone services
According to figures compiled by Etisalat, the number of telephones in UAE has risen in a decade, from just over 100,000 in 1981 to 409,640 in 1990, giving a ratio of 25 receivers per 100 inhabitants. Demand grows at 12% per annum, and exchange capacity exceeds demand by 10%. During the period from 1976 to 1990 the traffic flow in paid minutes increased from 25 million to 954 million on the national, and from 10 million to 229 million on the international level.

Facsimile and telex
Facsimile appears to be the fastest growing service of all. Since 1987, it has emerged as the most widely used message transmission medium. With the introduction of advanced equipment such as Group III machines, facsimile continued to be the most preferred and cost-effective business communication tool. Its rise has seen an accompanying, though not corresponding drop in demand for telex. While facsimile usage over five years from 1987 rose from 2,000 to 18,000, telex, in spite of greatly reduced charges, has declined from 6,000 to 5,000 subscribers.

Data communication services
The interface between computer and telecommunications technologies has greatly enhanced the opportunities for transferring information across data networks. Recent innovations in the field of advanced, reliable and speedy communication media have made considerable impact on networking. In the UAE, Etisalat has been quick to provide advanced media communication facilities for its customers. At the same time, data communication services appear to be gaining more recognition from the business world, as strategic assets for greater efficiency. The advent of more sophisticated office automation and PC-based networks, such as Local Area Networks and Wide Area Networks, has been met with specialized support services from Etisalat such as modems, multiplexes, and Local Area Network bridges.

The UAE's Packet Switched Public Data Network (EMDAN)

was launched a few years ago as the first network in the Middle East, with a capacity of 1,000 users. Following the introduction of networks in other countries, EMDAN users are able to access more than 68 networks worldwide.

The Electronic Mail Network (EMNET) is an addition to EMDAN, to provide an integration of message services, such as facsimile and telex, and at the same time to support Electronic Fund Transfer at Point of Sales (EFTPOS) using credit cards. Since its introduction in 1990 more than 340 users have been connected.

Etisalat also offers Service 500, which enables computer owners to access bulletin boards and databases on the Public Switched Telephone Network. This is being used increasingly by members of computer clubs.

Future development of Etisalat's range of services will be centred on the introduction of its Integrated Services Digital Network (ISDN), which has the capabilty of connecting telephone, telex, facsimile and computer to any other ISDN-based terminal worldwide. As such the UAE is entering the age of video conferencing and video telephony.

State of information technology
It is generally accepted that the driving force behind the transition to information-oriented societies in advanced countries is the computer, nowadays making such an impact as a decision-making tool for industry and business. The main technologies whose potential for information exchange and networking are considered here, include cost-effective data transmission services over the public telecommunication network. The range of available information technologies in the United Arab Emirates has already been discussed.

The computer marketplace
In the UAE, as in other Arab countries, the computer marketplace has flourished in recent years. In 1991 total demand for personal computers in the Middle East was estimated at 30,000 units per year, half of which was absorbed by the UAE.[17] According to figures published by the Emirates Industrial Bank in 1991, the value of the country's imports of computers increased more than twice between 1986 and 1989, even though their prices went down by approximately a third during the same period.

Although the production and assembling of computer hardware began as recently as 1989, the future of this field of industry looks promising. There were two computer manufacturing plants in operation in 1991, and a third that specializes in printers. Statistics from the Emirates Industrial Bank show that up to 50% of the components of locally manufactured computers are also produced locally, and that the country's annual production of computers will reach around 10,000 in 1993.[18]

Consequently, personal computer ownership is becoming increasingly evident. A study conducted by the Dubai Chamber of Commerce and Industry showed that nearly 25% of households in the UAE have computers.[19] There is a constant spread of computer literacy, apparently as a result of the numbers of private institutions that offer training courses. The role of the Ministry of Education in this process has also been remarkable. In 1988 it introduced computer education throughout the education system; all government schools were supplied with hardware and trained staff, and it was made mandatory for all private schools to follow suit.

The trend in industry is moving fast towards more professional applications of IT. The provision, by Etisalat, of wide-ranging and cost-effective data services over the public network, as well as connecting services between host computers and PC users, has been instrumental in spreading automation in the country.

Role of government in IT
The UAE government is taking a positive approach towards IT. Government offices are well equipped with computers and peripherals, and with networks between offices. The availability of most of the popular application software, such as word processing and spreadsheets in Arabic, has encouraged them to automate their operations much faster than was originally projected. Most automation developments appear to be taking place in municipalities, and in police and emigration departments. Secondly, awareness of the value of automation led the government to set up the National Computer Centre in Abu Dhabi. This was later upgraded to become the General Authority for Information (GAI). Its main duties include the co-ordination of automation in government administration. It also acts as a consultative body to government on information technology issues, and functions as a national training centre. Plans have also been drawn for setting up a central information network to link government departments, and at the same time be a national access point to the rest of the world. GAI currently subscribes to DIALOG and conducts literature searches for government organizations.

IT in libraries

It is generally accepted that the convergence of computer and telecommunication technologies is having great impact on access to information. Despite their general availability in the country, their advent in libraries has so far been slow. In his recent survey, Kalburgi[20] found that only some 50% of libraries have any computer hardware.

Academic and special libraries are among those who showed early interest in automation. The UAE University library, after years of apparently unsuccessful attempts to develop a home-made integrated system, appears to have decided to procure ready-made software. The Higher College of Technology Library Resource Centre uses the Canadian microcomputer-based software MICRO CAT for cataloguing and an OPAC, but the software developers have yet, at the time of writing, to develop a circulation module. The Abu Dhabi National Oil Company uses SOUTRON software in full integration environment. The library of the Dubai Chamber of Commerce and Industry has developed its own database on a mainframe, which meets all its library functions.

Automation in public libraries and the National Library is not yet a reality. The sole exception to this is the Dubai Public Library, which in 1991 introduced the Arabized version of CDS/ISIS, on microcomputers. The software does not, however, operate in a multi-user and multi-tasking environment, and therefore lack many of the capabilities offered by commercially available software.

One recent storage medium that is rapidly penetrating in libraries is CD-ROM. This is increasingly preferred by most academic libraries as being a cost-effective alternative to internationally available online databases. The UAE University has more than twenty CD-ROM platforms, distributed among its various service points, which are being used along with other online databases subscribed to by the library.

Printing and publishing

The printing industry in the UAE grew substantially in a relatively short period. Between 1975 and 1988 the value of paper production increased from US$15.2 million to US$100 million. There are at present some 85 commercial presses, compared to 19 in 1975.

Structural change in demand for publications, as well as competition between printers prompted them to diversify from office stationery to books, newspapers, magazines, and other reading material. Parallel developments in desktop publishing caused a temporary slump in the printing industry, but that was partly offset by a rise in demand brought about by a flourishing advertising sector.[21] Printers were also quick to adopt new technology, in order to keep abreast of the demand for publications and to beat rising production and material costs. The Emirates Industrial Bank reported that demand for locally produced print materials increased by 145% between 1981 and 1988. It also estimated that 65% of demand for locally produced printed matter was for informational, educational and entertainment purposes, and 35% as stationery. The major part of printed imports consists of books and journals published outside the country.

As with the printing industry, publishing in UAE has only recently started, and is still in fairly early stages of development. There is a large overlap between printing, publishing and bookselling, so that it is difficult to differentiate publishers very precisely. There are at present some 18 establishments that are almost wholly engaged in publishing. About 1,200 titles were published between 1981 to 1991.

It should be mentioned that publishing in this country faces a number of obstacles. Among these is censorship, and the low return on invested capital. UAE is not unique in this respect and such problems are cited as being major obstacles to growth in commercial publishing in the Arab world in general.[22]

Official publications are an important source of printed information in UAE. Exact figures of the volume of publication are not available, due to the diversity of official and semi-official bodies that produce them, and to the lack of a national organization with overall responsibility for collecting them. In order to make an estimate of their number, the recently started *Bibliography of the United Arab Emirates,* of 1991 was scanned for titles likely to have emanated from official sources. Out of 1,131 titles listed, 413, representing 36.7% were identified as official publications. It should be noted that the bibliography contains only the collection held in the National Library, which does not have comprehensive coverage of all the country's official publications. Most of the publications cited originated from the Ministry of Information and Culture, which appears to be the most active official publishing agency in the country.

Book trade

At present there are about 60 bookshops in the country, but only 10 specialize in bookselling. The rest are mainly stationery retailers and newsagents; activities that amount to 75% of the annual trade of bookshops. According to the Department of Culture and Information in Sharjah, Lebanon, Egypt and Syria are the main sources of Arabic books. They supply up to 80% of Arabic book imports, while the remaining portion is imported from other Arabic language countries. British suppliers are the source of 80% of the foreign book imports, with 7% from North America and 6% from India. Annual per capita spending on books is about US$25. The population of UAE is considered to be among the highest average consumer spenders in the world, with an estimated annual per capita expenditure of US$8,967. If that is so, the average inhabitant spends only about 0.1% of annual income on reading material.

Book fairs are a feature of cultural life in the Emirates, and are organized regularly by various cultural organizations, educational institutions and learned societies. Hence they play a fundamental role in the availability of reading material. Since 1982 the Sharjah Annual Book Fair has been widely recognized as a major cultural event, bringing together authors, publishers and readers from all over the Arab world. In 1992 it attracted 466 exhibitors, who displayed about 120,000 titles, and was seen by more than 110,000 visitors.

The Press

The UAE government views the press as an instrument of national policy. Such a view exacts strict control over content and orientation. Although there were several individual attempts to issue some form of newspaper as far back as the 1930s, the beginning of formal journalism only dates from 1965, when the Dubai Municipality issued the first regular weekly newsletter. After independence the government issued Federal Law no.15 of 1973, concerning publishing and printing, which stipulated that ownership of local newspapers and periodicals is limited to UAE nationals. There are at present 9 daily newspapers and some 80 other local periodicals, in Arabic or English. Standing at the crossroads between the Asian subcontinent and the rest of the Arab world, periodicals imported from those regions are usually on sale the day after publication. There are 8 daily newspapers, with an estimated daily printing of 225,000 copies. Arthur[23] estimated exposure to the press at 77% of the population to newspapers, and 85% to general interest magazines. Some 70 magazines are published and distributed free to employees and members of professional and business associations. Other specialized publications of high quality are also beginning to emerge, in Arabic from learned societies such as the UAE Writers Union and the Social

Scientists Society. Among the most influential Arabic publications is the daily *Al Khaleej*, with a circulation of 36,000 copies. *Al Itihad* is a more conservative national paper with moderate circulation. One of the most important features of the audience, which has implications for reading habits, is the place of oral communication in society. Despite rapid urbanization, person-to-person and group contact still appear to be the main channels for the dissemination of news.[24] The two English daily newspapers, *Gulf news* and *Khaleej times*, with broad international news coverage, have a circulation of around 50,000 copies each. These papers mainly address the non-Arabic speaking expatriates.

Censorship
In common with many developing countries, censorship in the UAE is prevalent enough to be regarded as an information policy issue.[25] Following the establishment of the federation, the government was quick to issue the Printing and Publishing Act (Law no.15 of 1973). This law defines the boundaries of public communication through the publication and distribution of reading material, sets requirements for licensing of new publications, and stipulates the punishments for violation of its codes. Any material that is offensive to Islam, the Arab nation, or the political system of UAE is considered illegal. The law also indicates penalties for publications that instigate hatred between members of society, or provoke religious or political unrest. Such legal control is justified by the government on the grounds of preserving the country's national heritage and culture, and maintaining peace and security among the different ethnic groups that constitute present society. The management of censorship is under the Ministry of Information and Culture, which has the jurisdiction of examining all publications before they receive permission for distribution. Authors who wish to print in the country are required to submit their scripts to the censor prior to publication. The censor is, in practice, more severe towards the audiovisual media, but the spread of satellite dishes, currently in 20% of households, is likely to whittle away the ability to exercise control over viewing.

Copyright law
The growth of UAE as a commercial centre under the declared *laissez-faire* policy, has encouraged pirating computer software and audiovisual products. The country is not yet a signatory of the Berne Convention, or of any other universal intellectual property agreement, nor does it have any bilateral copyright treaties with other countries. This situation has led to serious infringe-

ments of the intellectual property rights of overseas companies. The UAE was placed under the so-called Section 301 Watch List, because of its inability to protect US intellectual rights, and in response to this and other pressures from the West, the government issued its first Copyright Law in 1992, in what seemed an attempt to avoid sanctions under the United States Federal Law no.40, of 1992.

The UAE Copyright Law covers works of authorship, drawing, photography, and movement, and has been the subject of debate both locally and abroad. The most significant criticism came from the World Intellectual Property Organization (WIPO) which, in welcoming the law as a remarkable achievement in the area, suggested changes in 15 sections, in order to cover all forms of creative expression. The law was due to come into force in July 1993, but up to June 1993 its implementing regulations had not yet been issued by the Ministry of Information and Culture, the agency responsible for its enforcement.

Conclusion

From the data available, the country evidently continues along the path towards rapid modernization of communication facilities. It is also moving towards being an information society, but has yet to achieve that effectively. Economic and social development has not been equalled by the use made of potential information services. The country's telecommunication and technological facilities are still underutilized in the service of information.

In response to its present position as a centre of international trade, demand for information is showing gradually, and to an increasing extent. This is met, in part by collections in academic institutions, state-supported organizations, and industrial and commercial establishments. However, some components are missing that would enhance the level of information provision. First, there is an urgent need to develop a national information policy, and second, for an interactive network infrastructure that allows for linking the existing information components.

References

1   Arthur, Robin, *Advertising and marketing in the United Arab Emirates,* Dubai, Galdari, 1991.
2   Ali, Mohammed M., 'UAE economic development, 1975–1989', *Trade and industry,* **16** (183), 1991, 8–17.
3   Abdulla, Abdul Khaliq, 'Scientific reset in the United Arab Emirates', *Shuon ijtimaiyah* (Translated title; Arabic text), **7** (25), 1990, 57–72.

4   Masuda, Yoneji, *Managing in the information society*, Oxford, Blackwell, 1990, 161.

5   Sliney, M., 'Arabia Deserta: the development of libraries in the Middle East', *Library Association record*, **92** (12), 1990, 912–14.

6   Kalburgi, L. B., *An In-depth evaluation of development of libraries and information services in the United Arab Emirates after its independence: possibilities, probes and current boundaries of building up an effective library and information service system*, Karnatak University, Dharwad, India, 1992 (PhD thesis).

7   Ibid.

8   United Arab Emirates, Ministry of Education, *Annual report of educational statistics, 1991–1992*, Dubai, the Ministry, 1992.

9   Osama, Abdul Rahman, *The Dilemma of development in the Arabian Peninsula*, London, Croom Helm, 1987.

10   Kristelli, John A., 'Trade associations and new perspectives in library service: a study of the Indiana Chamber of Commerce library', *Journal of business and finance librarianship*, **1** (1), 1990, 57–65.

11   Hukins, Celia, 'Chambers of commerce and business information', *Business information review*, **8** (4), 1992, 37–44.

12   Misra, V. N., 'Challenge of emerging information society: national policy issues', *IASLIC bulletin*, **32** (4), 1987, 16–175.

13   Kalseth, Karl, 'Business information strategy – the strategic use of information and knowledge', *Information services and use*, **11**, 1991, 155–64.

14   Sakhanini, Isam, *The Arab Information Bank: a descriptive and analytical study: paper presented at the First Conference of the Arab Information Network*, Tunisia, Arab League, 1986.

15   Misra, op. cit.

16   Hernon, P., *United States information policies*. In: Schipper, W. and Cunningham, M. eds., *National and international information policies*, Walnut Street, National Foundation of Abstracting and Indexing, 1991, 1–48.

17   *Khaleej times; supplement*, 25 February 1991.

18   *Emirates Industrial Bank bulletin*, 1992.

19   Ali, Mohammed M., 'Computer development in UAE', *Trade and industry*, **13** (159), 1988, 10–16.

20   Kalburgi, op. cit.

21   Arthur, op. cit.

22   Abdulla, op. cit.

23   Arthur, op. cit.

24   Huraiz, S. Hamid, *Arabic language and oral culture*, Al-Ain, Centre for Historical Research, 1983.

25   Leonard, L. and Mara, R., *Information policies in developing countries*.

In: Schipper W. and Cunningham, M. eds., *National and information policies*, Walnut Street, National Federation of Abstracting and Information Services, 1991, 139–61.

Index

Abbreviations or acronyms only have been used for headings – see List of Abbreviations for full versions. Page references in italics indicate tables.

AACR 20
Abdellia library (Tunisia) 197
Abdullah, King 110–11
academic libraries
  Iraq 99–100, *100*
  Jordan 107–8, 114–15
  United Arab Emirates 245–6, 253
  see also school libraries; university libraries
ACML 214, 215
Adult Education Directorate (Bahrain) 76–7, 77
AIB 248
Ain Shams University (Egypt) *83*, 87, 91
Al Fatah University (Libya) 37–8
Al Itihad 256
Al Khaleej 256
Al Mafraq Hospital Library (Abu Dhabi) 233
Al Maktoum Health Centre Library (Dubai) 234
Al Wasl Hospital Library (Dubai) 234
Al-Aqsa mosque 106
Al-Azhar University (Egypt) 81–2, *83*, 87
Al-Haram mosque (Saudi Arabia) 141, 149
Al-Jabal Al Gharbi University (Libya) 37
Al-Kindi 214
Al-Musil University (Iraq) 99
Al-Mustansiriya University (Iraq) 103
Al-Zaherieh library (Syria) 190
Alam el maktabaat (Libraries World) 91
ALDOC 3–4, 7, 201–2
ALESCO 4, 20, 21, 201
Alexandria library (Egypt)
  ancient 81
  future 8, 93

Alexandria University (Egypt) 27, *83*, 89, 92
Algeria
  children's library services 55–66
  cultural centres 59–60, *61*
  LIS education 32–4, 41–4, 46–9, 49–51
  national library 13, *13*, 23
    functions 14, 15, 16
    resources 16, 18
  public libraries 57–9, *61*
  school libraries 61–4, *63*, *64*
ALIT 202
Anwar, A. A. 70
Arabian Advanced Systems 7
ARABSAT 4
ARISNET 4, 202
Assad National Library (Syria) *13*, 24, 191–2
  directorate and sections 192–3
  employees 194
  functions 15, 16, *16*, 194–5
  operations 20, 21, 22
  resources 16, *17*, *18*, 19
  use 193–4
Assiut University (Egypt) *83*, 86, 92
AUC (Egypt) 8, 82, *83*, 87, 92
audiovisual materials 19
automation *see* computers and computer systems

Bahrain 68–9, 79
  LIS education 69–79
  national library *13*, 15, 23
Bahrain Studies and Research Centre 76
Bait El-Alm (House of Learning AD 988) 81
Beit-el-Hikma (House of Knowledge) (Tunisia) 196
bibliographies, national 14, 195, 205

Bibliography of the United Arab Emirates 254
Bibliothèca Alexandrina 8, 93
Bibliothèque Générale et Archives (Morocco) 13, 22, 23
   functions 15, 16, *16*
   operations 20, 21
   resources 16, 17, *18*
Bibliothèque Nationale d'Alger 13, *13, 23*
   functions 14, 15, 16
   resources 16, *18*
Bibliothèque Nationale (Mauritania) *13, 23*
   functions 15
   resources 16, 17, *18*
Bibliothèque Nationale (Tunisia) *13,* 24, 205–6
   functions 16, *16*
   operations 20, 22
   resources 16, 17, *18, 19*
book trade in UAE 254–5
British Council 93–4
   libraries
      Algeria 61
      Bahrain 76
      Dubai 245
      Egypt 87–8
Bulletin de l'Informatiste (Morocco) 48

Cairo University 26–7, 28–30, *83,* 87, 89
cataloguing, national libraries 20
CD-ROM 7, 102, 126, 253
CDN (Tunisia) 202–3
CDS/ISIS 7, 21, 113, 124, 125
censorship in UAE 256
CERIST (Algeria) 33, 43, 51
chambers of commerce in UAE 247–8
Charter of Algiers (1976) 55
children's library services 1
   Algeria 55–66
   Egypt 1–2
   Iraq 101
   see also school libraries
children's literature
   Algeria 64–5, *64*
   China 109–10
CIP 20, 110

CND (Morocco) 15, 44, 47, 48
CNDA (Tunisia) 201, 202, 203–4
CNI (Tunisia) 199
CNUDST (Tunisia) 202, 204
collections, national
   library 17–19, *18*
college libraries *see* academic libraries
community colleges in Jordan 114–15, 122
computers and computer systems 4, 6–8, 90
   Iraq 102
   Jordan 116–17, 123–6
   national libraries 21–2
   Sudan 186–7
   Tunisia 199–200, 203–4, 208–9
   United Arab Emirates 223, 248, 250, 251–2
consultancy, LIS 155–6, 176–7
   Sudan 174, *175*
   in colonial period 156–7
   P. H. Sewell's mission 157–61
   J. S. Parker's mission 161–7
   P. H. Sewell's second mission 167–71
   other consultancies 171–4
copyright law in UAE 256–7
CPN (Algeria) 42
cultural centres (Algeria) 59–61, *61*
Cultural Foundation of Abu Dhabi 217, 244

Dagher, J. A. 171
Dar Al-Kutub Wal-Watha'iq *see* Iraq, national library
Dar-al-kutub al-wataniya *see* Tunisia, national library
databases *see* computers and computer systems
DBA 45
DDC 20–1
DESS 42, *42*, 43, 50–1
DEUA 33–4, *42, 42*, 49–50
DGJDPGD (Saudi Arabia) 142, 144
DIALOG 126, 248
dissertations 19, 195
DOBIS/LIBIS system 6, 87
Documentation and Information Centre (Sudan) 186–7
DPGS 42, *42*, 43, 51

DSB 42, *42*, 43, 44, *50*
Dubai Municipality (UAE) 21
Education Documentation Centre
  (Bahrain) 76
education, LIS 2–3, 26, 39
  Algeria 32–4, 41–4, 46–9, 49–51
  Bahrain 69–79
  Egypt 26–30
  Iraq 103
  Jordan 121–3
  Libya 36–8
  Morocco 30–2, 44–5, 46–9, 51–2
  Sudan 38, 187–8
  Tunisia 34–6, 45, 46–9, 52–3,
    199–200, 207–9
Education, Ministry of
  Bahrain 70–1, 72, 74
  Jordan 118–19, 120, 122
  Saudi Arabia 141–2, 143, 144, 150,
    151
Egypt 1–2, 8
  LIS education 26–30
  national library 6, *13*, 22, 23
    functions 14, 15, 16
    operations 20, 21
    resources 16, 17, *17*, *18*
  university libraries 81, *83*, *84*
    buildings and equipment 89–90
    characteristics of universities
      83, 85
    co-operation 91–3
    collections 86–8
    foreign assistance 93–4
    history 81–2
    role and organization 85–6
    staff 88–9
    users and services 90–1
Egyptian Library Association 91
El-Munifia University (Egypt) 27,
  83, 89
EMDAN 250–1
Emirates Armed Forces medical journal
  234
EMNET 251
ENA (Tunisia) 34, 45, 208, 209
ENSTINET 15, 92–3
ESI (Morocco) 30–2, 44–5, 47, 48
Etisalat College of Engineering
  (UAE) 246
Etisalat (UAE) 249, 250, 251

facsimiles (faxes) 250
Female Private Medical College
  Library (Dubai) 230
FMHS (UAE) 218, 219
'French Library' (Tunisia) 197
funding 5

GAI (UAE) 252
Garyounes University (Libya) 37
GDHMS (Saudi Arabia) 142, 144
General Directorate of Public
  Libraries (Saudi Arabia) 141–2,
    144, 149, 151
Gulf Wars
  first 96–7
  second 2, 9, 97
Gulfnet 8–9

Hashemite collections (Jordan) 117
Hasni, N. 198
hospital libraries (UAE) 231–5
hypermedia 7

IBM 6
Ibn al-Nadim 214
Ibn Sina (*Qanun al-tibb (The Law of
  Medicine)*) 214
ICL 6
IFLA Standing Committee on
  Theory and Research Panel dis-
  cussion (Manila 1980) 176
information policies, national 3–4
information technology *see* comput-
  ers and computer systems
Instituts de Bibliothéconomie
  (Algeria)
  d'Alger 32–3, 34, *42*, 43, 44, *44*, 48
  de Constantine 32–3, 34, *42*, 43,
    44, *44*, 48
  d'Oran 32–3, 34, *42*, 44, *44*, 48
Institute Ali Bach Hamba (Tunisia)
  34, 45, 207–8
INTERNET 7–8
IPSI (Tunisia) 34, 208, 209
Iraq 96–7
  academic libraries 99–100, *100*
  children's libraries 101
  LIS education 103
  national library 13, 23, 98–9
    functions 15, *16*
    operations 20, 21, 22

resources 16, 17, 18, 19, 98, 99
public libraries 101, 102
school libraries 100–1, 101
special libraries 102
Iraq–Iran war 96–7
Iraqi National Network for Libraries
    and Information Centres 102
IRSIT (Tunisia) 201
ISBD 20
ISBN 20
ISD (Tunisia) 34–6, 47, 52–3, 208
ISDN 251
ISSN 20
IUC 156–7

Jezira and Central Hospitals Library
    (Abu Dhabi) 232
JLA 16, 113, 121, 126–8
    and AACR2 20
    publications 14, 111
    and training 122
Jordan 104–6
    community college libraries
        107–8, 114–15
    information technology 123–6
    legislation 107–8
    library and information services
        history and development 106–7
    LIS education 121–3
    National Documentation Centre
        109, 110
    national library 13, 13, 23, 108,
        109–10
        functions 16, 16
        operations 20
        resources 16, 17, 18, 19
    NIC 119–21
    public libraries 108, 110–13
    school libraries 107, 117–19
    special libraries 108, 113–14
    university libraries 108, 115–17,
        116
Jordan Communication Format 121
Juma'a al-Majed Foundation for
    Culture and Heritage (UAE) 21

KACST 8–9
Kairouan mosque (Tunisia) 196
Khalifa, Hajji 214
King Fahd National Library (Saudi
    Arabia) 8, 13, 22, 24

functions 15, 16, 16
operations 7, 20, 21, 22
resources 16, 17, 18, 19
King Fahd University for Petroleum
    and Minerals (Saudi Arabia) 6,
    7
KISR (Kuwait) 9, 215
Kuesters-Schah, U. 198
Kuwait 1, 2, 6, 9, 16
    school libraries 131, 137–8
        facilities 136–7
        finance 134–5
        organization and distribution
            131–2, 133
        personnel 135–6
        resources 133–4, 133
        services 136
Kuwait University 9

Law of Municipalities (Jordan 1955)
    108
Lebanon
    national library 12, 16
lecturers 77–8
    see also education, LIS
legal deposit laws 14, 17, 110
legislation 4–5
librarians 2
    see also education, LIS; staff,
        library
library associations 2, 16
library schools 16
    see also education, LIS
Libya
    LIS education 36–8
    national library 13, 16, 23
Lindley, D. K. 173–4
literature, children's see children's
    literature

'madrasas' 81
Maghreb
    LIS education 41–53
    see also Algeria, Morocco, Tunisia
Mansoura University (Egypt) 83, 92
manuscripts 19, 117
maps 19
Mauritania
    national library 13, 23
        functions 15
        resources 16, 17, 18

medical libraries 214–15
United Arab Emirates 215–16,
217–18, 235, 237
Female private medical
college 230
Ministry of Health hospitals
231–4
NML 218–30, *220–1*, *226–7*,
228–9
Oasis private hospital 235
schools of nursing 230–1
Zayed military hospital 234
MEDLINE 223
microcomputers 90
Jordan 124–5
see also computers and computer
systems
MINISIS 7, 117, 124, 125, 126, 202
Morocco
LIS education 30–2, 44–5, 46–9,
51–2
national library *13*, 22, 23
functions 15, 16, *16*
operations 20, 21
resources 16, *17*, *18*
mosque libraries 81, 106, 141
Municipal Library of Algiers 58,
58–9
Munn, R. 172–3
Muta University (Jordan) 115, *116*

National Archives Centre (Jordan)
109
National Centre for Archives (Iraq)
98–9, *99*
National Committee for
Documentation (Tunisia) 202
National Conference for Educational
Development (Jordan 1987) 118
National Documentation Centre
(Jordan) 109, 110
national libraries 12–13, 23–4
functions 13–16
history 13
operations 20–2
resources 16–19
working hours 22–3
see also national libraries subhead-
ings under Iraq; Jordan; Syria;
Tunisia; United Arab Emirates
National Records Office (Sudan) 183

National register of current research
(Sudan) 186
NATIS 167
NDC (Sudan) 168, 174
New Al-Qassemi Hospital Library
(Sharjah) 234
NIC (Jordan) 119–21
NIDOC (Egypt) 92
NIS (Jordan) 120
NML (UAE) 218–20, *220–1*, *226–9*
NSTIC (Kuwait) 9, 215
nursing, schools of (UAE) 230–1

Oasis Hospital Library (UAE) 235
Offor, Richard 157
Omdurman Central Library (Sudan)
158, 159
Omdurman University (Sudan) 38
Orthodox Patriarchate Library 106,
107

PAAET (Kuwait) 9
Parker, J. S. 160, 162–7, 174
periodicals 14–15, 19
PGI 167
preservation of national heritage
5–6, 13–14, *14*
Press, the in UAE 255–6
printing industry in UAE 253–4
Printing and Publishing Act (1973)
(UAE) 256
public libraries 1, 15
Algeria 57–9
Bahrain 74–6
Iraq 101, *102*
Jordan 108, 110–13
administrative organizations
144–5
classification and cataloguing
150
collections 146–50, *147*, *148*,
149
distribution 142–4, *143*
facilities 150–1
goals and objectives 145
historical development 141–2
opening hours 151
personnel 145–6
user services 151–2
Tunisia 206–7
United Arab Emirates 243–5, 253

Public Libraries Directorate
    (Bahrain) 74–6
publishing industry
    Iraq *97, 98*
    United Arab Emirates 254

Qanun al-tibb (The Law of Medicine)
    (Ibn Sina) 214
Qatar
    national library 13, 24
        functions 15, 16, *16*
        resources 16, 17, *17, 18*

Rajagopalan, T. S. 171–2
Rashid Hospital Library (Dubai) 233
RETC (Bahrain) 70–1, *72*
*Revue de l'information scientifique et
    technique* (Algeria) 48
Revue maghrébine de documentation, La
    (Tunisia) 48
*Rissalat Al-Maktaba (The Message of the
    Library)* 128
Royal Scientific Society (Jordan) 126

Saudi Arabia 8–9, 140–1
    automation 6, 7–8, 22
    national library 13, 22, 24
        functions 15, 16, *16*
        operations 7, 20, 21, 22
        resources 16, 17, *18*, 19
    public libraries
        administrative organizations
            144–5
        classification and cataloguing
            150
        collections 146–50, *147, 148, 149*
        distribution 142–4, *143*
        facilities 150–1
        goals and objectives 145
        historical development 141–2
        opening hours 151
        personnel 145–6
        user services 151–2
    status of librarians 2
school librarians
    Bahrain 70–1, *71*
school libraries 1
    Algeria 61–4, *63, 64*
    Bahrain 72–3
    Iraq 100–1, *101*
    Jordan 107, 117–19

Kuwait 131, 137–8
    facilities 136–7
    finance 134–5
    organization and distribution
        131–2, *133*
    personnel 135–6
    resources 133–4, *133*
    services 136
Tunisia 207
United Arab Emirates 246
    see also academic libraries; chil-
        dren's library services
Sewell, P. H. 158–61, 167–71, 187
Sharjah Annual Book Fair 255
Somalia
    natonal library 12
special libraries
    Iraq 102
    Jordan 108, 113–14
    United Arab Emirates 246–7, 253
staff, library
    national libraries 16–17
        Syria 194
    public libraries
        Jordan 112
        Saudi Arabia 145–6
    school libraries
        Kuwait 135–6
    university libraries
        Egypt 88–9
    see also education, LIS
Sudan 181
    communications 182–3
    and consultancy 174, *175*
        in colonial period 156–7
        P. H. Sewell's mission 157–61
        J. S. Parker's mission 161–7
        P. H. Sewell's second mission
            167–71
        other consultancies 171–4
    Documentation and Information
        Centre 186–7
    education and research 181–2
    future development 188–9
    libraries, documentation and
        information services 183–4
    LIS education 38, 187–8
    national library 16
    obstacles to development of
        libraries and information sys-
        tem 185–6

Sudan science abstracts 186
Syria 190
  Assad National Library *13*, 24,
    191–2
    directorates and sections 192–3
    employees 194
    functions 15, 16, *16*, 194–5
    operations 20, 21, 22
    resources 16, *17*, *18*, 19
    use 193–4
Syrian national bibliography 195

TANIT 203
Tanta University (Egypt) 27, *83*, 89,
  92
Tawam Medical Library (Abu
  Dhabi) 233
telecommunications in UAE 249–50
telex 250
thesauri 21
theses 117
training *see* education, LIS
Training Directorate (Bahrain) 70,
  72
TUNIS 203
Tunisia 196, 211–12
  history of libraries 196–7
  information infrastructure 197–9
  information system 202–4
  information technology 199–202
  LIS education 34–6, 45, 46–9, 52–3,
    207–9
  national library *13*, 24, 205–6
    functions 16, *16*
    operations 20, 22
    resources 16, *17*, 18, *18*, 19
  public libraries 206–7
  school libraries 207
  university libraries 209–11

UCCI (UAE) 247
UDC 20
UNDP 4, 7, 30, 167, 171–2
UNESCO 155, 160
  and Alexandria library 93
  book coupons 5, 211
  consultancy missions to Sudan
    156, 157–8, 161–2, 171–2, 173,
    184
  and cultural preservation 5
  and information systems 4, 7

and LIS education 30, 167, 208
union catalogues 15
union lists of periodicals 15
UNISIST 167, 187
United Arab Emirates 2, 216–17,
  240–2
  academic libraries 245–6, 253
  Arab Information Bank 248
  medical libraries 215–16, 217–18,
    235, 237
  Female private medical college
    230
  Ministry of Health hospitals
    231–4
  NML 218–30, *220–1*, *226–7*,
    228–9
  Oasis private hospital 235
  schools of nursing 230–1
  Zayed military hospital 234–5
  national library *13*, 24, 244
    functions 15, 16, *16*
    operations 21, 22
    resources 16, *17*, *18*, 19
  policies affecting information pro-
    vision 249–51
  printing and publishing 253–7
  public libraries 243–5, 253
  school libraries 246
  special libraries 246–7, 253
  state of information technology
    251–3
United Arab Emirates University
  217, 245
University of Baghdad 99, 103
University of Jordan 115, *116*, 117,
  123, 126
University of Khartoum 159, 183,
  187
university libraries
  Egypt 81–94
  Jordan 108, 115–17, *116*
  Tunisia 209–11
  see also academic libraries
UNRWA 115, 117, 122
USAID 87, 93

VSO 87, 94
wilaya (Algerian counties) 58, 59, 62

Yarmouk University (Jordan) 115,
  116, 117, 122, 126

Zagazig University (Egypt) *83*, 92
Zayed Military Hospital (Abu
      Dhabi) 234
Zeituna mosque (Tunisia) 197

"You've come this far," he reminded her. "I won't drop you."

"Promise?"

"Promise." She bit her lower lip, released her grip on the airborne roots of a small tree, and slipped into his arms as if destiny had arranged it. A new shower of small sandy rocks cascaded along with her. He held her closely until she said, "Okay, I'm down."

He took a step back but kept his hands on her upper arms and looked down at her upturned face. There was a streak of dirt along her jaw, and he wiped it off gently, but it was the sweet curve of her lips that held him.

"Maybe we should get to work," she said softly.

"Yes," he said, and turning, looked over the side. The water was less than a foot below the waterline. Behind him, she asked, "Hadn't we better hurry up and tighten those anchor lines?"

He turned around quickly, and looked down into a pair of brown eyes. "Let's get one thing straight. There's only one skipper on *Ashanti*, and it's me."

The brown eyes narrowed and threw sparkling darts at him. "Then I'm glad I got down here in time for a good seat. I've never actually seen a boat turned into driftwood before."

He shook his head gently. "Listen," he said wearily. "I'm sorry—"

"Don't apologize," she interrupted. "You'll ruin the image I'm beginning to form of you."

"Image?"

"Of a stubborn, arrogant, cynical man. Am I far off the mark?"

He tried conjuring up a grin, which only served to send a shot of pain through his face. He supposed that accounted for the startled look that now hovered in the brown eyes. It seemed a little late for a witty retort, even if his brain was up to creating one. And besides, she was half right: even at his best he tended to be stubborn and cynical. He wiped a new layer of sweat off his forehead and stepped into the cockpit. Within seconds, he was tightening the lines on the anchors. Beside him the woman whose name he remembered was Catherine knelt next to the manual pump lever in the cockpit floor.

"Mind if I pump some of the Pacific Ocean out of your boat, skipper?"

Jake grunted, the pain in his head all but obliterating her words. Or was it the roar of the ocean beating his beloved *Ashanti* to death against the rock, a mountain of dirt only a stone's throw from the bow?

Catherine watched Jake pull on the anchor lines as she pumped endless quantities of seawater from the bilges. Muscles tensed and flexed in his arms and hands; his movements were sure and regular. For a second, she thought of the feel of those hands gripping her ankles, sliding up her body as, heart in throat, she'd trusted him to catch her as she slipped from the ledge above the boat. She still couldn't imagine why she'd felt so sure he would catch her, because he didn't look very good. She laughed softly as she rephrased her last thought. The fact was he looked very good; he might be slightly worn around the edges but it accentuated his masculinity and made him almost unendurably desirable. He also looked like a man teetering on the edge of control, and the barely perceptible swelling of the jaw she'd noticed that morning was almost twice as big.

Derek's clean-shaven face floated before her eyes. Maybe she should suggest he let his hair grow a little uneven and that he stop shaving for a day or so—

The boat began to move backward, against the waves, and Catherine fell back onto her bottom from her perch atop her heels. She heard an awful crunch as the hull ground against the rock. Jake had the anchor lines wound tight around the winches on either side of the cockpit and was dividing his energy between the two lines. She scrambled to her feet, let go of the pump handle, and took the starboard winch, smiling at his look of surprise as she quickly pulled on the line biting into her palms. He apparently decided she could handle the job and devoted himself to the port-side winch.

Ashanti afloat became a new entity. Sluggish from the water pouring through the hole in her side, but jaunty with the familiar sea rising beneath her hull, she danced drowsily over the ever-rising swell of the sea.

''Let your line go slack,'' Jake hollered.

Catherine unwound the line from the winch. Jake was pulling *Ashanti* towards the furthest anchor. She looked out to sea and saw that both anchors were marked with buoys. When her line became too short, she let it drop into the ocean, knowing he could retrieve it later. She got back on her knees and resumed pumping water from the bilges.

By now, *Ashanti* was on top of the second anchor. Jake walked the line to the bow of the boat and tied it off, then returned to the cockpit.

"Is that awful sound your cat?" Catherine asked.

He nodded. "She's not . . . happy with the situation," he said.

"No kidding."

Jake slid the companionway hatch toward the main mast and opened the small varnished doors. The cat shot out into the cockpit while Jake went down inside. He was back a second later.

"You'll have to keep pumping," he said. "She's taking in buckets of water. I'll start the engine."

"Amos said he'd have the cradle in the water by the time you got there," she told him. He nodded at her and disappeared inside.

Catherine hadn't been out in the bay for over a year. When her father had been alive, he'd taken her out fishing on occasion, always complaining when she invariably caught the biggest salmon. She understood his complaints were all make-believe, that he loved boasting to his buddies that his "little girl" caught bigger fish than they could. The bay had seemed a friendlier place when she'd been aboard her dad's skiff with the Evinrude motor sputtering away than it did today aboard this big yacht with a hole in its side and a bona fide grump for a captain.

She shook her head. What was Jake Stokes like when he wasn't working to save his boat while a toothache poisoned his system? She made a mental bet he was much the same as he was now, but the beginning of his apology sounded in her ears, and that beguiling grin he'd tried to conjure out of worry and pain played itself in front of her eyes. How long had it been since he'd slept decently or eaten anything?

The cat sat on the stern of the boat, her crossed eyes giving Catherine the once-over. "Instead of looking so superior, why don't you help?" Catherine mumbled, but the cat only meowed and proceeded to groom its sable-brown mask. It crossed her mind that this cat was about as opposite from Baloo as water was from dry land.

"You doing okay?" Jake asked as he popped up out of the cabin, almost smiling, his eyes lit from inside, apparently working on a second wind.

Catherine ignored the fact that her arm felt like falling off and said, "Sure."

"Good." He disappeared again, and a moment later, the engine sprang to life with a rat-a-tat rumble. The Siamese meowed loudly but didn't move.

Jake appeared again. He ran out onto the bow and began pulling on the line. Apparently he thought better of taking the time to reclaim all that line, and untied his end. The line sank down toward the bottom, but the orange buoy secured to it floated merrily in the swells.

He was back in the cockpit, his footsteps on the

decks as sure as Catherine's were on the mountains around Rocky Point. He stood behind the wheel and put the engine in gear. "Do you know a safe passage into the river?" he asked.

Catherine nodded. "Will your boat sink if I stop for a few minutes to show you?"

"I hope not," he said.

She straightened up and pointed. "The mouth is over there. Stay away from those old piers jutting out into the cove from the headland; stay in the middle of the channel. Then keep the red poles on the starboard side as you travel up the river."

"Red right returning," he mumbled, quoting boating traffic rules.

"That's right. Amos has an old railway lift. He'll have bright ties on the ends of the submerged cradle. He said he'll be out in a skiff to set the blocks once you're in the cradle."

"Has he done this before? I mean, with a boat the size of *Ashanti*?"

Catherine looked into his feverish sea-green eyes and decided to lie. "Of course. I'd better get back to the pumps."

By the time *Ashanti* made it into the calmer waters of the river, Catherine's arm was numb. She could hear the electric pump buzzing away, but she could also hear the fruits of her labor—water—washing overboard, so she kept pumping.

"Are we about there?" she asked, trying to see over the cabin and failing.

"Just about. Why don't you stop pumping and come help me get some lines ready?''

"Gladly." Catherine got to her feet again, her arm throbbing. She took a line from Jake and tied it where he pointed. Amos hailed them from his little skiff, pointing toward the gaily wrapped pipes that formed the ends of the submerged cradle. Catherine thought it was a good idea Jake couldn't see the condition of the contraption he was going to trust to pull his boat out of the water.

Jake yelled. "I see it. Thanks."

Catherine knew the railway consisted of an old flat-head gasoline engine, what looked like railroad tracks running into the water, a rusty cable, a few pulleys, and, she guessed, bailing wire and a wad of gum.

Jake expertly guided his boat into the cradle. Quickly, Amos was beside them, pushing wooden blocks down the pipes with one of his long oars until they were wedged in between the hull and the sides of the cradle. Jake and Catherine tied lines, then Jake pumped while Amos rowed ashore and started the engine, which they hoped would pull *Ashanti* out of the water.

In the end, it all went smoothly, though there were more than a few times when things seemed to shudder and shake, times which made Jake's drawn face pale and Catherine's heart stop. As soon as the boat was all the way out of the water, Amos propped a ladder against the hull, and Catherine climbed down. Jake followed.

He took a long walk around his boat. When he got back to Catherine's side, his eyes were wide. "I could use a stiff drink," he mumbled.

Catherine smiled. "You could use a good dentist."

"I don't need a dentist," he said as his cat howled from the deck like an abandoned waif. He climbed up the ladder, gently lifted her into his arms, and climbed back down.

"I got a bottle in the shack," Amos said and shuffled off towards the ramshackle wooden structure that housed the machinery for the old ways.

Catherine patted the cat on her sleek head. "I forgot her name."

"Pywacket," Jake said. He looked at Catherine and smiled, winced, and groaned. "Thank you for not mentioning the fact that this contraption your friend calls a boat ways is older than the two of us put together."

"You're welcome."

"And I also owe you a tremendous thanks for what you did today."

"Mr. Stokes, you're in terrible jeopardy of ruining that image we discussed earlier."

He smiled. "I hope so," he said. "I don't know what got into me." He carefully set his cat down on the ground. She sniffed the sea-scented mud before scampering off toward the tall weeds.

"I was afraid you were going to make me walk the plank," Catherine said.

"Was I that bad?"

She smiled. Before she could answer, they heard Amos.

"Found it," he called, waving a half-empty bottle of dark rum. He passed the bottle around and they each took a swig. Catherine sputtered a little and Amos slapped her on the back. She watched Jake take a second swallow. He very carefully set the bottle against his lips—not his teeth—and drank slowly.

"I had an abscessed tooth once," she said.

Jake stared at her. She ignored his gaze—not an easy task as his eyes made every inch of her burn with awareness—and continued her story.

"The dentist told me that people can actually die when the poison gets into the sinus cavity. In fact, he bawled me out because I waited a few days to come see him. Just out of curiosity, Jake, how long have you waited?"

"Not long enough to be taken in by this little story," he said calmly.

"Well, just let me know when you decide you can't take it anymore," she said. "I know a great dentist and I'll even drive you to his office. No, don't thank me—"

"I wasn't going to."

"Why aren't I surprised? It's just like I said. You're stubborn, Jake Stokes. Pigheaded and stubborn."

"Ah, and I thought you were beginning to like me," he said, conjuring up a devilish smile.

"I have work to do," Catherine said, and turned on her heels. She was halfway up Rocky Point Head before she gave in to the temptation to look back down at *Ashanti*. The skipper was nowhere in sight.

Not that it mattered, Catherine told herself as she resumed her climb.

Chapter Three

Catherine's living quarters were linked to the inn through a connecting door in the office. They consisted of four rooms: living room, kitchen, bedroom, and bath. Catherine's mother had died in childbirth, so it had always been just she and her father. While she'd been growing up, they'd lived in a cottage behind the inn, but he'd long ago rented that out, and while Catherine was away at school, he had taken to living in the small apartment so handy to the front desk. The welcome income generated by the cabin kept Catherine in the apartment, but the decor of the small apartment she now called home reflected her father's tastes and needs, not hers.

The living room was overly crowded with inexpensive furniture in a hodgepodge of colors and styles. Against one wall were several old framed black-and-white photographs chronicling the inn's construction and modifications, along with a few of the fishing camp and boat yard. There were pictures of her growing up as well, and some of Amos and her father holding strings of silver fish, their faces ruddy from a day spent out on the sea.

Catherine ran a finger over a photograph of her father and smiled. Maybe she kept these rooms the way he'd left them because it made him seem less gone, almost as though he would come shuffling through the door at any moment, smelling of dead fish and salt. What would he think of all the changes she'd made in the inn in the short time since his death? Would he approve, or be as horrified as Amos? Or more in character, would he even notice?

She perched on the edge of the vinyl avocado couch and stared at the stack of bills piled on the maple coffee table. Next to them was a shoebox of receipts Terry had presented her with that afternoon. In a flurry of efficiency she scooped everything up and carried it to the large rolltop desk where she spent an hour organizing, making out checks, and filing. That done, she closed the desk and stood, groaning as the muscles in her legs protested a day spent tramping around the rough headlands.

The one impact she'd made on her father's living quarters were the vases of fresh flowers from the inn's many gardens and some wild flowers from the headland itself. She stooped to pluck a wilted stalk of yellow lupine out of a vase and nip a dead iris from its stem so that there was room for the second flower to bloom. The window shades were open to admit as much sunlight as possible, and as she cracked open the glass to toss the dead flowers outside, she gazed past the wind-stunted trees at the Pacific Ocean. For a second she let her thoughts drift to her interrupted studies, to the plans she'd had to uncover the mysteries of the sea. She tore herself from this reverie when she realized it was getting late. Derek was coming to dinner.

Catherine closed the drapes in her bedroom and stripped off the soiled sweater and pants. She took a short shower, washing off the sweat and seawater she'd accumulated during her interval aboard *Ashanti*. It was impossible to think of the boat and not dwell on the skipper, she found. And while she twisted her mass of dark hair atop her head, she relived again the few minutes when she'd looked down into his face from the perch on the mountain's slope—the expression in his eyes, the curl to his lips, the feel of his hands wrapped around her ankles, the emotion that had risen like bubbles in an aquarium as his gaze burned into her soul.

This was ridiculous. Twice now she'd shivered at the memory of what? His eyes, the feel of his hands on her ankles? For heaven's sake, she hadn't lived twenty-five years without encountering a handsome male before. Take Derek, for instance. He was handsome *and* he was devoted to helping people, unlike the self-serving man on the sailboat. Only trouble was, she had a feeling she could gaze into Derek's eyes and absolutely nothing would happen. Was she thinking too much in physical terms? Wasn't attraction supposed to take place in the brain?

As she zipped up a pale peach-colored cotton dress

and slipped a pair of white sandals onto her feet, she
decided perhaps it was time to get to know Derek
better. He'd been hinting around for months, and she'd
been putting him off, citing the inn as the reason for
her hesitation to become romantically involved. "Let
me get this place back on its feet first," she'd said,
and though regret had filled his gray eyes, he'd nodded
with understanding.

Catherine found a matching shade of lipstick on her
dresser and applied a liberal coat to her full lips. *Time
to take the gloves off*, she told her reflection. Time to
look at Derek Prouse as a man and not a friend and
neighbor. Time to see if what she'd read was true, that
romantic feelings originated above the neck. She refused to think about *Ashanti*'s egotistical captain, or
the way his body was put together, or the way he moved
and smiled and looked at her. It was unnatural for a
woman her age to have no interesting man in her life—
no wonder she was looking at a man like Jake Stokes.
Deprivation, not genuine interest, accounted for her
runaway imagination and the silly shivers that period-
ically attacked her spine!

She caught sight of her reflection in the mirror and
sighed. Peach cotton? Without giving the action too
much thought, she unzipped the dress and began rummaging through her closet, looking for something a
little more daring, something that would announce to
Derek that the game—and the stakes—had changed.

"Look out, Dr. Prouse," she said as she pulled an

off-the-shoulder ivory silk chemise from within the confines of the closet.

An hour later, Catherine sat across the table from Derek Prouse. He was a medium-sized man with a boyish grin. He looked as though he played baseball; in fact, he looked as though someone should tattoo the words "All American" across his forehead. They'd met a few summers before when Catherine came home during summer break to help out at the inn. Derek, a new doctor in Madrone, the nearest town to the south, had been in residence. Now, he was one of the few who didn't act as though Catherine was defiling a national treasure by modifying the inn.

He leaned across the table, put his hand over hers, and whispered, "You must feel very satisfied."

She looked around the partially full dining room, saw the local art hanging on the walls, art that strayed towards seascapes, heard the chatter of satisfied customers, the occasional rise of a laugh or the tinkle of silver hitting china, and nodded. "I do," she said, not adding that a dozen more patrons would make her a dozen times happier. "The new chef is working out very well."

"I wasn't alluding to the inn," Derek said. "I was thinking of the fact that every male head swiveled your way when you entered the room. You look absolutely divine."

Well, well, well, Catherine thought, a smile of satisfaction toying with her lips. *Off to a good start!* She looked into Derek's gray eyes—which she decided on the spot to think of as smoldering—and let loose a smile of thanks. He really was a handsome man, she thought, with his sandy colored hair, fine features, and clean-shaven jaw with a small dimple in the middle.

"Have you ever thought of growing a beard?" she asked.

His hand touched his chin. "A beard?"

"Never mind. Derek, I'm so glad you came tonight."

A slow smile turned his lips. "Are you?"

Catherine stabbed a piece of endive, nodded at the portly couple from the deck—their name was Ring, she remembered suddenly, like a circus' main ring—and looked back at Derek. "Why do you sound so surprised?"

He shrugged. "I don't know. It just seems that sometimes we're not on the same wavelength."

Catherine found her gaze straying to the door. "Maybe all that's behind us now," she said.

His hand covered hers. "Do you mean it, Catherine?"

Just then, Amos barged into the dining room, Jake Stokes behind him. As the two men walked up to Catherine's table, Derek's hand slipped away.

Catherine was suddenly struck by the feeling that Jake and Amos were peas in a pod in some indefinite way. Both were in need of a shave, both smelled of salt, mud, water, and rum, and both had more life in their eyes than any man had a right to, although Jake's expression seemed to border on feverishness. Amos was bent and old, Jake tall and young. Both of them needed a good shower and a change of clothes. They both glanced at Derek but concentrated on Catherine.

"Don't suppose you have any fish on the menu tonight?" Amos said loud enough to earn him a few curious glances from the other diners. "Jake here is trying to bribe me out of some of that cedar by buying me dinner."

"Fresh petrale sole, fillet of red snapper, salmon with lemon-dill butter, scampi, abalone—"

"Okay, okay. See, Jake, I told you the girl would whip us up a bite to eat."

Jake aborted a nod as though the motion hurt too much to complete. "Looks as though she's a little busy to start cooking," he said, sparing Derek a longer look. His voice sounded fuzzy. Catherine found herself wondering if it was due to pain or dark rum.

"Forgive me, please," she said. "Derek, you know Amos, of course. This is Jake Stokes. His sailboat washed up on our beach this morning. Jake, this is Dr. Derek Prouse."

Derek laughed softly, and said, "You beached your boat? Boy, you must feel like an idiot. Say, did you hit your jaw in the process? It looks swollen. I'd be happy to take a look at it for you."

One or all of these comments earned Derek a glare from Jake that would have set driftwood on fire. The glare softened in an instant and with a lopsided grin, Jake said, "I'm fine, thanks. Well, Amos, that very

attractive waitress is motioning us to our table. Let's
not keep her waiting.''

"We'll have to settle for this fancy stuff," Amos
growled. "No fish and chips.''

"You don't need the grease," Catherine said fondly.
"Try the broiled snapper. And eat your vegetables.''

"You don't cook 'em enough," Amos grumbled.
"I hate crunchy vegetables.''

"Overcooking leaches all the vitamins out of vegetables," Catherine pointed out.

"Is she always like this?" Jake asked, his eyes twin-
kling.

"Always, since she was knee-high to a grasshopper.
Bossy little thing.'' The two of them moved off to one
of the empty tables. Catherine turned her attention back
to Derek.

"Now, where were we?" she asked.

He put his hand over hers again, and smiled. "We
were going to talk about us.''

Catherine smiled warmly. "Yes, us.''

The waitress showed up with their dinners. Catherine
sat back as she surveyed her plate. A charbroiled ten-
derloin of pork, marinated in soy sauce, garlic, and
red peppers, lay nestled in a bed of rice. Perfectly
cooked baby carrots were off to one side, a basket of
freshly cooked bread sticks nearby. Derek's salmon
looked just as delicious, which suggested that André's
ridiculous salary and temperamental nature might be
worth it after all. She wondered idly if she shouldn't
invite the loan officer from the bank to dinner some

night. Let the woman have a taste of what her venerable institution was financing.

"I've been trying to get close to you for months," Derek said, ignoring his meal.

Catherine had a forkful of rice halfway to her mouth, which she was reasonably certain made her look less interested in this topic of conversation than she should be. She put her fork down on her plate and said, "I know. I've had a lot on my mind."

"I know you have. But tonight, you look so lovely, and earlier, I got the feeling that maybe you were ready for us to . . . well, Catherine, to see if what we feel for each other is more than friendship." He raised her hand to his lips and kissed her knuckles. "I know it is for me. . . ."

Catherine, who had planned to hear these words, who had dressed for these words, who had desired these words, felt something the size of a football lodge in her throat. Now that they were out, she recognized the futility of it all. If she was going to be able to feel something for Derek, she would have felt it weeks ago, months ago, years ago. She felt a deep shame warm her cheeks; he was right—she had led him to believe she was ready for more. Now she knew she wasn't, that she never would be, not with him. Seemingly of its own volition, her gaze strayed to Jake's table; their eyes met, and she lowered hers. This was dreadful.

Jake wondered what relationship existed between Catherine Patterson and the doctor with the misguided sense of humor. He saw the doctor kiss her hand, saw the way her eyes looked troubled and then, amazingly, strayed to his face. She looked away almost at once, but he could still feel the dark intensity of her glance. His reaction to her startled him: he was moved to respond. He forced his attention back to his bowl of clam chowder.

At thirty-three, Jake had known his share of beautiful, exotic, exciting women. There was no doubt in his mind that there would be more in the future, but for now, Pywacket and *Ashanti* were the only females in his life and they were enough. There was no room for an innkeeper, as firmly anchored to the ground as the building itself. No room, no time, not now.

He had the world to conquer on a totally personal level. He was going to circumnavigate the globe in *Ashanti*. He was going to sail the little boat in and out of every port he could find, getting to know other people and cultures, stretching his stamina and courage to the limits. And he was going to take time to listen to the sea as well, time to stare into the night sky, taste the salt on his lips, feel the cool fingers of the north wind caress his face. He was going to rediscover the world and when that was over, well, then he had other plans. He was a man with plans, always had been. And he was a man used to fulfilling his plans.

"Have some bread," Amos said. "One thing that fancy chef does right is make bread." He pushed the breadbasket toward Jake. "Come on, boy. You're looking a little peaked. Something wrong with that soup?''

As he suspected Amos well knew, nothing was wrong with the soup, but everything was wrong with his tooth. Jake shook his head gently, regretted the action, and took a bread stick to shut Amos up. He bit down on it defiantly. He'd show the old man.

The ill-advised action sent a death-defying shot of one-hundred-percent pure pain straight through his jaw, up his sinuses, down his neck. It was as though someone with a jackhammer had started drilling the foundation for a hundred-story condominium right there in his mouth. This agony dwarfed previous pain and brought tears to his eyes, which he blinked away. Everything that had come before paled next to this.

''This has gone far enough,'' Amos said as he pushed himself away from the table. Jake saw him approach Catherine and talk to her. He saw her look at him and rise to her feet. A hasty conversation ensued between Catherine and her doctor friend, then she was at his table, by his side.

''Come on,'' she said. ''You're going to the dentist.''

Jake mumbled something about it being too late at night for a dentist, an idea she brushed aside. ''I have connections,'' she said. ''Derek is calling right now. Here he comes.''

''Dr. Hilton will meet you at his office,'' Derek told Catherine. ''You're sure you don't want me to—''

''No,'' she said succinctly, then she looked at her

doctor with kindlier eyes. "You go ahead and finish dinner. I'll be back soon." She turned back to Jake and added, "Are you coming?"

The pain had not subsided, not one iota. Jake took a deep breath. He knew he was at the end of his rope and that he'd have to accept help. He stood up and managed to say, "You *are* bossy, aren't you?"

She took his arm. "Yes, as a matter of fact I am."

The ride to the dentist's office took twenty years, or at least it felt as though it did. Jake was aware of Catherine beside him, of her small car eating up the miles between Rocky Point and the dentist's office, wherever that might be, and the darkness outside pressing against the windows. At first she didn't talk to him and he had mixed feelings about it. On one hand, the sound of her voice would be comforting. On the other hand, the throbbing of his head muffled some sounds, amplified others. He'd never been so aware of his own body, his own face, before. He was ashamed he'd let this get so far out of hand; he'd never before submitted to fear to the point where he forfeited control. It wouldn't happen again, he vowed. The car sped over a bump in the pavement. Jake swore.

"Sorry," Catherine said.

"It's my fault," Jake mumbled.

"Your fault I hit the old railroad tracks too fast?"

"My fault about the tooth. That it got so bad."

"That's true," she agreed.

He looked at her out of the corners of his eyes. The

inside dimness was temporarily illuminated by a large
overhead light outside a building that appeared to be
a barn, then the light faded as the small car put it behind
them. In that instant he'd seen her profile clearly. It
was wonderful, he decided before he could caution
himself not to think such thoughts. A smooth curve to
her forehead, straight nose, lush lips, rounded chin,
long neck—all the elements of beauty were there. With
her hair upswept, her profile looked as though it belonged on an old-fashioned cameo. It wasn't her beauty
that kept her in his mind, however. It was something
else about her, a certain spirit and independence that
shone through her skin. He put a hand on his forehead
to see if he was feverish, because his thoughts seemed
stranger and stranger.

"What are you staring at?" she asked as she slowed
down to manipulate a hairpin curve.

"You," he said with a sigh.

She turned to glance at him, then quickly away.

"You seem quite sure of yourself," he said.

In response, she chuckled to herself. "Well, things
aren't always what they seem," she said at last.

Hard to argue with that, Jake thought. He tried to
get a feel for the direction they were traveling, and
stared out the window to fix his position with the stars.
"South," he said at last.

"What?"

"We're going south."

"That's right."

"I can't think of a town south of here except San

Francisco. Please, tell me we're not going all the way to San Francisco.''

''We're not. That's about three hours away and trust me, in your condition, you wouldn't want to travel the road.''

''It's a hard one, huh?''

''Miserable. We're going to Madrone.''

''Then there's only one road leading away from Rocky Point Head?''

''That's right. Oh, there are a few old abandoned lumber roads, but this road leading south is the only paved effort. Madrone is a nice little town; in fact, it's struggling to become the new center of art and culture for northern California. From there, you can go any direction as long as you don't mind narrow twisty roads.'' She paused for a second and said, ''I don't know anything about you, Jake.''

''Like what?''

''Like where you come from. Is it Seattle?''

''What makes you think that?''

''It's painted on *Ashanti*'s transom.''

''It was there when I bought the boat,'' he said.

''Oh. So, where are you from, what do you do?''

''I sail *Ashanti*, that is, when I'm not busy beaching her.''

''But before that—''

''Before that, I spent months getting her ready.''

''You're evading my questions,'' she said. ''Why?''

He didn't know why. It wasn't as though he had anything awful to hide. He said, ''I've lived in Washington on and off for several years and I have worked at this and that. Right now, I'm not working at anything but sailing my boat.''

The first houses marking the outskirts of town appeared, then a gas station and a few dark stores and what looked to be a school. ''That still sounds evasive,'' she said.

Jake stared at Catherine again. ''Let me ask you a question. Why do you keep going out of your way to help me?''

This earned him a comparatively long glance. She looked back at the road and said, ''Here's Dr. Hilton's office.''

It took two hours. For the first hour or so, Catherine sat in a waiting room furnished in Danish Modern with a plastic plant collecting dust in a corner. She leafed through a couple of old magazines, then she called the inn to tell Derek things were taking longer than expected and that he might as well go home. When she sat back down, she found herself contemplating Jake's question.

Why was she helping him? The easy answer was that he was a stranger in trouble and it was only human kindness to offer assistance. The real answer, she suspected, lay deeper down and was trickier to access.

Her thoughts drifted to Derek, and before she could steer them away to a safer subject, she relived the awkward silence that had followed his gallant kiss of her hand. At least it had been awkward for her. Derek had seemed oblivious to her discomfort, tackling his salmon with renewed appetite, as though stating his intentions flatly had left him ravenous.

She'd toyed with her dinner, determined not to look at Jake again, determined not to look at Derek either. In fact, Amos' summons in Jake's behalf had come as a welcome reprieve.

The last hour of the wait, she spent thinking about the upcoming payment to the bank. She was short several thousand dollars; if the summer didn't pick up, she was going to default on the loan, and if that happened, she'd lose the inn. She jerked to her feet and began pacing. The inn had been in her family for nearly a century and by now the land alone was worth a small fortune. She was determined not to be the one to lose it all although common sense told her the process had begun way before her turn at bat had come.

Being summoned home to her father's funeral in her first year of graduate school had come as a total shock to Catherine. She'd planned on having years to pursue a career in oceanography before being needed at Rocky Point, but all that had changed. More shocks awaited. She discovered that everything had been put into her name to simplify inheritance, that the income from the inn had steadily declined as year after year went by without rate increases, without renovations. By the time Catherine left the lawyer's office, it was clear she'd have to jump in feet first, taking a giant plunge instead of cautiously wetting her feet.

A shadow of uncertainty haunted her steps. Maybe

she should have moved more slowly. Maybe she shouldn't have taken the bank note, shouldn't have depended on her ideas turning the tide. Yet what else had she had to rely on? The inn must stay in her family, that much was clear. It was her father's legacy, it would be hers. She wouldn't let go of it.

"I'll put an ad in the San Francisco newspapers," she told the fake plant. "I'll say something like, 'Get away to California's rugged coast for a week of gourmet dining, pristine beaches, art gallery tours in nearby Madrone, and very private contemplation.' I won't mention the fog or the roads or the—"

"Ms. Patterson?"

At the sound of the dentist's voice, Catherine twirled around. "Is he okay?" she asked.

Dr. Hilton was a small man with a shiny head and wire-rim glasses. He took the glasses off, polished them on his white coat, and perched them back atop his nose.

"Mr. Stokes will be fine," he said. "Thanks to you, that is. That tooth had abscessed, all right. He'll be on pain medication and antibiotics for a couple of weeks. I'll give you the prescriptions because he's still a little woozy, but I've got him pumped full of both of them, enough to last until tomorrow, so there's no need to try to fill them tonight."

"Okay," Catherine said as she took the prescription papers.

Jake appeared at the doorway. He looked as though he'd been in a barroom fight. Catherine stepped to his side. Jake fumbled with his wallet, then handed it to her. He said something that sounded like "Pay him," so she opened the wallet. There wasn't a lot of cash inside; in fact, by the time Dr. Hilton got his share, Jake Stokes was left with thirteen dollars. Catherine gave Jake back his wallet, stifling an internal sigh. All she needed was a sick, itinerant sailor.

"Let's go home," she told him.

Jake didn't argue or protest or make a snide comment. The lack of any of these left Catherine feeling the man must feel very poorly, very poorly indeed.

He was quiet on the drive home, quiet on the short walk to one of the redecorated cabins. It was chilly. While Jake closed himself in the bathroom with an emergency toilet kit Catherine kept on hand for guests who arrived without luggage, she built a small fire in the fireplace. Jake emerged amid the aroma of toothpaste and soap and began unceremoniously to strip off his clothes. Catherine hastened to peer into the fire, stirring the quickening blaze with a poker, looking back only when she heard the squeak of the bedsprings announce he'd gotten under the covers.

"This feels great," he mumbled.

She walked casually to the bedside. The quilt was puffy white eyelet; the array of pillows were covered in more eyelet or pastel flowered prints in polished cotton. His head rested against the pillows, his arms on the spread. The bedding hadn't exactly been chosen for a large outdoorsy-looking man with two or three days' of beard on his face, one with a lopsided grin and blazing green eyes. She smiled at him and he caught her hand, tugging on her until she sat down beside him.

"You're feeling better," she said as his hand burned her wrist. That description was stupid, she thought; his hand couldn't burn her wrist. But it did and she knew it. She was looking at his hand when he released her.

"I want to thank you," he said, his speech a little garbled, but easy enough to understand once Catherine got the hang of it. "The dentist said you saved me one heck of a long night."

"Well," she said with a sigh, "I guess you'd better thank Amos. He's the one who forced you into taking a bite of the bread stick. He said he knew your pride would get the better of you."

Jake closed his eyes. His lashes were dark smudges on the hollows above his cheekbones, and with his eyes closed, his face looked calmer, more peaceful. Catherine wondered if he'd fallen asleep. She fought the urge to kiss his forehead, or maybe taste the sweetness of his lips. She started to rise, as much to escape her own feelings as to leave Jake to his slumber, but he caught her wrist again. His eyes opened and, as usual, his gaze made her breath catch.

"You never answered my question," he said groggily. "Why do you keep helping me?"

"You have a lot of nerve saying I avoided your question. What about all mine?"

"You look like an angel in that dress," he mumbled. "Are you an angel, Catherine?"

"I suspect I'm a fool," she whispered to herself. As she began to rise, he pulled on her arm, his fingers brushing the scratch she'd received while scrambling down the hill unnecessarily. His strength belied the drowsy timbre of his voice. "A last request for a dying man?"

"You're not dying," she told him.

"Spoilsport."

"Yes, well, good night—"

"Come on, Angel, one little request."

Smiling, Catherine asked, "What's your request?"

He looked straight into her eyes and for a moment she thought he'd forgotten what they were talking about. It was as though he was weighing something in his mind. At last he said, "A kiss."

Catherine tried not to blink or show how disconcerted his request made her feel. "You've just had dental surgery," she said. "The last thing you need is someone kissing you."

"You'll be gentle, Catherine," he said softly.

Maybe it was the way he said her name, the way it sounded coming over those vocal cords, through those lips. Catherine leaned down close to him and cautiously pressed her mouth against his forehead.

"Not there," he mumbled as he touched his lips with a fingertip. "Here."

"Not tonight, not in your condition," she said softly. Her hand, seemingly of its own volition, was stroking his hair away from his face, gently touching his good cheek, discovering the curves of his sandpaper jaw. She drew her hand away.

"Another time—" he said.

"We'll see," she told him, but there wasn't a doubt in her mind that had his mouth been operational, she'd have welcomed the opportunity to harvest the deep kisses she could feel smoldering inside him, like embers banked in a stove. For a second, desire overcame caution and almost obliterated reality, and she stared at his mouth, memorizing the shape, speculating on the feel. The fire cracked and sputtered and Catherine drew away.

He was staring at her. "Promise," he said.

"Jake—"

"Promise," he repeated.

"Exactly what am I promising?" she whispered.

"A kiss. One simple kiss. Is that too much to ask?"

"Oh, I promise."

He closed his eyes.

She smoothed the blanket around his shoulders, trying not to touch his skin because she didn't trust her hands not to go making promises of their own. She'd never felt like this before—never felt such longing just to touch a man, just to feel his skin or breathlessly anticipate the brush of his hand. It was crazy, and she forced herself to think of him as an invalid.

In the end, he helped her out by falling asleep. His hand slid from her arm, palm upward; his breathing became deep and steady. She didn't know if he would remember the promised kiss once the morning came, but as she banked the fire and quietly let herself out of the room, she knew the image and taste and feel of him would linger in her mind a long, long time.

Chapter Four

Jake lay awake thinking. There was a time, he recalled, when a contractor he did business with got the concrete additive wrong on a project Jake was supervising. As a result, the concrete wouldn't set. It sat in the foundation troughs like gray mud, thick and stubborn and ugly. He decided that this was exactly how he felt, like unset concrete, like concrete that would never, even given a year of sunshine, set. He didn't like the feeling.

He opened one eye and saw that morning had come. The details of the little room, details he'd been too sick and too doped up with painkillers to notice the night before, assailed him now. Details like ruffles and flounces and pretty little flowers covering everything. It was like being trapped inside a dollhouse, he decided. A man like him belonged in an old wood boat with a cross-eyed, fishy-breathed companion, not in a little feminine room all tied up with with lace and bows.

Thoughts of Pywacket made him sit up slowly, like he was an old man who had been ill for a month. The cat was locked inside *Ashanti*'s cabin, had been since he and Amos had come up to the inn for dinner the night before. By now she'd be howling for breakfast and fresh air and company. Was she actually capable of wondering what had become of him? Even if she could reason, he decided, it was doubtful her thoughts would go further than the missed meal. Well, she could wait a little longer because suddenly, he was hungry himself.

From the night before, he vaguely recalled the hike up the hill, the soup, the bread stick. He more clearly recalled the snug fit of Catherine's dress, the ivory smoothness of her exposed shoulders, the glossy black of her hair, and her classic profile glimpsed in the dim interior lights of her car. Also clear was the memory of the doctor she'd introduced as a friend. It wasn't her expression that stuck with him, however; it was the doctor's. The man thought he was in love with Catherine. Question was, was she under the impression she was in love with the doctor? "We'll see. . . ." Jake muttered to himself.

"Mr. Moses is complaining about his bed," Terry said. She was standing over Catherine, her voice lowered so as not to alert the other diners to this dissension.

Catherine was seated at the table at which she'd eaten breakfast every morning since returning to the inn. She'd gathered her food from the buffet table; after the interrupted meal the night before, she was ravenous. With a distinct sigh, she put down the blueberry-cinnamon muffin she was about to engulf. Looking up at her cousin, she asked, "Why?"

"He says it's too soft. He says it hurts his back."

"You're kidding. He has the most expensive bed on the premises. I'd give my eyeteeth to sleep in that bed."

"I know. But he insists we find him a harder mattress or he threatens to pack his bag and his wife and check out."

Check out a whole week early, Catherine thought. A week at one hundred and fifty dollars a night.

"What about cabin 7-A?" Terry asked.

That was the cabin in which Catherine had stowed Jake Stokes, but for some undefined reason, she was reluctant to confess this to Terry. Thanks to the three couples traveling together who had rented three separate rooms just that morning, 7-A was the only refurbished cabin that wasn't rented by a paying guest. But how did she ask Jake to pack his borrowed toothbrush and leave when he was sick and broke? She couldn't.

Terry said, "You know, now that I think of it, I didn't see the key for 7-A on the board in the office. Did you rent it out last night?"

"Kind of," Catherine admitted.

"What do you mean?"

At that instant, the outside door opened and Jake walked in. He still hadn't shaved, and even though he'd put back on the old clothes he'd been wearing the night before—an ancient pair of jeans with threadbare knees and a black T-shirt—he managed to exude inordinate amounts of masculinity, which wafted in front of him like invisible steam from a cauldron of boiling water. Catherine found it next to hypnotic. Or was what preceded him, Catherine suddenly thought, her memory of his eyes locked onto hers?

Catherine heard Terry mutter, "Who in the world is that?"

"His name is Jake Stokes," she whispered. She'd heard a strange note in Terry's voice and wondered if Jake's inherent physical gifts affected every woman he met.

This question was answered by Terry's next question. "Who does he think he is? How dare he walk into this room looking like that? I'll speak to him—"

Catherine caught her cousin's arm. "No, you don't understand. . . . "

"He's the new gardener, right? Don't worry, Catherine, I'll set him straight."

By this time, Jake had zeroed in on Catherine and was advancing toward her table. He made what Catherine recognized as an attempted smile at Terry, but, thanks to the still obviously sore state of his jaw, it came off as a hybrid leer and did nothing to quell Terry's rising indigation.

"Don't you know any better than to waltz into a dining room in your grubby clothes during the brunch buffet?" Terry quizzed him softly.

Catherine was beginning to be glad her table was

separated from the other tables in the room. She said, "Terry—"

"No, Catherine, you're too easy with the hired help. This man should know not to—"

"He's not hired help," Catherine interrupted before Terry made a bigger fool of herself. She glanced at Jake, but, unwilling to look into his eyes, her gaze fell to his chest. She saw a small bright-blue stick poking out of his breast pocket.

"He's not?" Terry asked.

"Shall I tell her, or shall you?" Catherine asked Jake, addressing his neck.

"Go ahead. I'd kill for a cup of coffee, preferably laced with some of Amos' dark rum."

"The coffee is over on the buffet, but no rum. The dentist said you can't drink while you're taking the antibiotics."

"My luck," he said, and moved off toward the buffet.

Terry asked, "Mind telling me what's going on?"

So Catherine explained about the tooth and the dentist and admitted she'd tucked Jake into 7-A.

"Well, at least the cabin is making money," Terry said, "though what we're going to do about Mr. Moses—"

"This man has no money to speak of," Catherine mumbled, unaware until he cleared his throat above her head that Jake had returned with a mug of coffee and a bowl of oatmeal.

"I'm just a boat bum," Jake said to Terry, then he

looked down at Catherine and added, "May I sit with you? There's something I'd like to discuss with you, something about that cabin you put me in."

Catherine nodded because she'd finally met his gaze and she was temporarily unable to find her voice. It seemed to have retreated to her knees.

Terry sighed heavily. "I'll think of something to do with Mr. Moses." Glancing at Jake, she added, "Looks as though you have your hands full."

"I'll take care of Mr. Moses," Catherine said.

Terry nodded, cast Jake a longer and somewhat surly look, and left.

"I don't think she likes me," Jake said, stretching his long legs out to the side and crossing his ankles. He took a sip of coffee and sighed. "Delicious. I might live."

"You do look as though you feel better," she said.

"It's a little misleading. I woke up feeling like cement and now I feel like peanut brittle. The coffee is helping, though."

"Even without the rum?"

"Believe it or not, I don't normally drink my four food groups. It's just that the last few days have been . . . exceptional."

"That reminds me—Terry is going into town today. Shall I ask her to pick up the rest of your prescription?"

"Do you think she would?"

"If you either change your clothes or let her see you pulling a weed or two, I think we can talk her into it."

"Fair enough." Jake dug into his rear pocket and

produced his wallet. Catherine noticed he seemed star-tled to find nothing more than a ten-dollar bill and three ones.

"You asked me to pay Dr. Hilton last night," she reminded him.

"Oh."

"Listen, I could loan you money—"

"No," he interrupted, smiling. "That's not neces-sary."

"But you can't live on thirteen dollars—"

He reached across the table and set the bills next to her plate. "I have a little more stashed away. Please don't worry about me. I'm very self-sufficient."

"Is that right?"

"Normally. You don't think I always wash up on the beach, do you?"

"I have no idea what you normally do."

"Go ahead, take the money. If the prescription costs more, I'll get it to you later."

As reluctant as she was to take his last thirteen dol-lars, she was even more reluctant to start supporting this attractive self-acclaimed boat bum. She took the money.

As he carefully ate his oatmeal, Catherine tackled her muffin. She pretended to herself that she wasn't mesmerized by his sea-green eyes; she pretended she wasn't dying of curiosity as to how well he recalled the night before. Did he remember their conversation? Did he remember her promise? Was it all a blur to him, an incident that may or may not have been part of a dream? Was the fact that she was fantasizing about a promised kiss at nine in the morning an indication that she was going crazy? It was just a kiss, for heaven's sake. Inadvertently, she sighed.

"You're quiet this morning," he said.

"Just tired."

"About last night," he began, and Catherine looked up at him quickly.

"Yes?"

"Why are you so jumpy?"

"I'm not jumpy."

He tilted his head and stared at her. "Yes, you are," he said at last.

"No—"

"I was so spaced out on the pain medication that some of last night seems like it happened in a movie or I read it in a book. I remember you were there wearing a white dress. You were very kind."

"And that's all you . . . recall?"

"Is there more?" he asked with one raised eyebrow.

"Yes. No. I mean, of course there's more. I mean, you got into bed—"

"Which reminds me. I woke up to find myself in the buff. Did you—"

"No!" Catherine blurted out. Several heads turned their way, so she lowered her voice and added, "No, you were able to . . . undress and put yourself to bed. I just built you a fire."

"Thank you."

"You're welcome."

He pushed the empty oatmeal bowl away from him, leaned both elbows on the table, and said, "I appreciate having a room at your inn. I'm not quite up to par yet, but I'm sure that within a few days I'll be fine. What I'm trying to say is that I'd like to stay for a few weeks while I get *Ashanti* whipped back into shape."

"You mean stay up here at the inn?"

"Unless you're full."

Catherine nibbled at her lip and wondered how to broach the issue of rent. He saved her the trouble by adding, "How much is that cabin I'm staying in?"

"One hundred and fifty a night," she said.

He whistled.

"But there are less expensive cabins available."

"Are they all done up like that one, you know, with flowers and cute things?"

"You don't like flowers?" Catherine snapped.

"Flowers are fine out in fields or gardens and I've just recently become fond of them caught in a woman's hair, but I have to admit I prefer not to be smothered in them."

"You men are all alike."

He wagged a lazy finger at her. "Careful. That remark smacks of sexism."

"You're just like Amos. You want a man's room to look and feel and smell like a man's room. You think anything new or pretty will cling to your skin and scare away the fish or something."

"What?"

"Never mind. As a matter of fact, I do have a room

which is, shall we say, less decorated. The original cabins look just as they've looked since the beginning of time. Hordes of fishermen have tramped through their doors, scattering fish scales and stale beer and cigar smoke in their wake. I'm sure you'll feel quite at home.''

''Sounds like heaven. Why are you so defensive?''

''I'm not defensive.''

''Yes, Catherine, you are,'' he said softly.

She glared at him. ''Did you go to sleep Jake Stokes and wake up Sigmund Freud?''

''It doesn't take a degree in psychiatry to see that you feel—''

''Listen, will you please stop telling me what I do or do not feel?''

''Okay.''

''Good.''

They stared at each other a moment until Jake asked, ''How much do the old, smelly unimproved cabins rent for?''

The cabins normally rented for seventy-five dollars, but Catherine knew he couldn't afford that. After a brief hesitation, she said, ''Ten dollars a night.''

''Whoa! Quite a difference between uptown and downtown, isn't there? Do the cheap ones come with rats or snakes or spiders or something?''

Irritated with him, she said, ''Take it or leave it.''

For a second he narrowed his eyes and fixed her with an intense stare; Catherine had the odd feeling that she was looking at someone who had wheeled and dealed his way across many a boardroom table. But the second passed and he was back to being Jake Stokes, itinerant sailor in need of a shave. "I'll take it," he said, sticking out his hand.

She wondered if his touch would linger, but his hand was warm and dry and the shake was over before she could blink. "You can move out of 7-A and into 13-B any time you're ready," she told him.

Reaching into his pocket and taking the blue stick between thumb and forefinger, he withdrew his toothbrush. "I'm ready right now," he said.

A few minutes later, Catherine opened the door of 13-B. It was dark and stuffy and moldy smelling. She was glad. Let Jake loiter in this damp excuse for a room for a while, and he'd be begging her for flowers and ruffles!

"Your room," she told him, stepping aside and waiting for him to pass in front of her before moving to open the drapes. Sidling past her, he paused; she looked up at him and found his eyes staring straight down inside her soul. Did he realize how far his gaze extended? she wondered. Did he care?

"You're awfully good to me," he said softly.

"Don't push your luck."

"I'll find a way to repay you."

"Right." She stepped aside and opened the heavy drapes. Sunlight suddenly flooded the shabby room, falling on the faded pink chenille bedspread, making it look even uglier than it was. The old maple furniture was scarred and nicked, the surfaces covered with round bubbled patches suspiciously the size of a beer can. A tattered fake Oriental rug covered most of the mustard-colored linoleum floor.

"Home away from home," Jake said, dropping his toothbrush on the dresser. He took a long look around, his face curiously impassive as though noting the bleak surroundings in an impersonal way, and said, "I'll go down to *Ashanti*, rescue my cat, and bring a few things back. Would you mind if Pywacket stayed up here with me?"

"Not at all. She'll have competition, though. There's a big fat white cat named Baloo who lives at the inn."

"She'll whip him into shape."

"Veterinarian bills, how comforting."

"I'll pay them."

"How?"

Jake wrinkled his forehead and repeated, "How?"

"How will you pay a veterinarian bill or any other bill for that matter?"

"Listen, you seem to be under the impression—"

Catherine interrupted him. "I'm sorry," she mumbled. "I don't know what in the world is wrong with me. I shouldn't have said that; it was completely unnecessary and mean-spirited. And earlier, when you told me I was acting defensive, you were right. It's this place," she added, hugging her arms around herself and shuddering. "I get so worried about everything and—Oh, you don't want to hear my tale of woe."

He gripped her upper arms with firm hands and said, "Of course I do."

She shook her head. "Well, I don't want to start the day sniveling and whining." She looked over his shoulder at the room and said, "I think you'll be comfortable in here."

"Because it smells like the inside of an old shoe?"

"There isn't a flower in sight. It should remind you of your boat," she added, half wishing he'd move his hands, half hoping he wouldn't.

"You have a very poor impression of my boat, Ms. Patterson. When I get her patched up I want you to come aboard for the royal tour. At that time, I'll take an apology."

"We'll see."

"I'll take that as a promise," he said.

She cast him an anxious gaze, sure that his allusion to promises referred to the night before. But she found nothing but humor in his eyes, no hint of double meaning.

She moved and he dropped his hands. "The shower is built into the tub," she said as she pointed at the bathroom. "The gizmo that runs it is as ancient as everything else here but if you fool around enough, you'll get the hang of it." Checking her watch, she added, "I'd better go see if the new gardener has arrived. I'll see you later."

As she walked back toward her office, she felt his eyes on her, but once she'd climbed the stairs and looked back, she found that he'd closed the door to

his cabin. She started off toward the trail leading down
the head.

"You rotten little cross-eyed beast!" Jake snarled.
He'd returned to *Ashanti* to find that Pywacket had torn
open the bottom of an old loaf of bread and spread it
from stem to stern.

"You didn't like being locked up so you took it out
on the bread, is that it?" he asked as he scooped up
several gnawed slices of stale whole-wheat bread.

The cat was sitting atop the chart table. When Jake
yelled at her, she closed her eyes as though against a
stiff wind. When he stopped and picked up the bread,
she reopened them and watched.

Jake heard a rap against the hull, and then Amos'
voice called out, "Who you talkin' to, boy?"

"No one," Jake yelled. All this yelling was making
his face throb. He went to the head, found a bottle of
aspirin, and swallowed two with a swig from the fresh-
water pump. Too late, he realized the cat had dragged
an open bag of cotton balls into the sink. How many
other surprises had she planted here and there to express
her displeasure? Well, at least there was nothing in
that nasty little cabin Catherine had rented him that
Pywacket could hurt.

As he squeezed the water out of the cotton balls, he
looked in the mirror and winced. What a mess! No
wonder Terry had turned up her nose at him. And what
had prompted Catherine to treat such a derelict with
such graciousness?

She was obviously under the impression that he was totally broke. He'd tried to correct that impression, though he had to admit to himself he hadn't tried very hard; there was something refreshing in being judged on his own merits and not because of a name or the balance in a bank account. It was kind of liberating, and, truth be known, was one of the major reasons he'd embarked on this adventure in the first place. Was he to spend the next several months or even years correcting wrong impressions?

He could just hear himself: "Excuse me sir, madame, but I don't want to misrepresent myself. Yes, I'm on a rather small boat and yes, I pass myself off as a regular guy out to conquer the ocean, etc., etc., but it's only fair to also tell you that I'm very wealthy, rather successful, and could buy and sell you in the blink of an eye!"

He'd been young but industrious when his maternal grandfather brought him into the Hylord engineering firm. Neither his mother nor his father had had an interest in the business; in fact, they were both happily ensconced in New Mexico with a surprisingly lucrative art gallery. Jake, however, had taken to engineering like the proverbial fish to water; within a few years of college graduation, he'd secured several contracts in the Middle East to build oil drilling platforms, and by the time his grandfather died, had established himself at the helm of Hylord International, one of the world's leading engineering firms.

Technically not at the helm any longer, he reminded

himself. His handpicked replacement was there for now. From this day until whenever it was over, Jake Stokes had a different agenda and it involved *Ashanti* and the sea and little else.

No, he was Jake Stokes and that was all. He wasn't in this to lie to people, but he wasn't in it to admit to every pretty face he met that he was more than he appeared, either. Besides, was he? What did money have to do with who he was?

On the other hand, the woman obviously needed cash and it wasn't fair to stay at her inn without paying the going rate. The small pause before she announced the ridiculous rent hadn't gone unnoticed. She thought he was poor, and out of kindness had decided to subsidize him while he got his boat back in the water. Surely, while he waited for parts from San Francisco, he could help her out.

He'd noticed the disrepair of the inn and the problems a coat of paint couldn't hide, like that flat area where a few cars were currently parked. He'd walked across it that morning before going in for breakfast and had come away with an inch of mud caked on his shoes. What was it like in the winter? Did it flood? He could certainly help her with that—heck, the job was right up his alley. There were lots of things he could do to help and if he was clever and resourceful enough, she wouldn't end up feeling beholden to him. Old-fashioned word, beholden. It must have snuck through his subconscious, planted there by his grandmother or an old movie. He kind of liked it.

But he couldn't have Catherine feeding him and buying his medicine, taking money out of hand to support him. After he dropped the last of the soggy cotton balls into the trash, he went to the forepeak.

When he'd decided on this course of action—sailing Ashanti around the world—he'd realized he wouldn't always be near an ATM machine and should have a handy source of cash. Along with a carpenter friend, he'd built into the fore cabin a private safe. It required shifting the port-side cushion to the starboard, lifting out the board under the bunk, moving aside two sail bags and a case of engine oil, climbing into the now-damp bilges thanks to the tear in the hull, and contorting himself like a dolphin until he came to a small stainless steel vault with a combination lock. At least it was secure. Eventually he emerged, face throbbing, with enough cash to pay his room and board and effect repairs to *Ashanti*.

He was on his way up the ladder to talk to Amos about where to go in Madrone to order the boat parts he needed when he spied a chart of Mexico down on the quarter berth next to the empty Jack Daniels bottle. Normally the rolled charts were kept in a rack above, but this one had fallen. Evidence pointing to the culprit lay in the shreds of paper clinging to the blue canvas bunk cover; Cabo San Lucas had been reduced to a pulpy mess.

"Pywacket!" he yelled.

* * *

"What do you think?" Terry asked.

They were both standing in the deserted dining room looking out the big window to the gardens behind where the new gardener, a man of about thirty with stringy blond hair and wiry muscles, halfheartedly hoed between the hollyhocks and the shasta daisies. At this time of day, the dining room was empty; only André's voice, which rose and fell like ocean swells, filtered through from the kitchen.

"I think he'd rather be anywhere but here," Catherine said, "but we're the only job he can get and he's the only one who answered the ad and is willing to work for the paltry sum I can afford to pay him." Sighing, she added, "What about Mr. Moses?"

"Happily tucked into 7-A."

"He thinks the mattress will be firm enough?"

"He does. Besides, the Mrs. somehow talked André into fixing them a picnic and she was anxious to start driving. They're going north."

"On the old lumber road?" Catherine asked in surprise. The roads were numerous but rutted and difficult to maneuver.

"Yep. I warned them that it wasn't such a great road, but Mr. Moses says his truck is four-wheel drive and I couldn't forbid it."

"Of course not, but if they're not back by dinner, we'd better send out a search party. Did that other couple, the what's-their-names—wait, platinum hair tinged slightly green, that's it—did the Greens ever arrive?"

Terry, who was by now familiar with her cousin's convoluted manner of recalling names, nodded. "They checked in an hour ago. I gave them the Moses cabin. The wife is very interested in 'walking the streets of Madrone,' an exact quote that got my curiosity going until the husband added that she was a budding artist. I guess she wants to go gallery hopping." Terry's gaze suddenly darted to the side and she peeked out another window, her brow furrowing. "What's *he* doing?"

"The gardener?"

"No, your sailor friend."

Catherine moved to the window and watched as Jake walked out into the parking lot with a small shovel. He stopped and dug a hole now and again, kneeled to study the occasional skunk cabbage, ran his hand over the dirt. Keeping pace with him was Baloo, who seemed to be quite interested in the proceedings.

"I have no idea what he's doing," Catherine said. She noticed that Jake had showered and changed clothes. Dressed in pleated tan slacks and a semiwrinkled white cotton shirt, he looked incredibly handsome and virile. For a second, she remembered the texture of his skin, the way his lashes looked against his cheeks. He looked up at her as if her thoughts had penetrated the glass and wood and traveled across the yard. Caught staring, she waved weakly and he saluted, a mischievous grin on his face. Then he pulled a large weed out of the soft ground and dangled it in front of his face.

Terry said, "I don't trust him."

This shocked Catherine into turning to face Terry. "Why not?"

She shrugged. "He's too good-looking, too glib, and he seems to have you coming and going."

"What do you mean by that?" Catherine asked.

"You're interested in him."

"No—"

"Don't waste that phony denial on me, Catherine. You are too."

"That's crazy. I'll admit I enjoy watching him. There's something about the way he moves and his eyes—" She stopped abruptly when she noticed the knowing look that snuck over Terry's face. "He needs some help and I can give it, that's all."

"And that's why I don't trust him. He's charming you so he can take advantage of your natural kindness. Be careful, Catherine."

"You sound like the mother I never had."

"You're forgetting I'm older. I've been in love, I've been married. You need a lot more than that guy can offer."

"This conversation is absurd. You're always thinking that I'm in love with someone or someone is in love with me."

"Speak of the devil," Terry said, her eyes back on the parking lot. "Derek is here."

Catherine followed Terry's gaze. Derek had just pulled up beside Jake. He got out of his car and he and Jake spoke to each other for a few seconds, then Derek started towards the inn. Catherine groaned.

"What's wrong?" Terry asked.

"Derek. Terry, last night I realized that I'm never going to love Derek the way he seems to want me to. I like the man, but he doesn't . . . excite me. I guess that's the word; I'm not sure, I just know that we're not meant to be. I can't bear the thought of hurting him but I also can't mislead him anymore than I already have. . . . "

They both turned toward the door as they heard Derek's footsteps on the deck. Terry said, "I think you need to have your head examined, but leave it to me."

The door opened, and Derek stepped into the dining room. He took Catherine's hands and kissed her cheek, nodded at Terry, and then gestured toward the parking lot. "I see your patient is feeling much better."

"He seems to mend quickly," Catherine said. Derek still held onto her hands and she was fighting the unreasonable urge to pull them from his gentle grasp.

"The wonder of antibiotics," Derek said.

"Speaking of which," Terry said, "Catherine needs a few supplies in town and I was wondering if you could give me a lift. My car didn't sound so good this morning. I think it needs an overhaul or whatever it is they do to cars."

It seemed to take a few seconds for Derek to realize Terry was speaking to him. Once he did, however, his innate politeness took over.

"Sure, no problem." Then he turned to Catherine

and added, "After we get back, maybe you and I could go for a walk on the beach or a drive—"

"Oh, Derek, it sounds lovely, but there's so much to do here—"

On cue, André's voice rose like a geyser from the kitchen, scolding poor Sam. Catherine shrugged and said, "It seems my culinary genius has a short fuse. You'll excuse me. . . ."

"Of course," Derek said as he dropped her hands.

As Catherine hurried from the room, she heard Derek say, "It looks as though it's you and me, Terry. Let's go."

After Catherine ascertained that André wasn't really on the verge of deep-frying Sam, she walked outside to check on the gardener. She got no farther than the parking lot where Jake was once again digging a shallow hole. Baloo sat off to the left, peering into another hole.

"Looks as though you have help," Catherine said. "What exactly are you doing?"

He sat back on his haunches and fingered the dirt, then looked up at her. "Bet this place is a swamp all through the winter and early spring."

"Yes, but—"

"Which leaves you with no parking lot."

"It's not as though I have that many customers in the winter," Catherine admitted.

"But you will."

"What?"

"When you complete your renovations, there will be guests here twelve months a year. You need a parking lot, but even more important, this area slopes towards the inn. If it hasn't already wreaked havoc on the foundation, it will soon."

"Great," Catherine said with a deep sigh.

Jake grinned as he stood. "Not to worry. I figure a French drain running along about here," and he gestured from east to west, "ought to take care of it. I see an old backhoe parked off to the side there."

Catherine followed his gaze to the rusty hulk of yellow metal and said, "I think it's broken. I know Dad was trying to do something out here before he died."

"I'll take a look at the backhoe. I also noticed a pile of gravel pushed up against the bluff."

"I don't understand."

"Gravel goes in the drain. Your father must have been thinking along the same lines as I am."

"And neither one of you are engineers," Catherine muttered. "I should probably hire an expert."

Jake stared at her for a moment before saying, "I have . . . experience with this kind of thing."

She raised her eyebrows and regarded him speculatively.

"With machinery and drains and such," he said, expanding.

"Aha! You work construction, is that it?"

He scratched Baloo under the chin and shrugged.

"How do I know you know what you're talking about?"

"I guess you don't. Do what you like, but if you let me try to fix this situation it'll help me pay for my room."

She started to protest, but bit back the words. It did sound as though he knew what he was talking about, he was occupying an expensive room at a fraction of the cost, freeloading was bad for a man's character, and she was out of options. "Just don't make anything worse, okay?"

"Now, Catherine," he said with a glib smile. "Do I look like the kind of man to make matters worse?"

"As a matter of fact, yes, yes you do," she said, and resumed walking toward the garden.

Chapter Five

Jake stooped and ran a hand over the rusty railroad lines. He'd been crossing them for days, never giving them much thought, but now he stopped to consider where they went. He was on his way back to the inn after a long day spent chiseling the broken planks from the hull of *Ashanti*, and he was dirty and tired. What he wanted was a quick shower, a cold drink, and a sight of Catherine. He stood abruptly, wondering how she'd crept onto his list of after-work delights, shook his head, then started walking down the line.

It ended on the far side of the head. Past this point, the line disintegrated and fell away, the land part of a slide that looked several years old. He could see the rest of the track farther along the north side of the head. Presumably, the track had at one time circled Rocky Point Head, dropping off logs to ships anchored in the cove, then reconnecting and continuing—where? His engineer's curiosity had him wondering what the rest of the track looked like; actually, the track running between the boat yard and the head seemed to be in good repair.

He retraced his path down the weed-infested tracks until he intersected the trail leading up to the inn. As he arrived at the top of the trail, the wind hit him hard in the face, and he lowered his head. There was a storm coming; earlier, aboard *Ashanti*, he'd noticed that the barometer had dropped and now he saw a long line of dark clouds out over the horizon.

Catherine stood several feet away near the bluff, her back to Jake, her hair whipping. She was wearing a long multicolored skirt that had wrapped itself around her long legs. She also had on a thin blue sweater, the sleeves bunched up around her elbows. Red, yellow, and pink poppies tossed gaily by her side while the tall grass beyond her, bent low by the wind, shimmered silver in the fading light. In front of Catherine stood the lackluster young man she'd recently hired as a gardener. Jake ambled on over to find out what was going on.

"I don't know what you mean," he heard Catherine say.

"I mean it won't hurt them to do a little walking, will it?"

"Tom, if they've broken down—"

"Then they'll have to walk. Like I was saying, they could both use the exercise. Not like you, no sir. You don't need any more exercise, that's for sure. You're perfect the way you are."

Jake did not like the tone of voice or the choice of

words Tom used to compliment Catherine. He thought the younger man impertinent.

Apparently Catherine agreed. Her voice icy cold, she said, "All I'm asking you to do is drive down the lumber trail in your four-wheel-drive vehicle and see if Mr. and Mrs. Moses have gotten stuck somewhere."

"You'll go with me?" Tom asked, and this time, his words were joined by a sly glance that took in Catherine from head to foot.

"I don't think that's necessary—"

"Tell you what. You come with me and add a bonus, say a hundred bucks, then I'll go." Tom looked over Catherine's shoulder and his eyes met Jake's eyes. His expression didn't change, although Jake was pretty sure his own face was set in a scowl. The gardener leaned on his hoe and waited for Catherine to answer his proposal. It seemed to Jake that the man did a lot of leaning on that hoe.

"It would take you fifteen minutes," she said at last, as she caught her windswept hair in a gesture of irritation and brushed it away from her face. "Don't you think a hundred dollars is a little steep for fifteen minutes?"

"I need the money; why else do you think I'm working here? It's ruining my hands. Anyway, I don't intend to do extra work for nothing."

Jake had heard enough. He thought it high time he announced his presence to Catherine. "What's this all about?" he asked with an effort to keep his voice even.

Catherine twirled to face Jake. He saw her expression go from concerned to startled and back again.

"What's wrong, Catherine?" he asked.

"It's a couple of my guests, people named Moses. They've taken to picnicking every afternoon, but this is the first day they haven't shown up in time for their predinner cocktail. I'm trying to . . . coax Tom into helping me look for them."

Jake nodded at Tom. "Can't you help the lady out?"

Tom rubbed his thumb and forefinger together and leered at Catherine. "For the right incentive."

"Oh, forget it," Catherine said.

The gardener shrugged, then made a big deal out of looking at his watch. "Time for me to go anyway." He dropped the hoe and sauntered off. Jake thought Catherine's gaze would drill holes in the man's back, but he apparently suffered no ill effects.

"Are you really worried about these misplaced tourists?" he asked her.

She shook her head, but her eyes told a different story.

"I'll help you look for them," Jake said.

"I need Tom's four-wheel drive. The road they've been taking is deeply rutted and crossed with little streams. . . . Oh, who am I kidding? I'd better catch up with Tom and give him his money. I can't take the chance that the Moseses are stranded or lost. I sure don't want to ride with him, though."

Jake caught her arm. "What about that old Jeep I see parked beside the shack down at the boat yard?"

"It belonged to my father. It hasn't been run since he died. I wouldn't be helping Mr. and Mrs. Moses much if I got stranded out in the middle of nowhere."

They both looked up when Tom's truck roared into life and peeled out of the parking lot. They turned to see it come down off the headland road, cross the bridge above the fish camp, and disappear up the other side of the ravine heading toward Madrone.

"Too late to appeal to Tom's seemingly underdeveloped humanitarian side," Jake said. "Let's see if we can't get the Jeep started." He headed back down the trail, aware that Catherine had fallen in behind him. It crossed his mind that while he wasn't getting the hot shower or the cold drink he'd so desired, he was with Catherine. One out of three. Not bad.

Why aren't I surprised he got the thing running? Catherine asked herself as the Jeep engine roared to life. Jake slammed the ancient hood closed and climbed into the passenger side of the Jeep. She stared at him a moment. "Thanks," she said. "I can drop you off at the inn if you like. I know you're tired and now that the Jeep is running you needn't concern yourself with my problems."

"Give it a little more gas," he prompted. Then he added, "Who knows if the thing will continue running? I'd better come along."

"It isn't necessary—"

"While you're trying so hard not to inconvenience me, your poor little tourists are probably in a ditch somewhere fighting off bears, drinking the water out of their radiator, scratching their last will and testament into the dirt—''

''I get the picture,'' Catherine interrupted, hiding a smile behind a frown of fierce concentration as she guided the Jeep out of the shelter of the shack and toward the road leading up to the inn. She felt no fear at being alone with Jake, not like she'd felt at the prospect of riding with Tom.

''Besides, there's a storm coming,'' he said.

She spared him a quick glance and said, ''How do you know that?''

''Please, Catherine, I'm a sailor. It's my job to know things like that.''

She decided not to mention the grounding of *Ashanti*. ''How's your tooth?''

''All better,'' he said, bracing himself as she came up the crest and hit a rut. As they rambled past the inn and into the forest where the headland attached to the coast, Catherine said, ''I haven't thanked you yet for what you did. I mean with the backhoe,'' she added, brushing a long strand of hair from her mouth.

Jake was leaning over the seat back, rummaging about in the back. She heard him mutter ''Aha'' before emerging with an old baseball hat. It was white or once had been; now it was brown and streaked with rust. Stenciled above the bill was a picture of a salmon.

''Your dad's hat?'' he asked.

''Must be,'' Catherine said, glancing at it out of the corner of her eye.

He put his hand on the wheel and said, "You take it. I notice your hair keeps blowing in your face."

Catherine nodded her thanks. While Jake steered the Jeep, she bunched her hair through the adjusting hole in the back and tugged the cap over her head.

"Before I accept your thanks for the parking lot," he said, returning to the subject, "maybe we'd better see what happens when it rains. Tomorrow morning will be the test."

"So, you think it's going to rain tonight?"

"I'd bet on it."

"There's not a cloud in the sky," Catherine said, although thanks to the dense trees hovering around the lumber road, she could no longer see the sky.

"What do you want to bet?" he asked casually.

Catherine bit her lip. The Jeep scudded across a dry creek bed and up the next incline. "A favor," she said at last. "If it rains, I'll owe you one, if it doesn't, you'll owe me."

"Anything I want?"

"Or anything I want," she said. "Within reason. Nothing compromising or illegal or too expensive or—"

"All these qualifications," he said, sighing.

"Is it a deal?"

"Okay." He held out a hand which she shook briefly.

"And thanks for coming to my rescue," Catherine added. "With the Jeep and everything."

"About time I was the one doing the rescuing, isn't it, after all you've done for me?"

She shrugged.

He said, "Your gardener is a jerk."

"I know."

"Why do you keep him on?"

"Because he's all I can afford."

"I'd fire him and pull the weeds myself," Jake said.

"I'm sure you would," she said dryly, annoyed with his comment, although that was exactly what she wished she could do.

"I mean it," he said. "You don't need a guy like that hanging around an establishment like yours. He's lazy and rude and insolent."

Catherine braked the Jeep to a sudden halt, turning in her seat to face Jake. "Remember when I came aboard *Ashanti* and you told me there was only one captain and it was you?" she interrupted, her voice shaking with anger.

He nodded.

"Well, there's only one captain at the Rocky Point Inn too, and that's me."

He nodded again.

"And I don't appreciate you second-guessing my decisions or trying to influence me when it concerns things you can't possibly understand."

"Now wait a second—"

"Because you have no idea how . . . how complicated things are."

"Catherine—"

"Or how many different balls I'm trying to keep in the air."

"I know—"

"You're a boat bum, a man existing outside all the concerns that keep the rest of us awake nights. You've quit the day-to-day worry of living. You don't know or care about things like bank payments and lousy gardeners and money and staff—"

"I think you're beginning to repeat yourself."

"Don't you grin at me," she warned him.

"What's really bugging you?" he asked.

Catherine stared at her hands, which were clutching the steering wheel, and murmured, "I don't know what you mean."

"You're really not angry with me, are you?"

"Jake, you are an extremely irritating man sometimes."

"And you are an extremely beautiful woman who is uptight about two thirds of the time."

"Thanks."

"And a delight the other third. So what I'm asking is, what makes you so tense? You alluded to problems with the inn once before, remember?"

Catherine swallowed and shook her head. "It's not your concern. . . . "

"Even as a friend?" he asked. "Maybe I could help."

A bark of laughter escaped her lips before she could stop it. "I'm sorry," she said.

"You don't think much of me, do you?" he asked, but though his words sounded bitter, his eyes looked mischievous.

Catherine didn't answer because the truth of the matter was that she thought of him almost nonstop. He was such an enigma to her. On the one hand he seemed shiftless and yet on the other hand, concerned and capable and so incredibly good-looking, which shouldn't have anything to do with anything but did.

"I'm really not quite as worthless as you think I am," he said softly.

"I don't think you're worthless," she said quickly. "Quite the contrary. I think you're very able and kind too. It's just that. . . . "

"It's just that what?"

"My worries concern the inn. I need money and customers or the bank is going to foreclose on me. Lots of money. Thousands of dollars. So you see, you really can't help me unless you have fifty thousand dollars."

"Not on me at the moment," he mumbled.

She smiled indulgently. "You know what? I wouldn't take it even if you did. The inn has been in my family for generations and I am going to find a way to save it by myself or die trying. Besides, I got myself into this mess and it's my problem to get myself out."

His hand covered hers. "Amos said you left graduate school to come here to take over the inn when your dad died."

"Amos talks too much."

"He said you were studying to be an oceanographer."

She bit at her lip and said, "It doesn't matter now."

"How can it not matter? It's your dream, isn't it?"

"It was."

"And now you're tied to a piece of land—"

"Jake, please, I don't want to get angry with you again, so just stop. I've made my peace with my life. If it's enough for me, then it should be enough for my . . . friends as well."

"And are we friends, Catherine?" he asked softly.

"I hope so," she said, nodding, her eyes drifting to the sight of his brown fingers gripping her hand, and then she met his gaze in the gathering dusk. A flash of green held her; a wave of confidence flowed from him to her, replacing anger and melancholy with a feeling of peace. Her heartbeat slowed as she continued staring at Jake, and then when something in his expression changed, became more challenging, her heartbeat began to accelerate again, but not from anger this time. No, not from anger.

"Catherine," he whispered as he leaned across the gearshift knob.

She felt his lips touch hers. She drew away at once, but then his fingers were caressing her cheek, tracing the lines of her mouth, coaxing her closer again, and she was willing, very willing, to go.

"Remember your promise," he said softly, his breath warm against her skin. "The one you made on my sickbed? You promised me a kiss."

"Yes," she said, but just when their lips were about

to touch again, a high-pitched honk blasted the evening air.

They jerked apart and looked up to the top of the next hill. They saw a blue Chevy Blazer, a man's arm waving merrily out the driver's window.

"Mr. Moses?" Jake said.

"In the flesh," Catherine replied. "I guess they weren't in trouble after all."

"They are now," he said, pulling on the bill of her cap until her eyes were all but covered. Catherine pushed the cap back on her head, waved at the Blazer, put the Jeep in gear, and turned around, heading back toward the inn, switching on the headlights to blaze a path through the encroaching forest.

It poured all night long. Catherine lay in her bed and listened as torrents of water pounded the roof, gushed through the rain gutters, splattered on the pavement and decks. Before her father had died, she'd loved the rain. She'd loved the primitive music it created, the wild sense of life it always awakened in her. Now she worried about leaking roofs, draining parking lots, flooded gardens, guests leaving because they were bored staying inside. That thought led directly to worries about the bank loan—an endless, tedious cycle.

She thought about Jake. She thought about his mouth and the feel of his hand traveling her face. She touched her cheek and her chin, ran her own hand down her neck, retracing the trails he'd blazed a few hours earlier. He'd spoken of her promise; she'd been dying to throw herself into his arms and cover him with kisses! Who knew how long he'd be here; work was progressing very fast on his boat. She'd heard him tell Amos he'd have *Ashanti* launched within a month. Thirty days, then he'd put his boat back in the water and sail it away to the end of the world and she'd never see him again.

That thought made her heart ache, which was stupid because she barely knew the man. She had a month to rectify that, she thought to herself. A month to make memories that would last during the long winter ahead, to help her get through the problems with the bank and the inn and everything else.

And now, she was reminded as the sound of the rain once again seeped into her consciousness, she owed Jake a favor. A smile lifted the corners of her mouth as she closed her eyes and drifted off to sleep.

By the next morning, the rain was history. The sun greeted every blade of grass and every flower as though it had never been driven away, lusty in its blazing warmth and benevolent glow. The sun rarely shined on the North Coast with such a vengeance, and Catherine found her usual early morning solitude on the south deck was breached by clusters of the inn's guests, out enjoying the sun.

"Miss Patterson, Miss Patterson," one excited woman called. She was the woman with the bleached hair.

"Mrs. Green," Catherine said.

"I've got a problem, dear," Mrs. Green confided

in a voice loud enough to catch the attention of everyone present. She was a woman of about forty-five with black eyebrows, a jarring effect with her almost-white hair and lips painted flame red. She was plump and dressed in a flowing knee-length vest, wide-bottom pants, and a frilly blouse that tended to accentuate the negatives, but she also looked as though she couldn't have cared less what anyone thought. Bulky jewelry filled the neckline of the blouse, and Mrs. Green fingered one huge silver bead as she spoke.

"It's like this," she continued. "Jerry, that's the mister, he made friends with an old guy down at the marina. Amos, Arnold—some name beginning with an A. Anyway, the two of them have gone off fishing somewhere. They took our car, which means I'm stranded here at the inn."

"Is that really so dreadful on a beautiful day like this?" Catherine asked. She hadn't appreciated the use of the word "stranded," implying as it did that one would rather be anywhere else.

"No, dear, of course it isn't, not normally, anyway. But today was the day I was going to hit the left side of the street. We leave tomorrow, you know."

Hit the left side of the street? The meaning escaped Catherine until Mrs. Green explained, "There's the cutest little seascape in your dining room, and Terry said all the art in there is by local artists and it's all for sale. And the same artist has an exhibit in Madrone, but I've only seen the galleries on the right side of the street. And today Jerry promised to take me to town but then he went off fishing. I so wanted to see this artist's other work before deciding—''

Catherine wasn't sure what to do about this. She had a new maid to orient, rooms and laundry to check, the banker to call, so many things to do. As she hesitated making the offer she knew Mrs. Green wanted her to make, another voice spoke up.

''Isn't that just like a man?'' Mrs. Moses said.

She was a small woman, with wrinkled skin and naturally gray hair, dressed in jeans and a windbreaker. Catherine thought the two women were probably within two years of each other in age, but there all similarities ended. Mrs. Moses looked like a ''before'' picture in one of those glossy magazine pictures, and Mrs. Green looked like the ''after.''

''Hey, honey, I've got a car. My mister is sacked out in the sun and I wouldn't mind seeing an art gallery. Do you want a ride?''

''How nice,'' Catherine gushed, relieved.

Mrs. Green agreed and the two woman went off together toward the parking lot. Catherine followed along behind them, not to accompany them but to check out Jake's work.

The parking area was damp, but gone were the vast shallow puddles that had plagued that area of the inn for so many years. As Catherine walked across the dirt, she thought about Jake and wondered what ''favor'' he'd want to collect for correctly anticipating the rain. She also wondered again what it was this shiftless man had been doing with his life that would result in the knowledge and skills to fix this tricky drainage problem.

As she inspected the dining room and wiped down the old oak bar that took up half the lounge, Catherine thought about what Amos had said when she'd questioned him about Jake. "I don't care what he did before. I don't care who he is or what he is. The boy is hard-working and great with wood and that's enough for me."

This from the man who had been singularly unimpressed with Jake!

By mid-afternoon, the day truly was turning into a scorcher. Catherine settled a minor dispute between André and Sam, taste-tested a trial Foyot sauce intended for the grilled chicken that evening, and made her way to the bluff. She stared down at the marina, admitting to no one, especially herself, that she was straining for a glance of Jake.

Terry startled her by coming from behind and touching her arm. Catherine jumped.

"Sorry," Terry said. "What are you doing out here all by yourself?"

"Nothing," Catherine snapped. She shrugged and turned to face the inn. "It's hot, isn't it?"

"Muggy," Terry agreed. "That's why I interrupted your reverie. The air-conditioning in 8-A is on the blink. The man renting it is a little on the heavy side and he's complaining. Loudly."

"We only need air-conditioning one day a year,"

Catherine said, sighing heavily. "Do we have a vacancy we can shuffle him into?"

"Already tried that. I hate to tell you how many rooms we have empty and clean and ready to go, but he doesn't want to budge and I didn't want to insist without consulting you." Terry leaned closer and added, "I can't remember his name but I know he's a repeat customer. I didn't think you'd want to upset him."

Through Catherine's mind ran the words—heavy man, light on his feet, sweet. She said, "Mr. Sweet?"

"That's right."

"Okay, call Johnson, get him up here to fix the thing."

Terry nodded, but seemed in no hurry to leave. She faced the sun and smiled. "Feels good, huh?"

"Wonderful," Catherine agreed. "Speaking of wonderful, I've been meaning to ask you how your excursion with Derek went."

Terry's smile was noncommittal. "Fine."

"Just fine?"

She lifted one shoulder and added, "We have a lot in common."

"Like what?"

"Well, I have a nine-year-old son and he's got an eleven-year-old stepsister and we both like baseball and strawberry ice cream . . . silly stuff like that. I know he's in love with you—"

"Don't start that again," Catherine warned.

"Anyway, speaking of my son, I have to leave early

today. I left Mike at home instead of taking him to summer school because he didn't feel well.''

''Gee, I haven't seen Mike in weeks. It's nothing serious, I hope?''

''No, just one of those things that nine-year-old boys come up with to put a few gray hairs on their mothers' heads. I talked to him on the phone a few minutes ago and he said he feels better, but *I'd* feel better if I were at home with him.''

''You leave whenever you want,'' Catherine said.

''Speaking of leaving, what's the story on that sailor friend of yours?''

Catherine looked at Terry out of the corners of her eyes and smiled. ''I like him.''

''No kidding.''

''I mean it. He's different from other men.''

''He's unemployed, he's broke, he's taking advantage of you. Is that what you mean by different?''

Catherine frowned at her cousin. ''He may be some of those things, but he isn't taking advantage of me. Look what he did for the parking lot.''

Terry nodded. ''That's true, he did fix the parking lot. But don't forget that I know you're practically giving him a room here at the inn. It's the least he can do.''

''You just don't like him,'' Catherine said.

''I don't trust him.'' In unison, both their gazes darted in the direction of a sudden thumping noise. Tom was hammering in a row of stakes with the pan end of a shovel.

"Is that for the hollyhocks?" Terry asked.

Catherine nodded. "The wind battered them pretty heavily yesterday, and then the rain last night. I asked Tom to stake them for me."

Terry bit at her lower lip and said, "I should take the man a glass of iced tea. He's sweating."

"Good idea," Catherine said.

Terry hesitated. When she finally spoke, her voice was just a whisper. "You're going to say that I don't like anyone, but the fact of the matter is that I'd take your sailor friend over our new gardener and I don't know why."

"Maybe because he's insolent and rude and lazy?" Catherine suggested with a wry smile.

Terry nodded. "He stares off into space and acts as though he's better than everyone else."

Catherine said, "I hired him, I'll take him the tea."

"That's not necessary—"

"No, he's my problem, not yours. You go on home to Mike. And tell him 'hi' for me, will you?"

Tom took the frosty glass with both hands, the shovel handle tucked under one arm. He gulped the tea, wiped a bare forearm across his mouth, raked his eyes up Catherine and down again, and said, "Thanks. 'Course, you didn't have to do that."

"You looked thirsty," Catherine said, taking the glass and backing up, anxious to retreat. The man made her feel awkward and funny.

He leaned forward. "You don't need excuses to

come up to me," he said. "I've been thinking about it. I'd like to see you down on that beach, your skin all white, the sand black. No clothes."

That comment halted Catherine's steps. "What!"

He grinned with one side of his mouth. "You have nothing to hide."

Catherine, mortified, sputtered. "I assure you—"

"Just like this too, eyes blazing, all mad and flushed—"

"Ah, Catherine," another voice interrupted. It was Jake. Catherine turned to find he'd approached from the bluff. He was sweaty too, burned brown by the sun, his clothes old and worn and full of holes. His voice had been casual, as was his stance, but his gaze was directed at Tom and it was anything but pleasant. While she was very glad to see him, she wasn't about to stand there and let him rescue her again. She turned back to glare at Tom.

"Don't ever talk to me like that again," she said, her voice even and cool.

The gardener shrugged. He spared Jake a long look under stubby blond eyelashes, hefted the shovel, and brought it down on the narrow top of a wooden stake. It was the most energetic effort he'd expended so far.

Catherine moved away, and after a second, she heard Jake catch up.

"What a little helper that boy is," he said lightly.

She looked up at him and said, "Don't start with me."

"No, I mean it. He's just adorable, don't you think?

Full of compliments, hard-working, a real joy to have around.''

''Listen,'' she barked. ''I took care of him, didn't I? It's not necessary for you to drip sarcasm—''

''Me?''

''Or to feel as though you must defend my honor against anything that little twerp can come up with.''

''Obviously not. It was the last thing I had on my mind.''

''Really. Then why did you appear right then?''

''Because you're my landlady and I have a complaint.''

Surprised, Catherine said, ''Oh.''

''That's right. My shower doesn't work.''

They resumed walking around the deck toward the wing of older cabins. Baloo was sunning himself, his face turned toward the sun, his eyes squeezed shut. The big white cat was parked right in front of Jake's door. ''I warned you that the fixture is difficult,'' Catherine said.

''No kidding. But after the trickling showers on *Ashanti*, a good hot bath has been a treat. Until today. Today I spent under *Ashanti*, repairing the rudder, and I need a good shower. Truth is that I get the thing so far over and then it creaks and groans and I'm afraid I'm going to break it. Maybe there's a method you could tell me about. Or what about your handyman?''

''We *should* have a handyman, but the old one quit when Dad died and so now we just call on Bert Johnson when something goes wrong. He was here this morning fixing the air-conditioning. Instead of my calling him back, why don't I just show you how the thing works?'' she added, nudging Baloo out of the way with the side of her shoe. He'd taken to camping out in front of Jake's cabin.

''Fine,'' he said. He opened the door and they were greeted by a hoarse cry and a blur of creamy fur. Catherine hastily shut the door behind her to keep Baloo from coming in or Pywacket from getting out.

''Hello, you little tyrant,'' Jake said as he scooped the Siamese into his arms and scratched her ears. Catherine noticed the way the cat's tail wound around Jake's muscular arm, a pose she wouldn't mind imitating.

Honestly! she scolded herself.

''In here,'' Jake said as he gently set the cat on the bed and moved into the bathroom.

This was the first time Catherine had been in his room since she showed it to him several days earlier. She lingered slightly, taking in the personal touches he'd added in his short time of possession. There were two paperback novels on the nightstand, a pair of leather boat shoes tucked neatly under a chair. His prescription bottle and an empty glass were on the table as were a clean folded white shirt, thirty-five cents in change, and a rolled chart with a corner gnawed away. Draped over the back of a chair was a black sweatshirt jacket, and in the corner, a small shallow pan filled with kitty litter and two bowls, one empty and the other full of water. A blue box of cat food sat beside the empty bowl. The cat, sitting erect on the bed, stared at Catherine with crossed blue eyes.

Jake stuck his head out the bathroom door. ''Coming?'' he asked.

She went into the bathroom. Jake was standing in the tub, twisting the knob. Catherine reached past him and pulled the knob hard. ''Like this,'' she said, flooding Jake's shoes with cold water. ''Oh, I'm sorry, I'll turn it off—''

''A little late for that now. The shoes were dirty anyway. Look, I know how to get it into the tub, I just can't figure out how to get it up to the shower spigot.''

Catherine knew the handle had to be nudged gently but firmly, past the point where it looked and sounded as though it was going to break any second. Over the years, it had often unnerved people and one by one, she was doing away with the cantankerous things.

As Jake prepared to step out of the tub, Catherine smothered a smile and cranked the handle. Instantly, amid a roar of grinding metal, the water stopped gushing from the lower faucet and cascaded from the upper unit. In a matter of seconds, Jake was soaked.

She laughed. It was the first time in her life that she'd done something like that and for some reason she found the sight of him standing in a cold shower, fully clothed, extremely amusing.

He stared at her openmouthed.

''Your clothes needed washing too,'' she said, and started laughing again.

Suddenly, she felt two big hands grab her upper arms

and lift her off her feet. When she was set down, she too was in the tub, directly under the water spout, and now it was Jake who was laughing.

The color of his eyes, green like seaweed, mesmerized her. She saw him stop laughing. She saw him step closer, felt his hands leave her arms and wrap around her back, felt him pulling her closer. And although she was shivering from the cold water and ruining a perfectly good pair of leather shoes, she went eagerly, rising on her tiptoes so that her face would meet his and his kiss would land on her lips. In all that cold water, his mouth was warm, demanding. She recalled her midnight decision to grasp every moment with him that she could, and she closed her eyes and let herself be swept away by his warmth and strength.

It was Jake who pulled away, Jake who stared down at her long and hard, silent, intense, thinking. It was Jake who reached behind him and pushed the faucet in, first lowering the water flow, then completely turning it off. It was Jake who reached for a towel.

"I've heard of taking a cold shower," he said softly, blotting the rivulets which ran down Catherine's face, "but I believe a man takes those alone."

Catherine felt slightly rebuffed and a little confused. "Well, at least we've done away with that pesky promised kiss," she said, striving to keep her voice light, as though the kiss was just an empty flirtation and not a soul-quaking event.

"That's right," he said, grabbing a dry towel for

himself. "But you still owe me a favor, remember? For all that rain last night?"

She nodded. "You were right, of course. It rained and rained and rained. What do you want?"

"I'll think of something," he said, stepping from the tub and extending a hand to help Catherine do the same.

"Here we go again," she said, laughing as she dripped onto the threadbare bath mat.

Her comment seemed to startle him. For a second he almost glared at her face, but then his look softened and he bit at his lower lip. When he spoke, his voice was neither teasing nor sensuous. He said, "I'll make it something a little less personal. Extracting a promise for a kiss was rude at best."

She smiled coyly and touched his cheek. "I forgive you."

He caught her hand, folded it in his, and smiled politely. "I wasn't feeling well, of course."

"Of course."

"All that pain medication—"

"Yes," she said, extracting her hand from his. She didn't understand what had happened. Hadn't he enjoyed kissing her? Could she have enjoyed it so much if he didn't?

"Something impersonal," he repeated.

"Whatever," she said.

Chapter Six

Jake took a red bandanna from his jeans pocket and wiped his forehead. The heat wave was working on its fifth day. Not that he didn't like the heat; heck, this puny little wave wouldn't hold a candle to the temperatures he would encounter further south. But it meant that *Ashanti*'s hull was drying out faster than he'd like and if the parts he'd ordered in Madrone didn't hurry up and get here she'd leak like a sieve once he refloated her.

He stepped from one railroad tie to the next as he walked along the track. He looked up at the sun and figured he was heading north now; for the first mile he'd headed east. He told himself he wasn't the kind of man to think about one silly kiss, even if the woman he'd held in his arms was hard to put out of his mind. He smiled to himself at the memory of her laughter as she'd surprised herself along with him when she turned the shower on and drenched him. There was a deep well of fun lurking inside that woman, but most of the time she was so wrapped up in worry that it couldn't surface.

The inn was an albatross around her neck and she was too proud and too stubborn to see it. She had decided it was her mission in life to make the thing a going concern and by the set of her mouth and the tilt of her head, he knew she was the kind of person to work tirelessly to make it succeed. He'd seen her having dinner with an older woman the night before, one with a tight blond bun and a beautifully tailored red suit. The woman had carried a briefcase into the dining room and unfolded a sheaf of paper over her salad plate. He'd snuck a peek at Catherine's face and found her gaze glassy and her smile strained. He'd met enough bankers in his life to know that the woman in the red suit was one of them and that she was handing down some dire news.

He rounded a hill and was confronted with a chasm, more wide than deep. The tracks stopped abruptly where the trestle, according to Amos, had been washed away by a flood fifteen years before. Jake squatted to get a better view. Two hours later, after hiking up and down the ravine, he made an educated guess based on his years of engineering experience. The trestle was fixable. It would cost, but that's what Hylord International had—money. And he *was* Hylord International.

He had to see the other end of the line to make sure it ended where he guessed it did. He had to coerce Catherine into driving him to Madrone. Maybe he could bribe her with dinner, and then he remembered the favor she owed him. And with that memory, his senses were flooded with the sight and the smell and the feel of her.

He was not in love with this woman, he told himself. He felt deep compassion for her predicament and great respect for her generosity and her spirit, but he was not in love with her. He'd figure out a way to help her and do it in such a way that she wasn't even aware it was happening, and then he'd get back on his boat with his cross-eyed first mate and forget Rocky Point and the woman who lived here, as attached to her land and her mission as one of the bent cypress trees that dotted the headland she called home.

"What exactly are you looking for?" Catherine asked as they pulled into Madrone.

He couldn't very well say "the railroad tracks," so he played a hunch and said, "A lumber mill."

"Not a lumber store?" she asked, raising her eyebrows and sparing him a quick glance.

"Not a store. I need . . . a special piece of lumber milled," he lied. "And then I need to go by the marine store and pick up the parts I ordered." It had been almost two weeks since he'd first thought of the train and the trestle and the mill and it had killed him to wait until his parts finally arrived.

Catherine nodded. Jake looked out the window and saw, to his relief, the railroad tracks off to the right.

"Only mill I know of is Two Forks Lumber, but it's

not doing very well. The lumber industry is in trouble all up and down the coast, you know.''

"Yes," he said, agreeing.

And then, like a gift, she added, ''It didn't help any when the railroad trestle was destroyed. Now they have to truck everything out of here. Still, I hear they're going under. I'm not sure they'll be able to help you.''

"Will you let me buy you lunch after I'm finished?'' he asked, as much to change the subject as anything else.

She hesitated and he realized she was worried about his finances. He added, ''We'll buy a box of crackers and some cheese and maybe some fruit and go sit by the ocean.''

"Okay,'' she agreed, and then tossing him a playful look added, ''About this favor I'm doing to satisfy our bet—''

"Driving me to town?''

"Driving you to town. I want to know if you had to think long to come up with something so impersonal?''

"Oh, that. Listen—''

"I'm impressed, I really am, but I want to lay your mind at ease—you are absolutely safe with me.''

"Oh, brother.''

"I won't compromise you,'' she said, and he noticed she was struggling to keep the corners of her mouth from rising in a smile.

"You won't?''

"No kisses, no lingering looks, nothing.''

"I see," he said, using the same serious tone she'd used. "Well, thank you. I guess."

"You're welcome. Here's your mill."

Catherine spent the time Jake was gone on the beach across the street and down the hill from the mill. She took off her shoes, wiggled her toes in the sand, then found a gray log to sit against. Squinting her eyes against the sun, letting the wind tangle her hair, she stared out at the deep blue sea and let her mind wander, scolding herself every time it crept back to thoughts of the inn and Melinda Goodwinter, her "personal" banker who had come to the inn, eaten every bite of her *filets de soles Normandes*, and refused to even consider an extension on the loan.

She thought about her interrupted studies instead, the career she'd almost had. When those thoughts began to upset her, she shifted mental gears again, this time focusing on things she liked.

"I like Mike," she said softly, letting the fine grains of sand run through her fingers. It was true; Terry's son Mike was a good kid. He hadn't been around much lately and she decided on the spot to invite him over soon.

"I like hot dogs with lots of mustard and onions, beach fires, and Jake Stokes," she added, and spent the next several minutes recreating the man in her mind, everything from his incredible gaze to his broad shoulders to the way his voice sounded.

She jumped when the voice materialized behind her.

"Hello, beautiful," Jake said. He set a paper sack down on the ground and sat down next to it. Slowly, as though he were a magician pulling rabbits from a top hat, he withdrew a small bottle of wine, two plastic glasses, purple grapes, pâté, crackers, thin slices of Muenster cheese, and a tiny gold foil-wrapped box of chocolates.

"When did you buy all this?" Catherine asked in amazement.

As he uncorked the wine with a corkscrew built into his pocketknife, he said, "I finished . . . ordering my lumber about a half hour ago and saw you sitting down here. You looked so content, I walked to the corner deli and got this stuff."

"Did they have what you wanted?" she asked, accepting a glass of chardonnay.

He stared at her a second and then said, "Uh, no. They couldn't help me. I'll have to take care of it in San Diego before I go to Mexico."

"That's too bad."

He shrugged. "You were down here almost two hours. What were you thinking about?"

"Mike."

"I see . . . ." he said slowly.

Wondering if she detected a hint of jealousy in his voice, Catherine added, "Terry's nine-year-old son."

"Oh." He handed her a cracker smothered in pâté and asked, "What about Mike?"

"Just that I haven't seen him in a while. He's the only child in our family, you know." After she swallowed her cracker, she mused, "He may be the one I'm saving the inn for."

This remark caused Jake's eyebrows to raise. "You aren't planning on having children of your own?"

She shrugged. "I'm twenty-six years old and I work in an out-of-the-way place. I may never meet Mr. Right."

"What about the doctor?"

"Derek? No, he's not the one."

Jake leaned back on his elbows and fixed her with a steady stare. "How do you know?" he asked.

Catherine shook her head. "No, you don't. I'm not going to get into one of these 'woman meets man, man must have his mate' conversations with you."

"What does that mean?" Jake asked.

"You know what it means."

"Spell it out."

"No."

"Why not?"

"Because I promised you that you were safe with me today."

"Let's see. 'No lingering looks, no kissing, no nothing.' "

"That's right."

"How does explaining yourself fit into that scenario?"

She ate another cracker and said, "It falls under the category of suggestive conversations that tend to lead to lingering looks and then to kisses."

"Come on, Catherine."

She bit her lip. "Okay, but remember I warned you. I'm referring to the fact that you and I have been flirting since the first minute we met, give or take a few hours when you were in pain or I was mad. We've kissed, we've stared longingly into each other's eyes, we've exchanged verbal foreplay. But we're not right for each other and we're both smart enough to realize it."

"All that aside," he said with infuriating calm, "how do you know this doctor isn't the right man?"

Catherine popped a grape into her mouth and thought while she chewed. He really was annoying when he was single-minded like this. It made him seem very unlike a beach bum; didn't they have a more devil-may-care attitude? "What *is* your story?" she asked.

"You first," he said.

"Okay. Bluntly put, Derek doesn't make my breath quicken." The honesty of her words startled her, made her cheeks redden.

"Hmm," he said, and sitting back up, swallowed the last of his wine and folded a piece of cheese onto a cracker. "My story: I'm thirty-three, never married, on my way to Mexico first, who-knows-where second—"

"That sounds so wonderful," Catherine interrupted.

He stared at her a second before finally saying, "I wouldn't think it would appeal to you."

"Well, not for myself, of course. Go on . . . ."

"There's not much more to tell, Catherine."

"Oh, sure there is. Did you go to college, what kind

of jobs did you do before you checked out of the work force, are your parents alive—''

"Pretty personal stuff," he said with a lazy smile.

She nodded. "You're right, I'm prying. Of course, you've presented yourself as a rather romantic and mysterious figure, washing up in the mists, injured—"

He laughed. "Okay, okay. College, yes. I worked for several years in the construction business and my parents are alive and well in New Mexico. They own an art gallery. I haven't seen them in four years but I plan on visiting them before I leave the States."

"And your dreams?" she asked softly.

"Gloves off, huh?"

"In for a penny," she agreed.

"Okay," he said, sighing. "I'm off to see the world on my own terms while there's still enough of it left unhomogenized for me to see."

"So you just left . . . everything behind?"

"Yes."

"No regrets? No one you'll miss?"

"Not before now," he said, and when she looked at him suddenly, she found his eyes steady on her face.

"There's something I want to tell you," he said slowly.

Catherine's heart stood still. In a way, she didn't want to hear what he had to say; the differences between them were so vast, their futures so different. But she found herself leaning forward, anxious, breathless.

"I can pay my own way," he said finally and she

didn't know if it was what he'd intended to say or not. It wasn't what she had yearned to hear.

"You *have* been," she protested.

"No—"

"There's the parking lot drainage problem you solved—"

"I'm thinking of my room rent. Don't deny you've been subsidizing me. It isn't necessary. I asked Terry what the rooms normally go for and she told me and I paid her the difference."

"When did you do this?"

"Yesterday. I think she likes me better for it too."

"Terry never said a word."

"I asked her not to. I'm almost ready to launch *Ashanti* and move back aboard and I want everything between us to be . . . fair and out in the open."

Catherine nodded woodenly. She'd always known he'd leave but she hadn't thought about it being so soon.

"I have an idea," he added, as he topped the wine in both their glasses. "Why don't I take you and Terry and her son on a sail before I leave? I'll even take the doctor."

"All of them?" Catherine mumbled.

"Yes," he said softly.

Catherine met his gaze and asked, her voice soft, "Why?"

He didn't answer right away. At first his eyes delved deep into hers, and then he looked away toward the ocean. At last, he said, "You're right, you know.

About the pulse thing. I feel the same way so I think we'd better have lots of people around at all times, because, Catherine Patterson, you have your life and I have mine.''

''Yes,'' she said quickly, and though she wouldn't have admitted it to another person in the whole world, the only words he'd spoken that she wanted to hear had to do with his accelerated heart rate. ''Good idea,'' she added, making sure her gaze didn't linger on his face.

After lunch, they picked up the parts Jake needed to complete his work on *Ashanti*, and then they walked the raised sidewalks of Madrone. It had been a few months since Catherine had done this and she was surprised to see that three new galleries had opened and that the work was escalating from paintings to sculpture, pottery, textiles, and art photography as well. While the town wasn't on a par with Mendocino yet, it was growing in an unexpected way.

''Artists must like the sea air,'' she told one gallery proprietor. She recognized the art on the walls; two paintings by the same artist hung on the walls at the inn. *One*, she mentally corrected. Mrs. Green had bought the other.

''We've had several move here over the last few years,'' the owner said, agreeing. ''As traditional industries die out, they're being replaced by things that attract tourists. We've not only got three new galleries but two new restaurants and a bed-and-breakfast as well. What we need is more tourists, of course, but that's always been a problem for Madrone. I could sure use a few more customers.''

You and me both, Catherine thought to herself.

Late that night, after an evening spent avoiding the main lodge and hence Catherine, Jake used the phone in his room to make a call. Purely from a point of pride, he hated to do it, and it wasn't solely because he'd vowed to sever all connections with Hylord International for two years. There was also the factor of his beaching the boat seven hundred miles from home and being behind schedule. And then there was Catherine, always Catherine . . .

This was absurd, he finally told himself as he held the receiver in his hand. This was a business call, nothing else.

A week later, André's voice rang out over the soft sound of music and voices that filled the dining room. ''Imbecile!'' the chef shouted.

Catherine was in the act of leaning down to address a very good-looking man who had checked into the inn earlier that afternoon. His name was on the tip of her tongue. It had something to do with guns.

For a week, she'd caught only glimpses of Jake. It was as though the words and feelings tentatively addressed on the beach had driven a wedge between them. She kept hearing his voice, his proclamation that she had her life and he had his and she couldn't dodge the irrevocable truth of it. He was a free spirit, buffeted by wind and tides and all by choice. He was obviously not as broke as she had first assumed and the fact that he let her believe it for so long made her curious.

At the sound of André's voice, the man in front of a plate of bay scallops raised his eyebrows. When the second outburst rang out, he nodded as Catherine said, "Please excuse me."

He touched her arm lightly. "I will if you promise to come back."

"Of course, Mr.—" She hesitated while her mind skipped from gun to Winchester to Colt to Colton. "Of course, Mr. Colton," she said.

By the time Catherine interceded, Sam was backed up against a kitchen wall, his right hand clutched under his left arm, his eyes wide. Before him, six inches shorter but red in the face with rage, was André— armed and dangerous with a large wire whisk. He was shaking it at the young man as he hurled names and insults, distributing white drops onto the walls, the counters, and Sam's flushed cheeks.

"That's enough!" Catherine said sternly.

"He was whipping egg whites in a glass bowl!" André sputtered, backing down a few inches, but still brandishing the whisk.

Catherine said, "Sam, are you hurt?"

"I show him the copper bowl and he ignores it," André continued. "How will the whites attain volume?

I tell you, they will not. They will lie in the bowl like a melted cloud, like clogged—"

"Sam?" Catherine repeated.

André took a deep breath and moved a few steps away from the terrified young man. Sam held out his huge hand. His knuckles were bright pink.

"He hit me," Sam said.

Catherine looked at the chef. "This is too much—"

"I go to whack the whisk out of this heretic's hand and I hit his knuckles." André shrugged and added, "It is a mistake, though one I would not mind repeating."

"That's it!" Sam said angrily. "I've had it." He tore off his white apron, swiped it across his splattered face, and shoved it into Catherine's hands. "I can't take it anymore, Miss Patterson. That man is a lunatic."

"He whips egg whites in a glass bowl and I am the lunatic?" André queried innocently.

Catherine tried to oil the waters. "I know he's difficult, Sam, and he shouldn't have hit you—"

"It was a mistake!" André interrupted.

"He shouldn't have hit *at* you," Catherine repeated. "But please, don't quit. You're getting better all the time—"

"The boy is an oaf," André muttered. "He is an insult to my genius!"

"See?" Sam said. "Nope. I've had it. My cousin in Madrone has a gas station and he says I can get a job there. I'm taking him up on it."

"Sam—"

"Let him go," André said. "Who knows what he will do to a car, but at least his acts of brutality will not be centered on my kitchen!"

Catherine sighed deeply as Sam turned on his heels and stomped out the back door. She looked at André and said, "You're on your own now, Chef."

He shrugged again. "You will get someone else by tomorrow or I will abandon this outpost of humanity, this dreary fog-encrusted coast, this—"

Catherine left the room while the chef was still talking. Where in the world was she going to find someone André wouldn't mince into bitesize pieces? And by tomorrow afternoon? Impossible.

"I'll do it," Terry said the next morning as Catherine explained the situation.

Her offer left Catherine speechless for about thirty seconds and then she said, "But Mike—"

"Mike and I can move into a room at the inn until you can find someone to replace Sam. I'll help you out here in the morning, take a break when Mike comes home from summer school, then I'll help André in the evening."

"I couldn't let you—"

"You'd do it yourself if you could cook," Terry said, but Catherine wasn't so sure she would. She thought Sam had exhibited commendable control working with that temperamental self-acclaimed genius all these weeks; she doubted she'd last ten minutes.

"I'm sure I can do it. It's just for a while," Terry said.

"I could help with Mike in the evenings," Catherine said, warming to the idea.

"See? I'll take 13-A, the cabin next to your sailor friend. It has twin beds."

"My sailor friend is launching his boat in a few days or weeks, or so Amos says," Catherine said wistfully.

Terry nodded. She didn't say, "Good!" but the curt nod expressed her opinion of that development.

"It isn't as though he's taking advantage of me, is it?" Catherine said. She added, "He told me that he got you to give him the real cost of the room and that he paid the difference."

Terry still looked unimpressed. "There's more to that guy than meets the eye, Catherine. I have a funny feeling about him, like he's hiding something."

"Don't be silly. Anyway, I keep forgetting to tell you that Jake has invited us all on a sail when he gets his boat refloated. Even Derek."

"Mike will be thrilled," Terry said. "Who will hold down the fort?"

"Virginia Miller has agreed to come."

"What a doll. 'Course, she was your mom's best friend and I think she likes to take care of you. Anyway, that's great. Of course, Derek won't be able to make it."

"Why not?"

"You don't know?" Terry asked.

"Obviously not."

"He hates boats. He gets sick on them."

Catherine nodded. "Oh, yeah," she said, but she hadn't known. He'd never mentioned it and she'd never asked. "Well," Catherine said, "if you're sure it won't be too much of a strain to help André out for a week or so while I get an ad in the paper, I'm all for it."

Terry's gaze strayed out the window. "This time, let me help you interview the respondents, okay?" she said.

Catherine's gaze followed her cousin's. Tom was sitting on the slope, half hidden by huge bushes of yellow lupine. A lazy curl of blue smoke announced a cigarette, or at least Catherine hoped that was all it was.

"Why don't you advertise for a new gardener too?" Terry added.

"I'd like to," Catherine admitted. She could still see the look in Tom's eyes as he talked about the sand and her skin. She shuddered.

"Listen, Catherine, you've got to bite the bullet and get rid of that creep. He's just not working out and you know it. That's what happens with employees sometimes; they just don't work out and you find someone new. Let me help this time, okay?"

"All right," Catherine agreed. "But I hired Tom, so I'll fire him."

"This time we'll get someone who can double as a handyman," Terry said.

* * *

That afternoon, Catherine ran across the good-looking man from the restaurant. He was sitting on the deck railing, gazing seaward, a mug of coffee clutched in his hands. The heat wave was over, leaving Rocky Point Head enveloped in low ground swirls in the morning, but towards afternoon, the wind kicked up and blew it all away; the price for the sun was a cold wind that bit through sweaters and coats and chilled noses and hands.

He was dressed in a red sweater and black slacks. He'd been at the inn for two days now and the only words that had passed between them were those spoken before André blew up. Some guests liked to be alone, craved privacy, made it clear through words or actions that they were there to escape polite chatter. Some were very gregarious, openly inviting any conversation. The remote location of the inn meant that people sometimes felt like passengers on a ship, and a form of comradeship often sprang up out of nowhere.

He saw her staring at him and motioned for her to join him. He was a tall man in his late thirties with curly black hair and straight black brows over a pair of intense brown eyes. His clothes were expensive, his watch and signet ring top quality; even his shoes shone with a gloss not often seen at a rugged oceanside inn. He drove the latest model Mercedes, although Catherine had seen a rental car sticker in the window and assumed he'd rented it in San Francisco. All in all, he wasn't a typical Rocky Point patron.

"I hear there was mutiny in the kitchen last night," he said.

Catherine perched on the rail beside him. Baloo was taking his afternoon siesta on the ground below them, curled into a hollow to escape the brisk breeze. She said, "It was nip and tuck there for a while."

"Be that as it may, the scallops last night were excellent."

"Which is why I put up with our . . . temperamental chef," she admitted.

He laughed. "Talent is worth the extra effort, is that it?" he asked.

Catherine nodded. "Well, Mr. Colton—"

"Ross, please."

"Ross. How is your room? Any complaints about a lumpy mattress?"

"The bed is excellent," he said, taking a sip of his coffee. He held up the mug and added, "May I get you a cup?"

She shook her head. "No, thanks."

"Your rooms are very attractive," he said. "Did you hire a decorator?"

"Terry helped me," she said. "That's my cousin. You've probably seen her around the inn."

"The delicate-looking blonde?"

"Yes. She's a bundle of talent." Catherine waited a second and added, "Tell me something, Ross. You're a man staying here alone, do the ruffles and frills annoy you?"

His smile developed into a soft chuckle. "At first I

have to admit I was a little overwhelmed, but after a few minutes, I began to feel rather pampered. I'm in Madrone on business, you know, and it's nice to have such a pretty, plush place to retreat to.''

Catherine couldn't help being curious about what kind of business in Madrone could attract a man like Ross Colton. Maybe he was a successful artist or a prospective gallery owner. She said, ''Do you mind my asking why you're here?''

''Not at all. My company is buying a lumber mill.''

''You're kidding. Two Forks Lumber?''

''You know it?''

''I was just there a week or so ago. I didn't know it was for sale.''

''Everything is for sale if the price is right.''

''But why would you want an old lumber mill?'' she couldn't help asking.

''That mill has a huge inventory and lots of private forest; with proper management and responsible re-planting practices, it will yield lumber for years to come. We're going to rebuild the trestle so we can ship via rail—''

''The train!'' Catherine interrupted.

''That's right. A spur of it passes right in front of your inn and crosses the river above the road connecting your headland to the highway that travels on to Madrone and ultimately south.''

''I know,'' she said slowly. They were both quiet for a few minutes.

''I happened to walk across your spur when I went

down to the beach this morning,'' he continued. ''It's in remarkably good shape.''

''It is?''

He nodded.

''If I'm not being too nosy, may I ask how long you think it will take you to refurbish the rail line and rebuild the trestle?''

''Less than a month,'' he said. ''We're really rushing this project. Why do you ask?''

She shrugged and smiled but she didn't explain herself because her thoughts were like erupting buds on a dormant tree: fragile and unformed. In a whirlwind of impressions she saw downtown Madrone, growing into an art community despite its isolation. She saw colorful brochures picturing the Rocky Point Inn and the jutting headland and gaily painted shuttle buses running between the inn and the town.

''Catherine?'' Ross said. ''Are you okay?''

She nodded. It was just that with the mention of the train had come the idea that trains can carry people too.

Chapter Seven

Catherine trooped down the hill carrying a bottle of champagne wrapped in netting, Terry's son Mike close on her heels. The boy had been at the inn with his mother for two and a half weeks now and Catherine was loving every minute of it.

Mike was a gangly boy with straight straw-blond hair and huge blue eyes. He liked to talk about baseball and football, subjects Catherine was woefully ignorant about, but on the other hand, he never seemed to mind it that she didn't respond intelligently to his comments.

"Steve Young had a really good year last year," he said.

She assumed Steve Young was an athlete and said, "Oh?"

"He's not as good as Joe Montana, of course. No one is as good as Joe Montana."

"Of course not," she said. "Watch your step, Mike."

He jumped off the track and skipped along the trail ahead of her, calling over his shoulder, "Mom says we get to go to a Forty-Niners game this fall. Do you want to go too, Aunt Catherine?''

Though technically not his aunt, Catherine rather liked the title and she shouted back, ''I don't much like baseball, kiddo.''

This brought him to a halt. He turned on the path to face her and said, ''Aunt Catherine, the Forty-Niners are a football team.''

She felt like the unintentional straight man in a bad stand-up comic team. ''I knew that,'' she lied. She heard a far-off echo to the east, a relatively common sound since the trestle rebuilding had begun. She'd walked inland once with Jake to see how the project was coming and she'd been amazed at how quickly the thing was being constructed. In her head was the plan she intended on running by Ross Colton that evening; she resolutely pushed aside the jumpy nerves that ensuing conversation created inside her stomach as she dashed on down the hill behind Mike.

Amos, expansive in his role as chief boat launcher, strutted about the dock, operating his piecemeal machinery with aplomb, shooing adults and child onlookers aside with a gruffness ruined by the twinkle in his eyes. In a reversal of the process that had resulted in *Ashanti* being high and dry fifty-nine days earlier, the cradle and boat began to roll down the rails. When the water hit the top of the keel, Jake shouted and Amos stopped the momentum. Jake took Catherine's hand and helped her climb near *Ashanti*'s bow.

"How did you know to wrap the champagne in netting?" he asked as he held onto her hand. She was straddling the rails that held the cradle the big boat rested in.

"My college christened a research vessel the last year I was there. The department head wrapped the bottle like this. I don't know, though, Jake. Is it okay to christen a boat when she isn't being renamed?"

He shrugged his broad shoulders. "I don't know for sure. Can't hurt anything though, can it?"

"Waste of perfectly good bubbly," Amos growled from behind them. "Come on, tide's going to change in an hour; let's get this tub back in the water."

Catherine smashed the bottle—it took three swings to finally break it—and Jake climbed over the bow and onto the deck. She wished he'd asked her to come with him but he hadn't and she didn't want to be pushy. When he was aboard, she saw him opening the hatch and then Pywacket emerged from inside where she'd been locked. Within seconds, the svelte cream cat was sitting on top of the cabin, and while the human contingency darted and shouted and dashed, she sat washing her dark mask with a slender forepaw.

The boat entered the river with a swoosh. Jake carefully worked her away from the cradle until she was free and floating downstream. Waving at Catherine and Amos, he started the engine, turned her skillfully, and headed her toward the sea. Catherine knew his plan was to spend another week in the cove, but she also knew that she wouldn't see him as much, that an era with him had ended, and for this she was dreadfully sorry.

Jake anchored *Ashanti* in thirty-four feet of water and turned off the engine. The quiet assailed him. After a month and a half on land, the feel of the decks swaying beneath his feet was pure unadulterated bliss. Even the memory of Catherine standing on the dock, her hand wrapped around Mike's hand, couldn't totally depress him.

Mike was a nice kid. A little too involved in team sports for Jake's taste, but that was okay. He had an infectious grin. For the first time in his life, Jake wondered if he would have a son of his own someday, if that son would like boats and cranky Siamese cats and engineering. There was no way to know. Interests seemed to skip generations.

Pywacket yipped at the inquisitive sea gulls that landed astern of the boat, apparently waiting for Jake to clean a fish and throw the entrails overboard. He shook his head, dispelling thoughts of children. He grinned at the hopeful birds, grinned at the relentless waves running in from the south, at the sound of water lapping against the hull, at the feel of the decks, once again springy beneath his feet, the wind cold and damp against his face. This was where he belonged, where he longed to spend time, and if it suddenly seemed a little lonely, it was a feeling he'd get over.

He went forward to recheck the anchor line. After weeks trapped in that filthy boatyard of Amos', the

decks were covered with silt quickly turning to mud
as the moisture mingled with the dirt. Jake stripped
down to a pair of cutoffs, produced a bucket from the
stern locker, tied a rope to the handle, and lowered the
bucket into the saltwater. Washing the boat bucket by
bucket was cold, demanding, wet work. To Jake, it
was a little slice of heaven.

By the time the sun hit the horizon, he was ready.
The boat was clean and almost dry; he'd changed into
jeans and a thick Irish knit sweater to ward off the
chilly evening air. There was a pot of canned stew
simmering on the stove, a bottle of red wine open on
the table down below. Jake stood in the cockpit, looking toward the mouth of the river, listening for the
sound of an outboard motor. It was dark by the time
he finally heard it so he switched on *Ashanti*'s running
lights and within a few minutes, helped tie the incoming
skiff to the starboard side of the boat.

The man inside the skiff handed up a briefcase.

"Ross, you old landlubber. How's it going?"

Ross Colton took Jake's proffered hand and pulled
himself up onto *Ashanti*'s deck. He stumbled a little
as the boat rolled with the incoming waves. The slick
soles of his shoes didn't help any.

"I'm cold and I have no sea legs," he said.

"But no one saw you coming out here, did they?"
Jake asked.

"No. I rented a boat early in the day and then I
waited until I saw Amos drive up to the inn for his
dinner before I started out here. Still seems silly to me

to meet like this, Jake. Couldn't we have met at the inn?''

''I told you I didn't want Catherine Patterson to even think we might know each other,'' Jake said. ''Come on down below and have some stew.''

''Homemade?'' Ross asked as he followed Jake to the cabin door.

''Not exactly,'' Jake confessed.

''The special tonight at the inn—the special I am not there to eat—is hazelnut prawns.''

''The stew is warm,'' Jake said as he heard his friend's teeth clatter. As long as he'd known Ross, the man never remembered to dress warmly or casually enough for the water.

''I guess that will have to do,'' Ross said as he tickled Pywacket behind the ears and followed Jake down the ladder. ''And you'll be happy to know your lady friend was smart enough to take the bait.''

After several weeks of eating his meals at the inn, Jake found the canned stew less than appetizing. He preferred the hot bread made from a package, and the red wine, aged mellow and smooth. He turned down the kerosene lantern that hung above the table, casting soft yellow lights around the cabin, and cleared his throat.

''Okay, let's hear what she said.''

Ross took a sip of wine, cleared his empty plate away, and brought the briefcase up to the table. ''She approached me this evening around five,'' he began as he unlocked the case. "By that time, I had watched her watch you motor out to your anchorage. I know this isn't what you want to hear, but I swear she looked sad or something.

"Anyway, she stood on the bluff staring out to sea for a while, and then she seemed to shake her shoulders and make up her mind. The next thing she did was talk to that worthless gardener. The man left and she turned toward the inn. I barely had time to get my nose back in the book I was supposedly reading. For days I've been planting myself in obvious places, waiting for her to approach me because you said that you wanted the idea to come from her, not me, so I waited. Tonight, she finally came."

"And?" Jake prompted.

"She's as bright as you said she was. She ran over all the details of our operation, wanted to see all the papers, know all the companies involved. I had to tell her about Hylord International, of course."

"That's okay. She doesn't connect me with Hylord."

"Good. Anyway, when she seemed satisfied that we knew what we were doing, she said she had a proposition to make. She said she wanted to find a passenger car and hook it up to our lumber train. She said she would decorate it and fill it with champagne and caviar and overstuffed chairs, etc. She mentioned a brochure advertising the Rocky Point Express down in the Bay area. She'd make package tours. She talked about shuttles at the inn to get people into Madrone to tour the art galleries and I even believe she mentioned getting some of the galleries to underwrite some of the expense because of the increased exposure for their businesses. She understood that her car could be let off at the spur while our lumber train continues on into Madrone. She said she'd contacted the airport in Madrone and the rental car agencies, both of which were excited about the prospect of more customers. They assured her that they could handle those people who wished to make separate arrangements for going back to the city.''

''Did she mention where she intended on finding a railroad car?''

''I didn't give her a chance. You said to find one, so that's what I spent the first part of the week doing. I told her we happened to have an extra passenger car that wasn't going to be doing us any good and she was welcome to rent it.''

''And—''

''She asked how much. I told her a hundred, just like you said to. She said it wasn't enough, but that if I made it two hundred it was a done deal.''

''She thought of everything,'' Jake said with pride.

''She asked me when the trestle would be ready and when I said two weeks, she asked if we could make a trial run to see if it was feasible. I told her we could, that Hylord would underwrite the first trip, that all she had to do was get the advertising together and fix up the car the way she wanted it. So, three weeks from now—we have to wait two weeks to complete the trestle and get the car up here for her to decorate—it's all set to go.''

"I want you to handle everything yourself,'' Jake said. He knew he was repeating himself, but it was important. "I don't want anyone else to know I'm attached in anyway.''

"I understand,'' Ross said, handing Jake several papers from the briefcase. Since installing Ross as the temporary head of Hylord, Jake saw no reason to burden his brain with business papers, but despite his intentions, he looked them over. On the bottom of the stack was a bright-red folder with the Hylord insignia, a capital H and L intertwined in a crest, decorating the cover.

"What's this?''

"The papers concern the mill. That folder is our quarterly report.''

Jake tossed the report aside and thumbed through the papers. "We're going to lose money on this mill?'' he asked.

"Hand over fist. Should be a good tax write-off.''

"We'll have to keep it going for at least five years until this inn gets enough repeat and word-of-mouth business to get its feet off the ground.''

"We can keep it going until the end of time, if that's what you want,'' Ross said, taking back the papers and stacking them in the case. He clicked the locks shut and picked up his wine. "She's a nice woman,'' he added.

Jake nodded sullenly, suddenly missing Catherine and her warm laugh. ''Yes,'' he said.

''Beautiful too.''

Jake looked up at Ross. ''Your point?''

He smiled. ''She's in love with you,'' he said.

''No—''

''Yes, she is. I could tell by the way she watched you out here when she couldn't really see much but the general shape of the boat from that distance. I think she's determined to forget you, but it isn't going to be easy for her.''

''She's just interested in going sailing,'' Jake said firmly. ''For the boy's sake, I think. She's very fond of her cousin's kid.''

Ross looked at Jake over the edge of his glass and nodded. ''I see. Well, time for me to get back to the inn before they miss me. I'm having our attorneys draw up the papers. As soon as I get Catherine's signature, then I'm out of here. The deal in Mexico is coming to a head.'' He checked his watch, and added, ''I fly out of Seattle for Mexico City on the twentieth.''

''Better you than me,'' Jake said. ''I've sworn off planes for a while. Give me the ocean.''

Ross stared at his boss for a second and then he said, ''Jake, you *are* coming back to Hylord, aren't you?''

''In a year or two,'' Jake said.

Ross stood, but hesitated a second before moving off toward the ladder.

''Is there something else bothering you?'' Jake asked.

"No," Ross said quickly, but then with one foot on the bottom rung of the ladder, he turned around. "Since that night you called and asked me to look into buying the lumber mill and the train line, it's been clear that you're doing it for Catherine Patterson."

"So?"

"So, frankly, I've never seen you make a business decision based on figures as flimsy as these. You've always been a bottom-line guy. It's kind of out of character for you to rush to the aid of an individual."

"Spit it out, Ross," Jake said.

"Truthfully?"

Jake nodded.

"I think you're as in love with this woman as she is with you. I'm wondering what good can possibly come from this subterfuge."

Jake swallowed back his irritation. He'd invited the man to speak his mind and he did owe Ross for this and a dozen other little favors. He said, "You're right, kind of. We're . . . attracted to each other. But I'm sailing out of here next week and she's staying put, so we both know exactly where the other stands. The chance I'll ever see Catherine Patterson again is minimal. She'll never know about my involvement with Hylord. No one is going to be hurt."

Ross nodded slowly. The set of his mouth let Jake know that he remained unconvinced.

Catherine visited each empty room the next day. She earmarked pillows from some, chairs from others, framed paintings of cabbage roses and cut-glass lamps from still others, all destined to end up on the trial run of the Rocky Point Express.

She still couldn't believe her luck. What were the chances that an organization like Hylord International would become interested in a small lumber mill right on the eve of her impending financial disaster, that they would be powerful and rich enough to effect the changes necessary to help her in a such a short time, and finally, that the man in charge would be as gracious and accommodating as Ross Colton? They even had a spare passenger car!

She smiled to herself as she walked between cabins. It was a foggy day and the decks were clear of people. Even Baloo was happily ensconced on a wing chair by the potbellied stove in the office. She thought about Ross Colton again and wondered if he had met Terry. A man like him would be perfect for Terry and Mike.

There was so much to do! It was exciting and scary and she wished she could share it with Jake. With the thought of Jake, she found her steps diverting around the inn to the bluff. The world was a milky cloud of vapor, Jake's boat swallowed up and gone, just as it would be for real in one short week. She wondered if she should try to talk him into staying long enough to travel on the train with her. It would mean so much more if he were there.

Well, at least she'd finally worked up the nerve to fire the gardener. She'd expected Tom to argue or even threaten but he'd simply dropped his hoe, saluted her with his usual insolent sneer, and asked for his last paycheck. Buoyed by her success in ridding herself and the inn of Tom's presence, she'd immediately sought out Ross Colton and laid her plan at his feet; she'd been so relieved when he thought it not only viable but inspired.

Maybe the tide was turning. With that came the thought that it was time to dig up a photographer to take pictures of the inn. There was also the bank to call, the brochure to write, three newspapers to contact, and perhaps that Bay Area magazine in which to place an ad. She also needed a gardener/handyman and an assistant for the chef, and there was the upcoming sail and Terry and Mike . . . .

"And Derek," she said aloud, for walking towards her, she saw his tall figure and sandy hair.

"Hello," she called as she moved away from the bluff and walked to greet him.

"Hello, beautiful," he said, unknowingly echoing the words Jake had spoken on the beach a couple of weeks before. He leaned down and kissed her cheek. "Long time no see," he said.

Staring at him closely, Catherine took a step back. Derek was as handsome as ever and yet he looked like a stranger. His eyes were too light, his shoulders not broad enough, his face too clean, and his manner too soft and refined.

This is crazy, she thought. *Am I going to spend the rest of my life comparing every man I see to Jake?*

"I've been trying to talk to you for days," Derek said. "Weeks, even."

Catherine bit at her lip and said, "I've been so busy—"

"I know you have, and I don't have time now. I'm here to check out Mike."

"What's wrong with Mike?"

"I don't think much is wrong with him. He's got a fever—probably the flu. Terry will feel better if I check him over, though." They began walking towards Terry's cabin.

"I don't want to keep you," Catherine said, glad she wasn't going to have to have a heart-to-heart talk with him right that moment. There was so much on her mind, so many things to do, and there were her fragile emotions, shifting from euphoria about the train to distress about Jake's departure. She didn't think she had a frank talk with an ex-almost-lover in her.

He smiled down at her and touched the tip of her nose with his forefinger. "I'll talk to you later today then."

"Okay," she agreed, nodding. "And tell Terry if she needs to take time off to be with Mike that I'll cover for her."

Later that day, Catherine learned via Terry that Mike was okay, it was just a bug, and that Terry would be able to work the early evening dinner hour. Catherine geared herself up to help André for the late evening. She walked down to Amos' yard to avoid Derek.

Amos was absent, a sign over his door proclaiming

GONE FISHING! She was about to start up the hill when she heard her name and looked up to see Jake rowing towards the dock.

She felt her heart flutter at the sight and sound of him.

"Couldn't stay away from dry land, could you?" she hollered.

He docked the skiff and came ashore. As he walked toward her she was overcome with feelings she didn't even attempt to pin down. She let them wing freely about inside her, warming her cheeks, causing her heart to race, lifting her spirits.

"I have so much to tell you," she said, smiling.

He took her hand. "I can hardly wait to hear it all," he said.

Chapter Eight

J ake looked through the toolbox for a clawhammer. The shutters were banging on half the cabins and he was going to fix them because he was the new temporary gardener/handyman. He laughed to himself as he dug through the box, which seemed to be bulging with screwdrivers and little else.

Him a handyman! Boy, would Ross get a chuckle out of this. On the other hand, after Catherine told him all about the train and asked him to stay until the first run, how was he to sail away? It was only wise business practice to see an idea to completion, even if it was her idea. It was his money. It was only right to protect his investment.

Who was he trying to kid? This job kept him close to Catherine for three more weeks and he was so glad to hear she'd given that gardener the boot it was a small price to pay. Besides, she'd looked so cute as she said, "This will be a way for you to earn a little extra cash for your trip."

It was only September, still too early to go to Mexico. He'd have to wait until November when hurricane season was over. Giving himself eight weeks in San Diego to take care of outfitting and last-minute details, he was still on schedule. Originally, he'd planned on taking a leisurely land trip from San Diego to New Mexico to see his folks, but he'd put that off for now.

His motives for staying made him slightly uncomfortable. In a way, he resented Catherine for becoming important to him. Until he'd met her he'd been a man on a mission without a backward glance. He'd managed to sever ties to his business, at least for a couple of years. He'd said all his good-byes to friends and family except his folks but maybe they'd fly to Tahiti in a few months and visit him there. And now he was happy to be a temporary handyman. And gardener, he reminded himself at once, though he didn't know a rose from a rutabaga.

Saturday, he rowed ashore, beaching the small skiff on the fine sand on Catherine's side of the river. The fog of the last two days was history and there was an unusually warm wind blowing from the south. He glanced impatiently up toward the headland, wondering what was keeping his sailing guests.

After a half hour of waiting, he finally saw Catherine running across the sand toward him. Her long dark hair flew out behind her. He told himself he enjoyed looking at any pretty woman and that Tahiti and the rest of the world were crawling with more women than he could gawk at in a hundred years.

When she was closer, he called, "Where is everyone?"

Catherine came to a halt in front of him. She was out of breath, and propped her hands on her knees, hanging her head for a second before she spoke. It reminded him of the first time they'd met, on this very beach.

"Mike's fever is back. Terry and Mike can't come."

"Oh," Jake said. "I'm sorry. The boy isn't too ill?"

"I don't think so. Terry is calling Derek again."

"Is he a good doctor?"

"I think so, yes. Mike will be fine. Terry sends her regrets."

He nodded, then regarding Catherine out of the corners of his eyes, he asked, "What about you?"

"Well, my replacement came early and is happily holding down the fort so if it isn't too much work to take just one person sailing, I'm your girl."

"It isn't too much trouble," he said. "Besides, you're my boss now. I can hardly go back on my word to my boss, can I?"

She just smiled.

They rowed out to *Ashanti*. Catherine had been aboard bigger boats during college, but they'd been research vessels and as different from this sleek apparition as charcoal from diamonds. She felt a rush of anticipation as the bow of the skiff bumped gently against *Ashanti*'s hull. Catherine held on to the toe rail while Jake climbed aboard. She handed him the painter. He helped her on deck, then tied the skiff off at the mooring line.

Catherine removed herself to the cockpit so she wouldn't be in the way of the ritual Jake performed for preparing the yacht to sail. The boat moved like a totally different beast than it had the one other time she'd been aboard. It was springy and alive, almost dancing in the waves. She took the wheel when directed, and as he stood on the foredeck and cast the line aside, she steered *Ashanti* toward the open sea.

They sailed north, the wind behind them. When Jake took the wheel, Catherine caught her hair in a rubber band, stripped off her sweater, nudged Pywacket aside from the best seat in the house (atop the stern locker), and closed her eyes. The problems and headaches surrounding the inn seemed a million miles away. Every once in a while she looked toward the land, then out at the horizon, a distinct line of blue—crisp and as far away as forever.

Catherine insisted on making lunch. She loved looking through all the cupboards, marveling at all the storage space. She chose canned plums from England, hard rolls and canned butter from New Zealand, a round tin of cookies from Germany. She found a small stainless steel pot and brewed hot herbal tea, then looked around for a tray to tote everything on deck.

She'd searched the galley to no avail when she noticed a nice broad locker behind the settee. She unhooked the door and slid it open. The boat lurched just then and spilled magazines from the cabinet. She re-

stacked them and shoved them inside, but before closing the cabinet door, she spied a red folder on the cabin
sole. She leaned down and picked it up.

"Catherine?"

She looked up to find Jake standing in the companionway door. She tossed the folder in with the magazines and relatched the door. "Are you hungry?" she
called.

"Starving. Need any help?"

"You just steer this thing. Oh, where's a tray? That's
what I was looking for just now."

"Inside the stove," he hollered, and then he disappeared from view. His cat daintily descended the
ladder. She wrapped her body around Catherine's legs,
almost tripping her as she went back to the galley.

"The key to your heart is in your stomach, isn't it,
Py?" she asked the cat. "You're not so different from
Baloo after all."

Jake produced a small table from a cockpit locker
and attached it to the mast. Catherine set the tray on
the table, which was covered with a no-slip surface.

"We'll have to eat while we're going this direction," he said. "When we turn around, everything will
wind up in our laps."

"This is all so exotic," Catherine said after they'd
eaten. She was aware of him staring at her, his eyes
following her as she cleaned the table and carried
everything back down below. She'd just pulled her
sweater back over her head and plopped down on the
seat opposite him when he cleared his throat.

"Are you happy, Catherine?" he asked softly.

"Very," she said, looking at the thin band of brown land off to the east.

"I don't mean just right this minute," he persisted. "I mean in general. Like with your life?"

"I have the inn," she said slowly, meeting his gaze. "And I have Mike and Terry and friends. What more is there to want?"

"Nothing," he said, though his voice indicated he was disappointed in her answer.

Eventually, they had to turn around. Catherine learned how to tack back down the coast. It was harder going and later in the day, so that it began to get cold. "It's going to rain," Jake said.

"And you didn't predict it?" Catherine teased.

Jake smiled. He'd known the southerly wind would bring rain eventually, but he wouldn't have said one word that morning that might have put Catherine off the idea of sailing that day. He knew in his heart that these hours aboard with her were the best he'd spent on *Ashanti*. It made him want to cry when he thought of the weeks and months ahead without her.

What he yearned to shout at her was that she'd given up her freedom. She'd closed the door on everything she'd worked for during college, with some misplaced sense of loyalty to a building and a hunk of land. But he hadn't said a word because who was he to rob her of her purpose? In fact, he'd gone out of his way to protect her not only from foreclosure but from loss of pride. It was an integral part of her character. Would he love her if she wasn't exactly who she was?

The word *love* shocked him. He shoved it aside and barked at her. "Better find our foul-weather gear. Look in the starboard aft locker."

"Aye, aye, captain," she said, throwing him a grin and a salute and disappearing below decks.

When Catherine arrived back at the inn, she was wet and tired and happy. As she stepped onto the deck, she saw Amos standing under the eaves.

"You look like something the cat dragged in," he said fondly.

She reached up and kissed his cheek. "Where's Virginia Miller? I know I'm late—"

"Virginia is in the dining room wooing your guests like she has been all day long."

"Oh, dear. I'll go take a shower—" She stopped abruptly and laughed because she was already so wet. "I'll go dry off—"

This time Amos interrupted. "Don't be alarmed, but Mike is in the hospital."

"What?"

"Now don't get in a dither, honey; the boy is fine. It was his appendix, but they got it out in plenty of time and he's doing great. Terry said there's nothing you can do."

"I've got to go to Madrone at once," Catherine said quickly.

"That's what I figured you'd say."

"But the inn—"

"Virginia said she'd stay all night."

Catherine smoothed her wet hair away from her face. "Give me a minute to change clothes," she said.

"I'll drive you," Amos told her.

Catherine found Mike awake and Terry asleep in a chair beside the bed.

"Hi, sweetie," she whispered, alarmed with how pale the youngster's face was.

"I missed going sailing," he said.

She wished she could promise him a sail when he felt better, but by then it was likely that Jake would be gone. What an empty sensation that thought opened in the pit of her stomach! She said, "We'll do something else that's fun, okay? Like your football game or something. You go to sleep now."

His eyes closed. Terry hadn't woken up so Catherine went back out into the hall. Derek was standing beside the door, one hand rubbing his temples. He looked up when he heard Catherine's footfall.

"Amos said to tell you he's down in the cafeteria having some french fries."

She smiled wearily.

Derek took her arm and walked her toward the end of the hall.

"I blame myself," he said finally. "He didn't have all the symptoms, but I should have spotted—"

"Look, Derek," she interrupted. "He's going to be fine, right?"

"Yes."

"Then leave it alone. You saved him; we all owe you a lot."

He nodded. "Thanks, that's what Terry said too." He stared down at her a second and added, "This probably isn't the right time to tell you this, Catherine."

But you're going to anyway, Catherine thought to herself. His tone made her wary. In fact, it made her want to run down the hall and out into the night. She made herself stand still and say, "What is it?"

He swallowed hard and looked down at the floor. "It's Terry," he said at last. "Terry and me, that is. We've been spending a lot of time together recently and this emergency today cinched it, at least in my mind." Derek looked back at Catherine and took a deep breath. "I'm going to ask her to marry me."

Catherine had been so wound up in her own problems that this revelation made her speechless.

"I'm sorry," he said softly, touching her hand, misreading her silence. "But Catherine, honey, I think if you're honest with yourself you'll see that you and I were going nowhere. We haven't even seen each other, you know, like in dating, since early summer. In time, you'll find someone else, someone you'll love the way I love Terry."

She nodded woodenly. He leaned down and kissed her lips briefly, then he went back down the hall and disappeared into Mike's room. Catherine smiled wistfully, but by the time she reached the cafeteria, she was having to work to hide a fit of giggles. Terry and Derek. It was perfect. But it did make her wonder what else was happening right under her nose that she'd been too preoccupied to see.

The next morning, she covered for Terry by making the muffins. Once the guests at the inn discovered what had happened, they rallied and ate the muffins and didn't even complain . . . much. By Monday, Catherine had interviewed three people responding to the ad to replace Sam. Since Terry was still at the hospital, she let André help make the decision. They hired an older woman with very short, very straight gray hair. Catherine suspected one of the reasons the woman got the job was because André suspected he could bully her. Catherine wasn't so sure; she thought she detected an iron will lurking under the mild manner.

When Mike was released from the hospital, Terry took him to their own little house. Virginia Miller stayed on to help Catherine, who became more and more involved in preparations for the coming event. There was a shuttle bus to rent, reservations to respond to, the yet-to-be-renovated cabins to spruce up.

Mike recovered quickly and by the time Ross Colton appeared with the railroad car, was healthy again, which meant that Terry was back at work. Of course, Terry's feet barely touched the ground—Catherine gathered that Derek had popped the question—but she seemed invigorated by romance, working harder than ever.

The reservations poured in. Most signed up for the "Rocky Point Express Train Package," which included the train trip from Oakland, Hylord's point of departure, a room for three nights, and continental breakfast. Catherine spent many hours with André, poring over details of the menu, cautioning him against outbursts of temper. Actually, since Sam had left, André had quieted down to the point of near-normalcy.

And all the time, helping her at every step, was Jake Stokes. He was there to hammer in nails, change light bulbs, shore up dilapidated furniture, fix broken blinds, tinker with shower fixtures, mend fences and decks and stairs. Catherine spent as much time with him as she could, but the days didn't have enough hours and as it soon became apparent that Jake knew nothing about gardening, she spent much of her free time watering and pulling weeds. And meanwhile, there were always guests about, asking questions, needing things.

Pulling weeds did free her mind to wander, however, and she noticed it spent increasingly frequent hours reliving the time on *Ashanti*, the feel of the ocean swells, the cold rain pelting her face. She'd managed to bury her own deep feelings for the ocean for a year now, but they'd come rushing back on *Ashanti*.

She recalled looking up at the headland once they'd retied *Ashanti* to her anchor line in Rocky Point Cove. It had been raining hard by then, but she could see the inn through the silver rain, and it looked pristine, a world onto itself. The sound of the work being done on the trestle had echoed down the gorge and she'd seen her life presented to her like a still-life photograph. When Jake had taken her into his arms and kissed her, coming up from behind, his hands strong on her arms, his face warm through the cold rain, she'd blanked the inn out and for one brief second, flown away from the earth and her responsibilities. After the kiss they'd stared at each other for what seemed an eternity until at last he spoke, his voice husky. "I'll row you ashore," was all he said until the skiff reached the beach and Catherine stood in the rain and watched him row back to his boat and his cat and his choices just as she walked back up the hill to her own.

"It's bigger than I thought it would be," Catherine told Ross as she looked over the outside of the passenger car.

"Standard size," he told her. "I'm afraid it doesn't have seats and an aisle, however."

"Good," she said, her face lighting up with a smile. "I want to put small tables and chairs and an old loveseat aboard. Along with a bar and a buffet. I've arranged with a caterer in Oakland to help us out."

He nodded, his gaze drifting briefly to Jake's face. Jake smiled at him.

Seemingly flustered, Catherine said, "Oh, I am sorry, I forgot to introduce you two. Jake, this is my guardian angel, Ross Colton. Ross, this is Jake Stokes, a sailor who has been nice enough to help me out these last few weeks."

The two men shook hands. Jake was hoping Ross wouldn't say anything he shouldn't know.

"Well, I apologize again for being so late," Ross said, his attention back on Catherine. "We were three days late getting the railroad line cleared south of the trestle, but everything is in perfect order now. We'll be back for the car in three days. Will you have enough time?"

"Sure," Catherine said, and despite himself, Jake felt a wave of admiration wash through him. He really did like this woman's resolve and determination.

He watched her sign a sheaf of papers Ross produced from his briefcase. The rest of the train had departed for Madrone hours earlier, but Ross had come in a rented Mercedes and they both watched as he drove away.

"He's a nice man," Catherine said. She hitched her hands on her waist and looked at the car and smiled so widely Jake had to fight the impulse to kiss her mouth.

"It's not in bad condition," he said, and then pointed behind her. "There's Baloo. Maybe he fancies himself a train cat."

"Let's go inside," she said. They stepped up into the train car, Baloo on their heels. Ross hadn't been exaggerating when he said it was empty.

"It's so clean," Catherine said as she walked around the floor and peered out the windows. "And look at these lamps on the side of the coach, aren't they wonderful? We'll start decorating tomorrow." She paused a second as she watched Baloo rub against Jake's ankles, his purr a raspy staccato. "Do all cats like you?" she asked.

He bent down and patted the white head. "Seems so. Or maybe he just smells Pywacket on my socks."

"No, he used to sit by your door. Listen, Jake, I'm going down with the train and riding back with my guests, just to oversee things. Will you come too? You could bring the cat ashore and leave her with Terry."

Jake knew he shouldn't. The chances anyone would recognize him were remote, however, and he longed to share this one last adventure with Catherine. Still, there'd been that moment on *Ashanti* when she picked up the quarterly report and he'd thought she'd found him out. He'd stopped breathing for a moment. "Okay," he said at last.

"You don't have to," she said as though she sensed his caution.

"I want to," he assured her. "And Pywacket will be fine aboard *Ashanti*. We won't be gone overnight, right?"

"No." She looked up at him, a smile tugging on the corners of her mouth, and said, "I made my bank payment. I even have more inquiries than I have rooms or seats on the train so I'm planning a second trip already. I think I'll even get a start on the next payment coming due this winter."

"You must be very relieved."

She stared at him a second and said, "When are you leaving?"

He took a deep breath. "The day after we return up here."

"That's only a few days then."

"Yes. Well, I have to get to San Diego for some serious outfitting and any last-minute repairs I need to make after my beaching. Then there are the cupboards to fill."

"They looked pretty full to me already," she said.

"Man cannot live on canned food alone," he quipped.

"I've never even asked you where you're going," she said.

"Mexico first, as far as Cabo. Then across to Hawaii, and from there the South Pacific."

"Oh."

What would she say if he said, "*You could come with me, Catherine.*" Would she come? The desire to ask her was so strong it brought tears to his eyes, but by then she'd turned away and wasn't looking at him any longer. He was beginning to suspect that the prospect of living without him wasn't as horrendous to her as the idea of living without her was to him.

He swore under his breath.

"Did you say something?" she asked, turning.

"No," he mumbled, jerking damp fingers away from his eyes.

She stared at him a long moment, then biting her lip, she said, "You know, Jake, you don't have to go, do you?"

Chapter Nine

There was something hopelessly romantic about riding a train, Jake thought. The motion resembled being on a boat as it swayed and rattled and rolled down the tracks. The countryside was beautiful too, and he stretched out his long legs and watched Catherine as she plumped pillows, moved a table a half an inch, turned the lights bright, then dimmed them. She was nervous and excited and this was just the trip down to get everyone. She'd be a basket case by the time they came north if she didn't settle down a little.

He hadn't answered the question she posed a few days before. She hadn't expected an answer and he had none to give because the truth of the matter was that on one hand he *did* have to go and on the other, he was a gnat's breath from staying forever. But she didn't know the whole story. She didn't know he was behind the lumber mill and this train. If he told her now, would she accept it as he had intended, as a business deal, or would she be angry with him?

This was crazy. He was a sailor now, that was all. He didn't need Catherine or any other woman.

The forty-three paying customers all came aboard in festive holiday spirits. Jake had worn rust-colored slacks and a creamy white shirt, and Catherine watched him as he circulated easily, bearing a tray of canapés, chatting and smiling and helping. He looked gorgeous, his skin brown and healthy looking, his grin infectious. She loved his face. She peered for a flash of the green eyes, but he was busy listening to a young man expound about mutual funds.

This was yet another facet of Jake's personality Catherine was surprised to see. She'd discovered weeks ago that he was friendly and capable, but she had to admit a little shock at seeing him hobnob with the rich so easily.

In one corner of the car, a string quartet entertained the well-dressed passengers who sat around the floral-draped tables or gathered near the bar. It was amazing how many people were aboard, how crowded the car seemed, yet several had complimented Catherine on a novel new idea and pledged future referrals.

By the time the train rolled over the new trestle, Catherine knew she had a hit on her hands. Trips like this throughout the spring and summer would keep the inn and the restaurant and bar full. During the fall and winter she could gear them toward the proper holidays. The customers would help Madrone establish itself as a growing art community. She looked for Jake to thank him, to propose a toast to their success and, though she hated to think about it, to say good-bye. She had a check in her pocket for his wages for the last two weeks, but she owed him more than the money. In some indefinable way, his strength had been behind her all along, helping her over the obstacles. In some intangible way, she felt as though he was part of this endeavor.

He hadn't answered her when she asked him if he had to leave. In fact, after an awkward pause, he'd laughed and so had she. Of course he had to leave. It had been his plan all along; he'd never hidden that fact. Contrary to what Terry thought, Jake had been honest and forthright with her and trying to tie him down now wasn't only unfair of her, it was impossible. What could she possibly offer that Jake needed?

She greeted an elderly couple sipping coffee at their round table, assured them a room was waiting for their arrival, and turned to look for Jake.

Instead she found herself face-to-face with a woman in her late twenties. She had porcelain skin, platinum hair twirled around her pretty face, and diamond studs the size of peas on each ear. Her clothes were designer, so casual and perfect she looked as though she'd stepped from the pages of a fashion magazine. Catherine had noticed her the minute she came aboard because she was lovely and young and alone.

The hair made her look like a princess. Catherine had studied each and every person as they boarded.

Her memory now supplied the name Crown, Gillian Crown, like a princess' crown.

"This is fabulous," Gillian said, sipping from a glass of champagne. "I can hardly wait to get to your inn."

"It's rather small," Catherine admitted, suddenly nervous about the prospect of entertaining someone like Gillian for a week.

Gillian laughed. "But that's just what I want. Lonely beaches, cold mists, lots of sand and sea gulls. How colorful! I can hardly wait. Besides, Daddy said he'd send a plane to pick me up if I get bored."

Crown Aviation, of course. Catherine managed to nod.

Gillian leaned forward and said, "I want to know who that gorgeous hunk is."

"Which one?" Catherine asked, but she knew without asking who Gillian must mean.

"Right there," Gillian said, pointing through the crowd.

Catherine looked up and caught Jake's eye. Smiling, she said, "He's my associate."

Jake began walking towards them. She felt her insides warm at the sight of him.

"Introduce me," Gillian whispered.

Jake stopped by Catherine's side. He barely glanced at the woman standing next to her. For the last several years he'd been surrounded with women like this one: pretty, polished, pouty, and predictable. He'd once told Ross he called them "4-P." He knew it wasn't very nice to stereotype people, but he knew this woman's kind before she even opened her mouth.

When she did, it confirmed everything he suspected.

"Catherine, I don't need an introduction after all. I'm just going to be brazen and introduce myself." She stuck out her hand and said, "Gillian Crown. And you look familiar."

Warning flags. He stared at her harder. Did he know her?

She said, "Jake Stokes, right?"

He looked at Catherine who looked back at him, her eyes wide. She was still smiling but if he didn't get this socialite away right this minute, she wasn't going to be smiling long. He took Gillian's elbow and said, "May I freshen that wine for you?"

"What are you doing on this train, darling?" she persisted, resisting his grasp. She wasn't the kind of woman to be whisked away when she sensed an interesting story. He tried to subdue his panic.

"Jake is helping me," Catherine said. "Where do you know him from?"

"Are you kidding? Catherine, your little helper is Jake Stokes, head of Hylord International. Didn't you know that?"

Jake looked down at Catherine. He saw a flush spread up her neck and across her face. He said, "Catherine—"

"Is this what you're dabbling in nowadays, darling?" Gillian continued. Looking right at Catherine, she added, "Jake is always poking his nose into one thing and then running off to fix another. I'd heard via the grapevine that he was up to no good, but I never dreamed! Are you the new lady in his life? Lucky you, but don't get too comfortable with it because Jake's the love 'em and leave 'em type, aren't you, Jake?''

Jake finally recognized her. Harold Crown's obnoxious daughter, the one he'd dated once five years ago on the eve of her graduation from Vassar. She'd made a big deal about her father and how wealthy and important he was. Jake could remember being a little rude and totally disinterested but he had no idea she'd harbored such animosity toward him.

All this speculation about Gillian's motives was a delaying tactic so he didn't have to think about the bomb that had just landed at Catherine's feet. He finally cleared his throat. "Catherine—"

"You lied to me," Catherine said slowly.

"No, not really."

"Not really? What do you call it? You're behind this whole thing, aren't you? The lumber mill, the trestle, this train car?"

"Catherine, let me explain—"

But she turned and fled and he knew that it would be cruel to pursue her. He glared down at Gillian.

"Relax, Tiger," she said with a wicked smile. "She's not your type anyway. I'll take that champagne now."

"Get it yourself," he told her.

* * *

Catherine was the first one off the train. A smile, frozen on her face, greeted each guest as they disembarked. Gillian Crown was the last customer to leave and for her, Catherine turned up the wattage.

"I hope you enjoy your stay with us," she said. She could feel cracks in her facade, cracks starting down at her toes, traveling up through her legs and back, threatening to shatter her composure.

Gillian winked. "I'm sure I will, darling," she said.

After Gillian came Jake. Gillian tried to take his arm but he shook her off and flashed her an irritated scowl. She laughed. "This is so cute," she said, and made her way toward the shuttle bus for the short ride up the hill to the inn.

"Catherine," Jake said, pulling her toward him. "Listen to me, will you?"

"Later," she said, moving away. As the train left, she noticed the new insignia painted on each yellow car, an intertwined H and L in a crest. She immediately recognized it from the folder she'd noticed in Jake's boat and her feeling of betrayal almost suffocated her.

"Please—" he said.

Catherine motioned for Terry to drive the shuttle bus up to the inn, and when they were alone, whirled to face Jake. "What can you say?" she demanded. "For the better part of three months you've misrepresented yourself. You brought in Ross Colton. I feel like such a fool. How you two must have laughed over my naïveté."

"Oh, no, sweetheart, we never laughed—"

"Don't, Jake. When I think of the lies—"

"What lies?"

"You let me believe you were an itinerant sailor, broke, down on your luck."

"But I told you weeks ago that I could pay my way," he protested.

"How about Ross Colton?" she snapped. "You two pretended you'd never met. You didn't trust me!"

He gripped her arms again. "And if I'd offered you what you and Ross came up with, would you have taken it, Catherine?"

"No," she said softly.

"You see?"

"That's not the point. I feel like a fool, like I've been manipulated—"

"If you're referring to what Gillian said—"

"I know sour grapes when I hear it, Jake," she interrupted. "I don't give a hoot about Gillian. It's just that I thought you cared."

"Can't you see that I do?" he pleaded.

"No," she said firmly. "What I see is a power-hungry man used to moving this little pawn and that little servant and getting what he wants. I see a liar and a sneak. I see a spoiled, bored entrepreneur. I suppose I should be grateful to you for pulling the fat out of the fire, but I'm not. I'm just disappointed. I thought I knew you. Now I know I don't."

"I just wanted to help you," he said softly, dropping his hands. "I didn't know any other way to do it."

"So you lied to me."

"I didn't want you to feel as though you owed me anything—"

"That's what I mean. You didn't want to invest anything more in this place than your money. You were only passing through."

"It was more than that, Catherine."

"That's the operative word, isn't it? 'Was.' Isn't it time you were on your way?" With that last question, she turned and began climbing the hill, tears flooding her eyes, a breaking heart making her steps heavy and deliberate. She didn't look back. She told herself she was never going to look back. Not ever.

Catherine cried herself to sleep and awoke feeling dead inside. With a tremendous effort, she made herself get out of bed and dress in something bright and cheerful even though she felt like hiding under the covers or at best, donning mourning clothes. She made herself be pleasant to her new guests, made herself smile when Terry announced that she and Derek were getting married at the end of the month.

"And I was even going to invite your sailor friend," Terry said as she admired her diamond, "but I see his boat is gone."

Catherine was in the process of drinking a mug of coffee. She put the mug down and stared at her cousin.

"What's wrong with you this morning?" Terry asked. "You look dreadful."

"What did you say about Jake?"

''That he's gone. Didn't you know?''

Catherine didn't bother to answer. She rose and went outside, her footsteps leading her inevitably to the bluff. The cove was empty.

Chapter Ten

Mike looked adorable in his suit as he stood beside Derek in the role of best man. The wedding took place on the bluff, a spot Catherine had avoided for the past three weeks. She was dressed in pink, a color Catherine disliked but Terry had insisted upon. She didn't care enough to argue.

The wedding was attended not only by friends and Derek's family, but by all the guests currently staying at the Rocky Point Inn as well. Amos gave Terry away. Catherine had dreaded the wedding, knowing that her own lost love would prey on her heart, but she was mildly curious to see that it hardly phased her. She was more or less dead inside. It made getting through the days much easier.

"I'll be gone three weeks," Terry told Catherine at the reception. André had outdone himself. The tables were laden with beautiful trays of food. The centerpiece, an ice sculpture of a pelican, was busy melting in the afternoon sun.

Catherine nodded absently.

171

Terry touched her arm. "Are you going to be okay?" she asked.

"I'll take good care of Mike," she said.

"That's not what I mean."

Catherine shrugged. "You have a great time in Hawaii," she said at last.

"I'm worried about you. The inn is doing fantastic, André has calmed down to a rolling boil, the next payment is almost in the bank, and you act as though the world has come to an end. I know you liked that sailor, but honey, he's gone and you have to go on."

Catherine nodded.

"You've lost weight. There are big dark circles under your eyes. You look lost half the time and ready to cry the other half."

Catherine looked over her cousin's shoulder and spied Ross Colton walking toward her.

"Who invited him?" she asked.

Terry turned to see to whom her cousin was referring. "I did. We owe all this newfound prosperity to him, don't we?"

Catherine had never told Terry about Jake's deviousness. She hadn't been able to bear the thought that Terry would say she always knew Jake was a liar. She hadn't wanted to be driven into defending him.

She smiled at Terry and intercepted Ross. It was the first time since Jake left that she'd seen him. He looked embarrassed and uneasy.

"So, I guess you know that I know," she said without preamble.

"Yes," he said. He swallowed nervously and added, "Would it help to tell you that I'm sorry?"

"No."

"I didn't think so. You will go ahead with our agreement, won't you?"

She felt the strongest stirring of emotion since looking out into the cove and seeing that *Ashanti* had left. She said, "I would love nothing more than to throw this whole train concept back in Hylord's face. But the brochures are out there and people have reservations and the bank loan is a reality. I can't afford to be righteous, as your boss well knew."

"He never intended to hurt you," Ross said.

She held up a hand to silence him. "Don't."

"It's true, whether or not you want to hear it," Ross said. "Jake Stokes helped you because he's in love with you. It's as simple as that. And as complicated."

Catherine shook her head. She left him standing alone and went inside to her own rooms where she sat in front of the windows and stared out to sea.

She'd saved the inn. Thanks to Jake, she had everything she thought she'd wanted. She had security for Mike or for her own children someday; she had honor. But she knew deep inside she'd lost more than she'd gained and that in the end, she didn't have anything.

She looked around the room, at the mismatched furniture and the faded photographs, at the stacks of bills to be filed away or paid, at the shabby rugs on the floors. She'd lived in the apartment for over a year and yet it looked just as it had when her father lived here.

Was it really because not changing it made it seem as though he might return any second, or was it because she couldn't bear the thought that this was it, this was home?

How am I going to get through the rest of my life? she asked herself. *What am I going to do?*

What she did was knuckle down and make herself cheer up. In a fit of housekeeping, she got rid of almost everything in the apartment and redid it to her own taste. She told herself that the new furniture and rugs lifted her spirits. She played ball with Mike, raced him along the beach, and since school had begun, helped him with homework. She occupied her time so completely that she didn't have time to think.

She organized hot-dog roasts on the beach, Tropical Fever Night in the lounge, engaged musicians to entertain on Sunday afternoons. And as the wealthy tourists mingled with one another and spent money on just about anything she could think to offer, she kept note in her head. The winter payment—done. Next spring—on its way.

When a new gallery opened in Madrone, inviting one and all to "Meet the Artist," Catherine loaded three interested guests into the backseat of her car and, since Terry was still on her honeymoon, Mike into the passenger seat.

The gallery was in a converted hardware store. Gone were the hammers and power saws, the ceiling fans and shovels, and in their place, huge redwood carvings, shelves of etched glass, and walls painted bright white and covered with canvases. Catherine didn't much care for the featured artist's work. There were lots of sem-inude women with blurred facial features lying on the sand in arty poses; she wished she'd left Mike at home.

"It isn't too late for you," came a voice she rec-ognized. She turned to find herself face-to-face with her ex-gardener.

"Hello, Tom," she said, hoping he wasn't going to create some kind of scene.

He didn't answer her greeting, at least not in words. The leer was still there, accompanied this time with a smug smile. "How do you like it?" he asked, gesturing at the painting they were standing in front of.

Catherine looked at the dark-haired woman caressing a piece of driftwood and said, "It's not my style."

"It's you," he said.

"What?"

"I'm the artist," he told her.

Catherine felt her mouth drop open.

Seemingly pleased by her response, he expanded. "You didn't think I was really a gardener, did you? I'm an artist. It's in my soul. When you wouldn't pose for me, I used my imagination. That's what we artists do—we use our imagination."

Since Catherine felt the figure on the canvas in no way resembled her she could agree honestly with his proclamation. "I didn't realize what an active imagi-nation you had," she said. She remembered the con-versation he was referring to; she'd had no idea he meant that he wanted to paint her—not that it would have changed her response.

He nodded proudly. "I worked for you for money to buy paints. Now that you can see what I can do, I imagine you'll want to pose for me, this time in the flesh."

She didn't like the way he said the word "flesh." She didn't like anything about him, for that matter. She said, "Not really. Thanks anyway."

"Suit yourself," he said, and if he was offended, she couldn't tell.

He drifted off to talk to someone else. At her side, Mike asked, "Is that lady in the painting really you, Aunt Catherine?"

"No," she said firmly. "That's his artist's imagination." For the first time in weeks, she actually looked forward to something; she could hardly wait to see the look on Terry's face when she heard about Madrone's newest artist! Telling Jake about Tom also flitted through her mind, but she resolutely banished the thought of him.

Terry came back from her honeymoon tanned and revitalized. She tackled the inn like a storm trooper, and between the two women, there wasn't a blade of grass out of place, a speck of dust to be found, or a single guest whose needs weren't met. Derek was at the inn often, and Catherine reestablished the friendship with him that had been her mainstay during the months preceding the morning she first found Jake

Stokes' boat on the beach. She told herself she was happy.

She took long walks when she felt sadness creeping back into her heart. She liked to go to the marina and sit on the small dock. She liked throwing stale bread to the gulls and watching the alder trees across the river turn gold and orange and rust. Fall was coming. The inn had a big Halloween promotion going, and then there would be Thanksgiving and Christmas . . . .

Amos found her there. "Mind if I sit with you a spell?" he asked.

"It's your dock," she told him with a smile.

"Technically, it's *your* dock," he said.

She shrugged. Amos sat down and watched her feed the birds for a few minutes. Then he said, "I heard from Jake. He's in Ensenada, Mexico."

Catherine said, "I don't care."

"Confound it, girl! What matters in this world if not love?"

"Amos, listen to me—"

"No, you listen to me," Amos snarled. "I've been watching you; we all have. We're all worried about you. You've turned into a robot."

"That's not true," she protested.

"Yes, it is. At first you were a pitiful, sad little creature. I thought that was bad, but I think I liked you better that way than this efficient, cheerful—"

"Amos, I'm not going to talk about this," she warned him.

''You listen to me,'' he said in a tone of voice she couldn't ignore. ''I've known you your whole life. I was your dad's best friend, and though I loved the man, I didn't agree with everything he did. Saddling you with this inn, for one thing. Burdening you with it was selfish of him. He didn't want it either, did you know that? He let it fall into decay, but he wouldn't sell it because it was your heritage. Well, you've saved the place. Thanks to Jake Stokes and your hard work, this inn will endure. Now, get rid of it.''

''But—''

''But nothing, girl. Give the thing to Terry. She loves it like your granddad did and she's got Mike and now Derek. There's the cabin in back that you grew up in—let her have it. Do whatever you have to do, but don't allow yourself to stay here and spoil like a piece of rotten fruit. Go find your heart; the rest of us will carry on without you.''

Catherine sat on the dock long after Amos struggled back to his feet and left her alone with her thoughts. She tried to take apart his logic, but some of what he said made perfect sense. Her father hadn't loved Rocky Point Inn. He'd liked to fish and pal around with Amos, but his heart wasn't in being an innkeeper and she had always sensed the fact that he was unfulfilled.

Was she going to let the same thing happen to her?

Of course she wasn't, she realized with perfect clarity. She was going to go back to school and get her master's degree and then her doctorate. She was going to have the career she wanted and needed to make her whole.

But first, there was something else she had to do. She had to find Jake. Somehow, their futures were inexorably tangled. She owed him an apology. But more than anything, she had to look into his eyes and find what she'd lost.

Within a week, Catherine was free of the inn and on her way south. It was amazing how quickly it all came together once she stopped seeing problems and started seeing solutions. And even though the trickiest and potentially most emotionally risky task was still ahead, as the miles passed between Rocky Point and San Diego, her soul was filled with peace.

Once in San Diego, she spent the night in a small motel, then took off the next morning for Ensenada. She was full of everything she was going to tell Jake and ask him. She could hardly believe it when she got to the Mexican town and found *Ashanti* had sailed a week earlier. Jake was gone.

He woke up with the cat sitting on his chest. The anchorage was rolly and her claws were extended a quarter of an inch into his skin to keep her from slipping off onto the floor.

"Get away!" he barked.

Pywacket began purring.

He unhooked her and brushed her aside. Staggering to his feet, he glanced at the clock. Ten-thirty. It had been a hard sail to Bahia San Quintin the day before, and then he'd been up every hour or two during the night to check the anchor line. All in all, he felt miserable. For the first time that day, he thought about Catherine. He knew from experience that it wouldn't be the last time her image would cross his mind before he fell into exhausted slumber that night. He was almost used to the incessant yearning for her. And sometimes, especially at night when the black sky was so enormous it threatened to swallow him, he wondered if it was all worth it, and what he would make of his life from this point forward. Alone.

Catherine used her borderline Spanish to ask the man rowing the skiff to be as quiet as possible. They came astern of *Ashanti*. Jake's skiff was tied to a painter playing out behind the sailboat; the boarding ladder was down. She paid the man and climbed aboard, expecting at any second for Jake to throw back the main hatch and demand to know who was boarding his boat.

Nothing happened. As the Mexican skipper rowed his dinghy back to land, she crossed the cockpit and knocked on the open wooden doors. Nothing. She peered inside but it was dark and very still down below decks and had the feeling of emptiness. Stymied, she looked around the deck and spied a pair of bare brown feet near the bow. She walked forward and found Jake prone on the foredeck, an old white hat covering his face. The sound of his breathing suggested he was asleep. Pywacket sat next to him on the fore hatch, watching Catherine.

She knelt down beside Jake and lifted the hat. His eyes opened immediately and Catherine was struck by the sea-green intensity of his gaze, a color like the inside curl of a wave.

"I'm dreaming," he said.

"No," she told him. "But imagine how surprised I am to find your boat floating in the bay instead of sitting on the beach."

For long seconds he stared at her. He sat up finally and said, "I hadn't gotten around to beaching her yet. It just wouldn't be the same without you there to run to my rescue."

"Like you ran to mine?" Catherine asked softly.

"For all the good it did me."

"Jake—"

"Wait a second. How did you find me? Why are you here?"

"It doesn't matter how I found you, although I've driven three days straight and looked out at every anchorage I could find. I came to look into your eyes. I came to see if it's true, that you love me. I came to see if I love you."

He touched her face. "Well?"

Catherine nodded. She closed her eyes as his lips touched hers, and she felt her heart open and flood with sheer, unadulterated joy. When they finally separated, she cleared her throat and said, "Do you happen to need a crew for this voyage of yours?"

He hesitated so long she felt her mouth go dry. Was she presuming too much, had she burned the bridges between them? Just because she finally understood her own mind and heart, did it really mean she understood his as well? She said, "It's okay—"

He grabbed her hands and kissed her again. "You gave up your own dreams once before," he said slowly.

Catherine felt every ounce of pride flee from her body. Her heart was somehow outside her chest, beating wildly and freely, but exposed and vulnerable. She said, "Jake, take me with you. There's time. A couple of years from now, I'll go back to school and finish what I started, but all I want right now is to be with you on this boat."

"Are you sure?" he asked.

"I've never been more sure of anything in my life," she answered.

He stared at her for a second, and then he cupped her face. "Maybe if your last name was the same as mine," he said softly, kissing her softly.

"Are *you* sure?" she whispered.

"I've never been more sure of anything in my life," he said, parroting her words.

Catherine took a very deep breath. "We'll have to fly Amos down here," she told him. "It would break his heart to miss the wedding. And Terry and Mike and Derek—"

"And my parents," he said as he pulled her into his arms.

Catherine lay back against his chest. Her head was

exploding with all the news she had to tell him, all the apologies she wanted to offer, all the questions she had about this magical trip that would now be their honeymoon. But for the moment, it was enough to be close to him, to feel his heart beneath her cheek and the sun on her face.

She looked up when Pywacket screeched. The cat was on top of the cabin, staring down at them with crossed blue eyes. As if understanding that things aboard *Ashanti* were about to change forever, she yowled again.

"How am I going to explain you to the cat?" Jake whispered against Catherine's cheek.

She laughed. "You'll just have to find a way."